POLITE PROTESTERS

Syracuse Studies on Peace and Conflict Resolution
Harriet Hyman Alonso, Charles Chatfield, and Louis Kriesberg
Series Editors

Other Books by John Lofland

Doomsday Cult
A Study of Conversion, Proselytization and Maintenance of Faith

Deviance and Identity

Analyzing Social Settings
A Guide to Qualitative Observation and Analysis
(coauthor)

Doing Social Life
The Qualitative Study of Human Interaction in Natural Settings

Interaction in Everyday Life
Social Strategies
(editor)

State Executions
Historical and Sociological Perspectives
(coauthor)

Symbolic Sit-Ins
Protest Occupations at the California State Capital
(coauthor)

Protest
Studies of Collective Behavior and Social Movements

Peace Action in the Eighties
Social Science Perspectives
(coeditor)

Peace Movement Organizations and Activists
An Analytic Bibliography
(coeditor)

Polite Protesters

The American Peace Movement of the 1980s

John Lofland

SYRACUSE UNIVERSITY PRESS

First Edition 1993

93 94 95 96 97 98 99   6 5 4 3 2 1

Library of Congress Cataloging-in-Publication Data

Lofland, John.
    Polite protesters : the American peace movement of the 1980s / John Lofland.
        p.   cm. – (Syracuse studies on peace and conflict resolution)
        Includes bibliographical references and index.
        ISBN 0-8156-2604-5 (cl.). – ISBN 0-8156-2605-3 (pbk.)
        1. Peace movements – United States – History.   I. Title.
II. Series.
JX1961.U6L57   1993
327.1′72′0973 – dc20   93-23829

To Lyn

Contents

Figures

Acknowledgments

Each of this volume's seven main chapters has a different history and, therefore, differing debts that I want to acknowledge.

Mary Anna Colwell and Victoria Johnson are the second and third authors of a briefer version of Chapter 1, and I am grateful to them for permission here to use text from that treatment in a revised and expanded discussion. I thank Richard Healy, Lyn H. Lofland, Doug McAdam, Saul Mendovitz, Bill Moyer, and Carol Mueller for very helpful substantive and editorial suggestions.

Earl Molander was extremely helpful to me in gathering the material on city twinning reported in chapter 2. Beyond allowing unrestricted access to the files of the Ground Zero Pairing Project in Portland, Oregon, he was generous with his time in discussing city twinning, and he wrote an incisive series of comments on a draft of this chapter. Just prior to the research on city twinning, I had the good fortune to supervise two student projects on Beyond War, one by William Brigham, then a graduate student in sociology at U.C., San Diego, and the other by Ann McGuire, then a U.C., Davis sociology undergraduate. Their data began to force me to conceive "the consensus movement," and I am very grateful to them for having been my teachers. A number of people reacted in many helpful ways to this chapter in draft: Chadwick Alger, Martin Bennett, Joel Best, Paul Craig, Llana Davis, Dennis Dingemans, Carl Jorgensen, Louis Kriesberg, Lyn H. Lofland, John D. McCarthy, and Nick Milich.

As the discussant in a workshop where chapter 3 was presented, Carol Mueller made helpful suggestions that I have adopted. Lyn Lofland edited the text as well as pointing out many useful points of revision.

Sam Marullo critiqued chapter 4 in draft, and Doug McAdam offered beneficial commentary as the discussant in a session where it was presented.

Victoria Johnson is the second author of the analysis of citizen surges presented in chapter 5 and I appreciate her permission to use that material. As editor of *Research in Social Movements, Conflicts and Change,* the volume of this chapter's earlier publication, Metta Spencer provided very thorough and fine editing. I am much indebted to Lyn H. Lofland, Sam Marullo, David Cortright, Michael Mickler, and Richard Flacks for their cogent suggestions and supportive comments. I want most especially to thank John McCarthy and Metta Spencer for their detailed recommendations.

As editor of *Peace and Change,* Paul Wehr did an excellent job of editing chapter 6, which is reprinted and revised from that journal. Joel Best, David Cortright, Jo Freeman, Jen Hlavacek, Lyn H. Lofland, Sam Marullo, David S. Meyer, and John McCarthy made many valuable suggestions on previous drafts, and I am also grateful to each of them for other and diverse forms of help and encouragement. The anonymous reviewers for *Peace and Change* made excellent recommendations for revision that I have incorporated.

Sam Marullo is the second author of chapter 7, and I appreciate his permission to present this material. Douglas Bond, Christopher Kruegler, Ronald McCarthy, and Roger Powers had many helpful reactions to a draft I presented in the colloquium series of the Harvard University Program on Nonviolent Sanctions. David Meyer did an excellent critique of this chapter in draft.

Michael Ames arranged for an especially useful critique of the book in manuscript, and I am grateful to him for his more general and strong support. Mary Neal entrusted her collection of early-1980s materials to me, and I am extremely appreciative of this and other of her help.

I acknowledge with gratitude the permission of the following publishers to use previously published material in this volume:

Chapter 1, revised from "Change Theories and Movement Structure," in *Peace Action in the Eighties,* edited by S. Marullo and J. Lofland, Rutgers University Press, 1990, 87–105, is reprinted by permission of the Rutgers University Press. Copyright 1990 © by Rutgers, The State University.

Chapter 2, "Consensus Movements," in *Research in Social Movements, Conflicts and Change,* edited by L. Kriesberg, JAI Press, 1989, 163–96, and Chapter 5, revised from "Citizen Surges," *Research in Social Movements, Conflicts and Change,* edited by M. Spencer, JAI Press, 1991, 1–29, are reprinted by permission of JAI Press, Inc., Greenwich, Connecticut.

Chapter 6, revised from, "The Soar and Slump of Polite Protest," *Peace and Change* 17 (January 1992): 34–59, is reprinted by permission of Sage Publications.

Portions of the work on all seven chapters were supported by grants from the University of California Institute on Global Conflict and Cooperation and the Davis Division of the University of California Academic Senate to whom I am very grateful. My employment as a professor in the University of California is of a similar but much greater importance. A work of this kind is almost impossible without the support and freedom provided by such a position. In this sense, my most important debt is to the people of California who have created and sustained the University of California. At the University of California, Davis, I have a particular debt to Gary Hamilton, who, as chair of the Department of Sociology and at other times, has helped me in fundamental ways when I have needed it most.

A number of my compatriots in peace projects have been a special joy to work with or simply to have met, even if but briefly. As I have experienced them, each combines a grasp of our higher values with unusual degrees of moral courage and optimism. Although none is perfect and I do not agree with all their opinions and actions, in showing these qualities they have renewed my hopes for human betterment. My heartfelt thanks to Larry Agren, Marty Bennett, Elise Boulding, Dorothy Brownold, Felice and Jack Cohen-Joppa, David Cortright, Paul Craig, Dan Galpern, David Dellinger, Ilana Davis, James Douglass, James Driscoll, Barbara Epstein, Todd Gitlin, Ruth Hultgren, Randall Kehler, Louis Kriesberg, Kathy Mechling, Saul Mendovitz, Nick Milich, Earl Molander, Bill Moyer, Juanita Nelson, Oliver Northup, Richard Seyman, Gene Sharp, Stephen Souza, Dougas Walter, Barbara Weidner, Nancy Wellever, Anna Maria White.

Each chapter has its distinctive debts, but there are also several people to whom I am much beholden on all the chapters and on this book as a whole. Not surprisingly, I have already mentioned them several times. They are Lyn H. Lofland, Sam Marullo, and John McCarthy. They have fretted with me on virtually every aspect of the range of matters treated here, and it is not an exaggeration for me to say that I could not have completed it without their encouragement, sympathetic support, and way-opening advice in the hard times.

Above all others, I am obliged to Lyn H. Lofland, who has lived this book with me, and has given — even — the quintessential expression of love, the volunteer editing of much of its text! If only a slightly larger percentage of humanity possessed the breadth of her moral vision and the generosity of her spirit, the human species might just survive and even thrive. With love, this book is dedicated to her.

POLITE PROTESTERS

Introduction

In this volume I conjoin and, hopefully, achieve a productive melding of two topics: the American peace movement of the 1980s and the generic, sociological analysis of social movements. By means of this conjunction, I seek to broaden our understanding of both topics — to widen the ways in which we perceive the American peace movement while simultaneously advancing analysis of social movements as an abstract class of human striving.

I commingle the peace movement and generic sociological concerns with regard to *seven* major aspects of social movements. Four of these elucidate the peace movement (and social movements generically) as *structures* (that is, in static cross-section). These four aspects comprise the four chapters of part 1. Three of the seven treat dynamics of how movements change over time — their *processes*. These appear as the three chapters of part 2.

Peace Movement Structures and Processes

As a guide to the often detailed analyses of these seven aspects of the peace movement, let me overview the main concepts and arguments offered with regard to each and point out ways that the seven are related to each other and to additional matters.

Structures

The four structural aspects treated in the respective chapters of part I can be summarized in four rubrics: *change-theories, consensus movements, movement culture,* and *organizational profile.*

Change-theories. The strategic or goal-seeking activities of social movements embody theories of actions required to achieve desired social changes. Such conceptions are mostly unarticulated, and one task of the sociologist is to bring them to awareness and to analyze them as theories. With contributions by Mary Anna Colwell and Victoria Johnson, in chapter 1 I attempt such an articulation for the American peace movement of the 1980s. Six sometimes competing, contradictory, yet at times complementary theories of actions required to achieve desired social changes were encoded in that movement, theories centering on cognitively transcending, educating, intellectualizing, politicking, nonviolently protesting, and prophesying. Each theory appealed to clientele of varying social characteristics, and these clustered in distinctive ways. Each, in particular, was associated with different forms of emotional or interpersonal persona in the doing of movement work.

I treat these change-theories in the first chapter because understanding them is a key way to answer a yet more basic question about any movement: "What *are* these people doing?" The answer helps us understand exactly what is afoot, and this helps us more sensibly to answer a variety of other questions. Such other questions include: "Why are they doing these things?" "Who are they?" "How are they organized?" and "What difference do their actions make?" The notion of the "change-theory" spotlights what participants say they are doing, and such expressions are summaries of what they are, in fact, doing. The concrete activities in a movement vary enormously, but they are also variations on only a small number of basic ways of acting to achieve social change.

Consensus movements. The better to understand the "transcender" theory of how to achieve change that I introduce in chapter 1 (and its equivalent in other movements), it is helpful to distinguish between the "consensus" and "conflict" orientations within movements. This distinction in orientations, treated in chapter 2, calls attention to the degree to which participants identify and act on objective interests that are in conflict and seek in direct and detailed fashion to change social policy in view of such conflicts. What we can call "conflict movements" tend to so recognize and act while "consensus movements" do not. Signal surface features of consensus movements include the claim to be *nonpolitical,* or *nonpartisan,* and not to be *negative,* or *oppositional.* In one interpretation, consensus movement orientations are timid rebellions, disguised politics, or derailed dissents.

In chapter 2, I analyze city-twinning campaigns of the 1980s peace movement as instances of a consensus orientation. As a case study, it should be thought of as a closer and more fine-grained inspection of the *transcender* change-theory introduced in chapter 1. As depicted in figure 1.1, in the context of the entire movement, transcenders were on the order of 20 percent of all participants, and city-twinning campaigners were a modest proportion of all transcenders. Therefore, in chapter 2, we have a close examination of a special cluster within a cluster of the movement.

Movement culture. Social movements vary in the degree to which they exhibit culture. Dimensions along which they so vary include degrees of cultural consensus, distinctiveness, scope, elaboration, quantity, and symbolic expressiveness. I explain these dimensions in chapter 3, and I assess the degree of their development in the American peace movement of the 1980s with respect to the movement's values, symbolic objects, occasions of gathering, roles, participant persona, and social relations. Profiled in these terms and placed in comparative movement perspective, the American peace movement of that period is seen to have been culturally quite sparse at the movementwide level but relatively more "cultured" in several respects at a second tier of culture clusters. Theoretical implications of this pattern are discussed.

The six varieties of beliefs about social change explained in chapter 1 and the closer inspection of the consensus nature of transcender change-theory beliefs described in chapter 2 are subsidiary parts or aspects of the much broader phenomenon of the culture of a social movement. I begin with discussion of change-theories because the six variations we observe are the key principles on which people organized their actions. As mentioned, the six provide a fairly simple yet powerful answer to the question: What *were* these movement people doing? Having explained these basic forms of movement "praxis," in chapter 3, I have gone on to examine the broader ideational context in which these practices were situated, the context of culture.

Organizational profile. Social movements are exceedingly complex ensembles of a rich variety of formal and informal organizations that likely differ in significant ways from one movement to another. A necessary first step in analyzing such ensembles is to develop ways in which analytically to describe or profile them. In chapter 4, I attempt this by applying a modified and elaborated version of David Knoke and David Prensky's (1984) distinctions among *firms, bureaus,* and *associations* to the American peace movement. We find that while firms and bureaus were quite scarce, associations were abundant. Further to sharpen our perception of the peace movement's organizational profile, I then compare it to forms of movement organization and to the American military-industrial complex.

The concept of structure. The term *structure* has at least two pertinent meanings, and in order to avoid confusion I need to indicate the one I employ here. In one use, structure refers only to standing or "frozen" patterns of action and association in a social organization. Structure *is* the social organization conceived as a pattern of association. In this restricted use, there is then a contrast between (1) social organization as structure and (2) beliefs and/or culture. Relations between *structure* and *culture,* for example, are then explored. My use of the term *structure* also denotes social organization but is more inclusive. As treated here, reasonably static, or frozen, patterns of ideational content are also structure, including beliefs about how to achieve social change (treated in chapter 1), consensus beliefs (dissected in chapter 2), and *culture* (analyzed in chapter 3). In regarding both social organization and ideational content as structure, I can then contrast a static or cross-sectional (structural) view to a processual, temporal, or dynamic, view. As is evident, both the restricted and my expanded use of the term *structure* are valid; they are simply different.[1]

The first three of the four kinds of structure I am treating focus on the *ideational* content of movements, on forms of the beliefs or ideologies that we observe, while only the fourth deals directly with structure in the restricted or *harder* sense — specifically, the organizational makeup of movements. On the surface this may seem a clear imbalance of attention, but it is not. Over the last decade and more, studies of social movement have — rather mysteriously — neglected ideational content, preferring to focus on questions of macrostructural causes, mobilization of resources, and forms of acting.[2] I seek here to bring back to center stage the fact that movements are very much about people defining their situations.[3]

Identifying movement boundaries. In the first sections of both chapters 3 and 4 — on culture and organizations — I wrestle with the vexing and even imponderable question of the boundaries of the 1980s peace movement. How do we decide what or who was *inside* or *outside* that movement — or inside and outside any movement? This is a matter of practical and not simply theoretical pertinence. To speak of culture and organization requires that one have decided *what* culture is part of the movement (and what is not) and *which* organizations are *peace* (and which are not). I might have assembled my discussions of this problem into a separate chapter. I have not done this, though, because I want to stress that how one answers the boundaries question has important consequences for subsequent analyses — for, in these cases, analyses of culture and organization. Therefore, I have kept my struggles with this matter in the places where they make important, proximate differences.

Processes

The "big news" about the American peace movement of the 1980s was, of course, its "explosion" or "take off" in the early and middle years of the decade, which was followed by a slump into the doldrums, a pattern seen quite commonly in social movements. This *surge* offers us a new case with which to think about movements in rapid mobilization as a generic topic, and this is the relevance I pursue in the three chapters of part 2. Aspects of this process considered in part 2 can be condensed into a set of rubrics: *citizen surges, surge stages, surge soaring.*

Citizen surges. Assisted by Victoria Johnson, in chapter 5, I suggest that the dramatic rise of peace activism in the eighties is better understood by placing it in the larger context of citizen surges as a generic class of citizen action. I specify contours of this larger class, distinguish *uniform* and *multiform* surges, and describe the two major types of uniform surges — gatherings and organizations. Forms and scales of multiform surges are discussed, and I suggest that citizen surges are often conflated with social movements, interest groups, and mobilization, among other matters, and that identifying surges as a distinctive domain helps to correct some recent confusions and to end sterile debates. Ten major points involved in profiling multiform surges are explained and illustrated with the case of the American "peace surge" of the 1980s.

Surge stages. Surges of citizen activism exhibit a rapid and dramatic "soar and slump" dynamic that analysts have tended to depict — using analogies to organisms — as life-history trajectories or stages. But, because citizen surges are collective actions rather than biological entities, a more social model, such as that of a tenuously ratcheted and enlarging or contracting interaction spiral, may be more accurate. In chapter 6, this alternative approach is elaborated in terms of the nine major actors who are contesting in the rush of focusing and facilitative or inhibitive conditions and events. Distinguishing among the five phases of the American eighties peace surge — focusing, soaring, faltering, slumping, and percolating — this "interactive spiral" approach is applied to the initiating interaction spiral of that surge. Drawing from those data and the social movement literature more generally, I propose six principles of first phase facilitation, or *ratcheting*: supportive milieu, unengaged resources, the Darwinian parade of proposers, the striking proposer, the dramatic demonstration of feasibility, and the feasible-timely proposal.

Surge soaring. What is variously termed the *mushroom, explosion,* or *soaring* phase of social movements and other citizen action has primarily been analyzed in terms of prior causes rather than in terms of constituents and dynamics. With Sam Marullo, I seek, in chapter 7, to remedy this neglect by offering a scheme that facilitates such dissection and applying it to the 1981–1983 soaring phase of the American peace surge. We analyze this "peace soar" as a synergistic interaction of eight primary classes of events, suggesting that each tended to escalate the others in a spiraling process. Among other points, we conclude that the behavior of elite groups were particularly important in the eighties soar of peace activism and that political opportunity depictions of movements fit this case less well than a model of "new dangers."

⋘

These seven sociological analyses might not form as tidy a package of clearly and crisply interrelated studies as some readers might like. Instead, each chapter takes a concept (or a small number of them), and seeks to develop it (or them) using peace movement data. Readers who prefer what is sometimes called "a single golden thread" that strongly ties chapters together may, therefore, be disappointed. As desirable, in the abstract, as this may be, it also has limitations, one expressed well by Erving Goffman in introducing the four studies comprising his *Asylums*. "If sociological concepts are to be treated with affection, each must be traced back to where it best applies, followed from there to wherever it seems to lead, and presented to disclose the rest of its family. Better, perhaps, different coats to clothe the children well than a single splendid tent in which they all shiver" (Goffman 1961, xiv).

I do not, nonetheless, want to overstate the degree to which these seven studies is "free standing." Each treats the American peace movement of the 1980s, and all seven are, in this sense, about only one topic. At the conceptual and theoretical level, each deals with closely related topics of structure and of process. The three chapters of part 2 addressing dynamics are, in particular, separate developments of the single concept of "citizen surges."

Even though related in these ways, each chapter is also developed to make sense when read alone. This involves minor repetition in some places in order to provide background concepts, but I trust that such summary bridges are helpful rather than distracting in signaling continuity.

These seven slices of social movement reality clearly do not exhaust even the more important ways in which we can examine the peace and other social movements. In particular, I say little here about "activists"—that special class of persons who make things happen in a movement. Nor do I treat—in any central analytic fashion—the myriad campaigns that varied clusters of the peace movement launched over the course of the eighties. And I do not address, at least systematically, questions of the consequences, effects, or achievements of the eighties peace movement, a topic that has been of great interest to several other writers (e.g., Cortright 1991). The list of additional lively aspects is, indeed, a long one.

The Movement Studies Agenda

While there are many topics I do not treat, let me also stress that in addressing matters of structure and process I am helping to redress a significant imbalance of attention in the study of social movements. Broadly conceived, there are seven fundamental questions that one asks in any field of inquiry, including that of movement studies. These are the questions of (1) definition, or types, (2) structures, (3) frequencies, (4) causes, (5) processes, (6) consequences, and, (7) human agency or strategy in the construction of action.[4]

Movement studies scholars are notable for the extent to which, from the beginning of the subdiscipline right up the the present, they have virtually fixated on questions of causes, frequencies, and consequences. How movements are structured in various ways has been of little interest, and even processes have been investigated only scantily. This latter is especially puzzling because movements are very much about their very own rapid changes.[5] Therefore, while there are many substantive matters I do not take up, the seven studies presented here all press forward on structure and process frontiers that have been only scantily explored.

In the conclusion, I will expand on this depiction of the approach I have taken.

Polite Protest

Although, perhaps, not a "golden thread," one special theme does run through these seven studies, a theme I caption "polite protest," or more precisely, "the paradox of polite protest." This paradox is that even though citizens striving for global peace and justice over the 1980s formed a social movement, they mostly refrained from engaging in the kinds of behavior that we typically think of as quintessential movement action: abrasive protest or violence of a seriously threatening character. Instead, the peace movement was marked by a remarkable degree of genteel civility, restraint, and even affability. While its protest was paradoxically polite, its idealistic and even radical goals marked it as very definitely a social movement—one that has, with ups and downs, persisted for generations.

Some observers have thought that a pattern of polite protest significantly limited the American peace movement's effectiveness. Because it lacked a radical wing that was perceived as truly threatening, it did not exercise the "radical flank effect" (McAdam, McCarthy, and Zald 1988). The "radical flank effect" arises from moderates in a movement seeming all the more so because they are flanked by radicals who authorities and others perceive to be threatening. The message of the movement is, from the moderates: "You had better deal with us, because if you do not, you will be forced to deal with the radicals, who are much worse." Since the peace movement lacked a radical flank—a wing that was perceived by authorities as a serious threat to ruling elites—it also lacked a true *edge of menace* (cf. Marullo, Chute, and Colwell 1991, 255). For this reason, some commentators have observed, it exercised a great deal less leverage than have other movements.[6]

Conversely, yet other commentators suggest that it would be even more paradoxical or contradictory if the 1980s peace movement did *not* practice "polite protest," and was "truly menacing." The core values of the movement (described in chapter 3) demanded, in fact, that it *not* be like other movements in this "edge of menace" and "radical flank" manner. Instead, peace values required that ends and means be consistent as in the slogan often attributed to A. J. Muste: "There is no way to peace, peace is the way" (Larson and Micheels-Cyrus 1987, 258).

We need not, of course, see this as a debate. All the previous statements can be and are, I think, true: The movement did not have an "edge of menace"; it did lack the radical flank effect, but it did so for good ethical reasons; and, as a consequence, it was less effective.

But, none of this means that the peace movement was or is ineffective or that the increasingly numerous instances of polite protest movements are ineffective. Nor does it mean that polite protest is condemned always to a lesser degree of effectiveness. For we live as on a rapidly moving train in which the situation of the perception of collective actions is changing. On our new global television planet where the whole world is watching in a literal and not simply metaphorical sense, the dramaturgy and calculus of effective action may be changing radically. While polite protest may have been doomed to relatively less effectiveness in the media darkness of the pretelevision age, it may now become the strategy of choice in the cool, vivid world of the television image. Around the world, we increasingly observe movements that act in much the same polite protest manner pioneered and practiced by the peace movement and that do so with amazing effectiveness if not immediate success. This is not because ruling elites are more humane, merely that they are more constrained, constrained by the fear of the roving and probing television eye.

Peace Movement History

In taking a severely (and, some would say, austerely) analytic look at the American peace movement of the 1980s, I will be saying little about it in the chronological terms of story telling used by historians or about the history of the peace movement or movements more generally. Instead, I assume peace movement history and the relation of the 1980s surge to it. This omission might lead readers not conversant with this history to think the peace movement of the 1980s had no antecedents or even its own internal chronology. These would be incorrect inferences, and to forestall anyone making them, let me provide a brief account of these historical matters.[7]

Following the definition of Howlett and Zeitzer (1985, 54), the term *peace movement* refers to "a loose assemblage of groups and individuals often with dissimilar programs but in accord on seeking to reduce conflict or end war through achieving some change in foreign policy." While "loose assemblages" so focused have appeared in various periods and societies through history, distinctively peace "movement" groupings are ordinarily dated from the nineteenth century and found most prominently in Northern European countries and in the United States. Peace efforts prior to the nineteenth century have been characterized as largely "religious sectarian" in character and involved such groups as the Quakers, one of whom, William Penn (1644–1718), is sometimes called "the first real peace leader" (Howlett 1991, xxi).

More secularly oriented peace groups proliferated in early-nineteenth-century America, and that period is commonly pointed to as the beginning of a relatively organized American peace movement. It grew in numbers and strength up to the Civil War but was then eclipsed by that war. It began to grow again in the late-nineteenth and early-twentieth century, an upwelling Elise Boulding has treated as the first of four major periods of peace mobilization in twentieth-century America. "There was a peak in peace movement activity just prior to World War I, when a core of social reformers and lifelong peace workers helped launch a broad antiwar coalition that fought military preparedness and military budgets. . . . [But the coalition] . . . broke apart when Wilson declared war. Antiwar fervor turned into prowar fervor for all but the core of committed peace workers" (Boulding 1990, 21).

A second period of peace movement mobilization preceded U. S. entry into World War II. In the later thirties, there were "peace committees in two thousand cities and towns, organizations on five hundred college campuses, and nearly seven hundred nationally prominent men and women (not the old familiar peace workers) who donated their time traveling across the country to speak against military involvement in Europe" (Boulding 1990, 21). But, this surge, also, went into slump as events in Europe moved closer and closer to war.

The third major peace mobilization was against the war in Vietnam and was clearly the largest, longest, and most rancorous of the four twentieth-century peace surges. Stretching from the mid-sixties to the early-seventies, at its peak, it involved a very substantial portion of ordinary Americans and many sectors of the country's elites. And, unlike the first two surges, this one clearly had an impact on the course of a war.

The surge of peace activism analyzed in this volume is the fourth major peace mobilization of twentieth-century America, and it rose in opposition to the newly militant foreign policy of the administration of Ronald Reagan. Dissent from these policies crystallized in 1980 and soared in 1981–1983. Three-quarters of a million or more people rallied for a nuclear freeze in June 1982, and almost eleven million voted for one in November of that year. Dissent peaked in 1983 when the U.S. House adopted a freeze resolution and an alarming nuclear war film was nationally telecast, but the movement faltered as it focused forward to the November 1984 elections, the loss of which sent it into steep decline. A new period of fairly stable "percolation" was achieved by 1987 and continued into the 1990s.

I have mentioned only the four largest peace mobilizations in twentieth-century America. It must be appreciated, however, that there have been myriad smaller peace surges concerned with various war-peace matters in the twentieth and previous centuries. For example, even while the peace surge I will examine was in full mobilization, there was also a surge of antiintervention activism regarding American actions in Central America, focused especially on Nicaragua. Therefore, this brief and selective reporting of peace movement history should be taken as exactly that: brief and selective.[8]

Major surges of peace activism fill only a few of the total years over which we can say there has been a peace movement. In between these periods of surging, people in the peace movement continue to "plug away," so to speak, and to maintain what Nigel Young (1987) has termed one of several "peace traditions" that ideologically compose the movement. At times of surge, these continuing and preexisting peace traditions function as a base or core that importantly facilitates the new mobilization. (The 1980s instance of this facilitation is analyzed in chapter 6.)

At such times of surge, the inflow of new people, money, and ideas changes the movement so radically that some observers wonder if we are still looking at the same peace movement. The preexisting people, organizations, funding, and ideas are still there, but their numbers are so dwarfed by the new people, organizations, funding, and ideas that one is tempted to think in terms of newness and discontinuity rather than in terms of oldness and continuity. Looking at the long sweep of peaks and troughs (of expansions and contractions and of enormous diversity of philosophies and programs), one serious observer has rightly remarked: "It is arguable that there is no such thing as a single peace movement . . ." in the sense of "a continuous global or unitary social phenomena" (Young 1987, 138–40). While there is clearly something we can call a history of peace movements, it is a history marked by soar and slump discontinuities that are associated with pronounced internal movement division and fragmentation.

Voice, Data, Method

In the recent period, the "voice," or "point of view" of social science writing and analysis has come under intense critical scrutiny. Deconstructionists, critical theorists, and others have challenged the "voice from nowhere" posture they discern in social science writing. Although posing as objective and neutral — a voice from nowhere — social scientists are, in fact, merely and underneath defending exploitive hierarchies of all varieties — especially class, gender, and race hierarchies. The posture of professional social science is merely a mask for hegemonic domination, according to these critics.[9]

One can find clear instances of such defects in social science writing, and the main points of the critics of voice are ones about which we should properly be concerned and with which I agree. Despite the nihilism, sophism, self-delusions about their own authenticity, and the "New Columbus" posture[10] to which these critics tend, it is highly appropriate for them to raise these questions.

In that spirit, then, let me say the voice with which I speak in this book is that of a professional social scientist who also has certain values as a citizen and a human. Guided by larger commitments, my occupational allegiance is to the development of generic knowledge about social organization per se, the effects social organization has on humans, and the effects humans have on social organization.

My allegiance to professional social science is embedded in larger commitments to enlightenment values, to a human world informed by secular humanist ethics, and to political institutions organized on social democratic or democratic socialist principles. If we are to construct and sustain a world embodying such values and containing such institutions, one critical tool is, I think, unblinkered social analysis that is continually and critically reflective. In fact, professional social science as an occupation has arisen—and has quite properly arisen—as one (among many) roles that strive to realize enlightenment values, secular humanist ethics, and just social democratic institutions.

Within these larger traditions, my own specialized niche has been and continues to be the analysis of social movements—a rather well-organized scholarly enterprise that is definitely not a "voice from nowhere." It consists of several concrete, lively, and clearly identified arenas or forums in which there are ongoing debates over how best to understand social movements and to realize the values and institutions just mentioned.[11]

This, then, is the background and perspective I bring to my efforts to understand the American peace movement. Biographically, I first became actively involved with the peace movement in the early-1980s, and I did so for many of the same reasons that millions of other Americans became involved: the new militarism of the Reagan administration. In my case, there was the added factor that I had recently concluded my previous lines of research, and I was, therefore, available for new undertakings. There was, that is, a conducive conjunction between my personal fears of an American government run militarily amuck and my availability for new research enterprises. I think, however, that my interest would not have become a sustained one had it not been for a specific opportunity that arose in and as part of the "peace soar" of 1981–1983. Acting very much in terms of the kinds of "soar beliefs" that Sam Marullo and I describe in chapter 7, the University of California regents created and generously funded a systemwide research entity named the Institute on Global Conflict and Cooperation (IGCC).[12] Regental, as well as foundation funding, then provided a rather lavish two-week summer training session, the first offering of which was conducted on the University of California, Santa Barbara campus in June–July of 1983. Its purpose was to increase the number of UC faculty who taught courses on global conflict and cooperation, and I was one of eighteen faculty in that first group.

My background in international affairs, nuclear weapons, arms races, and the like was, to put it mildly, quite sparse, and it is only because of what I began to learn in those two weeks that I "turned the corner" on my lack of self-confidence about pursuing the general area of international relations and the peace movement as a part of it. Of quite considerable importance, living in a college dormitory with my fellow students and the visiting speakers, and informally associating with the likes of Herbert York, Herbert Scoville, Roger Molander, and a variety of other "heavy hitters" of the time, served to demystify and personalize the area in a highly accelerated manner.

It can be said, then, that I am myself a phenomenon of some of the phenomena I analyze in this book. In particular, when I write about a peace surge and all that it entails, I am among the unmentioned specific instances that are generalized about in the abstract categories I employ. Referring back to my mention of voice, this gives a special meaning to the seemingly bland declaration that the voice you hear is my own.

The Santa Barbara two weeks was not, of course, a peace movement event (communicating, in fact, a variety of messages) and did not in itself point to study of the peace movement. The movement became my angle of vision on international relations as an extension of my previous research work on movements. Informed by that knowledge, my central, initial objective was simply to familiarize myself with the entire movement. Achieving this turns out to have been more important than merely "getting up to speed" on "who is who," "what is what," "who is where," and the like. For, as I went along, exactly what *is* "the movement" proved elusive as I discuss in chapters 3 and 4. I became intrigued, in particular, with how little a great many of even important movement figures knew about (or cared about) what seemed to me important parts of the movement. If, therefore, the *anatomy* of the movement was not clear and shared, it was relevant for someone to take stock, as it were, and to try to decipher the elements making up this creature. Conceived as "change-theories," "consensus movements," "movement culture," and "organizational profile," deciphering such anatomy is what the four chapters on "structure" comprising part 1 are largely about. (In the conclusion, I formalize this concern as the task of "mapping the mesoscopic.")

It is this puzzle about the vagueness of movement anatomy that informed, to use an inflated term, my "research strategy." That strategy was simply to make a conscious effort to find out about, to visit with, and to participate with as *wide a variety* of peace movement people and organizations as was practically feasible. Since the early-eighties, this effort has meant traveling up and down the West Coast of the United States many times and across and around the nation on several occasions, not to mention very extensive involvements in the Sacramento, California, region, the area in which I reside. Let me list a few of these involvements and visits in order to provide a concrete sense of what this meant. This list is, however, not a representative sampling. Instead, it "over samples" more extensive involvements and more dramatic and varied episodes of participation.

Visits and Workshops:

· Campaign for Nuclear Disarmament activities, London, U.K., April– July 1981.

· Greenham Common Women's Peace Camp, U.K., July 1983.

· Workshop with Gene Sharp, Resource Center for Nonviolence, Santa Cruz, California, September 1983.

· Ground Zero, Poulsbo, Washington, July 1984.

· Citizen Exchange Council tour, three Russian cities, June–July 1985.

· Workshop, sociological research on war and peace, Institute on Global Conflict and Cooperation, University of California, Rancho Santa Fe, California, February 1985.

· Ground Zero Pairing Project, Portland, Oregon, June 1986.

Short-term Political Actions and Educational Activities:

· Yolo Citizens against the MX (shopping mall letter solicitation), fall 1984.

· Davis Freeze Voter, fall 1984.

· Davis, California, contact for the White Train Campaign, 1985–1987.

· SANE/Freeze, Test Ban Caravan, Washington, D.C., June 1987.

· March and rally in support of the United Nations Third Special Session on Disarmament, New York City, June 1988.

· Participant, persons organizing UC, Davis, campus talks by visiting peace personages, 1984–1989.

Civil Resistance Actions:

· Support member, Perishing Too affinity group, Davis, California, Livermore National Laboratory action, April 1984.

· Rally member (with a busload of Davis citizens), American Peace Test action, Nevada Test Site, February 1987.

· Civil Resistance arrests: American Peace Test action in front of the White House, June 1987; American Peace Test Action, Nevada Test Site, March 1988; Sacramento Pledge of Resistance action, McClellan Air Force Base, North Highlands, California, February 1991.

National Conventions of Peace Organizations:

· Consortium on Peace Research, Education, and Development, Berkeley, California, October 1985.
· First national meeting of paired cities leaders, Gold Lake, Colorado, April 1986.
· National Conference on Peacemaking and Conflict Resolution, Denver, May 1986.
· Mobilization for Survival, Weapons Facilities Network, New York City, June 1988.
· Physicians for Social Responsibility, Palo Alto, California, February 1989.
· SANE/Freeze, Cleveland, Ohio (merger convention), October 1987; Oakland, California, November 1989.
· War Resisters League, Marin County, California, August 1989.
· Peace Studies Association, Boulder, Colorado, February 1992.

Positions in Peace and Related Organizations:

· Organizing member, Uman-Davis Pairing Project, fall 1983; project secretary, 1985.
· Instructor, "Peace Institutions," Department of Sociology, UC, Davis, 1986–.
· Initiator and coordinator, minor in War-Peace Studies, UC, Davis, 1986–.
· Member, subcommittee on Nuclear-Free Davis, Peace and Justice Advisory Commission, Davis, California, 1987–1989.
· Member, Board of Directors, Sacramento SANE/Freeze, 1988–1989.
· Chair, section on the Sociology of Peace and War, American Sociological Association, 1989–1990.
· Member, Steering Committee, Institute on Global Conflict and Cooperation, University of California, 1988–1993.
· Member, Executive Committee, Peace Studies Association, 1992–1994.

As are other movements, the peace movement of the 1980s was a highly intellectual or at least literate affair in that its people produced written communications in profusion, especially communications sent through the United States Postal Service. If, as I did, one took out membership in a few dozen peace organizations and sent modest contributions to others, one's peace movement mail was several inches or more thick virtually every day. This was particularly the case during the surge of the early- and mideighties, declining toward decade's end. I read and saved all these communications and many other kinds of materials collected firsthand. With the aid of students assistants, these were filed by names of organizations and persons and by concepts used in this book, as well as by many other concepts. As this collection of written material approached a decade of age, it filled almost eight four-drawer file cabinets. In addition, in 1989, Mary Neal, a core early-1980s Freeze activist in California, very generously entrusted her collection on that period to me. Comprising the contents of seven substantial cardboard boxes, it was reviewed and filed with the other materials.

In addition, I purchased and read a reasonable portion of peace movement books published over the decade and developed a collection of videotapes on movement activities. Numbers of the former range in the low hundreds[13] and the latter in the several dozens.

Measured by the standards of social science fieldwork, this is a substantial amount of data collection. Indeed, field studies are not uncommonly based on "only" about one year or so of data collection, albeit the investigator is typically working full time, which, for the most part, I have not. However, the unit of investigation in a typical field study also tends to be smaller and more compact, as in a local group, scene or community, whereas, my unit has been an amorphous, nationwide milieux.

My peace movement observations may pass muster as social science fieldwork, but I am mindful that relative to long-time committed and influential movement people, my participation has been quite modest. I must, in particular, call attention to the fact that I have not been part of the leadership circles of larger national peace organizations (although I have observed many leaders at close range and am personally acquainted with a few).

Amounts and sites of participation are important, but they are not the only salient aspects of data collection. Also of great significance is the mind-set one brings to participation. In my case, immersion in diverse aspects of the movement has been guided in important part by the conscious desire to *understand* the movement itself. Although I have been guided by the expectations of whatever movement role I was occupying at any moment, I have *also* always been concerned to see how any given "moment" related to other movement "moments" and to yet other topics. Put differently, I have sought both to live the movement and to understand it. As is the case with all fieldworkers, I therefore have had a "dual consciousness"—the consciousness of a *participant*, whose tasks include believing and doing, and the consciousness of the *observer*, whose tasks include being reflective, critical, analytic, and comparative.

This dual consciousness of the participant and the observer is not my personal quirk or the collective peculiarity of social science field workers. Instead, it expresses a well-elaborated theory of social knowing (or epistemology), one holding that extensive personal involvement and participation ("member knowledge" or "intimate familiarity") are requisite to developing accurate and fruitful generic analyses of human social life and organization (Blumer 1969b; Lofland and Lofland 1984). It is only on the foundation of extensive personal immersion that one can avoid simply using one's preconceived notions about a topic as representations of that topic and can become sensitive to the shape of the topic as it *is* out there. Personal immersion does not, of course, offer any guarantee of discovering the truth; it only facilitates the possibility. But without personal immersion even that possibility is highly remote.

We need, however, to add to personal immersion the reflective or observer frame of mind just mentioned. Such a frame of mind is critical, analytical, and skeptical. Despite participation and immersion, in the observer frame of mind movement claims cannot pass undoubted and unassessed. This is especially the case for claims to uniqueness, excellence in diverse respects, and success — claims that are more commonly the products of morale needs than of reality. Application of this skeptical frame of mind inevitably results in social analyses that do not flatter the subjects of their attention. This is because official or preferred social reality always differs from the totality of social reality, a totality that always contains unofficial and unpreferred facts. It is the both elevating and dismal obligation of the social scientist to present this fuller reality — to show social undertakings in all their salient aspects — warts and all, as it is sometimes put. Acting on this obligation, in the chapters of this volume I report a number of matters that peace movement people will see as divisive, critical, or unsympathetic. Why do I have to speak about such things when there are any number of other and more positive things to which I might have attended more fully? The answer is that, beyond the sheer commitment to truthfulness, the pragmatic fact of the matter is that idealized and whitewashed portrayals are patently suspect. They are suspect because knowledgeable participants are as aware as I of the difference between preferred and total social reality in the movement.[14] Such participants would rightly recognize my whitewash.

Moreover, and in longer-term perspective, idealized pictures (1) inhibit if not prevent the building of truly powerful social scientific analyses that might be used in action and (2) present very misleading (and, therefore, damaging) models of inspiration of future movement activists. Regarding the latter in particular, movement organizers Madeline Adamson and Seth Borgos, authors of *This Mighty Dream: Social Protest Movements in the United States* (1984, 16–17) have pointed up that not to be fully truthful about movements — about, in their words, the "internal conflicts, . . . prejudices, false starts, and strategic errors" — is "a path to despair."

> Without access to a living tradition of mass action, it is easy for those who protest today to repeat mistakes, to feel isolated, to lose perspective, to lose hope. Yet a tradition which has been whitewashed to erase the harsh texture of struggle is of little aid to understanding the conflicts and setbacks of the present. Even its inspirational value is ultimately suspect. Social changes, once achieved, become part of the status quo and seem unremarkable to those who come after. It is the spectacle of change wrested from a stubborn adversary that sustains the spirit (Adamson and Borgos 1984, 17).

And, it is important to understand that the heroic people doing the wresting are far from perfect — just as you and I. As Adamson and Borgos put it, "To acknowledge this is not to diminish their heroic stature but to clarify it" (Adamson and Borgos 1984, 17).

≪-

We have in this volume, then, seven generic analyses of social movements that are based on my immersion in the American peace movement as simultaneously a participant and observer attuned to advancing social movement theory. It is my earnest hope the seven forms of understanding put forth here are of use to analysts of social movements, to peace movement participants, and to all other persons striving to increase the effectiveness of humane social movements in achieving democratic reconstruction of societies — a reconstruction for which there is an ever-increasing need.

Notes

1. Rytina (1992) elaborates a view of structure consistent with the one I offer here.
2. Among recent reviews revealing this neglect and commenting on it, see McAdam, McCarthy, and Zald 1988.
3. Classic but recently neglected analyses of movements stressing ideational content include Blumer 1969b; Turner and Killian 1987; Smelser 1963. A resurgence of such a concern is implied, however, in "new social movement theory" (Klandermans 1991) and in analyses of "framing" (Snow et al. 1986).
4. Lofland and Lofland 1984, chap. 7. The word *agency* is shorthand for the symbolic interactionist focus on how people construct their actions (Lofland and Lofland 1984, 114–17).
5. For commentary on and documentation of these imbalances, see, again, McAdam, McCarthy, and Zald 1988.

6. Thus, wags of my acquaintance have perversely misheard the term *polite protest* as "lite protest" and delight in transmuting that error into "protest lite"—that is, it's not the real thing but tries to imitate it.

7. Peace movement history blossomed over the 1980s, even to the point of justifying a large scholarly book surveying histories of the peace movement which is Charles Howlett, *The American Peace Movement: References and Resources* (1991).

8. In addition, I have not here treated peace movements in other nations. For a description that focuses on the different series of peak periods one sees in European movements, see Young 1987.

9. These newer critical perspectives are reviewed by Agger 1991, who also elucidates their relevance to various forms of sociological practice. While the language and posture of these critics is new, the concern itself is, of course, quite long-standing. (Like the rich, New Columbuses are always with us. Cf. Lyn Lofland 1990.)

10. Cf. Lyn Lofland 1990.

11. Among these, the one best known to me as a sociologist is the Section on Collective Behavior and Social Movements of the American Sociological Association.

12. Then California governor Jerry Brown and "transcender" intellectual Willis Harmon, both UC regents at the time, spearheaded IGCC's formation.

13. For a listing of books on peace movement activists and organizations classified by the six change-theories explained in chapter 1, see Lofland, Johnson, and Kato 1991.

14. Unfortunately, a number of people who have written on the peace movement either do not perceive this difference or are dedicated to concealing it. Sadly, not even peace movement corners of the world are free of sycophantic apologetics.

Part One

Structures of the
American Peace Movement

1

Change-Theories
Six Strategy Beliefs and Movement Clusters

As ends-means calculators striving to change social arrangements, social movement participants are in the business of propounding theories of social change.[1] Much such theorizing is, to be sure, hurried, pragmatic, uninformed, and at times naïve and inarticulate. This is in contrast to the kinds of features we associate with "professional" social theory—careful historical or comparative grounding in relevant data, articulate propositions that are logically interrelated, and studious consideration of competing theories and their relative merits.

Nonetheless, such differences ought not distract our attention from the fact that social change theorizing and acting is a central and ongoing process in every social movement. Social movement practitioners are practical theorists who devise hypotheses, act on them, assess their actions, confirm or revise the theory, and act again.

Such change-theory assertions are of two main sorts: declarations relating to *ends*, as distinct from pronouncements relating to *means*. Ends statements assert what is wrong with the current order of things, why that order, or aspects of it, are in error or are unjust, and what a reformed or revolutionized order ought to be. Ends declarations report where the movement wants to go and why (Cf. Wilson 1973, chap. 3). Means statements focus on how to get there and describe behavior needed to get there. Of central salience are assertions of *what the movement must do* to get there. These assertions are its "change-theories."

One task of analysts is to understand the exact character of these practical theories of social change, how those theories are formed, and how they are or are not revised in the light of experience.

23

We want, moreover, to take a broad view of the kinds of information we consider relevant to inferring the existence of one or another change-theory. We do not want, in particular, to confine our attention to only participant statements. Even though not articulated in the discourse of participants, consistent lines of action also express theories of change required to achieve social change. Simply because these "behavioral" change-theories are less than clearly verbalized, we do not want to discount or to overlook them.

Activist-codified Change-Theories

It behooves us, though, to begin with more articulated change-theories and to do so by acknowledging that a more-or-less standard set of means-end activities are in almost routine use in a great many social movements. Indeed, the numerous manuals on "how to do" movements published in recent decades contain a virtually codified set of such categories. Thus, Lee Staples' *Roots to Power: A Manual for Grassroots Organizing* (1984), anthologizes articles on what he terms "nuts and bolts" that are titled "Guide to Public Relations," "Research for Organizing," "The People's Lobby," "Actions From Start to Finish," and "Lawsuits for Leverage" (Staples 1984, xxi–xxii).

Staple's selections are informed by the "community organizing" tradition of movements, but equivalent conceptions are found in other traditions and these provide an activist-grounded starting point for understanding working change-theories.[2] In the American peace movement of the 1980s such manuals included American Peace Test 1988; Barash and Lipton 1982; Bobo 1986; Conetta 1988; Freeze Voter Education Fund 1986; Hedemann 1981 (and later editions); Jergen 1985; Moyer 1977; Plesch 1982; Robinson 1982; U.S. Out of Central America 1983; Wollman 1985.[3]

Change-Theories of the American Peace Movement

The change-theories I observed in the eighties peace movement were, in some respects, the same as many of those advocated in "how-to" movement manuals, but they were by no means identical. Instead, the set of them was broader and differed in other ways that we shall see.

In my experience, there were six competing and often contradictory, yet in some ways complementary, change-theories. These centered on, respectively: cognitively transcending, educating, intellectualizing, politicking, protesting, or prophesying. The middle four are close to those codified in movement how-to manuals (such as Staples 1984), but the two on each end of this spectrum are not commonly discussed in such manuals.

Transcender Theory: Promote Rapid Shifts of Mass Consciousness

The transcender theory of social change in the peace movement conceived international conflict as a giant error or misunderstanding. According to the theory, an honest reexamination would reveal the basis for the misunderstanding, and needed social changes would then come about quickly. Or, if there were, in fact, true disagreements, these were minor, insignificant, or inconsequential relative to a vast range of matters upon which everyone did agree. Therefore, rapid and significant change would occur once people achieved the proper realization. This most conservative of change-theories strode the "high road" of being "above" or "beyond" ordinary ways of thinking about war and peace, and "above politics."

Situated in the context of historic traditions of social change theory, transcenders were *idealists* in two senses of the term, and this combination of characteristics set them off from the rest of the peace movement.

First, they were idealists in the sense of the "realism versus idealism" used to characterize opposing approaches to the "realities" of international relations. Realism is a hard-headed "taking things as they are" between nations — which is a planet of states that act amorally and in a self-interested fashion in a field of chaotic and anarchic internation relations. Idealism, in contrast, holds that moral values can and should be brought into international relations — a view that realists see as naïve folly or worse.

Second, they were idealists in the sense of the couplet, "materialism versus idealism." Materialism stresses the role of people's objective circumstances in causing interest in or resistance to social change, while idealism stresses the causative role of what people believe in facilitating or inhibiting social change. Stated in extreme but clear form, idealism as a theory of social change consists, as portrayed by Brian Fay, of three claims. "First, that it is people's ideas . . . which solely cause social behavior; second, that in order for people to alleviate their dissatisfaction, all they have to do is to change their ideas about who they are and what they are doing; and third, that people are willing to listen to rational analyses of their lives and to act on these analyses" (Fay 1987, 24). As Fay documents, all three of these claims are quite contentious and decidedly out of fashion in the "higher intellectual circles" of, at least, the Western world. But, they were fashionably "in use" among the affluent classes who participated in the transcender cluster of the eighties peace movement.

Moreover, in the view of transcenders, the rational case for the irrationality and obsolescence of war was so obvious and overwhelming that mass change of consciousness could be expected to take place quite quickly. One organized expression of transcender theory — that of Beyond War — had even adopted Everett Rogers's (1983) theory of diffusion of innovations into its formal scheme of social change, propounding that at a certain percentage of adoption in a human population an idea was unstoppable. No systemic or collateral changes in social, political, or economic structures seemed necessary. Such a theory was understandably attractive in emotional as well as philosophical terms to the upper middle class and wealthy who tended to be its adherents.

Theories of social change vary in the degree to which they feature rapid and dramatic "triggers of change" as distinct from small, incremental, and evenly paced steps to change. Transcender theory was very much toward the "trigger" end of this continuum and was partial to characterizing events as "epochal." The character of such triggers was, however, relatively benign, involving, for example, glitzy, high-tech events, such as satellite-televised "space bridges" and publications of books such as Beyond War's tellingly titled *Breakthrough* (Gromyko and Hellman 1988).[4]

Educator Theory: Communicate Facts and Reasoning

Construed narrowly, the term *educator* refers to people who are employees of educational institutions, that is, of schools. Although, some people in the movement were educators in this narrow sense, I use the term in a broader fashion to include all people who (1) collected and (2) disseminated information on war-peace subjects and who did so (3) in a continuing and reasonably systematic fashion in order (4) to provide instruction. Understood as a theory of change and action, to educate was continually to process, update, manage and systematize a *flow* of information for purposes of communication to broad and public audiences.

These features of their activities set educators off from the transcenders on the one side and the intellectuals on the other. Like educators, transcenders disseminated information in a systematic fashion for instructional purposes. Unlike educators, they managed no incoming flow of data. Instead, having generated their "input," transcenders simply "shut down." Efforts to collect information ceased because appropriate courses of action had already been decided upon. Additionally, transcender communications reflected exclusively their theory of change. In contrast, the content of information disseminated by educators related to numerous theories of change and activities within the peace movement.

Educators and intellectuals largely shared a theory of social change.

The latter, however, claimed not only to receive and disseminate information but also (1) assertively to collect, select, manipulate, and mold it and (2) to arrange it in terms of novel concepts, numbers, and arguments. That is, in their collection, processing, and presentation of materials, educators tended to be passive, while intellectuals tended to be active.

Of course, the line between educators and intellectuals was vague and subject to dispute. Some people worked both sides of the street, and some who considered themselves important intellectuals were disparaged by others as mere educators (as in "he or she merely writes textbooks").

The more important core beliefs in the social change theory of peace educators were the same as those of educators in general, namely, a faith in the utility of facts and reason in searches for truth and the efficacy of facts in promoting appropriate actions. A quintessential educator slogan might be, "You shall know the truth, and the truth shall make you free."

A large number of people reading these words are educators or, at the very least, extensively and, perhaps, overly exposed to educators. It is, therefore, important to stress that the belief that facts and reason lead to desired social changes must be bracketed and treated as searchingly as we treat any other social movement belief. As a piece of ideology, it was *not* accepted as true throughout the movement. In the view of many in the movement to the "left" of educators, there was ample evidence that facts and reason had little or nothing to do with much of what people (particularly war system compromised people) thought to be true or with what they did. Or, if facts and reason were used (by, especially, high-ranking members of the war system) they were tortured and twisted beyond recognition. Along a different dimension, one classic peace button declared, "Knowing is not enough/Act for peace and justice": and one peace paraphernalia merchandiser, Donnelly/Colt, used that slogan as a self-critical logo on its order forms. As analysts of social movements, then, we must not inadvertently accord a special cognitive status to educator theories of social change simply because of the unavoidably cozy relations all of us have had with them.

Intellectual Theory: Produce New Facts and Reasoning

As indicated, the core social change beliefs of intellectuals were similar, if not identical, to those of educators, but these beliefs were more strongly held. To go beyond systematizing and disseminating — the core activities of educators — to *creating* data and ideas committed one, by its logic, to the belief that facts and reasoning and, specifically, new insights, would lead to desired social changes. As phrased by leading intellectuals of the Institute for Peace and International Security:

Those who set the [political] agenda have significant, perhaps decisive power. . . . A powerful tool against war and the arms race, however, is unfettered imagination. The national security state cannot endure the release of political imagination, the invention of new language and new ways of thinking about and oragnizing the US global role.

Washington is the place where decisions are made. It is not, however, the place where all the power is or where the most effective campaigns are always fought and won. The real political battle is between those who innovate and introduce ideas intending to set the foreign and military policy agenda (Sasson, Solo, and Walker 1988, 3, 2).

The change theory of the ordinary intellectual was not, of course, that new concepts and facts *directly* brought about the social changes sought. Rather, through dissemination to educators and through educational relations — particularly with politicians — they and others using the new concepts and facts generated by the intellectuals would create the appropriate change. To recycle and use anew the classic phrase employed by Katz and Lazarsfeld (1955) in studying the effects of media on political opinion, intellectual theory envisioned a "two-step flow" in which the intellectual was the fount of new inspiration, facts, and reasoning that provided the direction for educators and, especially, for action-involved politicians. Actually, this is at least a three-step flow, for the great public presumably looms out there as the target of all this.

Transcenders, educators, and intellectuals alike exhibited the idealism that beliefs were what really mattered though, presumably, all three also looked to changes in domestic and international law as the ultimate outcome. Few stated this as an explicit objective (and some decried politics) but the *logic* of all their positions was that the public, once enlightened or educated, would act through their equally enlightened or educated legislators to bring about the desired end.[5]

Educators and intellectuals differed from transcenders in their views about the speed of change. The latter, as we have seen, conceived of dramatic triggering events producing rapid social change. In educator and intellectual theory, by contrast, the image was one of change achieved slowly and incrementally.

Politician Theory: Undertake Political Electioneering and Lobbying

Liberal parliamentarianism was the change-theory of the *movement politician,* a term I use broadly to refer to citizens who so oriented themselves as well as to office holders or activist members of political parties. Through public reasoning and dialogue in the legislative and electoral process, peace policies could be achieved by building majorities in a democratic process. Change required building "credibility" for feasible and realistic policies that could thereupon muster a preponderance of support.

Among populations of the Western, industrial nations this is, of course, the most familiar and famous of theories of social change. It is the official state ideology of virtually all nation-states and *the* elite-sanctioned manner — now even in nations of the former Soviet Union — in which to set about changing things. It is, of course, simply a *theory*, one to be inspected as dispassionately as the other five before us. (Its less than "of course" status within the peace movement was communicated by such slogans as "Don't vote — it only encourages them" and "If voting mattered, they wouldn't allow it.")

The central concepts of this liberal parliamentarianism were *feasibility, realism,* and *compromise.* In order to "get" one had to "give." One settled for less than what one wanted in the tug and pull of competing interests. Further, one scaled one's desires to assessments of what was possible, meaning that one scaled down one's aspirations even at the start in order to achieve the possibility of a majority (cf. Solo 1988).

Like the theories of educators and intellectuals, peace politician theory tended to a slow, even tortured, image of how social change occurred. The Byzantine legislative "battle" was the centerpiece of its activities. There might be moments of exhilarating victory, but such successes were neither rapid, dramatic, nor glamorous achievements.

Protest Theory: Force Issues by Noncooperation and Disruption

One key tension in some social movements is between those whose change-theories lead them respectfully and conventionally to *present* movement issues and those whose change-theories lead them to *force* movement issues. The four theories of seeking change just described were all respectable and conventional. They employed showmanship, education, intellectual analysis, parliamentary politics, lobbying, and electioneering. They all presented rather than forced. Such approaches presumed a faith in and a trust of authorities to listen to reason and respond in satisfactory measure.

The essence of "presenting" was to allow opponents the option of ignoring you. They did not have to watch your television show, buy your newspaper, take your course, read your book, pay much heed to your lobbying, vote for, or even vote *on* your candidate or issue. And, in fact, most opponents seemed most often overwhelmingly to ignore such peace movement "presentations."

This was (and eternally *is* for change-seekers) a constant frustration. None of the four theories were very strong on telling their practitioners what to do after one had been ignored or turned away for the *n*th time. This weakness opened the way to the idea that, perhaps, showpersonship, education, reasoning, lobbying, and electioneering were not sufficient as strategies of achieving change. Opponents might have very powerful reasons for not wanting to be educated by or to reason with you. They might not want to know what you have to say. In fact, your proposed social change may threaten or undermine their interests and well-being. Stated more generally, to educate and reason with people, you have to have their attention and "openness." If they will not pay attention or are opposed to your cause, you are simply out of luck.

How then might you get people's attention? Generically, the answer is to act in ways that interfere with or *disrupt* the target's cognitive or physical routines, that upset either their expectations about ordinary behavior, or their capacity to perform their own ordinary behavior. In either event, the object is to make the target believe that he or she has no choice but to attend. Once you have the target's attention, the more "presentational" kinds of social change theories and actions can be used. However, forcing tactics might still be needed because the target is likely to want to leave as soon as possible and must continuously be discouraged from doing so. These were the central points of protest theories.

However, in the view of peace protesters, such forcing had to be nonviolent. Protest "how-to" literature commonly contained lists with headings like "Basic Concepts of . . . Gandhian Nonviolence" and such formulations as "Four Basic Principles [of] . . . of Nonviolent Direct Action" (American Peace Test 1988a, 1).

Basic concepts included:

1. "Sat"—which implies openness, honesty, and fairness: Truth.
2. Ahimsa—Refusal to inflict inquiry on others.
3. Tapasya—Willingness for self-sacrifice (American Peace Test 1988b, 5-6).

Fundamental principles counseled:

1. Define your objectives.
2. Be honest and listen well.
3. Love your enemies.
4. Give your opponents a way out (American Peace Test 1988b, 5-6).

These concepts and principles were often also translated into a set of concrete rules of action as in:

1. All activities must be strictly nonviolent in action and tone.
2. All participants must undergo . . . nonviolence training.
3. No property will be damaged.
4. All activities will be open and public, not secret.
5. No participant will bring or use any illegal drugs or alcohol.
6. All participants must freely accept the legal consequences of their actions.
7. All participants must agree to follow the directions of the decision-making body (American Peace Test 1988b, 7).

Protest theory itself divided internally in terms of beliefs in the relative efficacy of *noncooperation* versus *intervention.* Noncooperation as a theory of how to achieve social change worked off a contrast with "lobbying, . . . petitions . . . [and] massive marches" in which these were portrayed as having little or no effect because none of them "hit them at the bottom line" (Cole n.d.). The "bottom line" consisted of money and, perhaps, bodies and, therefore, not providing one or both to corporations and/or the United States government was a key route to change. Corporations, in particular, were believed to be a target that the movement had missed by excessively focusing on Congress and the military. As profit-oriented entities, corporations were theorized to be more responsive than government bodies to economic pressure (Cole n.d.). Other prominent forms of noncooperation with government and corporations included draft and tax refusal, boycotts, and alternative investments.

Noncooperation theory was espoused and practiced in a relatively minor fashion compared to intervention theory. The literature published by protester-intervention organizations very explicitly propounded that "no significant social change movement has ever succeeded in [the United States] . . . without civil disobedience playing a significant role in its activities. The American revolution, the abolition of slavery, the labor movement, women's suffrage, and the civil rights movement all employed civil disobedience as an important and often central tactic" (American Peace Test 1988b, 3). The need, therefore, was for repeated and ever-larger and changing forms of mass intervention.

This central proposition was often combined with a theory of the social psychological effects of protest acts on the larger society and on those who engaged in them. As regards the larger society, "nonviolent civil disobedience . . . demonstrates the firm commitment of a movement. . . . It highlights the . . . moral . . . issues at stake. It galvanizes group solidarity and dramatically seizes public attention and respect. It generates funds to continue and expand the movement. It forces politicians to act" (American Peace Test n.d., 1).

Effects on participants were encapsulated in the concept of empowerment. To protest, especially in ways that resulted in arrest, was to undergo a change of self in which one spiritually and psychologically *felt* stronger and *was* stronger. In addition to such effects of the protest act, the process of participating in equalitarian organization was believed to produce the personal transformation of empowerment. Such organization was also frequently termed "feminist process" and "assured those with little political experience or intellectual self-confidence that they . . . [would] be heard" (Epstein 1991, 183). In extended form, this was a theory of social change in which "transformation of consciousness is a greater priority than the dismantling of institutions or the seizure of power. [S]elf transformation . . . [becomes] an important part of building a movement and working toward a better society" (Epstein 1991, 192).

The "trigger of change" dimension of protest theory was clearly closer to the transcender image than to those of educators, intellectuals, and politicians. In both, change had to be rapid and dramatic although protesters and transcenders clearly differed in the *kind* of trigger they envisioned. For transcenders it was a rather joyous transformation of consciousness — a so-called new way of thinking—whereas for protesters the trigger was a *jolt,* an intentionally created political crisis that gave politicians little option except to make the changes demanded by the protesters.[6]

In these depictions of change-theories, I am focusing on the general principles that grounded, or theorized, approaches. This focus clarifies the logic of change-theories, but in so doing it downplays the fact that some practitioners of a theory might personally believe a change-theory in only a qualified way or not at all. More clearly to acknowledge this fact, let me briefly report some of these variations for the case of protest theory. Protesters varied, specifically, with regard to how they felt about nonviolence as a philosophy versus a pragmatic tactic. My impression was that a *first,* and large, portion of protesters seemed not to have given much attention to nonviolence as a philosophy. They had not, that is, studied the matter, agonized about its demands, and rejected it. Instead, nonviolence as a philosophy was little understood, and nonviolence was perceived as simply a practical form of political action. These were the *naïve pragmatists.* A *second* tendency consisted of members of churches who had given attention to the philosophical meanings of nonviolence and to some degree supported those meanings. They had not, though, embraced it as an encompassing and total way of life in the manner we found among the prophets. They were the *qualified believers.*

In a *third* tendency, nonviolence was embraced as a philosophy of life and integrated with several other themes. Barbara Epstein (1991) has conceived these themes and the lifestyle they supported as the "nonviolent direct action movement" (or NDAMers), an orientation Epstein thinks was born of the "blocked cultural revolution" of the late-sixties and that first appeared as a political force in the antinuclear power protests of the seventies. It was less visible as a movement in itself than as a component of other movements, working — in succession — in the antinuclear power, feminist, peace, and antiintervention movements over the seventies and eighties. The NDAMers', or neocounterculturalists, pertinence to protest theory is that they were likely the largest portion of the "radical" protesters in the eighties peace movement. As an orientation, this consisted of "dedication to nonviolence, opposition to any hierarchical structures or relationships, a view of revolution . . . as having more to do with the transformation of the way people live than with seizing power, and a reliance on personal experience and moral witness" (Epstein 1991, 56–57).

A *fourth* tendency consisted of the people who also understand nonviolence, consciously rejected it as a philosophy, adopted a radical political perspective in its place, and acted nonviolently for only pragmatic reasons. We might call them the *sophisticated pragmatists* (Ryan 1983). The most politically extreme of the sophisticated pragmatists seemed concentrated in an organization called the No Business As Usual Action Network (NBAU). This organization sought to "break . . . out of the confines of 'protest-as-usual.'" The choreographed, light-hearted and routinized character of liberal protest was eschewed in favor of actions that "propel . . . [protest] to much higher levels" and "change the terms of debate, analysis, and action." Thus, campuses had to be turned into "zones of disruption," there had to be "No Religion As Usual," and world war had to be prevented "no matter what it takes," this last phrase being one of the NBAU's oft-repeated slogans. I need to stress, though, that this strain to violence was found among only a tiny number of participants in some movement actions. It was so small, in fact, that although its existence must be reported, its size and presence do not justify raising it to the level of a significant theory of social change seen in the eighties movement. The *absence* of such advocacy and action seemed, to the contrary, to be the key feature of the eighties peace movement. (In contrast, the idea that violence-causes-positive-change has been an extremely important change-theory in a great many other social movements.)

Prophet Theory: Affect Deep Moral Regeneration

Prophet theory of social change centered on the assertion that the war system, the state, the power elite (or other abstractions) were not, per se, the enemy. Instead, the evil (if that it be) was in ourselves — *all* our selves, members of the war system or not. Therefore, the goal was to "seek change from within, . . . to engage deeply the spirits of both sides of a conflict" (Douglass 1987, 94). "Spiritually based nonviolence," or "civil disobedience," was an act of striving to overcome the evil in ourselves that "lies in our cooperation" with nuclear war, for "when we cease cooperating with evil at its source in ourselves, it ceases to exist" (Douglass 1987, 96). Further, "when we accept responsibility for nuclear war in the hidden dimensions of our own complicity, we experience the miracle of seeing [for example] the Nuclear Train stop and the arms race end. To paraphrase Harry Truman, the bomb stops here" (Douglass 1987, 96). Civil disobedience properly understood, then, was, not "an act of defiance but an act of obedience to a deeper, interior will within us and within the world that is capable of transforming the world. . . . To live out the kingdom of God through such an action is to live in a loving relationship to our brothers and sisters in the police force, in courts, and in jails, recognizing God's presence in each of us. It is also to accept responsibility for an evil that is ours; as we are, so is the nuclear state" (Douglass 1987, 97).

In the view of Jim Douglass, a leading peace movement prophet, civil disobedience was, so conceived and motivated, an act of prayer and love. It was "divine obedience." Indeed, Douglass observed, civil disobedience done in defiance rather than in prayer and love was "the right deed for the wrong reason. . . . Civil disobedience, like war, can be used to mask the emptiness of a false self" (Douglass 1987, 96). It followed that protest acts of the prophets were conducted with an air of religious solemnity, very much in contrast to the carnival/liberation/jubilation atmosphere often prevailing at liberal protest actions (and the edge of anger expressed by the hard-left protesters sometimes present). Prophets such as Jim Douglass were, thus, not supportive of such protest atmospheres and, in fact, were infrequently seen at them.

Significant social change, then, required profound inner transformation, an overcoming of "the arms race within" (the title of a video documentary on Ground Zero, Poulsbo, and the Puget Sound Agape Community). The nuclear arms race and the war system were not merely errors in understanding — matters correctable by reason and education, or the tools of greedy and contending elites — although those factors might be involved. The causes went far deeper and signified something basically gone awry in the human spirit that required spiritual revolution. Prophets typically cast this "far deeper" matter as a radical form of Christianity, of which there were two main versions. Radical Catholicism was prevalent among prophets and particularly associated with the Plowshares network. In other networks, evangelical Protestant Christianity with a commitment to social justice was central as espoused by, among others, the Sojourners Community. (Both are profiled in Epstein 1991, chap. 6.)

As articulated by Trident II Plowshares member Frank Panapoulos (1986), prophet theory, as a mode of action, had three levels. At the first and most basic level, adherents strove to build *life-sharing* communities among themselves. Premised on such communities, the second level required actually beginning disarmament by literally "beating swords into plowshares" or equivalently engaging in disarming actions. Two forms of "beating swords into plowshares" acts were especially prominent. One, what were called *plowshares* actions often involved illegally entering a military installation and physically damaging (mostly in a very minor fashion) nuclear missile equipment. Hammers might be used to bang on missile nose cones or silo protective doors; blood might be spilled on equipment. These actions were accompanied by prayer and other religious ceremony. The prophets waited until authorities arrived and they quietly allowed themselves to be arrested. This was a mild and fleeting form of *occupying* combined with planned and symbolic property damage. Two, a similarly mild and fleeting form of blockading was undertaken, as in the "white train" actions on the railroad tracks leading into the Trident submarine base near Poulsbo, Washington. Police were informed that a group of prophets intended to sit on the tracks and to block an approaching train that was carrying nuclear weapons. They sat; police warned them they must leave or be arrested; they were arrested and taken off the track. These acts, too, were accompanied by religious ceremonial activities.[7]

On the third level, an adherent was nonviolent, asserted that he or she had a responsibility to engage in disarming action, and accepted the consequences of those actions. In doing all of this, one hoped that "people will see the truth of the action . . . and act on it in their personal lives. Our goal is a chain reaction of Plowshares actions around the country. Short of that we hope for people to alter their lives by engaging in *some* form of resistance" (Panapoulos 1986, 6, emphasis in the original).

Use of the term *chain reaction* suggests the degree to which prophet theory conceived change as occurring rapidly and dramatically. As a theory, it would seem to lie toward the "trigger" and crisis end of the change continuum. Panapoulos further observes, "To me, a million people taking the risk of *occupying* and *remaining* at nuclear weapons . . . sites would shut the system down, creating the moral crisis atmosphere necessary for disarmament to begin" (Panapolous 1986, 6, emphases in the original). Prophet actions, such as those of Plowshares, then, looked toward such a day (although yet other prophets did not explicitly envision such outcomes, reasoning instead that resistance was simply the "right" thing to do).

Viewed as a social role rather than a theory of achieving social change, the prophets might also be termed "nonviolent revolutionaries," or "saints." Its participants were marked off from other theories also conceived as social roles by (1) commitment to a Spartan life-style of simple and sometimes communal living; (2) embracement of a radical religious philosophy in which opposition to the war system was a central concern; and, (3) engagement in dramatic acts of moral witness as a way to communicate this concern. This complex of features evokes the classic prophetic figures of the Judeo-Christian sacred texts. It has, therefore, seemed most appropriate and even necessary to invoke the ancient image of the prophet in this modern context. The similarity was so striking, indeed, that commentary on it was not uncommon, as in William Sloane Coffin's observation that the Berrigans "are prophets . . . [and] like all prophets, they are without honor in their own time" (Coffin 1984, 93).[8]

As is evident, as both a theory of social change and social role, prophets were radically discontinuous with the other theories and roles. Save for the neocounterculturalists, other members of the peace movement were more-or-less ordinary folk in the sense that they looked, acted, and lived pretty much like people in the social classes of which they were members (e.g., middle class public sector employees, upper-middle-class professors, etc.). Most members of the peace movement were distinguished from most Americans merely and most importantly by their peace activism and associated beliefs. Such was not the case for the prophets who, instead, carved out a distinctive, religious way of life whose most evident larger counterparts were certain forms of Catholic monasticism.

Change-Theories and Movement Clusters

Using a strategy of pure or ideal typing, I have exposited the six main theories of how to achieve social change seen in the eighties peace movement. This serves to hone our perception, but it results in a clarity for which we have paid a price, the price of decontextualization. In presenting change-theories in sharp relief, I have extracted each from the social location in which it was found and ripped each from the social organizations in which they were differentially embedded.

The contextual fact is, however, that change-theories were not espoused randomly and conjoined willy-nilly with other social matters. Instead, the six had decidedly different conjunctions with a great many dimensions of social organization, and I must now begin to repair the imbalance I have created by elucidating these conjunctions.

Dominant Orientation

Peace movement organizations tended to adopt one or another of these six theories as their dominant, even if not exclusive, orientation and to specialize in one type of change action, even though they might also engage in other types of actions. For example, Grandmothers for Peace and its moving spirit, Barbara Wiedner, were practitioners of protest theory although both Wiedner and her organization did more than protest. The organization's "statement of action" in fact listed nine "tasks": meditation and prayer for peace; speaking out for nuclear disarmament; participation in vigils; supporting other peace groups; educating themselves and others; voter registration; promoting peace studies in schools; making contacts with grandmothers in other countries; and, "when necessary, participating in nonviolent acts of resistance" (Grandmothers for Peace 1987). Only two of these nine (vigils and resistance) were "protest." However, protest acts were viewed by her and her group and by advocates and enactors of other movement change-theories as the feature that provided Wiedner and Grandmothers for Peace a distinctive identity and raison d'être. Much the same applied to most other persons and groups. I speak, therefore, of differentiating directions, distinctive competencies and dominant tendencies rather than totally exclusive features.

Clusters

Peace organizations of the same or adjacent theory perceived a shared "community of interest," selectively interacted with one another, and were partial to one another in undertaking joint activities. These selectively interacting "communities of interest" formed the six clusters of the movement. As will be elaborated, each presented a distinctive profile of activities; relations with other movement clusters, the war system, and the public at large; characteristics of activists; forms of organization; modes of financing; features of membership; and, cultural and emotional persona.

In this conception of clusters, I am proposing a model of movement structure that is similar but not identical to the segmentary-polycephalous-reticulate (SPR) model formulated by Luther Gerlach and Virginia Hine (1970) as characterizing several movements they studied. In their analysis, these three terms have these meanings:

1. *Segmentary.* A movement is composed of diverse groups, or cells, which grow and die, divide and fuse, proliferate and contract.

2. *Polycephalous.* [A movement] . . . does not have a central command or decision-making structure; rather, it has many leaders or rivals for leadership not only within the movement as a whole but within each movement cell.

3. *Reticulate.* These diverse groups [are] not . . . simply an amorphous collection; rather, they are organized into a network of reticulate structure through cross-cutting links, "traveling evangelists" or spokespersons, overlapping participation, joint activities, and sharing of common objectives and opposition (Gerlach and Hine 1983, 135).

The terms *segment* or *segmentary* also mean that a movement "is composed of a great variety of localized groups or cells which are essentially independent, but which can combine to form larger configurations or divide into smaller units" (Gerlach and Hine 1970, 41). Two features in this passage require underscoring. One, the groups or cells that compose the movement are "essentially independent." Two, such units can and do nonetheless "combine to form 'larger configurations'." It is these essentially independent units combining into larger configurations that are segments.

I do not doubt that SPR is an accurate characterization of the movements Gerlach and Hine studied. Moreover, as a matter of general direction, SPR correctly depicts structural tendencies observed in the eighties peace movement. My concern, however, is that SPR suggests a greater degree of organization that seemed to obtain. The term *segment*, in particular, suggests "larger configurations" of more definite shape and clearer boundaries than was the case. The term "polycephalous" suggests multiple leaders of a stature, following, and degree of rivalry that is stronger than actually seen. In fact, a concept of *acephalous* seemed to apply as well as *polycephalous*. The better to denote this greater degree of amorphousness I, therefore, prefer to speak of the peace movement as having had "clusters" rather than segments.

Liberals Versus Radicals Within Clusters

Save, perhaps, for the transcender and prophet clusters, each of the other four divided internally in terms of mainstream-liberal versus radical perspectives regarding how much change was thought to be needed. There were substantively "liberal" versus "radical" educators, intellectuals, politicians, and protesters. Within clusters, liberals and radicals agreed on their theory of how to make change, but they disagreed on how much change was needed using that theory. Liberals envisioned more restricted and socially "surface" changes than radicals, who called for a wide range of thorough-going and "deep" social changes.

Liberal-Radical Similarities Interlaced Clusters

Although it was only a main tendency, as we proceeded through the list of change-theories and their embedding clusters, the degree to which the leaders and members were socioeconomically privileged and culturally "upscale" declined. At the transcender extreme, leaders and members were quite affluent, and at the prophet extreme, leaders and members embraced a life of economic simplicity or even poverty.

The four middle segments were rather more complicated in that the economic level tended to divide between liberal and radical versions of educating, intellectualizing, politicking, and protesting, with the radical being the less affluent. Even so, compared among themselves, the educators and intellectuals tended on the whole to be more affluent than the politicians (with the exception of office holders) and the protesters. (A major reason for this was that the activities of the former two tended also to be ways they made their living, while the latter two were involved predominantly in volunteer and unpaid forms of citizen activism.)

Cluster Sizes

The great news about the peace movement of the eighties was, of course, its "surge"—the phenomenon analyzed in part 2 of this volume. Adopting a moderately restrictive conception of *membership* I estimate that the movement started the decade with about a quarter of a million members and perhaps twenty-five hundred organizations. As it surged toward middecade it may have had as many as ten million participants involved in perhaps eight thousand organizations. In the late-eighties, membership declined, though the number of organizations continued to grow (even as some older ones closed their doors). By the decade's end, about half a million people were involved in some seventy-five hundred associations.[9]

Viewed in terms of clusters, I estimate the relative strength of each as shown in figure 1.1. The politicians were by far the largest cluster in terms of participants, followed by the transcenders and educators. The intellectuals, protesters, and prophets, indeed, formed a kind of second tier, having only on the order of a tenth to a quarter of the membership of the larger clusters.

Figure 1.1
Clusters of the American Peace Movement:
Estimated Number of Organizations and Participants , Later Eighties

Cluster	Number of Organizations	Number of Participants
Transcenders	2,000	100,000
Educators	2,000	100,000
Intellectuals	200	10,000
Politicians	2,000	250,000
Protesters	1,000	50,000
Prophets	300	10,000
Total	7,500	520,000

I would further estimate that the overwhelming majority of movement people — perhaps four hundred thousand — inclined in the liberal direction, while some one hundred thousand leaned in the radical direction.

Degree Conflictful: Talkers Versus Doers

Theories of social change can be ranked in terms of the degree to which they are conflictual — that is, the degree to which executing them brings one into a contentious relation to the targets of change and produces a combative relationship with opponents. Indeed, I have so ranked the six theories of change presented previously, ranging from transcending as least conflictful to prophesying as most conflictful.

The variable *degree conflictful* may be thought of more specifically as having at least two components. First, did the theory of change require only *talk?* or Did it mandate some regular form of *action?* In addition to the sheer uttering of words with movement content, by *talk* I mean the activities of writing and researching *and* activities attendant to supporting these in a sustained way, most especially the activities of raising the funds that made concerted talking, writing, and researching possible. Talking, in the narrow sense of uttering words with movement content, includes the activities of public speaking, television and radio appearances, and the concatenation of these into "tours."

Second, we can ask, "Talking (or doing) to *whom?*" Some important variations are to people in one's cluster, the public at large in a general and disembodied fashion (as through articles, books, and television appearances), people in other movement clusters, and participants in the opponent world. Termed differently, What are typical objects of the talk (or action)? Who is targeted?

In these two terms of talking or doing to whom, the transcenders, educators, and intellectuals were the least conflictful. Their activities consisted mainly or totally of talk, and the talk was heavily directed to their own clusters or to the "public at large." Such targeting may be thought of as indirect or unfocused generalized propaganda as distinct from directed and direct social pressure.

The activities of "doers" entailed talking, of course, but went on to support the talk with persistent efforts to bring it *directly* to the attention of members of the opponent world. By directly I mean that, as a regular matter, the doer came into the immediate physical presence of members of the opponent world for the purpose of speaking about movement topics or against opponent policies and, perhaps, also for the purpose of performing acts which would communicate the seriousness of intent (e.g., acts of civil disobedience or resistance). Such targeting was *focused* and the three clusters that moved in this direction – the politicians, protesters, and prophets – may be thought of as doers. They sought to "make problems" for opponents, to initiate situations that made it difficult if not impossible for opponents to ignore the movement. This was in contrast to the talkers who, by definitional dissimilarity, could safely be ignored by opponents.

Cluster Risk and Substantive Radicalness

There are yet other dimensions along which the six clusters can be ranked, and I want especially to call attention to the degree of *risk-taking* each involved. Regardless of the degree of change they believed necessary, all talkers were engaged in relatively low levels of social risk taking. In contrast, the doers subjected themselves to the possibility and reality of social disapproval, legal action, financial punishment, marginality and unemployment, and bodily harm.

Such risk taking seemed to be associated, moreover, with beliefs that supported and facilitated it – beliefs that were more left or radical on the whole than those of the talkers. (Substantively, these beliefs were more left in the sense of greater advocacy of equalitarian social arrangements and wide, democratic participation.)

The spectrum of ideological variation across the six clusters was really quite impressive because leaders and members differed on much more than sheer right-left talk in a narrowly political sense. The spectrum ran, instead, from a focus on technocratic arms control perspectives, toward one end, to focus on the ultimate existential features of human life, at the other end.

Forms of Organization

As will be explored in detail in chapter 4, there were several affinities among change-theory clusters, forms of organization, and sources of funding. Toward the right wing of the movement, one observed preference for traditionally bureaucratic and hierarchical associations in which centrally formulated policy was executed through a series of organizational levels. This was the tendency especially among the transcenders. The suggestion, also, is that in the case of organizations like Beyond War, there was a particularly close fit between its change-beliefs and its relatively hierarchical organizations (Brigham 1990). The tendency in the middle clusters (especially among liberal educators, intellectuals, and politicians) was toward democratic organization (the classic preference of American voluntary associations). Hierarchy as a principle was more likely to be accepted — including the unproblematic utilization of paid staff — but upper-level activists were selected and controlled through elections and other voting. However, the world is complicated, and smaller and less affluent groups of mainstream transcenders often also adopted the familiar practices of parliamentarianism — elected leaders, voting, public meetings. And, like the transcenders, *liberal* educators tended to accept mainstream forms of organization, namely, bureaucracy and parliamentary democracy in voluntary associations.[10] The two clusters furthermost to the left — the protesters and the prophets — were more partial to equalitarian organization, to associations in which leaders were deemphasized and policies were, ideally, adopted by consensus. The radical protesters, indeed, objected to the practice of bureaucracy and parliamentary democracy. Concepts and practices of equalitarianism and consensus decision making took their place.

Low Strife and Muted Tension

Despite all the differences and, therefore, potential for strife that we see in the foregoing, the level of intramovement conflict was quite low. Although people in each cluster might have reservations about what others were doing (if they even knew what others were doing), such skepticism was far short of the disdain or even hate seen in many other movements.

The mild and muted character of conflict was, in part, a function, first, of the narrower range of cluster change-theories and their ideologies than seen in other movements. It had, for example, no equivalent to such formations as the black power wing of the civil rights movement of the sixties or of the Earth First! faction of the environmental movement of the eighties. Second, the differentiated character of the tasks and social composition of each cluster made it possible for each to field its own programs in relative independence of other clusters. Low cluster interdependence meant that one could "get by" without much relation to many other clusters and, thus, the strife born of interdependence-frustration.[11] Third, here as elsewhere, one cannot but be impressed with the role of "peace ideology" in holding strife in check.

This overarching pattern notwithstanding, there were, nonetheless, tensions among the clusters. Let us examine some main forms of these.

Transcenders and others. People in clusters to the left of the transcenders sometimes voiced the opinion that transcenders were, unhappily, shallow dilettantes in the quest for peace. David Mixner's aborted PRO-Peace March was responded to by many nontranscender peace groups as "simplistic and shallow" in terms of its assertedly "nonpartisan" message and methods (Cordes 1985–1986), and these groups only grudgingly endorsed the effort. *Far* to the left, people did not like to think of the transcenders as part of the peace movement at all. Such feelings clearly functioned to discourage relations.[12]

However, distancing was not always successful. In particular, educator efforts were vulnerable to being overwhelmed and even captured by a rapid influx of transcenders. Thus, the transcender enterprise of city-twinning that arose from Ground Zero's campaign of educating people about the Soviet Union was decidedly not what was planned or intended by Ground Zero leaders Earl Molander and Roger Molander (Molander and Molander 1990). Instead, after an initial activation, the Molanders sought to forge a broad-front educational phase that would than act as a transition into a political participation phase in which U.S. policy was changed. In their view, the movement skipped or truncated the educational phase and entered political participation prematurely, was educationally unequipped to manage opposition, and failed to have policy effects because of this educational deficit. As conceived by Ground Zero, city-twinning — the particular educational activity — was simply one device for focusing attention and not intended as the main theme — which was education about the Soviet Union as part of the broader educational phase of movement building. Alas for the Molanders and their associates, the bulk of recruits to city-twinning had their own and different ideas about it — transcender ideas. As a consequence and ironically, Ground Zero leaders were the major force in starting city-twinning but among the least happy with what it became.

On a lesser scale, exuberant transcenders sometimes overwhelmed gatherings of other clusters with their numbers, enthusiasm, and — most important — monetary resources. For example, the 1986 annual conference of the educator organization the Consortium on Peace Research, Education, and Development (COPRED) was held on and near the campus of the University of California at Berkeley, the geographical region of which also happened to be a hotbed of transcenders. The time of the COPRED conference coincided with the desire of a number of transcender organizations to promote their programs, and they became heavily, even overwhelmingly, parts of the extremely open COPRED conference programming. Swamped in transcender rhetoric, many of these taken unawares educators were, in turn, puzzled, amused, and angered (e.g., Crews 1986). Beyond differences in the specificity of their respective realms of discourse, each style signaled their dissimilarities through their very attire and grooming: shabby academics and other peace types mingled with people in expensive three-piece suits and fur coats.

In addition to such social class factors, transcender sheer ignorance of an older "peace culture" found among groups further to the left functioned to inhibit cluster relations. Being ignorant, transcenders tended to think they were doing many things for the first time, when, in fact, certain practices had taken place in some movement clusters for many years. Thus, when the founder of a well-known transcender group featuring "mothers" as key actors was inspired to organize a commemoration of Hiroshima-Nagasaki in her large Southern California City, she thought that she was the first person or organization ever to organize such an event. In fact, historic peace groups in that city had organized a commemoration for many years, and it had come to have certain traditional features. These groups were, therefore, offended that the transcender-leader acted as though she was a pioneer and thereby swept aside tradition by ignoring it. Even after this matter was put straight and a coalition to organize the commemoration was formed, there were other "cultural conflicts." The transcenders' idea of "security" for the event was to hire a private guard company and to encourage the presence of city police. This again offended peace groups to the left, who had a tradition of training and fielding their own volunteer and nonviolent march-rally monitors, explicitly eschewing reliance on public or private police. The leader of the transcenders acceded to this more traditional cultural practice, and transcenders were recruited to undergo training in nonviolence in order to function as monitors, an experience that was itself, as reported by one War Resisters League trainer, a trauma for all concerned.

Politicians and protesters in ambivalent alliance. A second form of intercluster tension obtained between the politicians and protesters. Politicians seemed both to reject and to embrace protest as a strategy. At the level of formal and official policy of organizations, pronouncements on protest were somewhat negative but also permissive and even supportive although not embraced as organization programs.

This ambivalence crystallized most strongly at the yearly conventions of the Freeze in the early- and mid-eighties. The Freeze had stalled as a political line of action, and some people argued that protest was necessary for further progress. But resolutions endorsing and adopting protest failed to gain majorities at Freeze conventions, opponents arguing that protest would only alienate the public at large. Finally, the proprotest minority formed a new protest organization, the American Peace Test (APT). APT members did not, however, cease membership or participation in the Freeze (SANE/Freeze [S/F] after the 1987 merger). Instead, APT functioned as a S/F "rump" group that made protest activities more acceptable because APT was now a formally separate entity and its members no longer lobbied to have Freeze-S/F adopt protest policies and actions. For example, at the merger convention in 1987, the de facto head of APT, Jesse Cocks, served, without public controversy, as an S/F delegate from Nevada; the convention unanimously endorsed the February 1988 "reclaim the test site" action, and APT organizers conducted program-listed and, therefore, de facto–endorsed workshops on APT philosophy and the "reclaim the test site" action.[13] The relation was not without its tension, however. At the end of a SANE/Freeze video documentary on a joint S/F-APT June 1987 lobby day and protest in Washington, D. C., the narrator (popular music personality Casey Kasem) declared that the joint action was a "tribute to the maturity and diversity of the movement that it could include in one event both lobbying and protesting." Such a declaration is, of course, only necessary when an alliance is problematic.

Neocounterculturalists and the middle class. The deepest division in the movement was only in part indexed by change-theory differences, liberal-radical tendencies, or variations in specifically peace ideology. This was the difference between the *nonviolent direct actionists,* or *neocounterculturalists,* on the one side, and the middle class, on the other. The latter vastly outnumbered the former, but the former's much greater commitment and life-style orientation to the movement gave them power and impact beyond their numbers. Accepting of the lower wages and Spartan life-style it imposed, they were especially likely to be employed as staff in otherwise middle-class peace organizations. Barbara Epstein has characterized neocounterculturalists she observed in Northern California over the eighties in these terms: "Most are in their twenties and early thirties, though there are a substantial number in their forties and some even older. Most, though not all, are of middle-class origins; many are downwardly mobile, through various combinations of choice and necessity. Many have college degrees. . . . Many have parents who expected them to be professionals, or perhaps to enter business. Instead, they are likely to have found less stable jobs in the social services, as clerical workers, or perhaps in alternative businesses such as health-food stores" (Epstein 1985, 47–48). Demographically, this is not a dramatic profile. Its interest resides, instead, in the culture elaborated among them, a culture Epstein characterized as "quite extensive" in the San Francisco Bay area, where "it is made up of people who, by the standards of white middle-class America, live culturally unconventional and often economically marginal lives. These people inhabit a milieu in which feminism, environmentalism, and anti-militarism are assumed, and in which there is a good deal of contempt for the consumerism of the mainstream middle class" (Epstein 1985, 48).

Neocounterculturalists and the middle class came into most frequent and intense contact in the protest cluster, where, perhaps, the largest number of protests were coalitions of affinity groups drawn from both cultural orientations. One of the earliest and largest of these coalitions — the Livermore Action Group (LAG) — was referred to humorously as, indeed, a coalition of "Montclair housewives" (Montclair being an upper-middle-class neighborhood in the San Francisco Bay Area) and "hippies" (Epstein 1985, 47).

Neocounterculturalists were distinctive in the degree they were striving to develop a set of cultural alternatives to mainstream American culture — an alternative set of heroes, songs, myths, icons, and array of institutions — a cultural content that is conveyed in Epstein's description just given. In its own way it took seriously the admonition that "you can't beat something with nothing."

The interactions of counterculturists and the middle class was further complicated by the fact that the counterculturalists differed very considerably among themselves. Here is Epstein's summary statement of her longer description of the tendencies she observed in simply the Livermore Action Group:

> LAG brought together former Abalone affinity groups, especially anarcha-feminist ones, a more spiritually-oriented section of the counter-culture that identified with Paganism and witchcraft; activists who leaned more strongly toward Marxism than had any groups in the Clamshell or the Abalone; Quakers; Catholic and Protestant pacifists; feminists; environmentalists; lesbian activists; rural countercultural groups; veterans of the anti-war movement of the sixties; peace activists who had been involved

in left politics since the thirties; and middle class, middle aged people who had never been involved in political activity before, many of whom came in contact with LAG through Bay Area churches (Epstein 1991, 125–26).

Moreover, women of countercultural leanings were particularly active as organizers and leaders in the protester cluster, and, among them, lesbians were an especially important component. Epstein (1991, chap. 5) characterized this component as a "major element" and estimated that they were about one-third of those jailed in some LAG actions and a "large majority" of participants in women-only protests, such as the Women's Pentagon Action and the Seneca Peace Camp.

Such divergences and tendencies between and among the neocounterculturalists and the middle class were not strongly supportive of cooperative action and were muted, but ongoing, sources of difficulty as Epstein (1991) documents.

Prophet isolation. The prophet cluster seemed relatively insular vis-à-vis the rest of the movement. Educators, intellectuals, politicians, and liberal protesters had at least some interlacing relations, but less so with the prophets. Even relations with what seemed to be the "closest" cluster — the protesters — were rather cautious. Investing *protest* with religious meaning, a great deal of protester action seemed insufficiently serious to prophets. This uneasiness was particularly noticeable at protest sites selected by *both* protesters and prophets — such as the entrance gate of the Nevada Test Site. While associations such as the Franciscans held solemn and moving ceremonials with names such as Lenten Desert Experience, APT staged colorful and sprawling actions with names like Reclaim the Test Site. With a note of sadness and resignation in his voice, one prophet described the latter to me as an unfortunate "Woodstock in the desert."

Qualified in the various ways just reviewed, I would generalize that clusters adjacent to each other were more comfortable with one another than with clusters that were further removed. Thus, joint programs between transcenders and educators were observed as in the ability of Vivienne Verdon-Roe (a leading transcender maker of films) and Helen Caldicott to share the same stage on the transcender topic of "The Courage of Commitment" and in promotion of Verdon-Roe's film, "Women for America, For the World" (Palace of Fine Arts, San Francisco, Calif., November 10, 1987).

Transcenders and educators expressed, in contrast, uneasiness about

"politics," the de classe "antics" of protesters, and the solemnity of prophets. This was particularly apparent among transcender and educator groups
formed in the liberal professions (doctors, lawyers, architects) and in business. The executive director of a coalition of seven such groups in a large
east coast city put it this way to a workshop on "coalition building" at the
1989 national meetings of the Physicians for Social Responsibility:

> We really keep it as a professional coalition. . . . There are groups
> that are wonderful and active, and many of us . . . are members of Sane/
> Freeze or Women's Strike For Peace but [such groups] are not in the coali-
> tion. They kind of are very important to us but there is a difference.
> We are now talking to an audience that is very different, we are not
> talking to ourselves in the peace movement. [Our city] . . . has a very
> strong conservative power base. The peace movement, even the word
> peace, [causes them to say] . . . , "oh god, here we go again. . . ." And
> they have never before thought of themselves as members of the peace
> movement. . . . To this day some of them resist the word "peace move-
> ment." And they do understand that we work really close with all the
> other groups, with Sane/Freeze. We have a great relationship, but they
> [peace groups] also know that if we run an event they are not going to
> be co-sponsors.

Uneasiness was of course reciprocated from the other end of the spectrum.

Conclusion

I have addressed two basic matters about social movements in general
and the American peace movement of the eighties in particular. First, I
have explicated the sense in which the ensembles of change-seeking organizations we call social movements espouse diverse theories of how desired
social changes can be achieved. Using materials provided by the American
peace movement of the eighties, I have specified six such theories. Because
we are speaking only of the peace movement, I do not claim these six are
the only theories found in movements although — impressionistically — I
do think most of them occur quite commonly in other movements. Comparative analysis of other movements is obviously in order, however.

Second, I have suggested that such theories were embedded in "clusters"
of like-theoried movement organizations. These clusters themselves had
complex relations to one another. Among other relations, they were interlaced in certain ways and could be arrayed in terms of the degree they were
conflictual and risk taking.

Notes

1. This chapter is a revision and expansion of Lofland, Colwell, and Johnson 1990.

2. The works of Saul Alinsky (1946, cited in the 1969 ed., 1972) are classic, of course, and there is an exceedingly rich and broad set of manuals in the tradition he pioneered.

3. For a more complete listing see Lofland, Johnson, and Kato 1991, an analytic bibliography of almost seven hundred books on peace movement organizations and activists that indexes social change manuals and codes them in terms of the six clusters discussed in this chapter.

4. One splashy transcender conference held in early 1988 was characterized by its organizers as an "epochal event" under the banner of "A New Way of Thinking: Social Inventions for the Third Millennium." Transcender imagery is further conveyed in Ken Keys, Jr., *The Hundredth Monkey* (1982), several hundred thousand copies of which are said to have circulated in the early- and mid-eighties. For expanded discussion of transcender theory and practice see Mechling and Auletta 1986 and chap. 2, this volume.

5. It was likely, in addition, that laws governing the activities of tax-deductible nonprofit organizations (which prohibited more than an insubstantial amount of effort to influence legislation) were significant in causing this gap between what would appear to be the logic of educator and intellectual theories and what actually took place (McCarthy, Britt, and Wolfson 1991). Conversely, the logic of politician theory presumed the importance of educating the public so it will undertake appropriate lobbying and electoral action.

We must recognize, moreover, that some intellectuals did engage in forging connections between ideas and politicians. For example, in the late-eighties, the Institute for Peace and International Security (whose change-theory is in the text) set about quite explicitly to carry ideas of "common security" into the political arena through grassroots political action: "Political power and short term success demand that the peace movement redefine the larger security agenda and engage in what right wing architect Irving Kristol calls the 'war of ideas.' In fighting to give legitimacy to our ideas, we push back the boundaries of what is now considered reasonable or politically possible" (Sasson, Solo, and Walker 1988, 2–3, emphasis deleted).

6. A professionally articulated version of protest theory is presented by Piven and Cloward 1979. The social psychological side of being jolted into believing in the need for social jolts is nicely portrayed by Todd Gitlin in his account of his personal conversion from politician to protest theory in the presence of a Pentagon official who was defending U.S. government civil defense plans: "The world went obvious on me. *Men such as this were not going to be persuaded to be sensible.* They were grosteque, these clever and confident men, they were unbudgeable, their language was evasion, their rationality unreasonable, and therefore they were going to have to be dislodged. . . . I left the Pentagon a convinced outsider (Gitlin 1987, 96–7, emphasis in the original).

7. For accounts, see Laffin and Montgomery 1987; MacQueen 1991; Epstein 1991; McNeal (1992, chaps. 6, 7). Even though acts of civil resistance took up a rather small part of prophets' time, they were not unimportant on that account. On the contrary, they were central to the identities and activities of prophets. Commonly, court trials ensued in which the argument was made that it was necessary to break a minor law in order to stop the ongoing commission of greater crimes against peace, war crimes, and crimes against humanity — inchoate crimes continuously committed by the U.S. government. Processes of appeal and jail sentences took up further time.

8. Along the same lines, Francis Anthony Boyle (1987, 6) quotes Ramsey Clark as declaring, "Our jails are filling up with saints."

9. These are order-of-magnitude estimates that are extremely sensitive to one's definition of what "is" a peace organization and who "is" a participant or member. Variations in
defining both these concepts and the important differences they make for estimations are
treated in chapters 3 and 4.

10. Formal courses of instruction associated with this cluster were reported to differ
somewhat from courses on other topics in that they were more informal and supportive.
The idea, some professors felt, was that the study of peace itself inherently required a more
equalitarian and community atmosphere (Harris 1990). Educator organizations that were
also economic enterprises experimented with forms of worker ownership and control, as
found in New Society Publishers.

11. See, however, the accounts of conflict reported by Benford and Zurcher (1990) and
Rogne and Harper (1990).

12. A well-known radical intellectual recounted to me an occasion on which a member
of Beyond War approached him after a talk he had given in order to say that he had just
lectured the exact beliefs of Beyond War. Exasperated, he exclaimed: "Lady, if that's true,
I give up."

13. More publicly, at the movement-historic APT action of March 12, 1988, the president of SANE/Freeze, William Sloane Coffin, gave the rousing final speech and call to resistance action and was himself among the first of the 1,260 arrested that day.

2

Consensus Movements
City Twinning and Related Activism

In the 1980s, a special if not new type of social movement surged in America.[1] Its outstanding feature was that, although it addressed matters that were definitely political in the ordinary meaning of that term, movement members claimed their enterprises were *nonpolitical, educational, nonpartisan,* or *humanitarian.* Prominent instances in the *war-peace* domain included Beyond War, PRO-Peace (the aborted Great Peace March), Mothers March for Peace, Peace Links, the Ground Zero Pairing Project, and Citizen Diplomacy, Inc., among dozens of other efforts labeled "citizen diplomacy." In the *poverty-hunger* domain, we saw the Hunger Project, USA for Africa ("We Are the World"), Live Aid, Band Aid, and Hands Across America. And, in several domains of *criminal and civil justice* "alternative dispute resolution" and similar "peace-making" efforts proliferated, embodied in hundreds of new movement organizations (MOs) dedicated to "dispute resolution." Traveling somewhat alone but in the criminal justice neighborhood was Mothers Against Drunk Driving (MADD).

I seek here to elucidate features of this, the *consensus movement,* as a generic type, to explore its appeals, and to relate these generic features and appeals to conducive conditions of the American eighties.

Consensus and Conflict Movements

To isolate a type is to imply other types, to imply other categories to which the proposed category is to be contrasted. In this case, consensus movements need to set against the vast bulk of what we commonly think of as garden variety, run-of-the-mill "social movements." Such movements have in common the fact that they seek in direct and detailed fashion to change the behavior of authorities or officials (the *establishment*) and/or social arrangements controlled by such persons. A program of action targets authorities and demands are made. Disagreement and dispute with authorities are openly asserted and pressed. Negotiation over differences is undertaken with an eye to bargaining and settlement. All of this is *political* in that each side views itself as being in a contest over the future substance of social policy. It is also political in the sense that "sides" are taken up among conflicting social policies. And, it is political in the sense that both sides correctly perceive and act on the recognition that *some* people are being asked to give up things — to change their behavior — for the benefit of *other* people. The unjustly skewed distribution of class, status, and power is perceived and is at the root of the common intransigence that authorities quite rationally (in short-term calculations) display. For such reasons, ordinary movements are inherently antiestablishment (cf. Traugott 1978). As a class, these statistically common movements may be termed *conflict movements*.[2]

In contrast, a key feature of *consensus* movements is that even though the programs of action they undertake imply, by their logic, conflict or politics in the senses just described, they deny that this is the case. Instead, they espouse versions of "nonpartisanship" and phrase their aims and programs (and other matters I will analyze) in ways that achieve a facade of consensus. Indeed, I argue that consensus movements are disguised or timid politics (as politics are classically understood), a way of safely posturing as social movements without the problems of real conflict that genuine — that is, conflict movements — engender. Consensus movements are subterfuge conflict movements; they are derailed dissent and the disguised rebellions of timid rebels.

The distinctive character of consensus movements can be clarified by further contrasting them to what Roberts and Kloss label "cultural alternatives to social movements," or "nonmovements," which they define as "a social or collective solution to a problem that does not attempt to influence the labor or property relations of a given society. . . . Nonmovement collectives depend on psychological reorganization rather than social change to solve social problems" (Roberts and Kloss 1979, 57, italics omitted). These authors review various forms of therapy, religion, and countercultural retreat as examples of such nonmovements. Consensus movements are like nonmovements in avoiding clear reference to labor and property relations but unlike them in, nonetheless, believing that they are addressing "social problems," that is, questions of social policy. Additionally, their mode of address centers on achieving mass changes in perception or consciousness as distinct from *psychological reorganization*, the focus of nonmovements. A scale of the degree to which movements are open and direct in their dissent would rank conflict movements highest, nonmovements lowest, and consensus movements somewhere between the two.

I want to develop this view of the consensus movement and its contrast with conflict and "non" movements using materials on what is called, variously, "sister cities," "paired cities," or "city twinning." Begun in the early-eighties, city twinning was a variation of a larger set of efforts called citizen diplomacy (Shuman and Williams 1986), which was itself an element of the larger peace movement cluster that, in chapter 1, I termed the *transcenders*. The empirical materials I present were collected in the course of my membership in the Uman-Davis Pairing Project (Davis, California) dating from September 1983; participation in the First American-Soviet Sister City Conference, Gold Lake, Colorado, April 1986 (a gathering of almost all the principal movement figures); inspection of the Paired City files at Ground Zero headquarters in Portland, Oregon; and, perusal of the large amount of written material its participants produced. (Quotes below credited only by city and state name are drawn from newspaper accounts and letters in the files of the Ground Zero Pairing Project.)

City twinning provides a case for close scrutiny, but it cannot be treated in isolation. As just noted, it was an element of the transcenders in the peace movement. Moreover, transcenders were themselves simply one form of many other consensus movements of the eighties. After reporting on city twinning, I analyze salient aspects of these numerous consensus movements and how they formed a context for city-twinning, for transcenders, and for the peace movement per se.

Citizen Diplomacy and City Twinning

As social movement enterprises of the eighties, *citizen diplomacy* referred to the efforts of ordinary people in the United States to establish relations with ordinary people of the Soviet Union (as well as with citizens of other nations the U.S. government defined as enemies). This form of reaching out was distinguished from Track Two diplomacy, which also referred to extraofficial and informal contacts by private citizens, but such contacts were undertaken (1) between citizens who were not "ordinary" for (2) the purpose of achieving specific diplomatic settlements at high government-to-government levels. Citizen diplomacy aimed to build a generalized kind of good will and understanding, while Track Two diplo-

macy aimed to achieve specific national accords through the use of amateur diplomats who had special relations to figures in governments or some
special credibility with the public at large. Thus, the Reverend Jesse Jackson's diplomatic endeavors were Track Two rather than citizen, as was the
role of Alec Smith, son of Ian Smith, in the transition from Rhodesia to
Zimbabwe.

The earliest and most active *organizational bases* of these citizen diplomacy efforts were religious and occupationally based associations. The
most common form of activity was the goodwill delegation and tour. The
Citizens' Exchange Council and Anniversary Tours were among the more
active organizations arranging the details of these efforts although — as is
the mark of a social movement — other such "travel" organizations burgeoned across the United States in the early-eighties.[3]

In 1982 and 1983, an additional organizational basis of citizen diplomacy came into important play, the *city*. This new base had two main,
proximate sources of inspiration. First, in Gainesville, Florida, Steven and
Natasha Kalishman determined to form a sister-city relation with the Soviet city (Novorossisk) in which Natasha had lived and worked as an Intourist guide and where she had met Steven on one of her tours when he
was there as a member of the United States Merchant Marine. Married
and settled in Steven's hometown of Gainesville, she remained on good
relations with her home city and her country. The couple, believing Soviet-
American relations could be improved by sister-city links between their
two cities, participated in the formation of a local organization with that
aim, secured a resolution endorsing the idea from the Gainesville City
Council, and set off for Novorossisk in June 1982 to propose the linkage.
Novorossisk officials accepted, and the relation began. In city-twinning
circles, that experience came to be called "the Gainesville model" and about
a dozen American cities tried a similar direct approach with some success.

Earl Molander, a professor of marketing at Portland State University,
and his twin brother, Roger, an ex-National Security Council nuclear strate-
gist (Molander 1982) were the second source of the new city-to-city citizen
diplomacy. Working in the basement of his Portland, Oregon, home, in
mid-1983 Earl matched or "twinned" 1,052 American and Soviet cities. Using the network of Ground Zero nuclear war gaming chapters already existing around the country (Alpern 1982), educator, religious, and Freeze
activists with whom they were in contact, and skillfully garnering publicity, the brothers aimed to have 1,052 "community portraits" "launched"
to the respective paired Soviet cities in a "first strike" on November 23,
1983 (1,052 was the number of U. S. intercontinental ballistic missile [ICBM]
silos at that time [Ground Zero 1984]).[4] Striving for arresting images, the

effort's slogan was "let the first strike be a knock on the door." The number of community portraits actually sent is uncertain. Diverse sources claim that it was close to a thousand although my inspection of Ground Zero Pairing Project files puts it closer to three hundred. The scale and complexity of this outpouring was, nonetheless, quite an impressive "collective behavior event" and bespoke a special sensitivity in America in late-1983 — one that I try to explain later in this chapter and in the three chapters of part 2. By mid-1986, almost sixty replies had been received from Soviet cities.[5]

Before proceeding to detailed discussion of city twinning, I need to enter an extremely important caveat regarding the need sharply to distinguish among the *plans,* aims, or intentions of the organizers of the Ground Zero Pairing Project and the actual *development* and *outcome* of this branch of city twinning. In publications (e.g., Molander and Molander 1990) and in personal communications, Earl Molander and associates have explained that the consensus movement that arose (in part) from Ground Zero efforts was decidedly *not* what was planned or intended by Ground Zero leaders. Instead, and as I described in a different context in chapter 1, after the initial activation of the antinuclear war movement, they sought to forge a broad-front *educational phase* that would then become a transition into a *political participation* phase in which U.S. policy was changed. In the Molanders' view, the movement skipped or truncated the educational phase and entered political participation prematurely, was educationally unequipped to manage opposition, and failed to have policy effects because of this educational deficit. As conceived by Ground Zero, city twinning was simply one device for focusing attention and not intended as the main theme, which was education about the Soviet Union as part of the broader educational phase of movement building. As I will document, recruits to city twinning had their own and different ideas about city twinning — the consensus ideas that I describe. As a consequence and ironically, Ground Zero leaders were the major force in starting city twinning but among the least happy with what it became.

City Twinning as a Consensus Movement

The consensus features of city twinning may be elaborated with respect to its guiding ideas (or ideology); emotional motif; social locations, identities, and attitudes of its core activists and their relation to the traditional peace and other movements; and, community responses to the twinning enterprise.

Ideology: Commonalities

The city twinning movement did not have an ideology in the formal sense of a codified creed that one could neatly reproduce as representing its beliefs. Instead, participants were guided by a set of less-than-formalized collection of ideas that one encountered repeatedly in writings and in conversations. Therefore, the orderly list of guiding ideas I present below makes city twinning seem more systematic than was actually the case. As long as this is understood, I assume it is not a problem. I describe what appear to be the five major guiding ideas.

Soviet people are like you and me. Central to citizen diplomacy was the premise that ordinary Soviets wanted what movement members wanted: a peaceful world where people are left alone to work, to raise their families, and to enjoy leisure without the threat of war, especially nuclear war. These three matters of work, family, and recreation were stressed rather than political and economic matters.

> The everyday life of the Soviet citizen is clearly not radically different from that of his or her U.S. counterpart. . . . [local activist] "We have the same problems, the same hopes, the same daily business" (Newspaper account, Petaluma, Calif.).

> The theory of the letter-writing campaign is that the similarities extend far beyond economics, climate, and latitude and longitude lines: People living in the two small cities share the same aspirations and worries. . . . The goal . . . is to find the common ground on which peaceful relations between the two world superpowers might be built (Newspaper account, Medford, Ore.).

> "But the most important thing is we have something in common," said [a high school junior] referring to the common quest for peace. "To have something in common is to understand each other" (Cornwall-on-Hudson, N.Y.).

> Both governments have their faults and problems. But the two countries have to go beyond the obvious differences and understand each other on a simpler level. Americans and Russians attend school to learn, work for a living, and play for recreation (Newspaper editorial, Brattleboro, Vt.).

> The goal . . . is to reach out, on a community level, and find common ground . . . under the clang of mayhem and missiles that goes on almost full-time between the Kremlin and the White House (News story, San Juan, Wash.).

The idea was phrased more grandly in an Associated Press wire story claimed by Ground Zero to have appeared in more than one thousand newspapers in late 1983: "In Tucson Arizona . . . [an] organizer said, 'Its about time we recognized each other as brothers and sisters'."

The community-portrait cities and towns so enthusiastically launched in late-1983 and later were conceived as "humanizing rather than glamorizing" the respective cities and were designed to "let the Soviets know we're just people too" (Waterville, Maine). In these portraits, the meaning of "pair," "twin," or "sister" would be drawn out, as in, "Our cities, as you know, have a great deal in common. Both our cities have roots in the frontier heritage of our nations; both of our economies and populations have boomed in the last 40 years, with the mining industry playing a major role; we both have institutions of higher learning; and our two communities take pride in furthering the arts and culture" (Mayor of Tucson, Ariz.'s letter to Novokuznetsk). Or, a project may simply make a bold declaration. "In the Soviet Union there are cities virtually identical with cities in the United States" (Flyer, Bellingham, Wash.).

The "like you and me" theme was *prescriptive* as well as *descriptive*, a mandate for actively selective perception and not simply an empirically neutral observation. Steven Kalishman's *Citizen Diplomat* editorialized, "Everyone is familiar with the differences between the economic and political systems of the United States and the Soviet Union. But who looks for the commonalities, the shared concerns, the mutual problems? The American and Soviet peoples are not enemies. Our enemies are hunger, disease, poverty, nuclear war, fear, mistrust, and ignorance" (Dec. 1984, 3).

Face-to-face contact with Soviets reveals our alikeness. The cornerstone of citizen diplomacy was the idea that the essential identity of the aspirations of Soviet and American people would become obvious when ordinary people from the two sides talked to each other directly, or short of that, sent one another diverse artifacts that communicated one's ordinariness. Direct communication was the key to mutual recognition of the identity of basic aspirations. Direct talk fostered friendship, and friendship stimulated further and broader communication. The bonds built through all forms of citizen diplomacy would serve to reduce hostility between the two superpowers through — implicitly — creating pressure groups within each society that would eventually force the two governments to moderate their policies with regard to one another.

From the start, the Gainesville wing of city twinning centerpieced face-to-face contact with a Soviet twin and encouraged travel, having sought itself to organize tours. The trip of Natasha and Steven Kalishman in June 1982 become almost iconic, an emblem to emulate.

58 STRUCTURES

The importance of face-to-face contact as a guiding idea was dramatically suggested by the fact that it was originally *absent* in the plans of the Ground Zero wing of city twinning. As mentioned, when initially conceived by Earl Molander, community portraits were intended only to initiate educational mail correspondence between people of the two nations. Paired Cities was simply one more educational project in the series of projects that Ground Zero had organized starting with Ground Zero week and the simulation game FIREBREAKS (a series later including Wildfire, a nuclear proliferation game-simulation and educational campaign). Once launched, though, the Paired Cities campaign took on a life of its own. Beyond correspondence, twinners around the country got very interested in elaborating their relation to their paired city by *visiting* it. Many soon found that their Ground Zero assigned city was "closed" to foreign travel—commonly meaning it simply had no Intourist facilities. For the purpose of correspondence and education such inaccessibility was of little or no importance, but local twinners wanted *more!* There has not been a systematic canvass of the numbers, but, impressionistically, I estimate that groups in perhaps two dozen American cities traveled to the Soviet Union in the 1984–1986 period in hopes of somehow, despite travel restrictions, getting to their twin. Some made it. Some did not. The fate of these forays became legendary adventure stories among twinners, some being tales of triumph, others being high comedies of "so near yet so far," and a few touched with the sadness of frustration and a note of tragedy. Yet other cities desired and laid plans to travel but did not actually manage to do so.

The point of all this is that local twinners created a ground swell of sorts for face-to-face contact despite the fact that the Ground Zero plan had not envisioned it. (However, once the interest in travel became apparent, Earl Molander made efforts to facilitate it, including personal trips to Moscow and conversations with relevant officials there and in the U.S. His efforts were unsuccessful, but that is another story.)

More intellectual twinners articulated the theory of social conflict and resolution underlying the guiding idea of face-to-faceness. "Tension and conflict between the countries cannot be explained completely by incompatible interests and objectives, but rather that to some extent ignorance and isolation foster groundless fears and tensions. . . . Increased knowledge and personal communication can eliminate some of this baseless fear" (Project brochure, Milwaukee, Wis.). Contacts, therefore, "decrease the tension, antagonism, fear and mistrust which underlie and fuel the arms race" (Project explanation, Baltimore, Md.).

Differences are educative not divisive. Differences between communism and capitalism (or however one wants to label it) were minor differences *compared to* the common interests. Indeed, the two peoples had much to learn from each other. The differences could be and were enriching rather than divisive, or at least, differences that "we" did not like were simply legitimate variations on ways of living. For example, "we" had a great deal to learn from "them" about mass transit, sewage systems, construction, industrial technology, and a host of other matters, including a sense of responsibility for all "our" citizens with regard to providing universal employment, housing, education, and medical care. Likewise, there was much "they" could learn from "us." Phrased most generally, we could well adopt some of their collectivism, and they could well adopt some of our individualism.

Citizen diplomacy is nonpolitical. What we had to learn about matters we had in common and what we could positively borrow from one another among matters in which we were different were enormously more important to talk about than specific political differences — *discussion of which was to be avoided.* National leaders in citizen diplomacy generally (e.g., Shuman and Williams 1986) and city twinning specifically enjoined projects to be carefully nonpolitical not only in communications with Soviets but in relations in the local community. The mission was friendship, not political posturing.

As an organization, Ground Zero declared in flyers that it "does not lobby for any particular political approach. . . . Instead it focuses on creating . . . [an] informed citizenry" and publishes materials that "take no positions on any issues." In a newspaper interview, Natasha Kalishman declared "I do not care for the Soviet government . . . and I could care less for the American government. It really makes no difference to me" (quoted in Robinson 1984b). Instead, a reporter characterized her as believing that "breaking out of nationalistic thinking, setting government aside entirely for awhile, may ultimately be the only way to peace" (Robinson 1984b).

Many twinning projects appeared to screen communications with Soviet cities for political content, following instructions provided by Ground Zero as to what *not* to send or to say.

Rule no. 1: This effort will be absolutely non-political. Nothing will be included which deals with American or Soviet domestic or foreign policy (Flyer, Milwaukee, Wis.).

PRINCIPLES . . . ABSOLUTELY NO POSITION OF A POLITICAL NATURE WILL BE ENDORSED (Flyer, Eu Claire, Wis.).

The best way to achieve world peace, [said a fourth grader] is to avoid "big arguments" and "just be friends" (News story, Chapel Hill, N.C.).

A committee of volunteers will screen the materials before mailing . . . keep the tone of your message non-political and uncritical of either country. Emphasis on American affluence in a word or photo is also inappropriate (News story, Sacramento, Calif.).

Quest for the nonpolitical sometimes gave rise to a stress on the innocuous and bland in public presentations designed to assuage fears of communicating with Soviets. "[A] Proponent spokesman . . . told the Council it was 'just people' who were involved. 'We'll be dealing with very innocuous things, . . . like people sending teacups and quilts back and forth'" (News report on presentation to the City Council, Sebastopol, Calif.).

Among the sixty or so Ground Zero–inspired cities receiving responses from paired Soviet cities, complications arose, for, many of the responses from Soviets did contain "political" statements.

[The Soviet writer] focused his message on international politics rather than city to city relations [as the Waterville writer had hoped] (News story, Waterville, Maine).

The Soviet friend who replied [to a nine-year-old who had written of his two pet gerbils] didn't speak of gerbils. . . . Instead he wrote of war, peace, intervention and the buildup of nuclear arsenals (News story, Chapel Hill, N.C.).

[The reply received] was . . . short . . . and a bit testy about why the U.S. wasn't interested in making peace (Letter to Ground Zero, Jefferson City, Mo.).

Soviet responses consisted of more than this aspect, however, and tended to be constructed on the model provided by the packages Americans sent. There was, therefore, more than sufficient "nonpolitical" material also in the packages received to make it possible to downplay the political parts of Soviet responses. In instances where the question of being political was in some sense "forced," the nonpolitical guiding idea prevailed, at least in cases I have seen. Thus, Davis, California's, paired Soviet city suggested that "it would be desirable for you to reject the plan for the militarization of space." The question of how to respond to this Soviet request was debated by some fifty people at a general meeting of the Davis project, and while most participants opposed "star wars," the large majority also voted to avoid stands on "political questions," and this decision was communicated to the Soviet city.

From the bottom up. Consensus versus conflict as movement orientations are, of course, matters of degree. Movements, in reality, only tend to be dominantly one or the other. While tending strongly toward consensus, city twinning did not entirely avoid conflict themes. The most central of these addressed the question of why city twinning (and citizen diplomacy more generally) were required in the first place. What difficulty rendered it necessary? Little conversational time and press space were devoted to answering this question, but the answer was, nonetheless, there: governments had failed or, at least, governmental approaches were not entirely adequate.

> We feel the governments have not been effective in handling the nuclear issues at all, so perhaps we can approach it on another plane (Associated Press wire story, statement by Erie, Pa. organizer).

> We feel that the two governments must be by-passed and that the common people must become involved. In this way only is there any hope to avoid a nuclear war that will destroy the whole planet (Vista, Calif.).

> The governments aren't talking to each other, the people have to talk to each other (Core activist quoted in news story, Twisp, Methow Valley, Wash.).

> "Things don't seem to be working very well from the top down," says [an organizer] of Reagan and Andropov, "It's important to try from the bottom up" (York, N.Y.).

Often, nonetheless, this possibily conflictual starting point was construed to have *conciliatory* implications for the relations of city twinning to governments. Thus, "The time has come for individuals to take responsibility for creating a climate for peaceful relations, so that politicians will have a basis for negotiation. The core of the problem . . . is the lack of communication between the *people* of both countries, not the governments. . . . Peace . . . requires involvement at every level: individuals, organizations, social institutions, communities, and finally, national governments will follow" (*Citizen Diplomat*, Dec. 1984, 3, emphasis in the original). Indeed, this statement virtually blames ordinary citizens for poor relations between the superpowers. But the editorial in which this conciliatory statement appears also concludes with Dwight Eisenhower's famous "get out of the way" statement, a quote encountered often in city-twinning literature. "I believe that the people in the long run are going to do more to promote peace than governments. Indeed, I think that the people want peace so much that one of these days governments better get out of the way and let them have it" (Quoted in the *Citizen Diplomat*, Dec. 1984, 3).

There was, though, ambivalence about the antigovernment implications of such declarations. "Among the artwork was a picture of the two countries shaking hands which . . . [the paired-city chair] said is entirely possible with the infant step she and the students have taken. 'The Soviets said this was the only way it was going to work. It would have to come from the people and not our leaders.' Instantly she covered her mouth in an attempt to take back what she had just said. 'I hope I don't get into trouble for saying that but what have the governments done?'" (Aberdeen, S.D., news story on children's art work received from the Soviet paired city).

Emotional Motif: Joy

Like forms of collective behavior (mass actions and crowd occasions), social movements vary in terms of their dominant emotional motif — fear, anger, and joy being the three most commonly dominant. Thus, panicked crowds, collective reactions to natural disasters, red scares, and mass delusions are among episodes conceived as variations on the dominant emotion of *fear*. Mob attacks, lynchings, ghetto and communal riots, mass vilification, and numerous kindred patterns are alike in exhibiting a dominant emotion of *anger*, or hostility. And, ecstatic congregations, revivalist crowds, crazes, fashions, and fads, among other forms, are similar in their dominant emotion of *joy* (Lofland 1985, chap. 1, 2).

Paralleling these distinctions among mass and crowd behavior, social movements may also be distinguished in terms of the emotion dominantly exhibited by the modal participant. In so distinguishing, I think an early and salient realization is that cases of social movements that come immediately to mind are almost all dominated by emotions of either anger or fear. The idea of a joyful social movement is an oxymoron, an expression on the order of that oft-cited example, "military intelligence."

As indicated at the outset, social movements are, virtually by definition, centrally about *objection*, about *dissent*, about *protest*; that is, about *conflict*. To be about these things is to be about anger and fear. People who are targets of movements are doing things that are morally noxious, and that fact generates — of supposed necessity — moral indignation (Turner and Killian 1987: chap. 13). Moral indignation and its accompanying sense of injustice are stimulated and supported by anger and fear. Hence, these dominant emotional motifs.

However, the dominant emotional motif of the modal participant in city twinning (and consensus movements more generally) was quite different, tending, instead, to variations on joy, or, perhaps, more accurately, to upbeat cheerfulness, friendliness, optimism, graciousness, and good will. Fitting together with the ideology of commonality, movement members bore good news rather than bad and extolled new possibilities more than they condemned social evils.

Here is a sampling of activist statements in letters of thanks for help received written to Ground Zero headquarters or appearing in newspapers:

Our launch [Ground Zero jargon for the act of mailing a community portrait] has generated excitement and hope for the future (Sheboygan, Wis.).

This has been a very positive project for us. The public response has been warm (Higganam, Conn.).

Thanks to you [Ground Zero headquarters] the people of Bellingham [Wash.] really seem to be having fun for a change instead of counting missiles.

There is an exciting opportunity open to everyone on San Juan Island [Wash.] to regain our sense of hope in the future of our world, and to take action as collective individuals, in spreading this hope to others (Newspaper article inviting public participation).

I am thrilled by the concept of pairing Russian cities with American cities (Reston, Va.).

Some joyous news about the Montpelier [Vt.]-Nikel Pairing Project. . . . We were delighted with our portrait.

Enthusiasm runs high (Duluth, Minn.).

I receive many anonymous calls just saying "great idea!" . . . Many spoke to me of seeing this as one of the few positive acts toward world peace within their control (Petaluma, Calif.).

The Pairing Project is a precious gift to mankind (Auburn, Calif.).

The key terms signaling certain emotions — above and in twinned city writing and talk generally — included enthusiasm, joy, thrill, positive, warm, excitement. We do not yet have comparative studies, and I, therefore, only hazard the guess that scrutiny of ordinary conflict movements will not discover the use of words such as these with any notable frequency. (There is, however, yet another sort of movement in which such terms are much more familiar, the religious movement, using the term religious in an ordinary way and illustrated by such groups as fundamentalist Christian sects and Asian-inspired new religions.)

Core Activists: Mainstream Peace-Progressives

To whom was such a set of guiding ideas and and its emotional motif appealing enough to generate collective effort (1) to assemble a "community portrait" and (either entailed in or following on the portrait) (2) to create a grassroots citizen organization dedicated to establishing and/or sustaining a relation to a Soviet city and to educating the local community about the Soviet Union?

1. Two impressions of statistical tendencies pertaining to cities themselves may be offered. One, lists of cities sending materials or otherwise reaching out to a Soviet city and receiving responses tended prominently to be either medium size or small in population. Ground Zero's 1986 list of fifty-five cities it knew had received replies from the Soviet twin also provided city populations. Eighty-three percent of the American cities had populations of one hundred thousand or less, 72 percent were fifty thousand or less, and 43 percent were twenty-five thousand or less. Two, the small cities and large towns tended also to be college or university cities and towns. The core activists of the two founts of city twinning — Gainesville and Portland — were closely associated with universities in their respective cities. The Paired City list of replies received was a virtual roll call of college towns (except that some of the largest and most famous of university cities — which were also the most political — were not present, e.g., Ann Arbor, Madison, and Berkeley).[6]

2. This association between twinning and college towns seemed not to be an instance of the "ecological fallacy" (there might be twinning in such cities, but it had no relation to the local institution of higher education). Instead, members of peace-oriented and religious organizations related to colleges often functioned as core twinning activists. Or, if this link were weak, students and other college-involved people played important roles in twinning efforts, as members of audiences, as suppliers of materi-

als for communications to twin cities, as translators into and out of Russian, and in other roles.

3. While quite visible, colleges were not the only source of core activists and other support. Peace committees of mainline churches (especially the Unitarians, Methodists, Presbyterians, Catholics, and Congregationalists) and members of the historic peace churches per se (especially the Friends) were quite evident. In some locales, this took the form of an interdenominational peace group. (As elaborated in the section on causes in this chapter and addressed in chaps. 5, 6, and 7 of this volume, twinning came on the scene in a period of heightened activism on the part of these church groups.)

4. Teachers in elementary and high schools sometimes appeared as core organizers and used, indeed, their students as workers in twinning activities. In some places, civic groups, such as chapters of the American Association of University Women or the League of Women Voters, were the organizing vehicle. (The strength of this link to colleges, churches, and schools was especially plain in the many instances where core activists used the *letterhead stationery* of their respective institutions in communicating locally and nationally on twinning matters, a use also signaling the unproblematic [consensus] character — in their eyes — of twinning activism.)

5. There was an especially intriguing pattern of the emergence of ad hoc groups who stood, socially, pretty much alone as a new social formation that did not depend on college- or church-embedded core activists and facilities. The members of such groups were often also members of a local college, sympathetic church, or school, but those memberships were not critically salient to the functioning of the new twinning organization (although those memberships were obviously salient to an explanation of why the members would become core activists in a new twinning organization). In at least one instance, a city council (Grand Forks, N.D.) appears to have given an ad hoc group de jure recognition as a Nuclear Preparedness Task Force.

As groups, twinners had to hold meetings and, therefore, to meet in some *place*. The places selected and provided were themselves clues to how twinners thought of themselves and how others viewed them. Aside from homes of core activists, which does not seem especially common, groups typically met in churches, senior centers, libraries, student religious centers near college campuses, peace centers, schools, and even the "community rooms" that savings and loan companies make available to community groups.

Demographically, core twinners spanned the age grades, but tended to be forty and older, slightly more women than men, and quite noticeably upper–middle class in life-style orientation if not economic reality. Politically, they tended to liberal democratic, but, again, the nonpolitical ideology muted this fact. Occupationally, many of the core activists were ministers, school teachers, upper–middle-class housewives of the civicly active sort, professors, and assorted small business entrepreneurs. Others were retired from sundry occupations.

Equally as important as the question of who they were is the question of who they were not. First, as is likely obvious but needs, nevertheless, to be said, they were not to any visible extent of a right-wing political persuasion nor were they drawn from organizations exhibiting that orientation (e.g., the American Legion) although some fairly conservative types did turn up, proudly proclaiming that twinning was "not a matter of liberal and conservative." Second, they were also not drawn to any important degree from explicitly left-progressive political circles and organizations. Indeed, among political groupings, the left-progressives seemed almost studiously to have ignored citizen diplomacy, neither joining nor attacking it (in contrast to the right, small numbers of which sometimes attacked twinning, as discussed later). Third, in only a case or so were the core organizers neocounterculture in life-style. Indeed, the single clear instance of this I came upon in the Ground Zero files stood out in dramatic and engaging contrast to the massively mainline peace-progressive character of the bulk of the participants. Along these same lines, only a handful of what would conventionally be defined as eccentrics seem to have achieved any visibility in local twinnings.

Last, and in line with the central notion of the nonpolitical, core activists publicly disavowed association with what they called "the peace movement." Despite the fact that some had done peace lobbying, with the Freeze for example, or had been involved in peace centers, peace committees of churches, and peace churches, activists did not want to be defined as part of the "peace movement." The substantial minority of twinners who were also involved with Beyond War likewise derided the peace movement. (This, nonetheless, was only the dominant tendency. In a few places, groups such as the Fellowship of Reconciliation, Women's International League for Peace and Freedom, Physicians for Social Responsibility, and Health Care Professionals for Social Responsibility were publicly the organizing vehicle of pairing.)

All these generalizations are, of course, only tendencies in the composition of core activists in twinning and many groups were, in fact, quite mixed. This mixing was captured nicely in the characterization given by a key activist from a small California city in responding to a Ground Zero questionnaire asking the question "Could you specify what elements of the community were represented [at your 'kick-off meeting']?" The activist responded that 10 percent were young radical, 75 percent were mainstream, and 15 percent were older Quaker types — long-term organizers.

Mainstream Community Response: Enthusiastic Support

It is one thing to "capture the imagination" and enthusiasm of core activists of the social features just detailed, it is entirely another to make any headway in stimulating the interest of the bulk of the community. What is remarkable about city twinning is the ease with which a broad spectrum of mainline city groups was prepared actively to support it. This ease, of course, was, in part, a function of who was asked to what.

Mass community portraits and educational events. In the Ground Zero Pairing Project, the initial request was for materials to be included in a community portrait to be sent to the paired Soviet city. Ground Zero supplied a list of categories of things to include that was used as a model around the country. The categories included a petition urging peace and a paired relation signed by ordinary citizens (sometimes many hundreds of them), peace letters and art from school children, newspapers, city histories, maps and Chamber of Commerce-type descriptions of the city, and, most importantly, resolutions from the city government endorsing the paired relation.

People soliciting, constructing, and donating materials constituted a second level of twinning participation, a level involving, if only signing the petition is counted as participation, many hundreds of citizens. A news story summary of the Erie, Pa., package typifies organizational participation. "Among organizations who helped . . . were the Erie Area Chamber of Commerce, the Manufacturers Association of Erie, Saint Vincent Health Center, Interchurch Ministries for Northwestern Pennsylvania, St. John's School, Mercyhurst College, Presque Isle Park Office, Erie Philharmonic, Erie Museum Guild, L'Arche Community and the Erie Community Foodbank." These community portraits ofttimes weighed more than twenty pounds and cost fifty or more dollars to send.

Connected to and beyond these packages, twinners staged many educational events (mainly talks and movies) about the Soviet Union which seem to be satisfactorily attended. Cities receiving replies commonly displayed the Soviet materials in the local public library, a sure-fire indicator of centrist acceptability.

Political endorsement. In only a few instances did city councils and mayors turn down requests for endorsement of a twinning effort although there is a sampling problem here in that officials of strongly conservative city governments were likely not asked because of presumed futility. Often these endorsements were cast in the form of the ornate proclamations and resolutions, containing "whereases" and "now therefores," that political bodies are wont to issue. Substantively, these documents contained the themes listed above as the guiding ideas of city twinning ideology and sent "sincere best wishes" (Holden Village, Wash.) or "warmest greetings" (Green Bay, Wis.).

Media. Especially noteworthy was the amount of positive coverage local newspapers were happy to give twinning. Beyond polite story-responses to press releases, papers commonly did *feature stories* on twinning. These stories typically profiled core activists and highlighted accounts of the activities of schoolchildren who were drawing pictures with peace themes for the community portraits.

(Parenthetically, I want to call attention to the sophistication with which core twinners "managed" local media. As one might suspect based on their social characteristics, just detailed, they were savvy about "press releases" and "media events." For example, the physical act of mailing the community portraits was commonly a press event, typically depicted in a newspaper *photograph.*)

Even further, although less frequent, a reasonable number of newspapers published editorials endorsing twinning. A core activist in a small Oregon city reported to Ground Zero, "the editorial I've enclosed [endorsing city twinning] is the ONLY pro-peace editorial this nearly-fascist publisher has ever written. You have no idea what a breakthrough it is to have the [newspaper] publisher . . . do something positive!" The editorials themselves echoed the ideological themes detailed earlier and encouraged citizen participation:

> Show your concern for your county and its future; write a letter to a Soviet (*Spectator,* Eau Claire, Wis.).

> We . . . heartily endorse the project. . . . Efforts to forge communications . . . can draw on the similarities between people everywhere and indeed foster a climate of understanding (*Davis Enterprise,* Davis, Calif.).

As one indicator of media coverage, the almost two file drawers of materials that constituted the twinning files at Ground Zero's Portland office consist largely of photocopied news stories sent in by twinning projects (and, as is evident, a large portion of materials in this report are from those stories). In the Gainesville wing of city twinning, the several hundred page manual on how to do city twinning that Citizen Diplomacy, Inc., published consisted almost exclusively of photocopied news stories on the four cities defined as using the "Gainesville model" (Citizen Diplomacy, Inc. 1985).

Business. Local businesses like to advertise and one measure of the "social safety" of an activity is the degree to which such establishments are prepared to associate their advertising with it. The magazine of Citizen Diplomacy, Inc., *The Citizen Diplomat*, carried advertising by Pepsi Cola, a chiropractor, local restaurants (including Snuffy's, which featured "gourmet burgers," Sonny's Real Pit Bar-B-Q, which provided "He-Man Portions," and Burger King), Superfleece Sheepskin Seatcovers, and jewelers. The Boulder, Colorado, twinning project at one point had a coupon tie-in with McDonalds Hamburgers, and the Davis, California, project benefit movie had its ticket printing paid for by a regional pizza chain in exchange for an ad and discount coupon on the tickets.

Conscious mainstream breadth. In both the Ground Zero and Citizen Diplomat wings of city twinning, there was conscious effort to construct twinning in as mainstream and inclusive a manner as possible. Many twinning organizations had an honorific board of advisors who did little, but who were selected to provide a broad face of legitimacy to the community. When the Tallahassee, Florida, twinners were preparing to ask Krasnodar to be their sister city, beyond securing a unanimously adopted resolution from the City Commission, they also had letters from the president of Florida State University, the secretary of state, the Florida State University student body president, the county superintendent of schools, chair of the school board, and the president and vice-president of Florida A & M University, "as well as other church, business and community leaders." The Eau Claire, Wisconsin, community portrait, as summarized by core activists, had similar features. "Between thirty and forty organizations, churches and groups are contributing letters, gifts, or signatures for the letter of greeting which will be part of our package. Numerous businesses have generously donated gifts for our greeting. Our city council, U.S. Senator Kasten, State Senator Moen, and perhaps other elected leaders are contributing letters." Other projects were perhaps not as ambitious as these but moved in that direction. (On a more mundane level, Steven Kalishman related to a city twinning organizing workshop that his magazine, *Citizen Diplomat*, was significantly assisted by volunteers from the Greek letter societies at a Gainesville university, all of whom needed "community service" projects and defined his enterprise as such.)

Distancing the political Right. In a few communities, anti-Soviet rightists were prompted to oppose twinning, but they were typically unsuccessful. Core activists and mainstream community influentials convincingly reiterated the guiding ideas of city twinning. Their success was perhaps related to the relative implausibility of common rightist claims, which included portraying Ground Zero as a Soviet front and the twinning project as a massive intelligence-gathering operation, as in the following: "Molander . . . has come up with a diabolical scheme to persuade American citizens to provide the Soviet military with the vital information necessary to target the most important American cities with their swarm of ICBMs. . . . Gullible victims of this scheme are asked to be voluntary spies for the enemy by sending to the 'sister city' basic demographic data about your community, including . . . description[s] of your local business[es] and factories [together with photographs of] local families in the neighborhood settings and the sourrounding countryside" (Letter to the editor, *Bellingham Herald*, Wash.) Other rightists feared "leading credibility" to the Soviets and "educating people that everything is all right in Russia" (News report, Paradise, Calif.).

Distancing the political Left. As mentioned, core activists sometimes had peace-related backgrounds or had been involved in the Freeze campaign. Such linkages potentially posed a community response problem; namely, rejection of city twinning as a mere, soft-headed "peace movement" scheme. This, however, seldom happened, in part because core activists themselves carefully drew a distinction between "peace movement," left-liberal, or "protest" activity and city twinning. A Wisconsin activist reported to Molander, "Throughout our activities we never mentioned nuclear war or the local peace coalition. We tried to distance ourselves from a political stand or any label that would cause people not to participate." A York, N.Y., activist described himself as "not into the really hard-core peace movement. . . . The peace movement has a negative, antigovernment image. . . . We're just average people concerned about our family and the future. . . . I'm not the kind of guy who stands on the corner with a sign."

As chance would have it, another and much more radical and political organization also used the name Ground Zero, or more precisely, the Ground Zero Center for Nonviolent Action. Located just beside the Trident submarine base near Poulsbo, Wash., that Ground Zero conducted campaigns of nonviolent civil disobedience and was perhaps best known for its work against the "white trains," the railway trains transporting nuclear bombs around the country. *That* Ground Zero was definitely not nonpartisan, and confusion of the two organizations in a few communities caused some difficulty for city twinning. However, Ground Zero, Poulsbo, seems not to have been well-enough known for such a confusion to occur in more than a handful of cases. (And, it is indicative, I think, of the selective attentiveness of the media that Ground Zero, Portland, always garnered *vastly* more media coverage than Ground Zero, Poulsbo, despite the fact that both aimed for media presence.)[7]

⋘

City twinning, then, displayed a distinctive and "consensus" profile as a social movement. Ideologically, it stressed commonalities, inclusiveness, and reconciliation. Emotionally, it was upbeat and even joyous. Its core activists were mainstream peace-progressives, and community response to it was supportive and enthusiastic.

Surging Consensus Movements in the Eighties: Leading Ideas

Were city twinning the only instance of its type—the consensus movement—we could, perhaps, say that it was not important politically or sociologically. But, in fact, the decade of the eighties abounded in instances of campaigns and movements that were dominantly consensus in character. In the peace movement, this was the orientation of the transcender cluster, and I mentioned a variety of other instances in the opening paragraph of this chapter. Enumerating them exceeds the space available, but I want, nonetheless, to report what appear to be the leading *ideas* that animated them, for the five ideas I have described as guiding city twinning are only particularized applications of these more general concepts.[8]

Correct Awareness Causes Positive Social Change

One of the most important of these leading ideas was the conception that correct *awareness* translated in some fashion into the social change one sought. Therefore, the prime aim of a consensus movement organization was the *alteration of awareness* rather than of social conditions. Slogans and key organizer statements appropriately stressed changes of cognition as in

"The End of Hunger is an idea whose time has come" (Hunger Project).

"What we wanted to do all along was raise awareness" (Ken Kragen, organizer of Hands Across America).

"The splitting of the atom has changed everything except our way of thinking, and thus we drift toward unparalleled catastrophe. . . . We require a substantially new manner of thinking if mankind is to survive" (Statement attributed to Albert Einstein, frequently quoted in consensus movements).

"Beyond War: A New Way of Thinking" (formal name of the organization Beyond War).

The most extreme formulation of this overarching idea held that *sheer thinking itself* could cause positive social change. Operationally, such thinking was called *meditation* and was claimed to be most effective when done by many people at the same time. It followed that *mass meditation* was in order, and groups such as Peace Is Possible Now organized it, including a New Year's eve worldwide meditation, which, in 1986, was claimed to have involved "400 million persons in 77 countries gathered in living rooms and auditoriums to visualize world peace or reaffirm personal commitments to peace" (Cordes 1988, 76). (Some groups believed, additionally, that the effect was enhanced if one also held crystals while mass meditating [Cordes 1988, 76].)

Educational and Dramatic Events Are the Levers of Awareness Alteration

If awareness were central, then technologies of its alteration were critical to movement action. Constrained by the ideas of "no enemies" and "lovingness" (discussed in the next sections), techniques of awareness alteration ran to milder forms of educational efforts and showy — even glitzy — events. Toward the milder end of this restricted spectrum of options lay traditional book, pamphlet, and brochure publication. Toward the more showy end lay such activities as megaconcerts televised worldwide; "space-bridges"; attempts at cross-nation marches by thousands of hikers; hand joining by millions of people; a transworld Earth Run; among others.

In a World of Correct Awareness, Everyone Lovingly Resolves Conflict

In the consensus view, if people could get beyond their false perceptions they would see that other people were really quite well meaning and any differences of opinion and aspiration that might exist could be worked out peacefully and in a loving fashion.

One large cluster of consensus movements was California-Esalen based, inspired, or in strong affinity with it, as in the Noetic Institute, the Ark Foundation, and Business Executives for National Security. Also enamored with the newest computer and communications technologies, this cluster formed a pocket of "humanistic techies" who combined techy talk with Esalen vocabularies that stressed such terms as: heart, trust, love, unity, awakening, transformation, healing. (The musical compositions of Robby Gass were virtually ideal-type expressions of these themes as in his "Bridges of Love.") Such California-inspired ideas permeated the larger surge of consensus movements.

Other People Are Not Our Enemies, Only Our False Awareness

One's only true enemies, therefore, are one's perceptions, not other people. The Beyond War Creed ranked this sentiment among its main provisions: "I will not preoccupy myself with an enemy" (Plowman 1986). A leader of the neighborhood conflict resolution movement declared as a major principle in a plenary speech to a "peacemaker" conference that his movement was "not a challenge to institutions."

Traditional Left-Right Politics Are Obsolete

The consensus world was a world beyond political left and right as historically understood. On being asked his politics by Russian dinner table companions, techy guru Joel Schatz "gestures at his place setting. 'Reagan here', he points at the knife; 'Anderson here,' he moves his finger a few inches to the plate; 'Democrats — here,' he moves his fingers a few inches more to the fork; 'Me — *there*,' he raises his whole arm and points at the ceiling" (Hochschild 1986, 31). Or, as other gurus have put it, and other transcenders have often repeated, "Not left or right but out front."

This led to searches for "common ground" that transcended left-right divisions and one consensus movement organization was even organized around marketing an interaction process that purported to facilitate The Search for Common Ground (the organization's name) and to find it. A host of newly formed organizations likewise focused on the *process* (as distinct from the substance) of conflict resolution, that is, the *means* of finding consensus. By the mid-eighties, such process-oriented associations were convening a National Conference on Peacemaking and Conflict Resolution. The third annual one, in 1986, was organized on the theme of "Peacemaking and Conflict Resolution as a Social Movement" and attracted almost a thousand participants. Also in 1986, the World Future Society, "went with the flow," to borrow a phrase, and organized its annual meeting around the theme "Conflict Management and Conflict Resolution," a gathering that featured leading consensus movement figures.

Left and right were obsolete in another sense that tied together with the loving resolution of conflict. Traditional politics involved "enemies" and confrontation and opposition. Beyond *substantive* objection to left-right thinking, there was objection to the *emotional* motif of "negativism" and of oppositions.

⋘

If such were the leading ideas of consensus movements, how might we understand their social sources in the eighties, and what consequences might they have?

Consequences of Consensus Movements

Movements obviously have many kinds of effects on diverse aspects of the societies in which they emerge. Consensus movements of the American eighties impress me as having at least the following important consequences. (I leave aside the question of the possible "functions" of such movements, a phrasing that would imply some sort of "system necessity" and self-maintaining stability as distinct from simply effects.)

1. As I have implied, one prime consequence was to retard the development of conflict movements on the same topics. Consensus movements drained off energy and talent that might otherwise be available for more openly oppositional politics. In such a fashion, ruling elite policies were less challenged and, therefore, protected. In this perspective, government and corporate assistance to consensus movements that were so amply provided was immanently sensible. If Ronald Reagan could significantly defuse questions of poverty, hunger, and homelessness as federal policy issues by standing in the Hands Across America line, the price was cheap at many times what he paid. (This same effort had, also, 750 "corporate angels" [*People Weekly* 1986].)

2. This *structural* defusement had, as its *social psychological* counterpart, the participants' sense that participation had made a difference and that one had, therefore, already made the world a better place. "It gives them a release," observed one student of the Hunger Project. "It reassures them rather than arousing them, which is what would be needed for real social action" (Divoky 1980, A26). Or, in the phrases of other critics, they were engaged in "frivolous masturbatory exercises" that were "Tupperware parties for yuppies." But, in the eyes of participants, even if a difference

was not visible, it was surely there. Among the slogans circulated in consensus movements was an (ironic) quote from Gandhi: "Everything you do will seem insignificant, but it is still very important that you do it" (quoted in Shuman and Williams 1986, 23, and Landau 1984).

Such consequences of consensus movements need to be distinguished from the more familiar *co-optation* consequences that flow from conflict movements. Co-optation is the process of adroitly absorbing dissident elements into leadership structures in a way that mitigates their impact on policy. Dissidents are accommodated, but in a fashion far more minor than they originally had in mind. Consensus movements of the eighties seemed not to have achieved even the limited but real success represented by co-optation.

With respect to city twinning specifically, Chadwick Alger (1985, 8) has offered a more optimistic and sanguine view, suggesting that "the very notion of relations among cities, as distinct from the state view of the world, is a significant break from tradition. [City twinnings] . . . can be viewed as building blocks for alternative worldviews." This is surely possible, and in the absence of relevant research the question is open, empirically. Here I can only enter the anecdotal evidence that when I asked several city twinners to read Alger's analysis or told them about his view, they were more distressed than delighted with the idea that there was something called "state ideology" that they were implicitly challenging with their city-twinning activities. They seemed, instead, uncomfortable because Alger painted them — positively to be sure — as subversive of a dominant ideology of their time, the ideology of statism. (Perhaps, though, Alger's theory of consequences applies better to future participants in future movements that derive from those of the eighties.)

3. As consensus movements evolved in the eighties, they became ever-more spectacle and "good time" oriented, turning problems raised into occasions of celebration and festival. The climactic Hands Across America was asserted by some to be the Woodstock of the eighties (*People Weekly* 1986), a profoundly contradictory construction that transmuted poverty into a rock festival. Looked at in terms of consequences, this was a mystified portrayal of social inequality and injustice, a "newspeak" rendering of social arrangements in which it becomes appropriate not only to feel that in doing nothing one has done something (consequence two) but to be joyous about it on a spring Sunday in the sun. Richard Reeves's rendering of the consequences of Hands Across America expresses the point clearly for Hands specifically and for consensus movements generally. "I thought the whole thing was a sentimental exercise, substituting sentimentality for commitment, pretending that there is an equation between volunteered

feelings and societal obligations. "Caring" isn't enough, but "doing" takes more than volunteering a Sunday afternoon. It takes taxes and determined government" (Reeves 1986). Writing in the *New Republic* in 1988, Richard Blow summed up these several consequences for at least the more New Age–oriented of consensus movementeers.

> It's true that New Agers are anti-war, pro-environment, anti-nuke, pro-feminist. What makes them different . . . is their approach to the resolution of these issues. Instead of seeing them as political concerns . . . [they] completely depoliticize them. Under the guise of non-partisan change, . . . [they] address issues in ways guaranteed to offend no one. They never tackle issues; they hug them.

> [They do] not . . . deny differences between people, but . . . deny that they matter. It's an attempt to create an egalitarian society based not on equal distribution of wealth or property, but on spiritual equality—a sort of socialism of the mind. (Blow 1988, 27, 26).

4. At a more general and intellectual level, the conceptions of society and social change promoted by consensus movements had the effect of, in the views of critics, *mystifying social causation and social change* by portraying social problems as merely isolated matters of incorrect awareness, ignorance, and lack of direct or personal relationships. Hunger, in a more conflict view, for example, involves more than an "idea whose time has come." Instead, it is part of a "web of results of larger social and political ills" concerning "social justice in developing countries, . . . existing inequitable structures, . . . [and] rapid population growth" (Divoky 1980, A26). War-peace focused consensus movements were regarded by critics as 'New Age,' fuzzy thinkers [who promote] high-tech yuppyism and 'I'm okay, you're okay' symbolism, and a dearth of substantive dialogue. . . . If one were to believe the[ir] gospel of superficiality . . . , one would think that the only thing needed for an end to violence and war would be a simple change in people's attitudes" (Crews 1986, 3). Such consensus views, continued the critics, operated at the intellectual level the same as they did at the structural and social psychological levels (numbers one and two): to support the existing order. Thus, the Hunger Project was claimed by detractors to "encourage . . . uncritical thinking . . . , the kind of thinking that makes the problem of hunger worse. . . . While [the Project] urges people not to take a position on the causes of hunger, such a non-position actually supports the status-quo. . . . Silence or an amorphous anti-hunger 'concern,' whether we like it or not, puts us on the side of those forces now actively generating hunger" (Divoky 1980, A26).

If these were among the likely consequences or effects of consensus movements, from where did they come?[9]

Causes

Among the complicated sources of surging consensus movements, I want to single out three that seem to me to have special salience. The first relates to the long-standing and chronic poverty of political culture in the United States; the second refers to some special developments of the early-eighties; and the third focuses on pains of social movement participation as structured by the first two factors.

The Poverty of Political Culture and the Wealth of Boosterism

At the broadest level of constraining, directing, or conducing social conditions, there was (and is) the much-discussed poverty of American political culture and organization (e.g., Burnham 1982). Under conditions of social distress, the lack of culturally and organizationally developed political alternatives made consensus responses more credible simply because they lacked competition. Distress over the direction of the U.S. government had little other direction in which to go, especially under conditions of the exhaustion of liberalism, discussed next.

The central ideas of consensus movements and the impulses of members seem to me quite critical of larger social arrangements *but* critical in a restricted, muted, and very indirect way *and also* either ignorant of (or lacking in imagination about) *how more politically* to act on the perception that international and other social relations were headed in perilous directions. Consensus movements at least allowed one to act in some seemingly responsive fashion.

The consensus movement emotional motif was not itself fortuitous. Rather, it was borrowed from or modeled on the complex American traditions of civic boosterism, positive thinking, and the cultural myth that fuller communication promotes improved social relationships (Myer 1965; Halmos 1966). In this mindset legacy, conflict, politics, and impersonal, distant relations are "negative" and to be avoided, as opposed to direct, personal interactions that achieve consensus and get beyond politics, which are "positive."

The Embattlement of Liberalism

One proximate stimulus to the rise of citizen diplomacy in its myriad forms was obviously the advent of the Reagan administration's military buildup, its belligerence toward the Soviet Union, and the belief that the Reaganites were preparing to fight and "win" a nuclear war. Other key proximate stimuli included the failure of the campaigns to stop deployment of Cruise and Pershing missiles in Europe, the failure of the Freeze campaign, and the semifailure of the anti-MX campaign. These several efforts were more conflictual in orientation, and they were not successful. In the context of these failures and of a massive military buildup, Reagan also ideologically outflanked the peace and moderate left, commencing with his star wars speech of March 23, 1983.

More broadly and in domestic affairs, the Reagan administration was dismantling public-spirited government efforts across the board, and traditional liberalism was not able to develop an effective response to these changes. Such a dramatic *Right Turn* (Ferguson and Rogers 1986) set the stage for millions festively linking hands across America in timid and derailed dissent, grasping onto civic boosterism for lack of any more substantial and credible political culture to give shape to their concerns.

The Exhaustion of Negativism: The Style-Substance Dilemma of Activism

As discussed, conflict-oriented movements are about objection, dissent, and protest. To be about these things is also easily to be about anger and fear. People who are targets of movements are doing things that are viewed as morally noxious and that fact generates — of supposed necessity — moral indignation (Turner and Killian 1987, chap. 13). Moral indignation and its accompanying sense of injustice are both stimulated and supported by anger and fear, hence, these dominant emotional motifs.

Reactions to movements as anger and fear. Participants in and observers and targets of movements are troubled by expressions of anger and fear. Indeed, their troublesome nature are a reason to exhibit them to targets of movements. Anger, in particular, is often intended to generate fear in targets of movements. However, cycles of anger and fear between movements and targets take their psychic toll, a toll labeled and elaborated on by Robert Coles (1964) as *weariness.*

Weariness and wariness. At some psychic level, actual and potential participants in social movements understand the conjunction of dissent, anger, fear, and weariness. That understanding retards becoming involved in movements in the first place and prompts participants to quit.[10] City-twinning leader Steven Kalishman phrased it this way in his speech to the first national conference of Soviet-American twinned cities: "It's a positive program, its not negative. People go away feeling good about themselves and what they are doing. . . . The nature of the peace movement has been negative to a certain extent. . . . It's not very pleasant talking about nuclear war . . . and violence and hunger and all the other things that concern us in the world. It's just nice to have something positive to do to complement that."

The possibility of "feeling good" was founded on city twinning uniting rather than dividing people. In another talk at the same conference, a veteran peace radical, who became a leader in city twinning, characterized it as a "tremendous reconciling force," going on to say, "As a long-time peace advocate who has always done things that a lot of peace advocates do — you know, angry rhetoric against all the warmakers — [I know] there's a lot of reconciling to do between peace advocates and lots of conservatives." Such reconciliation was linked in the minds of some with the method of movement action. In the same talk, Kalishman made these connections among mode of action, emotional state, and being negative. "The sister city program will accomplish more than me marching with a sign, chaining myself to a weapon, or throwing blood on something. It's a positive thing that will really accomplish a lot if we make it comfortable and safe for the people who are in political power to participate and by not ever embarrassing them in front of their constituencies by taking political stands that are going to hurt their careers."[11]

In the war-peace arena of the early-eighties, there was an added and vastly more dreary dimension. The campaigns of the period involved countless portrayals of the horrors of nuclear war, horrors dramatized in several motion pictures, by depicters of "nuclear winter," in the clinical deadpan delivery of Jack Geiger (in the widely shown video "The Last Epidemic"), as well as in innumerable other ways. (The iconic event in this period of drenching the country in the horror of nuclear war was likely the film "The Day After" broadcast by ABC-TV on November 20, 1983). People in the city-twinning movement were veterans of this cultural orgy of nuclear horror.

Many people were, therefore, understandably wary of more conflict-oriented movements as they also "burst" upon the scene.[12] At one level, techy guru Joel Schatz was correct when he declared, "'How did I get into the peace movement? I'm not. The peace movement is mostly people who sit around and talk about how terrible it is that the U.S. and the Soviet Union aren't talking to each other. That's a waste of time. What you've got to do is to do it; to go out and talk to the Russians. It can be done. That's what I'm going to do this week'" (quoted in Hochschild 1986, 30).

The dilemma of wariness and injustice. To be wary of movements is not necessarily to be without moral sensibility, a sense of injustice, and a desire to see social policy changed. But wary people live with a dilemma:

to act in a movement is to become involved in debilitating anger and fear; not to act is to suffer a stinging discrepancy between social reality and one's belief in a more just and moral world.

Resolving the dilemma. The tensions of this dilemma can and are dealt with in several ways. A *first* and most evident resolution has already been described and needs only now formally to be recognized: grit one's teeth and experience the anger and fear so commonly dominant in movements. A *second* is simply and consciously to live with the stinging discrepancy of doing nothing.

Among persons aware of movement anger and fear, a *third* resolution could be attractive: leap into the embrace of an ideology of self-cultivation and benign love for the cosmos and all its creatures. Rennie Davis provides the archetypical instance. As a more general class of organized enterprise, Roberts and Kloss (1979, chap. 4) term this solution "nonmovements," or "cultural alternatives to social movements," and they cite various forms of psychotherapy, self-improvement schemes, religion, and countercultural retreat as examples. Seen only rarely and for brief periods, but of the utmost sociological and moral significance, in a *fourth* resolution the person objects and protests with persistence but manages to do this without the anger and fear that so commonly accompanies movement action. The dominant emotion or emotions are, instead, closer to compassion, empathy, and cheerfulness (cf. Douglass 1983). This is the resolution adopted by the prophet cluster of the eighties peace movement although they (in their special lifestyle) are far from the only people who have adopted it.

Consensus movements can be a *fifth* resolution. The impulse to resist noxious social arrangements persists but attaches itself to an ideology that is bland, centrist and "mushy," an ideology that has enough latent and implied substance to provide a sense of doing something relevant, but not enough to create overt conflict. Hadley Cantril concluded his analysis of Moral Rearmament — the great consensus movement of the thirties — with an observation that is as fresh and cogent today on this matter as when published in 1941:

> [Moral Rearmament] has gathered momentum . . . essentially because it shows certain bewildered people a way to interpret their personal troubles and the larger social problems of their world without endangering their status. It provides a psychological mechanism whereby they can escape the responsibility of dealing directly with conditions they realize are not right and just. It attracts to itself people who want to improve these conditions without injuring their own positions and who want to avoid an alignment with existing institutions or ideologies which assume

that individual problems cannot be solved without collective action (Cantril 1941, 168).

Dissent is there, but it is derailed dissent; rebellion is entailed, but it is a timid and disguised rebellion.

Concluding Question

To me, the distinctive feature of the consensus movement as a social formation is the manner in which (1) fresh-minded and attitudinal idealism and emotional joy and good will (the emotional motif variable) combines with (2) ideas that are vacuously consensual and embracing and seemingly devised to mute obdurate differences in objective social interests (the substantive conflict-consensus variable).

This consensus package needs to be set against the classic conflict package in which (1) jaded cynicism, anger, and fear (the emotional motif) combines with (2) ideas that identify differences of objective social interests and target people who are "the other side"—the enemy (the ideological substance).

These consensus and conflict packages are of course only two of the four possibilities created by the conjunction of the two variables of emotional motif and conflict-consensus substance. The question to me is: To what degree must these two variables combine in these ways? Does attitudinal idealism have an affinity with substantively bland ("mush") politics? And conversely, do cynicism and mush politics not easily and often combine?

If there are such empirical tendencies, what is the social psychology of these relations? More precisely, in what directions do the causal arrows run? Does idealism cause political mush or does political mush cause idealism? Does cynicism cause political substance, or does political substance cause cynicism? Or are these reciprocating relations that evolve in complicated and interdependent cycles?

Assuming such connectional tendencies, they are, nonetheless, only tendencies, even if they are strong. The really important question, I think, is: Under what conditions can there be successful and strong linkages among (1) programs of political substance (of conflict rather than of political mush); (2) generous and humane idealism; and, (3) an emotional motif that is upbeat, joyous, and inclusive? Put differently, when are the major tendencies to the contrary confounded or overcome? This is an empirical question and a first step in answering it is to identify cases in which counter-tendency links have clearly been forged.[13] Such cases are not overly evident or abundant, and careful searching is in order.

Notes

1. This chapter is revised from publication as Lofland 1989. Although unusually popular in the American eighties, consensus movements were not confined to that period, as seen, for example, in Moral Rearmament, a "moral renewal" movement that boomed in the 1930s (Cantril 1941) (and which apparently experienced a revival in the eighties), and as seen in the many nonpartisan versions of environmentalism that abounded in the early-seventies.

2. It would be reasonable to call them *political* movements if that term did not have such narrowly electoral meanings.

3. The practice of good will travel to the Soviet Union was, of course, of several decades standing as was the work of the Citizen Exchange Council and Anniversary Tours. The reference here is to the eighties upsurge in this form of activity under the new label "citizen diplomacy." Interestingly, the surge of Americans traveling to the Soviet Union in 1983–1984 was still below the levels of the late-seventies. The journal *Surviving Together* (Institute for Soviet-American Relations, 1987, 55) reports these State Department figures on visas issued each year for travel to the USSR (rounded to the nearest thousand):

1976: 66	1982: 28
1977: 58	1983: 40
1978: 53	1984: 35
1979: 44	1985: 45
1980: 13	1986: 44
1981: 22	

4. Features of community portraits and what was involved in assembling and sending them are described in the section on "Mainstream Community Response: Enthusiastic Support."

5. For advocate discussions of citizen diplomacy more generally as a class of peace movement action, see Shuman and Williams 1986 and Warner and Shuman 1987. The latter has an especially useful alphabetized appendix titled "What You Can Do" that lists thirty-nine activities from animals through mountaineering to youth.

6. A list of all cities that sent packages irrespective of whether a response was received has not been compiled. In correspondence, Earl Molander reported his impression that this much larger set of cities would not be, in the vast majority, college towns.

7. The activities of Ground Zero, Poulsbo, are reported in their newspaper, *Ground Zero*. See also Douglass (1983, 1987, 1991) for accounts of the organization's philosophy and program.

8. Mechling and Auletta 1986 provide an extremely helpful and insightful treatment that parallels and in some ways elaborates the one I offer here but focuses only on the sociorhetorical structure of Beyond War. For further discussion of Beyond War, which may well be the prototypical instance of eighties consensus movement organizations, see Faludi 1987 and Gelber and Cook 1990. Jay Rosen 1986 offers a useful characterization of the role of television tycoon Ted Turner in the eighties surge of consensus movements.

9. Cf. Hadley Cantril's (1941) comment: "The appeal [of Moral Rearmament] is sufficiently general and vague to satisfy all tastes. 'Never in my long experience in Washington

have I found anything on which all parties in both Senate and House have so thoroughly agreed as on America's need, and our own need, for this new spirit,' is the dubious tribute paid moral rearmament by the late Speaker Bankhead. At times these tastes seem horribly irreconcilable. For example, the leaders of two warring nations both sent messages simultaneously to Buchman advocating moral rearmament. Cabled Generalissimo Chiang Kai-shek, 'Glad focusing world attention on this all important question of moral rearmament'; cabled the Japanese Prime Minister, 'Believing necessity of moral rearmament for solution of world problems, sincerely hope for every success of your noble movement.' But neither Generalissimo nor Prime Minister laid down his arms" (Cantril 1941, 167–68).

10. Consider, for example: "He worked in the anti-war movement, the civil rights movement. But 'there came a period when I was tired of being against everything. I'm basically an optimistic person and I wanted to be for something'" (Milich [1986] in an interview with international economic cooperative activist-executive David Thompson).

11. The common dominance of anger and fear may well be related to why movements so commonly occur in brief waves or spurts. If people cannot live by bread alone, they also cannot live by fear and anger alone.

12. Note the image of angry explosion contained in this and other common ways to label the start of movements.

13. Joel Best has suggested that contemporary movements focusing on threats to children exemplify the fourth possibility in this motif-substance typology — the conjunction of a cynicism motif with consensual substance. Counter-tendencies that make this possible are obviously also of great interest and are explored by Best (1987, 1989).

3

Movement Culture
Sparse, Uneven, Two-tiered

Social Movements are related to culture in three major ways: (1) they are
partly *molded by* the cultural traditions from which they draw at the time
of their formation or surge and which affect them as they develop over
time; (2) aspects of the cultures created and/or celebrated by movements
sometimes diffuse into the larger society and are among the *causes* of subsequent societal culture; and (3) culture is a dynamic and variable aspect
of movements per se, a *feature* of them as social formations.

I want here to elucidate this third kind of relation between social movements and culture and to do so in terms of how culture varies in formal
ways across movements. By definition, all movements exhibit culture, but
how they do so is quite diverse along several dimensions that I want to
inspect.

1. Movements vary with respect to the degree that their participants
agree on or *share* the same complex of cultural items, be they items that
are distinctive to the movement or not. This is the question of sheer cultural diversity versus consensus within movements.

2. Holding aside (or "constant") cultural agreement or sharing, movements vary in terms of the number or proportion of their cultural items
that are *distinctive* to the movement. At one extreme, a few movements
elaborate a wide range of movement-distinctive cultural matters; at the
other, participants are almost culturally indistinguishable from other members of society.

3. Cultures can be quite narrow or situation-specific in *scope* or quite
wide, specifying appropriate beliefs and actions for every circumstance
and topic.

4. Within particular kinds of cultural items, we observe variation in degrees of *elaboration* or complexity.

5. Some forms of culture—particularly items of material culture—vary in terms of their sheer numbers or the *quantity* in which they are produced, a matter related to complexity but not the same as it.

6. Specific items of culture and the array of cultural matters differ in the degree to which members emotionally and positively experience them as expressing or embodying their values and life circumstances, as providing occasions of transcending the mundane in *expressive symbolism* (Jaeger and Selznick 1964).

These six dimensions, and others we might use, allow us to profile movements in terms of the degrees to which and ways in which they "do culture." Movements tending to higher values on these dimensions are—in a noninvidious and technical sense—"more cultured," "culturally rich," or "culturally developed." Movements that are "lower" in these respects are "less cultured" or "culturally poor." Of course, we are also likely to find that all these dimensions do not move in concert, and, further, different classes of cultural items may have varying profiles even when there is an overall movement pattern.[1]

Viewing these dimensions in composite and, thus, as a variable, culture is but one of a large number of other variables that are pertinent in analyzing social movements. The point of isolating culture as something that differs among movements is to be able to relate it in a more articulate manner to such other variables. Thus, the rich versus impoverished cultural profile of a movement may have complex relationships to such variables as degrees of mobilization potential and achievement, persistence and resilience in the face of adversity, retention of participants, and achievement of success in campaigns.

It is evident that these six dimensions of cultural variation are all *formal* rather than substantive; that is, they do not make reference to the specific *content* of culture, the particular goals, activities, and the like espoused and enacted by a movement. One might well object that any discussion of culture must address such content—that a purely formal discussion misses the essence of culture, which resides in the specific goals and values guiding conduct. My answer to this question is that the substance of culture is obviously important, and it is, indeed, something we need to take account of in complete analyses of social movements. I offer these formal matters as additions to rather than substitutes for the analysis of substance.

My strategy in analyzing dimensions and degrees of movement culture is to focus on the case of the American peace movement of the 1980s and in these terms. But, as I inspect dimensions of its culture, I will also make reference to similarities and differences between it and other movements. In so doing, I hope to increase our appreciation of the differentially cultured character of social movements more generally.

Three Global Constructs Specified

In order to proceed with this task, I need first to specify what I mean by the global and diversely defined concepts *social movement* and *culture*, as well as by the third and equally ambiguous term, *the American peace movement*.

Social Movements

In recent studies, social movements have mainly been conceived as enduring collective efforts to achieve or resist social change in oppositional action directed to ruling elites. Joseph Gusfield has characterized this as the "linear" conception of movements, a view of them as sharply pointed, rationally calculated, organizational engines in which "the unit of observation is an association organized to achieve change" (Gusfield 1981, 319).

Gusfield contrasts the linear view with a more "fluid" image that stresses "the cultural side of movements — the transformation of meaning — [in which] . . . the focus shifts away from the short-run search . . . for goal realization and toward the less political parts of human life in long-run perspective. Society rather than the State become the area of analysis."[2] So attuned, we are more prepared to "see" movements as diffuse, sprawling, halting, and slowly lumbering trends, accretions, or lessenings. Their beginnings and ends are ambiguous or even indeterminate; their programs and other activities are often inchoate and faltering and beginning ever again; their edges are ragged and blurred; their goals are unclear and their goal achievement is problematic, if assessable at all.

One of these models is not truer or better, than the other, only different. Each serves to sensitize us to alternative kinds of questions. In Gusfield's terms, "movements are not only linear and directed, they are also fluid and undirected."[3] At different periods in time, though, one rather than the other model may be more pertinent. For example, in the early-eighties, peace activism soared or exploded and a linear model for understanding it is very much in order — as provided in the three chapters of part 2 of this volume. The soar period passed, of course, as it does in all movements, rendering a fluid model once again of special relevance.

In order most accurately to capture the culture of movements — and specifically of the peace movement, I, therefore, think we need to use a fluid model, a model, indeed, that harkens back to the classic distinctions between *general* and *specific* movements (Blumer 1969a) and that, as Gusfield observes, "blur[s] the line between trend and movement."[4] Or, in other contrasting images offered by Gusfield, we are looking at a "ripple in the water rather than a shot in the dark."[5]

The Peace Movement

Among other merits, a fluid perspective on movements encourages us to see that movements are often quite indefinite and ambiguous affairs. In many instances, they are drifting fogs without definite form. In the case of the peace movement, as I made my way through the jumble of social entities that were in someone's view part of the movement, I observed several trends that prompted me to exclaim, "Movement, movement, who's got the movement?" Trends evoking this exclamation included the following:

1. People who were leaders and other activists in what they thought of as prominent peace organizations were often ignorant of the existence of other people, organizations, and events considered by these latter and others as also prominent in the movement. And, these latter reciprocated the compliment with their ignorance of the former. All, nonetheless, considered themselves important movement figures and thought of their organizations and events as the mainline of the movement.

It is no accident, I think, that in any given year several persons and organizations were at work compiling lists and directories of peace movement organizations. Literally dozens of national, local, and topical directories were published over the decade of the eighties.[6] The continual appearance of such works is puzzling until one appreciates that this kind of work was responding to widespread lack of knowledge, or puzzlement about, what "is" the movement among that small number of persons who even bothered to ask themselves that question.

2. Some organizations and leaders who said they were very concerned about peace and operated programs to achieve it also vigorously said they were *not* in the peace movement. Such disavowers were, nonetheless, classified as peace movement participants by *yet other* people who asserted who was *really* in or out of the movement!

3. The label "peace movement" was but one of a rather large number of labels used over the decade and featured the word *movement.* Here is a list of more frequently encountered terms:

freeze movement	sister city movement
antinuclear war movement	nuclear disarmament movement
antinuclear weapons movement	arms reduction movement
disarmament movement	anti-intervention movement
antiwar movement	anti-imperialist movement
arms control movement	peace and justice movement
citizen diplomacy movement	sanctuary movement

The matter was further complicated by frequent use of many of the above words in "softer" versions that avoided the "harder" word *movement* as in these terms: action, project, campaign, task force, mobilization, initiative, alliance, committee, council, network, federation, center, group.[7]

4. Among those people who knew of one another and thought that all of them were in the movement, knowledge of one another's recent or almost-recent activities was frequently quite sparse or nonexistent.

5. Joint actions — events and coalitions — among what participants defined as "peace movement organizations" rarely consisted of more than a few dozen of the several thousand organizations that *other observers* considered part of "the movement."

I want to be careful not to overstate these tendencies and to recognize that people were highly variable in the breadth of their conception of the movement and the degree they were knowledgeable about campaigns and persons. A small percentage — perhaps 2 or so percent — were, in fact, highly knowledgeable and formed a tiny minority of experts on the movement.

The pervasive ignorance and diversity I sum up in these five trends needs to be addressed at two levels, the practical problem of inclusion and the epistemological problem of "constructing" or "imputing" social formations.

As a practical matter, an analyst who wishes to discuss a movement or some aspect of it is confronted with the problem of who and what, according to whom, *is* the movement? The answer, of course, needs to be: It depends on who you ask and the conception of "social movement" you are using.

And, as another practical matter, we discover that some rather than other people we ask are regarded by yet others as knowing the right answer to the question of who or what is in the movement. These knowers-of-the-right-answer are those few people who undertake explicitly to decide what *is* the movement in the concrete sense is what is in or out of it. The most influential of these delineators are, commonly, historians, social scientists, and compilers of peace movement directories, all of whom start with the assumption that there *is* a movement of which some people, organizations, and events are a part and others are not. They write histories and other accounts that are of necessity explicit in "reading in" and "reading out" items that "are" and "are not" the movement. But, given what we also know about ambiguity of the reality out there (as in the five trends just listed), all such readings are, if considered closely and seriously, highly contentious.

What, in a particular case, is called the peace movement is very much the *creation* of any given observer and is likely to be expansive or restrictive as a function of the observer's predilections. In this sense, "fluidity"—a la Gusfield—is not simply a perspective on movements but an inescapable epistemological feature of them. If the reality out there is a myriad of scattered, inchoate, and frequently independent actions, events, and organizations, what is the degree to which the observer brings a movement into cognitive existence in the very act of asserting that "it" *is* there? And beyond this, such repeated assertion of a pattern of movement can be self-fulfilling. The movement comes to exist as a consequence of the prior presumption of its existence. In believing there "is" such a thing, there actually *is*, for practical purposes, such a thing. I do *not*, however, intend this only in the sense of the self-fulfilling prophecy—although that operates. Instead, inchoate reality "out there" is amenable to a variety of orderings. "Peace movement" is simply one ordering. "Peace movement" is a category for coding the raw outpourings of events. Because of the ambiguity of events and the abstractness of the category, coders continually find that there *is* a movement.[8]

I am not saying there was no such thing as the peace movement in the eighties. Instead, I am warning against our being blithe and unreflective on the question of what a movement is. With regard to the peace movement, I have come to the view that it is impossible to formulate criteria of inclusion and exclusion that will be both clear and acceptable to all reasonable evaluators, especially as such evaluators include participants, who, as indicated, were quite varied in their knowledge of and conceptions of "the movement." About the best we can do is strive for very fluid criteria that will be acceptable among people most dedicated to the task of analyzing movements—thought even this audience is prone to reasonable disagreement.

In the case of inclusion in the peace movement, we look to such obvious but far from infallible criteria as a person or organization: (1) regularly using the words *peace* and *war* (in their ordinary meanings) as salient parts of their ongoing activities; (2) favoring peace over war as a laudable goal; (3) eschewing policies that "advocate as the primary route to peace increased military strength, increased military spending, or military superiority by one nation or alliance over another" (Bernstein et al. 1986, 37). To repeat, this, and any other set of earmarks for the peace movement is, for the reasons just reviewed, unavoidably ambiguous and contentious. These are, nonetheless, pragmatic guides.

Culture

The term *culture* labels the collection of values, ideas, and practices that are publicly regarded in positive terms, enacted to a degree, and officially rewarded in a collectivity. Inspecting the parts of this definition, culture is, first, *ideational*, an assortment of cognitive categories that, second, specify *positive preferences* for goals to be pursued in life and ways to act in pursuing those goals that are superior to other possible goals and ways of acting. In this way, *cultured action* is to be distinguished from action that is defined by actors as merely expedient, neutrally habitual, or necessary but abhorred. While culture is, at its core, ideas about positively valued "things" of all sorts, it is also, third, about *action* that flows from those ideas that is to some degree, and fourth, *rewarded*, at least officially if less often in reality.

This use of the concept of culture is carefully limited in two ways. One, I use the word *collection* in referring to the constituents of culture because I think it is hazardous to assume that the items making up a given culture have much logical interrelation, are logically consistent, or form anything we would feel comfortable calling a "system." Cultures can consist, instead, of an ad hoc assortment of values, beliefs, and preferred actions (although this may create some strain). Two, we should not assume that all — or even a majority of — members of a collectivity "share" a given culture in totality or even many of its elements. A culture may be, for example, robustly espoused, practiced, and celebrated by some segment of a collectivity but not be known at all, or hardly known, to other segments of that same collectivity. Or, if it is known, all or some of the culture may be rejected. Indeed, if we added to our definition the requirement that culture be *shared* or a matter of *consensus* in the sense of universal knowledge, belief, and enactment among members — or almost all — there is likely nothing we could call culture. Nonetheless, the notions of *shared* or *consensual* are still relevant to understanding culture if we connect them to the appreciation that culture is a matter of *uncontested public profession* in some collectivity. Ideas, ideals, and the like that are a matter of *formal* and *public* proclamation, assent, and approval are cultural items, even if hardly at all enacted or privately believed, or enacted and not privately liked.

In being about ethereal ideas about ideals and their enactment, culture has proved a difficult matter to analyze. As put by Gary Fine, it has been difficult to get beyond regarding culture as "an amorphous mist which swirls around society members" (Fine 1979, 733). One way to move forward is to think about a limited number of prominent social locations in a social formation where culture can most easily be observed. By the term *social location* I mean aspects of a social entity where matters of a cultural nature are conspicuously exhibited. In reflecting on the peace movement, seven locations in that social formation have struck me as such conspicuously exhibiting culture. These are

1. Expressions of general *values* that are distinctive enough to justify asserting there is a movement in the first place.

2. Material *objects* and associated iconic personages that express culture.

3. Everyday *stories* circulated among participants.

4. Characteristics of the movement's *occasions*.

5. Specialized cultural *roles*.

6. Ways in which these and other roles are expressed in the *persona* exhibited by participants.

7. Features of desired *relations*.

These seven can also be thought of as operationalizing bridges between the extremely abstract concept of culture, on the one side, and the minutiae of everyday life as it swirls around us, on the other.

These social locations or places in which to look for culture are *also* places in which to assess the degree of development of each of the six formal dimensions of culture I explained at the outset. Our analytic task is, therefore, to inspect *locations* of culture vis-à-vis the *dimensions* of culture. This relationship is displayed graphically in figure 3.1, "Dimensions and Locations of Culture."

Peace Movement Culture

As one might surmise, a truly detailed inspection of each of the conjunctions shown in figure 3.1 is a virtually encyclopedic task that would run hundreds of pages longer than all but the most diligent would want to write, much less to read. I will, therefore, speak in summarizing rather than in highly detailed ways about the strength or degree of development of each of the six dimensions with respect to each of the seven social locations.

Figure 3.1
Dimensions and Locations of Culture

Dimensions

Locations	Sharing	Distinctive-ness	Scope	Elabora-tion	Quantity	Expressive-ness
Values						
Objects						
Stories						
Occasions						
Roles						
Persona						
Relations						

Values

In order to say there is a social movement at all, a collection of persons must, by definition, share at least one goal or value they espouse and seek to achieve.

Shared. In the case of the peace movement, the very name required that all its participants seek peace. This is obviously not definitive, though, because opponents of the peace movement were also claimed to be seeking peace (as in the official motto of some American military units "Peace Is Our Profession"). The peace sought was one, in addition, that did not involve or minimized the use, or the threat of use, of violent or military means. The behavior of the U. S. leadership and the views of the bulk of the population in early 1991, for example, demonstrated that peace values of even this minimal sort were not widely held. That is, in early 1991 the peace movement clearly supported the prolonged use of sanctions against Iraq as opposed to the use of military means. However, when military violence began in January of that year, only about 12 percent of the U.S. population opposed it — a rough measure of at least potential peace movement membership at that time.

This value preference for social order founded on other than organized violence or threat of it was associated with a number of other value trends that were widespread but not necessarily universal in the movement. These included reservations about (or rejection of) hierarchy in human affairs as regards, especially, political divisions, social class, race, and gender. To various degrees, nationalism was also rejected and replaced with ideals of global citizenship and welfare. Charles DeBenedetti summarizes these tendencies of what he terms "the peace subculture" in this fashion: "The peace subculture speaks of forbearance within a culture that has flowered on conquest. It speaks of reconciliation within a society that works better at distributing weapons than wealth. It speaks of supranational authority among a highly nationalist people who dislike all authority. It speaks of a just global order to governing officials anxious for preeminence and profit" (DeBenedetti 1980, 199).

Such values and the sentiments associated with them marked off the peace movement as a very small minority of American society. Yet even within the movement, the more specific these abstract notions became and the more topics were introduced, the less accord we observed. That is, as we moved down the "ladder of abstraction," all these values were subject to myriad and often conflicting understandings, especially when specific targets and programs of action were discussed. Though united at the broadest level, at the ground level, "the movement" became a virtually inchoate jumble of disparate enterprises.

Cluster variations. This jumble was most clearly seen in differing conceptions of *how to go about* seeking peace. As I discussed in chapter 1, if we ask, "What were people in the peace movement actually doing?" we see quite striking and potentially conflictful variations among six peace clusters. Having analyzed the six in chapter 1, let me here recapitulate them in a capsule form that focuses specifically on cultural implications.

1. Transcenders. Furthermost to the Right in the spectrum of the six clusters were the relatively affluent and middle-class professionals who stressed consciousness raising about the obsolescence of war and the construction of positive citizen-to-citizen relations to people in other countries, especially — in the eighties — with people in the Soviet Union. Their faith was that shifts in mass consciousness could occur with some rapidity and a "world beyond war" could, therefore, be established. Prime vehicles of citizen action for such transcenders included impressively dramatized gatherings and conferences that changed people's views and group travel exchanges with other nations.

2. Educators. Transcender belief in the possibility of rapid and broad changes in mass consciousness set them off from the less dramatic and more measured approach of educators, using that term here to include traditional employees of educational organizations but also encompassing all persons involved in systematic efforts to assemble and disseminate peace information, which includes publishers of magazines and books, audiovisual materials, and the like. In dedicating themselves to continuing courses of

instruction and other presentations of information, educators expressed their faith in the efficacy of facts and reasoning as ways to advance the cause of peace.

3. Intellectuals. A third cluster also centerpieced the belief that facts and reasoning were central to the quest for peace, but they were different from educators in being the producers or creators of such material rather than simply its disseminators or presenters. As a species of the general class of intellectuals in American society, they were oriented — in terms of values — to other intellectuals and not simply to clusters of the peace movement. As one example, unlike persons in other movement clusters, intellectuals placed a high value on being critical and reflective in their own work.

None of these three clusters needed to enter the political fray directly. Each was — by its own logic — rather more genteel and indirect in its approach. The three to which we come now were inherently more oppositional or conflictful and, therefore, expressed different cultural values.

4. Politicians. The mildest of the three more conflictful clusters consisted of persons engaged in ordinary political action and, therefore, in the culture of mainstream politics. Governed by the careful civility of political strife, peace politicians tried to build support for what they considered credible and feasible policies. Key cultural values of politicians included practical realism, flexibility, compromise, and "give and take." (At the level of adornment, "dressed-up" attire and careful grooming were the order of every working day.)

5. Protesters. Efforts at mainstream political change were frequently unsuccessful, giving rise to the idea that more forceful — though still peaceful — action was required. Such forceful action was often labeled "nonviolence" and centered on orderly forms of civil disobedience or resistance. Persons who were most active and persistent in such protest action tended also to participate in a broader cultural dissent from American society, a dissenting cultural movement trend sometimes termed the neocounterculture or *nonviolent direct action movement* (Epstein 1991). And, though neocounterculture people had a large influence on the practice of protest, they often found themselves in coalitions with liberal, middle-class people who also believed that ordinarily mainstream political action lacked sufficient force.

Further, the educator, intellectual, politician, and protester clusters all contained a liberal-radical division over conceptions of the nature of the political order and, therefore, of the extent of necessary change. "Peace liberals" thought that peace programs were achievable within the current political order of things and were reasonably comfortable working with and within the Democratic party, especially. "Peace radicals," in contrast, felt that a wide range of political and social changes must occur before significant progress on peace matters could be achieved, and they doubted that the Democratic party could be a key vehicle for such changes.

6. Prophets. Discontinuous with the preceding five clusters, several networks of radical Christians undertook to violate laws relating to the military in attempts both symbolically and literally to "turn swords into plowshares." Although they represented a very small proportion of the entire peace movement, the persistence of, and publicity given to, these prophetic souls propelled them into a cultural importance well beyond their sheer numbers. Their life-styles of voluntary simplicity or poverty, combined with their prophetic condemnation of dominant institutions, conjured up images of Biblical prophets, to whom, indeed, several commentators explicitly likened them.

It is crucial to appreciate that each of these six clusters embodied a genre of culture that also existed *outside* the peace movement: upper–middle-class boosterism; professional education and journalism; scholarly and intellectual work; politics; neocounterculture dissent; radical prophetic religion. This external grounding may not be very apparent in the case of the prophets, so let me elaborate. First and most centrally, the prophets were Christians, albeit ones who had a more self-sacrificing and self-demanding conception of Christianity than is common. Second, their Christianity centerpieced nonviolence, or to use an old-fashioned term, *pacifism.* These ideals counseled gentleness and lovingness in all relations, notions endemic to mainstream culture albeit practiced in carefully selected ways. Third, at the level of daily living, their life-style was that of the working poor or the impoverished, circumstances they shared with something like thirty million Americans in the eighties albeit prophets were voluntarily poor while millions of other Americans were not. On the other hand, prophets were also dramatically divergent from their host society. Prophet culture seemed, indeed, much like the kind of "primitive" Christianity reportedly found in the first century Roman Empire. The apocalypse envisioned was natural and nuclear rather than supernatural and cosmic, but the culture of the end-time and the means of salvation were rather similar.

I indicate how these six clusters differed in terms of symbolic objects, occasions and and so forth as I treat each of these topics. At the moment, I want only to mention the additional matter of *variations in basic ideas* as espoused in differing clusters. The focus of each cluster already signals different ideas about practical activities, but these had implications for yet other notions. For example, among transcenders, one encountered various kinds of "new age" notions such as embodied in the well-known "parable of the hundredth monkey," which alleged that telepathic communication of "energy" at key times results in "critical mass" changes of mass behavior (Keyes 1982). Or, as a second example, prophets spoke frequently of the need for widespread and deep moral regeneration, suggesting that mainstream politics were superficial and futile. Such ideas were not received enthusiastically in other clusters, to say the least, and there were many other instances of deep differences and lack of intercluster agreement.

As discussed in chapter 1, based on these very large differences alone, we ought to expect the peace movement to have exhibited quite considerable internal movement conflict. But, in fact, it did not. This was, in part, because people in each of the clusters needed rarely to cooperate with one another—and, as suggested previously, might be ignorant of one another. To the degree there was awareness, relations among the six were rather like those among the more respectable and less respectable branches of families: as long as they keep their distance we need only be mildly embarrassed by them and try mostly to ignore them. In addition, among the more knowledgeable, diversity of approaches was voiced as a cultural value.

I conclude that while there were shared values sufficient to justify saying there was a peace movement, these were small in number and exceedingly abstract. As these values were operationalized at specific levels of action, there is a significant degree of cultural diversity and the potential for "cultural conflict."

Symbolic Objects

In cultural perspective, the symbolic objects of a movement (or any social formation) are all those material items that participants view as giving physical expression to their values, including remembrances of its successes or trials and hopes for its future. Such objects are of at least five main kinds: movement identifiers, iconic persons, key artifacts, central events, and symbolic places.

Some few social formations are strikingly lush in symbolic objects of these sorts, especially religious organizations, which are prone to generate elaborate special buildings, garb, ceremonial objects, and even elaborate statuary. Others formations generate very few and may even explicitly oppose elaborate symbolic objects, yet the few they do generate may be quite distinctive (as among, for example, the Quakers and the Shakers).

The peace movement in its totality tended definitely to the minimal side of things. It was difficult to identify more than a few all-purpose identifiers, iconic persons, key artifacts, defining events and symbolic places that were widely known and revered. However, the clusters I have out-lined did not lack in abundant *candidates* for movementwide symbolic ob-jects, and some clusters were much richer along these lines.

Identifiers. The Christian Cross and the Jewish Star of David are, of course, preeminent examples of all-purpose symbols of two social forma-tions. The nearest equivalent for the peace movement would be the "peace symbol," but this was not, in fact, used all that frequently and was not even known to some younger peace participants. It has the additional prob-lem of not clearly symbolizing anything, and its historical origin and mean-ing was even disputed.[9] Perhaps more widely (but far from universally) employed was the white dove, a figure that may be rendered in a great many ways. During the eighties, the mushroom cloud of a nuclear explo-sion was seen frequently but was an icon of less than positive appeal.

Beyond these, there was nothing of movementwide scope. Instead, there were a variety of competing organizational logos, among the more strik-ing of which was the green and blue representation of the planet Earth used by Beyond War and the broken rifles of the War Resisters League.[10] It was telling that the largest single organization of the peace movement — the merged SANE/Freeze at almost two hundred thousand members in 1987 — had enormous difficulty selecting a name for itself. The decision simply to join the tag names of the two organizations together was the result of a lack of any symbolically resonating alternative. The logo that was subsequently produced — a spread-winged dove under an image of the Earth — looked to many more like a militaristic eagle of world domination than a dove of "global security" and was soon dropped.

Persons. The phenomenon of the charismatic leader is perhaps the fullest developed case of persons as symbolic objects and was definitely not seen in the peace movement. One needs only to think of the symbolic status of such people as Karl Marx, V. I. Lenin, Adolph Hitler, Mao Tse-Tung, and Sun Moon in their diverse movements to appreciate this quite vast difference.

The two strongest candidates for iconic movement personages were Mohandas K. Gandhi and Martin Luther King, Jr. Knowledge and rever-ence of them was quite wide in the movement, but, then, each was well known in the general culture anyway. Ironically, neither is most impor-tant historically for his work against international war or for peaceful al-ternatives to war. Instead, each led nonviolent struggles against unjust rulers inside his respective nation. It was their philosophies of nonvio-lence rather than their antiwar work that made them attractive to the peace movement.

A further irony is that the historical record of peace activism does not lack in impressive personages who might have been raised to the level of movementwide iconic figures but were not. In fact, one observed a puzzling degree of amnesia regarding outstanding leaders of both the distant and recent past and even of the present. This may, in part, be a function of the clustering "ghettoization" I have previously described: people tended to pay attention only to matters within their own clusters and, even more narrowly, within their cluster's liberal or radical wings. But there may be more to it than that. One observed as well a sheer *disinterest* in remembering historic figures and in promoting their relevance to the present and future. (There was, however, some cluster variability in this. More politically radical participants and the prophets did tend to iconize past leaders more than did liberals, so that articles and books on A. J. Muste and Dorothy Day, for example, were more common than articles and books on Jane Addams, Janet Rankin, or Norman Cousins.)

The dearth of iconic figures and the disinterest in generating them were likely related to attitudes toward hierarchy that I mentioned at the outset as among the core values of the movement.[11] Democratic and anti-hierarchical sentiments tend to undercut iconic reverence. Such sentiments appeared to extend also to living recent and past leaders — to such people as Noam Chomsky, Helen Caldicott, William Sloane Coffin, and David McReynolds — none of whom was very widely known in the peace movement much less beyond it.

Even so, a few figures did approach the iconic for some people within their own clusters. For clusters inclined to ordinary politics, such people included Norman Cousins, Benjamin Spock, William Sloane Coffin, Randall Forsberg, and Randall Kehler. For the pacifists, iconic people included Thomas Merton, Dorothy Day, and the Berrigan brothers. Among liberal intellectuals Kenneth Boulding, Johan Galtung, and Roger Fisher were accorded the highest degrees of such preeminence. Intellectuals who were more left leaning would also point to figures such as Noam Chomsky. Among transcenders, Armand Hammer and Samantha Smith enjoyed at least period vogue.

Artifacts. One intriguing way to look at a movement is by inventorying the more easily transported physical objects that are "part" of it. Such inventories will vary across movements in terms of the number of objects, their size and weight, market value, distinctiveness, and the like. Presumptively, the higher its rank on these dimensions (comparatively speaking), the more materialistic the movement as well as the more cultured. However, social movements in general are rather modest affairs in terms of transportable artifacts, and the peace movement seemed to differ little in this regard.

Artifacts may be divided into those endowed with symbolic value or expressive symbolism by participants and those regarded as mere neutral instruments. Following Jaeger and Selznick 1964, the terms *symbolic value* and *expressive symbolism* refer to objects employed by people

in order to continue and sustain meaningful experience. The wearing of black respects and prolongs the experience of mourning, of confronted death. Festivities rich in symbolism can help consummate an experience that would otherwise be brief and incomplete. In the presense of the symbol, people respond in ways that nurture rather than attenuate the experience. Moreover, having had "an experience," [humans] . . . create a symbol of it in order that the experience may be re-evoked and relived.

[Expressive] symbols help to provide focus, direction, and shape to what otherwise might disintegrate into chaotic feeling or the absence of feeling. . . . By serving as vehicles of response, symbols can help transform a "mere" feeling, a vague somatic tension, into genuine emotion. Thus symbols do more than sustain emotion. They contribute to the emergence of emotion as a uniquely human attribute (Jaeger and Selznick 1964, 662–63).

One further way, then, to scrutinize the artifacts observed on the bodies of participants, brought to their gatherings, and found at places of movement habitation is in terms of which, if any, of those artifacts is fondly regarded (has symbolic significance) as distinct from merely used. Prime candidates for such expressive symbolism in movements might include certain prized posters from past campaigns, particular copies of certain books and other publications, unusual souvenirs from past striking events, and photographs of movement people. My impression is that the peace movement was remarkably sparse in all these respects. While offices and gatherings were certainly stocked with "literature" and related movement-distinctive artifacts, little of it had more than a transitory and instrumental significance.

Only a few objects were endowed with symbolic significance beyond one or a few clusters. Of some currency were "paper cranes" resulting from paper crane ceremonies as well as one or more panels from The Ribbon. The Ribbon was a project conceived by Justine Merritt of Denver as a "band of fabric panels sewn end to end [to be] wrapped around the Pentagon in Washington on August 4, 1985 to mark the 40th anniversary of the atomic bombing of Hiroshima" (Keller n.d.). Each panel of cloth or other material was 1.5 × 3 ft. and stitched or painted with motifs and messages of peace. Originally, it was estimated that 1,535 panels would be required to circle the Pentagon, but response around the country was so enthusiastic that several times more than that number were actually created and used. After the circling in 1985, the panels continued to be displayed at peace meetings of many kinds.[12]

Events. The histories of humans striving are punctuated by space and time compressed actions in which long-term and diffuse fears and/or aspirations are rendered momentarily visible in decisive victories or defeats. The crucifixion and "resurrection" of Jesus and the signing of the Declaration of Independence are examples of such events for their respective forms of human striving. Each is commemorated and celebrated as an occasion of value clarification and rejuvenation. Iconic events are, of course, as much constructed as objectively "perceived." Therefore, many more episodes are candidates for use than actually get constructed, and the degree to which a movement "has" them tells more about the level of its cultural enterprise than about its history (though not all events are equally suitable for iconic construction).

In the peace movement of the eighties, there were no unambiguously movementwide iconic events. The anniversary of the dropping of nuclear bombs on Japan, August 6 and 9, 1945, was a strong candidate for iconic status in the mideighties but it faded by decades's end. During the period of heightened activism over the dangers of nuclear war, August 6 and August 9 were days of considerable *and diverse* commemorative activity of many sorts. I stress the "and diverse" because each of the clusters engaged in its own favorite form of action: slick commemorations, educational gatherings, scholarly treatments, political expressions, protest arrests, religious ceremonies, as well as innovative variations on each of these. Media coverage provided a collage of forms, sending mixed, perhaps even mixed-up, messages. For example, the Associated Press reporting on the forty-third anniversary in 1988 noted that

> the observances [included] vigils outside nuclear weapons plants, a mountain climb in New Hampshire, a bicycle ride in California and the signing of a scroll in Boston. . . . At the Washington Monument . . . protesters arranged 30,000 warhead-shaped cones to form a 'ban-the-bomb' symbol. . . . Actor Martin Sheen was among 64 people arrested for . . . trespassing at the Nevada Test Site. . . . At Seal Beach Naval Weapons Station in California, 24 protesters were arrested for trespassing. . . . [In] New Hampshire, six women tried but failed to hang peace symbols on . . . the seven-foot mushroom-cloud-and-eagle emblem of the 509th Bombardment Wing at Pease Air Force Base. . . . Residents of Portland . . . awoke Saturday to find the pavement scattered with thousands of pale "shadows" painted by anti-nuclear activists. (Associated Press 1988)

When the peace movement slumped in general in the late-eighties, so did commemorations of the bombings. It is worth noting also that, as an iconic event, the bombings presented two difficulties. One, to commemorate them was to commemorate death and disaster without any compensating notes of birth and renewal (rather as if Christians were to commemorate Good Friday without Easter Sunday). Iconic events may be, as I have just said, constructed, but their selection cannot be entirely arbitrary. Two, as the prime vacation month of the American year, August is not an auspicious period to celebrate an iconic event of any sort.

The many other events that could have been selected for elevation to iconic occasions all had the difficulty of eliciting reverence from only a limited segment of the movement as in, for example, the founding the United Nations or the birthday of a leader. Other occasions could be said to be "celebrated" only in a highly abstract sense as when a United Nations declared Day of Peace set for the third Tuesday of September was promoted by some "transcender" organizations who asked cities to "declare peace and schools . . . [were asked] to teach peace" (Peace Links Connection 1988, 4).

Another way to develop iconic events is to "piggyback" on established symbolic days by *overlaying* their existing symbolism with peace symbolism. Efforts to do this for two days — Good Friday and Mother's Day — are of particular note. As an American Peace Test spokesperson put it: "We are very sentimental as a culture about Mother's Day, . . . which made it even more powerful to be speaking out for peace on that day. . . . [There was] something inherently wrong with arresting women on Mother's Day" (Nancy Hale quoted in Rice 1987, 12).

Places. Some movements generate spaces or places that are defined as recalling and expressing noble values. The peace movement was stronger on this cultural matter than on some others although not much so. For while there was (and is), in fact, quite a variety of actual and potential "peace places" in the United States in the forms of peace trees, walls, rose and other gardens, parks or sections of parks, buildings, and even (in Chicago), a small and struggling but serious Peace Museum (opened, November, 1981), knowledge of any of them was limited and occasions organized around them were sparse.

Sometimes a *single,* particular place gets defined as *the* revered place of a movement. The peace movement had no such place in the United States although candidates for it might well have included the Isaiah Wall peace memorial across the street from the U.N. headquarters in New York, the U.N. headquarters itself, the peace organization building at 777 United Nations Plaza, or the Methodist Building at 100 Maryland Avenue, North East, Washington, D.C., across the street from the Supreme Court. Internationally, there are of course several memorials to nuclear war victims in Japan.[13]

During the eighties, some people took the creation of peace places as a special task in their lives. T. J. David, manager of a tire store in Sacramento, was among such dogged cultural entrepreneurs. Over the course of six years in the mid- and late-eighties, he "traveled more than 35,000 miles and spent more than $30,000 of his own money planting World Peace Rose Gardens" on church properties (Hoge 1988). David told a reporter "It's so much fun doing this. . . . It's my biggest expense, but the way people react when they see the roses makes it more than worthwhile" (Hoge 1988).[14]

In contrast, some peace movement people seemed quite reckless about candidate and key peace places. At the time of the merger of SANE and Freeze, SANE-owned property at 711 G Street South East in Washington known as the Ben Spock Peace Center. But, as part of the merger, and throwing tradition and reverence for place aside, it was sold to raise cash for operating expenses and to allow a move to "high tech" and high rise headquarters in a more upscale neighborhood—a move that, along with other changes, left what had been the largest American peace organization in rootless disarray.

Stories

In the materials I have reviewed in previous chapters, we see that peace movement people (1) espoused distinctive values, (2) propounded varyingly liberal versus radical substantive beliefs about desired social changes, and (3) put forth six, diverse theories of the actions required to achieve those changes. These three activities do not, however, exhaust the "ideological work" that one observed in that movement or that we see in other movements. To read the writings of movement members and to listen to them talk among themselves is to encounter a stream of what we might think of as "movement stories," or, when compressed, as "movement slogans"—a kind of argot. I am referring here to "homely folk" tales, pithy sayings, and special labels that contribute to a movement's distinctive cultural ambiance. In his classic depiction of social movements, Herbert Blumer calls attention to such storytelling as the "popular character" of ideology in "the form of emotional symbols, shibboleths, stereotypes, smooth and graphic phrases, and folk arguments" (Blumer 1969a, 111).

Movements vary in the degree to which such stories circulate among the members. In some few movement organizations, ordinary language is so laced with such argot that day-to-day talk and common movement writing is virtually unintelligible to outsiders or, if intelligible, is seen as strikingly novel and/or alien. The peace movement in toto had not moved very far in such a direction, but it did have a number of widely circulated stories. One category of these, what we might call "social change" stories, were really stories in the narrow, literal sense, and as a group, they held out hope that social change in war-peace matters could be achieved. One variety was the "critical mass story" that had as its dominant theme the idea that "small actions make a critical difference." The Hundredth Monkey story, recounted previously, was the transcender version of a critical mass story although it was certainly heard among more than transcenders and was sometimes shorn of its original mystical telepathic communication element. Another critical mass story was called "The Weight of Nothing," which told how an individual snowflake weighed nothing, but en mass (3,741,952, to be exact) they broke off the branch of a tree. In the Fall of 1988, the Friends Committee on National Legislation (FCNL) printed up The Weight of Nothing Story on a sheet suitable for posting and in a mail solicitation urged people to post it "as a reminder that your political action is not in vain." This story was also said to be an appropriate answer to the question, "How can my small voice have any impact on the political decisions of the Federal government?" (Snyder 1988, 1). Sloganized versions of critical mass stories included the declaration that "everything you do will seem insignificant, but you must do it anyway." The moral of such stories, of course, is that in the right context, a small action can make a great difference, and a great many small acts are needed to build the right context for a last act to make *the* difference.

A second class of rather widely heard story featured the theme that even massive social change that seems impossible can come very quickly. Its most common version was the "War Is Like Slavery" story, which argued that in the early–nineteen hundreds, slavery in the United States seemed a natural and unalterable feature of society, yet through human effort, it was abolished, and war is the same. While it might now seem an unavoidable feature of human society, it can be abolished if we simply set ourselves the task.

These two kinds of stories were intended to boost morale and respond to the David-Goliath imbalance that existed between the war system and the peace movement. A widely posted and reprinted quotation from Margaret Mead played on both themes: "Never doubt that a small group of thoughtful, committed citizens can change the world. Indeed, it's the only thing that ever has."

A third genre of story gently mocked the war system. Widely circulated versions ran:

It will be great day when our schools get all the money they need and the air force has to hold a bake sale to buy a bomber.

Strength through peace [a mock inversion of the militaristic "peace through strength"].

The degree to which a movement features *humor* or friendly ridicule of its opponents in the little stories that circulate tells us a great deal about participants' attitudes toward such adversaries as well as their attitudes toward themselves. I know of no current way to measure the amount of humor in a movement and can only venture the suggestion that at the movementwide level, peace movement people were clearly, if not highly, appreciative of humor. Popular orator (in the political cluster) William Sloane Coffin, an experienced preacher, was especially adept at humorous utterances, and the use of humor was fairly common among speakers. Considered in terms of the different clusters, my impression is that humor was most common among the protesters and especially among the neocountercultural protesters. The names of their "affinity groups," in particular, were often intended as humorous plays on words as in Scum of the Earth (a group who dressed in the punk style of the eighties), Communist Dupes, Perishing Two, Salt and Pepper (older people), Sunflower Brigade, and Soviet Agents.

There were even neocountercultural affinity groups organized around humor, comedy acts, and comedy troupes. The Communist Dupes, or "the Dupes, as they were affectionately called" (Epstein 1991, 143), were one of the better known humorous affinity groups of the eighties. Among their more notable actions was the production of "cardboard posters of the sort that government agencies sometimes put up in public places. . . . [A]ttributed to the Federal Emergency Management Agency, . . . they were entitled 'IN CASE OF NUCLEAR ATTACK' [and gave instructions to] '. . . Remain Calm . . . Avert Eyes [and ended with] . . . Comfort the Dying . . . Isolate Corpses to Prevent Spread of Disease.' The posters were extremely convincing; one would not have thought, at first glance, that they had been issued by anyone other than the government" (Epstein 1991, 143). The Dupes were San Francisco Bay area residents, and early one morning about thirty of them boarded the Bay Area Rapid Transit system and put up the posters. Yet other Dupes rode the trains and "point[ed] out the posters to passengers and ask[ed] what they meant. One man said, "Well, it's a joke, but it's not really a joke" (Epstein 1991, 144). Two of the Dupes interviewed by Epstein "said that this was exactly the kind of response they wanted" (Epstein, 1991, 144).

Humor was part of a larger motif of *playfulness* that the neocounter-culturalists, especially, injected into the cultural life of the peace movement protesters. Although acts of protest were preeminently serious — perhaps more serious in many respects than the core acts of other clusters — they were often accompanied by a sense of absurdity. The very deadliness and seriousness of the opponents one was engaging — members of the U.S. war system — perhaps demanded that one ask, "Can you war system folks really be serious about this? Surely you are perpetuating some kind of colossal put-on and joke that you will reveal as such if we tweak you enough."[15]

Occasions

The occasions on which movement participants assemble face-to-face provide many opportunities for richer or poorer cultural expression. Even gatherings that are instructional or worklike in character — as opposed to celebrations per se — can vary in the distinctiveness and extent of cultural enactment.

At the level of the peace movement as a whole, there was no distinctive culture of gathering which made the gatherings distinguishable from social movement occasions as a generic class. The quintessential forms of movement occasions staged by the peace movement — the march and/or rally — were, by and large, formally identical to marches and rallies of other social movements: marchers carried banners and placards, rallies involved a parade of speakers from the organizations in coalition punctuated by "folksy" musical entertainment.

However, at the level of the six movement clusters there was considerable distinctiveness to and elaboration in gatherings, including the fact that marches and rallies per se were not regarded as appropriate in all clusters. Transcenders, for example, preferred indoor programs in plush concert halls or resorts. Beyond War was perhaps the preeminent producer of what can be called the *glitzy high-tech public relations event.* Over several years in the eighties, they used satellite television communication to hold nation-scale "meetings" in which groups gathered at dozens of locations to watch televised "down-linked" programs. In some versions, these meetings were on a global scale and a few formed a "space-bridge" to the Soviet Union. These events celebrated communication per se and often made awards to persons or organizations who were defined as working for peace.

The transcender *plush conference* was the logical extension of the glitzy event. Ensconced in a mountain resort, a suburban conference center, or a lavish big city hotel, several days of talks by and with prominent transcender activists were organized, including an annual "symposium" staged at Aspen by John Denver's Windstar Foundation, registration for which, in 1986, was $425 a person, with lodging priced "from $50 to $150 per night."

While "glitz" was a cultural tendency in the transcender cluster, not every event displayed much of it. More ordinary, garden variety transcender "educational gatherings" tended toward the culture forms of the lecture, panel discussion, or video. Slightly elaborated, one-day annual "peace fairs" were organized in many communities. Many of these featured *children* and, indeed, children figured quite centrally in transcender culture.

Irrespective of the degree of glitz, transcender peace occasions drew heavily on the cultural forms of ordinary middle-class entertainments, such as concerts, coffees, and teas. The similarities, indeed, prompted wags to deride the home-staged ones as "Tupperware parties for yuppies." Such a characterization also applied to the "peace travel" that was, over the eighties, such a prominent part of the transcender cluster repertoire of actions. Rather than visit the Bahamas for pleasure, one went to Russia for peace.

Transcenders faced the special cultural problem that events staged for peace, even glitzy events, created the possibility of *appearing* to be a declasse "demonstration," and presentational work had therefore to be done to forestall such an unintended message. One form of guarding against that message was publicly to *predefine* one's event as *not* a demonstration. Here is an example from Davis, California, in 1984, a year that transcender women organized a Mother's Day Walk for Peace. Three women who were current or recent members of the Davis City Council (and each of whom had or would soon serve as mayor) signed a letter printed in the local daily paper supporting the upcoming walk. "The event is . . . not a demonstration, but a simple, dignified statement by mothers and children and families. . . . Like may [sic] of you I've never been much of a 'marcher,' but the compelling nature of the issue and the dignity of this particular event make it worth supporting. When better than Mother's Day to express the ultimate concern for our children" (Motley, Evans, and Poulas 1984). Distancing is managed by means of the juxtaposition of *demonstration* and *marcher*, on the one hand, with *dignified* and *dignity*, on the other.

The peace movement appears to have had a particular proclivity for the long-distance, multiple-week *march* or *walk* as a mode of dramatizing its messages. The practice extends back several decades and was especially frequent during the eighties. The most famous of these in the eighties was first organized as PRO-Peace by David Mixner and conceived on an unprecedented scale and sophistication level. Initially envisioned as a "mobile city" with newspapers, a radio station, schools, and a variety of other stationary modes of social organization not ordinarily seen in marches, the sheer scale of the undertaking—which made it difficult to finance and recruit for—led to collapse almost immediately after leaving Los Angeles in March of 1986. However, it was resurrected as the Great Peace March and a cross-country march was completed (Folsom, Fledderjohann, and Lawrence 1988). Following it, in the late-eighties there were several Soviet-American Peace Walks, one climaxing in a "first-ever Soviet-American stadium rock concert" (Kenney 1988) and other less well-publicized marches.[16]

While the classic march and rally were the predominant forms of peace gatherings over the eighties, women of more radical direct action and feminist persuasions early-on in the decade "broke away from the traditional rally format . . ." and introduced an "esthetic" that "allowed greater participation and personal expression," and made a more striking impact (Epstein 1991, 162). According to Epstein, these innovations started with the November 17, 1980, Women's Pentagon Action, an event that

> began with a march through Arlington Cemetery. As the women approached the Pentagon they were joined by drummers and by four women carrying large female puppets, each symbolizing a different stage of the demonstration: . . . black for mourning, . . . red . . . for rage, yellow, for empowerment, white for defiance. . . . In the first phase of the demonstration, some women planted cardboard tombstones . . . on the Pentagon lawn . . . while the rest of the women stood in a circle around them, wailing in grief. The red puppet was then brought to the center of the circle, the women shouted, crowded together, and began to chant, yell, and bang on cans. The yellow and white puppets then led the women around the Pentagon [in a line] . . . which was extended by ribbons held by and linking the women. When [the lines] . . . met, the women had encircled the Pentagon (Epstein 1991, 161–62).

This demonstration also went beyond symbolic display in a subsequent defiance stage in which some women "wove the doors to the Pentagon shut with brightly colored yarn while others sat in the doorways" (Epstein 1991, 162). Motifs of circling, bright colors, tombstones, weaving, and kindred practices were adopted into many subsequent demonstrations in which more radical protesters appeared.

On a somewhat smaller numerical scale, a second breakaway from the ordinary march and rally also began in the early-eighties. Members of some religious orders and mainstream religious congregations began holding religious services at the gates of war installations. Commonly scheduled on Good Friday, some of these evolved into ecumenical services that deemphasized the distinctions between Protestant and Catholic ritual. One of the longest running and most frequent of these was the Lenten Desert Experience centered on the main gate to the Nevada Test Site. Among more conventional religious peace groups, Pax Christi may have been the decade's champion of distinctive, elaborate, and expressive occasions, for it devised quite impressive variations on Catholic religious ceremony.

Finally, over the eighties, what one might think of as sporadic and short-lived innovations in culture that had rather limited careers emanated from a variety of sources.

• As part of the 1988 Disarm the Seas Campaign, the Bay Area Peace Navy "staged an 'aquatic play' for audiences along the waterfront. Their peace fleet of sailboats, speed boats and kayaks circled a 100-foot replica of a nuclear submarine, which experienced a 'theatrical' nuclear accident" (Jacobson 1988, 9).

• As part of the same campaign, "In San Diego, the Channel Zero Theater Group staged a skit near the harbor. In it, the personnel of a sea-launched cruise missile unit, who carried a shiny 20 foot replica of a Tomahawk missile, killed Third World figures and took King Neptune into custody to dramatize the consequences of U. S. naval intervention" (Jacobson 1988, 9).

• Some circles of prophets adopted the practice of pouring blood on war system property in order to "mark . . . an object as Other" (MacQueen 1991, 67, italics deleted).

The music sung (or or not sung) at movement occasions is always, of course, of particular cultural interest. Despite the ferment I analyze in chapters 5, 6, and 7, there was no distinctive peace movement anthem. Instead, the most performed musical compositions were "imported" (or should one say appropriated) from other movements. These included "We Shall Overcome" (of civil rights origin, a song that is now the global all-purpose movement anthem), "Singing for Our Lives," (by Holly Near, first associated with gay rights), and even "Amazing Grace" (of Christian origin). At the turn of the decade into the nineties, even a nonmovement song titled "From a Distance" enjoyed vogue in some peace circles.[17]

Roles

While culture pertains to everyone, "everyone" does not have an equal relation to it or an equal role in its creation, elaboration, preservation, chronicling, performance, or dissemination. Instead, some people are likely to "do" culture much more than others. And, movements differ in the *de-*

gree to, the *variety* with, and *numbers of people* which are engaged in these specialized cultural roles.

Specialized culture roles may be divided into those that create and elaborate culture and those that are particularly occupied with disseminating it.

Creators. One key category of culture is the ensemble of concepts, assertions, precepts, presumed facts, and other cognitions labeled "knowledge." This body of knowledge is mostly created by people who work at that task with continuity and diligence. These are, therefore, "knowledge workers," otherwise called "intellectuals," "artists," and "scholars." So, too, the products of knowledge workers divide roughly into items that are more "scientific," or "analytic," versus "artistic," or "humanistic."

1. Analytic. Institutions of higher education and journalism along with private wealth (foundation based and individual) have created an infrastructure on which has risen a social class of intellectuals, numbers of whom function as the continuing culture creators (and elaborates) of several social movements, the peace movement among them.

Over the eighties, peace movement intellectuals were rather modest in number and vigor of creation/elaboration as compared to the intellectual clusters of other movements in that decade, such as those of the environmental, left, feminist, and minority rights movements. Nonetheless, peace intellectuals numbered in the several thousands if we are not overly strict in our conception of what is an intellectual. Their numbers can be gauged by the memberships of their leading and allied organizations, several of which had less than a thousand members and among which there were overlapping memberships.[18] Nonetheless, their products accumulated, and over several decades they created a quite substantial literature consisting of thousands of books and articles in about a dozen scholarly and semischolarly journals.[19]

As I stated at the outset, I am more concerned here with the structure or form of culture than with its substance. Nonetheless, it seems worthwhile to discuss briefly just what these intellectuals were working on over the eighties. What kind of writing were they doing?[20]

First, the work was done in the formats of several traditional scholarly disciplines, including physics, political science, history, law, philosophy, and religion. That is, the methods and approaches of peace intellectuals differed little if at all from those of intellectuals of other types. They were political scientists, historians, lawyers, physicists, ethicists, or whatever, who happened to treat war-peace matters. Thus, like other historians, peace historians dug out primary source material and analyzed it. Like other political scientists and sociologists, peace social scientists calculated statistics on the war-peace behavior of nations. Like other philosophers and lawyers, they carefully dissected the morality and legality of war system institutions and activities. Like other policy analysts, they dissected concepts of "national security" and ideas of "common security" or "alternative security." The culture they created, then, might be different in *content*, but it was not different in *form*.

Second, some of the questions they addressed were similar to, or the same as, many of the questions addressed by their competitors — the mainstream "defense," or, if you will, war intellectuals. Their answers and some of their questions were, however, different. A brief listing of what appear to have been the ten main questions addressed by peace intellectuals in the eighties should illustrate these similarities and differences.

1. Scale, Structure, Changes? What is the sheer scale and structure of the war system of the United States, other countries, and the planet? and How is its scale and structure changing over time in response to what other kinds of changes?

2. Processes? What are the processes of the U.S. and other war systems? What, precisely, is going on within them? How do they work?

3. Causes? What are the causes of the U.S. and other war systems? Why is there a military-industrial complex in the United States, in other contemporary societies, in societies of human history? What are its historical, economic, political, psychological, and other underpinnings? Is it driven by psychologically pathological forces?

4. Goals and Motives? Why do the U.S. and other war systems act as they do? What are the U.S. military-industrial complex's motives and aims, as stated publicly and as held secretly and/or unconsciously?

5. Effects? What are past, current, and likely effects of the U.S. and other war systems on economies, human rights, the environment, and other matters?

6. Technical Adequacy? Which doctrines, programs, and weapons of the war system are technically adequate or inadequate within the frameworks of ends and means used by their promoters?

7. Geopolitically Adequate? Which geopolitical analyses offered by the war system leaders are accurate or inaccurate?

8. Morally Adequate? In what ways are various aspects of the war system morally and ethically good or bad or legal or illegal?

9. Alternative Policies? By means of what national and international policies, programs, and actions can war systems be made safer, reduced in size, or eliminated altogether?

10. Citizen Action? By means of what citizen actions can government policies that maintain and expand the military-industrial complex be changed?

Although peace intellectuals tended to develop distinctive answers to all these questions, they were, perhaps, most active and distinctive in answers to question nine, alternative policies. Beyond an entire journal devoted to more technical ideas (*The Journal of Peace Proposals*), the literature was filled with concepts and plans of diverse scope proposing alternative local, international organizations, and global organizations, images of the future, and concepts of security.[21]

On the assumption that a cluster of dedicated culture creators and elaborators is important to a movement, it becomes relevant to ask, Are the ranks of creators and elaborators filled with adequate numbers of people who are energetic and talented? That is, a movement can presumably have too few intellectuals and/or have intellectuals who are neither especially talented nor especially energetic. It can, in these senses, be "under cultured."

I assess the peace movement of the eighties to have been relatively fortunate in at least having a few intellectual contributors of some distinction in the major areas where its movement-mandate demanded intellectually credible writings. However, the *amount* of talent in each of the creative areas was less than abundant, and it was not clear that these ranks would be replenished.

In addition, the degree to which a cluster of intellectuals is important to the public credibility and influence of a movement likely varies from movement to movement. As I argue in chapter 7, the matters of concern to peace movements are such that intellectuals are probably *more important* for public credibility and influence than is the case for other movements. Peace movements tend to be about topics that are remote in the experiences of most people — about, that is, foreign affairs, war preparations, and distant military deployments. Having little or no personal experience against which to check ruling elite claims about such topics, people tend to defer to the judgments of those who claim to know those topics better. Therefore, people who claim expertise *and* who *disagree* with the policies of ruling elites — peace intellectuals — probably play a larger role in influencing people about these matters than they do influencing people on topics closer to immediate experience.

Their unusual salience to the public standing of a movement makes it important for us to examine peace intellectuals with more care than might be the case with other movements. I have just described the kinds of questions they mostly asked, and this tells us about their abstract, theoretical enterprise. It does not, however, provide us a picture of them as people who also performed social roles that were, in important part, roles as *public intellectuals* — a role that some observers think is declining but which was much in evidence among peace intellectuals of the eighties (Jacoby

1987). These roles ranged from specialization in narrow and weapons-technical topics, on the one side, to dominant concern with wide and globally political matters, on the other.

1. The Atomic Scientists. Virtually from the moment of the detonation of the first nuclear weapon at Alamogordo, New Mexico, on July 16, 1945, some scientists who worked on that weapon have thought that the American government has had inadequate policies regarding it and have carried on technical and other criticism of successive regimes. Expressing themselves in such organizational forms as the *Bulletin of the Atomic Scientists* and the Federation of American Scientists, they were a key, legitimizing element of the peace movement in every decade, including the eighties.[22] (Unfortunately for the peace movement, this "magic" generation of scientists who, by their presence at the "birth of the bomb" have been thought to have unusual wisdom and have been accorded high stature, cannot, by definition, be replenished. Also, unfortunately for the movement, subsequent generations of weapons have not created equivalent numbers of defecting scientists of such high stature.)

2. Technical Defense Critics. However, there were at least a few such subsequent defectors and combined with people who had scientific credentials but who had not been inside the weapons complex there was, in the eighties, a cluster of intellectuals who carried on criticism of the war system at technical levels. The milder of these critics were commonly associated with the Arms Control Association and the Union of Concerned Scientists. Intellectuals of this specialization worried, though, that their ranks were thin and thinning and that there were few if any established programs that might result in their replenishment.

3. Expert Policy Critics. The first two varieties of intellectuals credibly criticized the "hardware" of the weapons system (as well as other matters). Allied with them were intellectuals who lacked "hardware credentials" but who had mastered the details of the structure of war preparations, of "force structure," "forward deployment," "extended deterrence," "minimum deterrence," and the like. A number of them were retired military officers of high ranks and policy-level service, as organized, for example, into the Center for Defense Information and exemplified by Col. Robert Bowman.

4. Political Analysts. Attuned to materials generated by these three specializations, a yet broader and "softer" set of critics addressed themselves to the political and economic meanings and motives of evolving war-peace policies and placed these in historical perspective. Noam Chomsky was, without doubt, the preeminent figure of this genre over the eighties, albeit he was among the more radical of them.

5. Ethical-Legal Analysts. All the specialists mentioned worked fairly

"close in" to the hardware and polices of the war system in their criticisms and suggested alternative policies. Stepping back somewhat, a number of analysts frontstaged basic moral and legal questions they saw raised by the war system in general and by particular parts of it. On the moral side, leaders of religious denominations were especially critical of the moral logic of nuclear weaponry in the perspective of the criteria of a "just war." On the legal side, the Lawyers Committee on Nuclear Policy sought to specify ways in which a variety of war system policies and acts were violations of international law. Some crafted legal bases of "civil resistance" to nuclear weaponry (e.g., Boyle 1987).

6. Psychological-Existential Analysts. Concerned about yet broader matters, a varied set of analysts argued that hardware, policy structure, political programs, and overt matters of ethics and legality failed to come to grips with deeper, underlying problems. One needed, in addition, to probe the psychological and existential levels of human functioning. The depth and breadth to which these analyses went varied, but all saw the underlying problems of humans as quite profound. The theses of such analyses included a human propensity to death and destruction in the hope of renewal; the workings of an aggressive, masculine ethic; a human need to project personal defects as enmity and a need for enemies.[23]

7. Peace and Conflict Researchers. Attuned to one or another degree to all the above types of work, but not featuring any of them, a somewhat more "removed" cluster of intellectuals strove — on the surface at least — to develop a dispassionate but also morally engaged science of the causes of war and peace. This specialization was most prominently associated with efforts to establish "peace research" as a legitimate form of intellectual enterprise in higher intellectual circles. One measure of the accumulated work of peace and conflict researchers over the eighties is provided by the fact that the first peace studies textbook, in the sense of an expensive and large tome issued by a standard textbook publisher, appeared in 1991. Textbooks represent a significant advance investment by a publisher who is gambling on a large adoption; thus, any topic with "a textbook" has been assessed by the publisher to have "arrived." Titled *Introduction to Peace Studies* (Barash 1991) and running 613 double-column pages, it provided twenty-four chapters organized around four topics: the nature and frequency of war, causes of war, paths to negative peace, and paths to positive peace. Johan Galtung, regarded by many as the founder of peace studies, wrote the introduction.[24]

8. Peace Scheme Developers. Sometimes overlapping with peace and conflict researchers, a nonetheless distinctive genre of intellectuals concentrated on devising schemes of political and other arrangements that would

reduce or eliminate war and/or preparations for war and or devising plans for how to get to such a peaceful world. Efforts of this sort were quite varied in scope and focus and included enterprises in which groups of people tried systematically to "image" an alternative peaceful world, detailed plans for a new world order in a radically revised form of the United Nations, and rethought conceptions of "national security" (as in "alternative security") and nonmilitary civilian defense.[25]

9. Peace Action Strategists. Individual intellectuals tended to specialize in one or another of the above roles, even though they might do additional kinds of work in a secondary way. This ninth is rather different in this respect. Although a fair literature was produced, the task of criticizing past movement strategies and proposing new ones was not the major undertaking of any significant number of people. Instead, it was a preoccupation of a great many but was addressed in a way that was secondary to other work.

10. Preservers and Reporters of Movement History. Culture creating and elaborating intellectual roles of the nine types just described is rather different from work centered on preserving historical records of peace movement matters and working such records into formal histories. This latter role is culture creating and elaborating in the sense that history is created *socially* in the acts of preserving and analyzing it. A history that would not "exist" is created by acts of assembling it. Comparatively, over many decades, the peace movement has been quite striking in the degree and variety of organized entities which have sought to preserve the records of organizations, the papers and other artifacts of peace activists, and sundry memorabilia. Over the eighties, the diversity and complexity of these collections advanced to the point of justifying publications that listed institutional and individual peace archives.[26] From these and other sources, several dozen historians have written a variety of histories of the peace movement, including a new wave of analyses of the eighties. Suggesting the distinctiveness of their consciousness, peace historians formed themselves into a Council for Peace Research in History. (Although engaged in a different kind of intellectual work, social scientists who apply their cognitive schemata to the peace movement have played a similar role as creators of peace movement history. Indeed — mirrors within mirrors within mirrors — this book is an example of such work.)

2. *Humanistic.* While not as numerous and productive as the analytic intellectuals, over the eighties there was also a substantial force of more "humanistic" peace culture creators and elaborators. Literary items — primarily novels that took war and peace as themes from a peace point of view — were, perhaps, the largest single class of products. The impressively

large number of science fiction works dealing with nuclear war resulted in a genre of books analyzing *them* (e.g., Brians 1987) and a scholarly association and newsletter devoted to their study (*Nuclear Texts and Contexts*, published by the International Society for the Study of Nuclear Texts and Contexts)!

There was no notable outpouring of stage plays, musicals, or musical compositions although there were some works of these sorts, including the widely performed play "Peace Child."

Disseminators. While creators and elaborators of a movement's culture obviously also disseminate it to a degree, culture is probably most effectively spread when people set about doing it in social roles geared to that objective. Also any manner in which any participant promoted the peace movement was, of course, also an effort, in a general sense, to spread peace movement culture. I want to address here, however, the narrower topic of disseminating peace movement culture per se and not the vastly broader range of activities constructed to promote the movement and its programs.

There are at least three major sorts of these specialized disseminator roles, not all of which appear with much force in all movements and which were seen quite unevenly in the peace movement of the eighties.

1. Culture retailers. The creators and elaborators I have described produced a wide variety of materials that could be assigned monetary value and offered to a market. Given such a supply, we can then ask: (1) How many retailers of distinctively peace movement culture were there in the eighties? (2) What was the scale of their operations? and (3) What was the range of their offerings? While not "small time" when compared to other social movements, I am struck that when compared to cultural offerings in many nonmovement areas (e.g., for even something as specialized as the Macintosh computer), the peace movement provided quite "slim pickins" answers to all three of these questions at both the movementwide and cluster levels.

Social movements are enterprises centered on ideals and ideas, and *publications* treating such ideals and ideas as the key items to retail in social movements. Many of them were retailed in the peace movement but on a puzzlingly small scale and in a very scattered fashion.[27] In many areas of human interest there is a central periodical that carries pretty much all the latest and most important news, as with, for example, *The Chronicle of Higher Education*. At the more developed level there may be a daily or weekly newspaper and a weekly or monthly "slick" magazine. In the decade under scrutiny here, there was no newspaper issued daily, or *even* weekly. There were perhaps two dozen newspapers issued monthly around the country, but these had very limited circulations. Even a monthly slick news magazine — *The Nuclear Times* — existed precariously for seven years in its initial incarnation. Begun with "start-up" funding by foundations, by the time this funding stopped, it had not yet achieved sufficient subscribers to survive.[28] There was also no movementwide peace publishing house. And, the array of paraphernalia one associates with a movement — buttons, posters, books, pamphlets, stationery, T-shirts, bumper stickers, videos, leaflets — had not resulted in a supply house of any appreciable size.

In all these areas of periodicals, books and paraphernalia, then, one found economic enterprises that were very small and, for the most part, economically quite marginal. Moreover, most enterprises catered primarily to only one or another of the six clusters. For example, New Society Publishers, the most distinctive peace publisher, catered heavily to the protester and prophet clusters. (In the late-eighties, however, a few mainstream publishers did expand their peace offerings, albeit temporarily.) The leading paraphernalia producer was Donnelly/Colt, an enterprise which consisted primarily of two people — a couple whose respective last names were Donnelly and Colt. Cultural "items" were more generally offered not by profit-making organizations but by one or another of the leading organizations of a cluster who did this as sideline operations designed to support and augment their more major activities. Notable in this regard were the Fellowship of Reconciliation, the Women's International League for Peace and Freedom, and the War Resisters League (all of whom who were more radical than liberal in culture and politics).

2. Artistic performers. Movement-based or movement-oriented dance, drama, comedy, music, and kindred performers in troupe or solo form differ in the degree to which they can make a living from a movement or must depend on broader audiences. Speaking comparatively, it appears there have been and are very few movement-sustained artistic performers. Movements, that is, tend to be so small that any performer must reach out beyond one or a few of them in order to make a living. Such generally movement-based but broader-reaching performers have, of late, included Pete Seeger, Joan Baez, Holly Near, Jackson Browne, Bruce Cockburn, and Tom Paxton.

In the specifically peace realm, it was difficult during the eighties to identify any performers who were able to make much of a living from a primarily peace movement audience or with a primarily peace movement message. There were, nonetheless, a few professional performers who *included or endorsed* peace themes, Joan Baez being the preeminent example along with, to a degree, Holly Near. Kris Kristopherson also moved in this direction later in the decade even in the face of concert audience boos, walkouts, and patrons' requests for their money back (especially frequent at county fair concerts). Parttime and amateur troupes, groups, and solo performers were much more common — perhaps abundant — but none was widely known. Among these were comedy acts such as the Atomic Comics, the Plutonium Players, and Dr. Bossin and His Home Remedy for Nuclear War.

3. *Formal educators.* One of the largest groups that could make a living at peace movement work (relative to all paid movement workers) were people who offered instruction in peace topics in formal curriculum of instruction from kindergarten through postdoctorate levels. Though ranging "merely" in the several tens of thousands (making them a mere trace in education as an occupation), they were likely at least half or so of all the people who got a paycheck for peace movement work.[29] Peace educators disseminated the kinds of ideas and ideals I have described. At the K–12 level, their particular focus was on nonviolent conflict resolution skills in situations ranging from global confrontations to school yard confrontations. Some also promoted peace culture as a philosophy of the classroom itself and strove to create an equalitarian and cooperative learning atmosphere that was thought superior to the ordinary hierarchical and competitive structure of formal education (Harris 1990). Peace approaches in formal education grew considerably in the eighties and though they remained a small cultural force, over the longer run, they may prove to be among the more important cultural elements of the peace movement.

Persona

By means of the term *persona* I want to call attention to styles of interaction — to motifs of emotional expression and physical gestures commonly enacted and culturally approved by participants in a social organization. Personae are enormously complex composites of myriad features that are, nonetheless, discernable as identifiable "packages" of ways of speaking and interacting. Major matters of variation we are often pointing to when attending to an actor's persona include the degree to which it is "cool, contained, and analytic" versus "fiery and emotional," or friendly, warm, amiable or loving versus angry, distant, or hostile. Sometimes, we can think of persona as involving a dominant emotional content, forms of which include anger, fear, joy, shame, and cool civility, among many others.

Personae are real as social facts, but it must also be appreciated that they are subjective and subject to contentious perception among varying observers. For example, one prominent movement spokesperson was commonly perceived as an "infectious personality," who buoyed up all around him and delivered humorous, learned, and inspiring speeches. Looking at exactly the same behavior, his detractors regarded him as a loud-mouthed buffoon, who masked his inability actually to lead with glib, artfully delivered rhetoric. Because he was perceived as the former much more commonly than the latter, his persona, as a *cultural fact*, was the former rather than the latter. Therefore, in treating persona as cultural items, we need not adjudicate the "real reality" although such an adjudication might be necessary for other purposes.

The topic of persona is especially relevant to the study of social movements because movements are so integrally about objection and protest or conflict. Authorities and others are being targeted with "demands" that they — the authorities — would rather not hear, much less grant, and such a mismatch of desires is fertile ground for angry and aggressive interpersonal personae. That is, for these reasons, the situations of social movement people are more stressful than the situations of persons in ordinary life and, therefore, are more likely to call out and culturally to sanction personae that are hostile and snarling. Indeed, the upstretched arm with a clenched fist is among the classic all-purpose symbols of social movements, and this gesture is only one element in a larger persona motif of anger that is often associated with movements.

The American peace movement of the eighties, however, strode a different cultural pathway. While there was no single and elaborate persona at the movementwide level, the core similarity of diverse personae one observed involved a remarkable degree of cordial civility. Indeed, over the decade of the eighties, the single prominent spokesperson who tended *not* to exhibit such cordial civility was the subject of rather sharp criticism from other prominent movement people. I speak of Dr. Helen Caldicott — called Helen Holocaust by her critics — who was characterized as "direct and blunt, eschewing the need to be moderate and respectable" (Neal 1990, 177). Other terms applied to her persona included "hysterical" and "shrieking."

Cordial civility was a movementwide interaction trait, but it tended to be embedded in a very large number of diverse personae. Some of these were associated with a particular culture, and some cut across them. At the movementwide level, that is, participants were definitely not "persona clones" (a charge sometimes made with some justification about social movement members).[30] The better to understand this diversity, let me describe a few personae that were of particular salience in the eighties or that I have found most intriguing.

Restrained alarmist. Following from their class culture and primary activities, the persona of liberal educators tended, during the eighties rise of public fear over nuclear war, to stress a dispassionate disclosure of the "facts" of nuclear war. Norms of professional restraint conduced a bland (and cordial) emotional display. Given the horrifying substance educators were often called on to present, the *contrast* between these horrors and the speaker's personal calm itself became a matter of notice. The archetypical case of this was made available to wide public viewing in the videograph "The Last Epidemic," which contained the unremittingly deadpan and monotonously delivered speech of Dr. Jack Geiger, describing the effects of a nuclear blast on the city of San Francisco (Thierman 1980). Geiger's clinical dispassion served to make the horrific content, indeed, all the more riveting in the eyes of many viewers. Moreover, such a persona was explicitly planned and carried out by the Physicians for Social Responsibility as a way in which to maintain "professional credibility" (Neal 1990, 174).

Cool intellectual. Liberal and radical intellectuals alike tended to what is commonly termed a professorial persona—a measured, restrained, dignified, and cool style of interaction that is also commonly perceived to be dull. Even so luminous an intellectual as Noam Chomsky was remarkably lusterless as he described the amazing adventures of American capitalists bent on global domination. A few intellectuals, however, tended to more flamboyant, upbeat, and "can do" persona—as was the case with Carl Sagan's spirited and quasi-prophet public presentations.

Gee-whiz enthusiast. Among transcenders, one prominent persona featured upbeat cheerfulness, friendliness, optimism, graciousness, and good will. Fitting together with the ideology of commonality (described in chap. 2), transcenders bore good news rather than bad and extolled new possibilities more than they condemned social evils. Rank and file transcenders commonly exuded an emotional motif of warmth and embracement, greeting everyone with apparently sincere cordiality, perhaps seeking to incorporate and enfold humankind at the level of encounters. In the words of one member of Beyond War, "You can't build a world beyond war angrily."

Transcenders did not, however, have a corner on varieties of gee-whiz enthusiasm. In particular, protest events featuring highly organized and even scripted acts of civil disobedience often possessed an aura of cheerfulness and a festiveness that was almost carnival in atmosphere and crowd ambiance. Some younger and teenage protesters appeared even to approach civil disobedience as fun "pranks." For example, one group of five teenagers with whom I became acquainted in preparation for, during, and after a mass arrest in front of the White House in 1986 had found it great fun earlier that day to scout Washington, D. C. novelty stores for the cheap hand cuffs they then used to lock themselves into a human chain and to the iron picket fence fronting the White House.[31]

Spirited grandmother. Some personae involved conscious playing against stereotype, as for example, the stereotype of the "kind, gentle, little old grandmother who never does or says anything offensive." An incongruous persona was, thus, created when older women proclaiming "grandmother" as their central identity engaged in acts of civil disobedience. On some occasions, members of Grandmothers for Peace would intentionally get themselves arrested on the eve of or close to major holidays so as to generate press reports that there would be no going "over the fields to grandma's house" for the holiday since the judge had sent the grandmothers to jail. This was, of course, a press "ploy" and one the press found hard to resist, especially when the founding grandmother, Barbara Wiedner, was involved. Wiedner, whose dimpled countenance and Grandmothers for Peace sweatshirt featured the heart symbol for love, was a surefire subject for "oh, that's so cute" newspaper photographs.

Assured elite. Participants in the liberal politician culture cluster tended to emulate the persona of mainstream politicians, the people they wanted to influence. They inclined, therefore, to variations on the style of the cool, civil, rational persuader who carefully considers objections to his or her positions—a style well established inside the belt of freeways encircling Washington, D. C.

Current and ex-government officials who participated in the peace surge of the eighties were of course, embedded in American professional-political culture, and they exhibited the appropriate male persona of dress suits, careful grooming, extreme politeness, and cordiality in the face of conflict and strife. Prominent (though temporary) members of the eighties American peace movement included Robert McNamara, William Colby, and even George Kennan, none of whom ever lost his "cool" and all of whom, except in the approved ways during occasions of platform oratory, kept their voices well modulated.

Some of these ex-officials were simply dissident members of the American ruling elite. Their cultural worlds were those of the lower reaches of the upper class and the higher reaches of the upper–middle class, with all this means for life-style preferences and involvements. These are the worlds of expensive three-piece suits, cuff-links, and well-shined shoes. Their emotional persona was one of relaxed, calm, and open reasonableness. They were imputed to be expertly knowledgeable, unusually intelligent, highly capable, and uniquely experienced—and they enacted such qualities in their demeanors.

The lower-rung varieties of beltway personae blended with the well-groomed and sleek persona expressions of real privilege, affluence, and wealth. Although their numbers were quite small, the peace movement of the eighties did have an important strata of such persons, mostly among the transcenders, and including Don Carlson, San Francisco Bay area developer, businessman, and leader of Business Executives for National Security (BENS); Richard Rathbun, the president of the Beyond War Foundation and, of course, Robert E. "Ted" Turner of Turner Broadcasting and his Better World Society. Well suited and groomed, they exuded the persona of the executives they were.

The female variation on the assured elite persona carried many of the above features but added rather more optimism, warmth, and cordiality. Leading exemplars of it included Linda Kroc Smith (moving spirit of Mothers Embracing Nuclear Disarmament and an heir to the McDonald Hamburger fortune), Barbara Marx Hubbard (an heir to the Marx Toys fortune), Vivian Verdon-Roe (film producer), Rama Vernon ("founder/director," Center for Soviet-American Dialogue), Sharon Tennison (Center for U.S.-USSR Initiatives), and Betty Bumpers (Peace Links). These were well-groomed and affluent women of a physical appearance and manner commonly associated with media celebrities, and, indeed, they photographed well and had a certain "star quality."

Solemn believer. Seen most conspicuously among the prophets but also among the liberal middle class, people who engaged in acts of civil disobedience exhibited a persona of solemn and serious religiosity. While a kind of festiveness prevailed at larger and "mainstream" scenes of protest, at yet other protests and in some sectors of mainstream protests, one had the sense of being at a religious ceremony rather than at a protest gathering.

For some of the liberal middle class, peace work — especially involving protest acts — was a serious and religious business in which group prayer was common. This account by one Grandfather for Peace conveys the ambiance of religious solemnity on an occasion of crossing the cattle guard and being arrested at the Nevada test site:

> Thirty-one grandmothers, grandfathers, and grandchildren walked their beliefs across the cattle ground and were arrested. . . . I felt I was watching something divine and I'll never forget that tearful sight of watching my friends being handcuffed and hauled away for citations.

> After the violators were taken away, the rest of us formed a circle and held hands quietly for a few minutes. I noticed there were flowers laid down on the road where the violators had crossed the cattleguard. I picked

up the flowers and with the help of one of the grandmothers . . . we taped a sign [and the flowers] up . . . to the barbed wire fence next to the "NO TRESPASSING" sign (Bost 1987, 6).

Among people in the prophet cluster, the core emotion of the kind of persona described in this quotation was generalized into a life-style. Prophets presented themselves as profoundly sorrowful, sad, solemn, and gentle. They bore news of profound tragedy which required cosmic humility. They defined the human situation as one of momentous existential calamity about which they had to speak peacefully and in sympathy with our common plight. Their emotional message was grief, sorrow, and suffering with the hope of redemption.

This modern prophet persona was clearly quite different from that of the prophets of classic biblical fame, who marched out of the desert angrily to denounce the ruler, the people, or both for their derelictions. Staff held high and shaken for emphasis, the biblical prophet proclaimed the condemning message of an angry and wrathful god. This is all in very strong contrast to eighties prophets, who were gently imparting the tragic message of a sorrowful god. One of the meanings of this persona was that these are not exactly "fun" folks. Their detractors, indeed, were prone to characterize them in such uncomplimentary terms as holier-than-thou, sanctimonious, and "creepy."

≪-

These capsules serve to communicate something of the range and variety of personae in the eighties peace movement and to give some substance to my claim that a theme of cordial civility ran through them. While there was no peace movement persona per se, there was a definitely civil and polite cast to the varieties of interpersonal styles that were expressed. But this list certainly does not exhaust the range of personae one observed in the broad and far-flung precincts of the eighties peace movement. Others, important ones, in particular, that I have not tried to "capsulize " included variations on the neocounterculture or "hippie" motif — distinctive physical features of which included long hair, denim pants, and flowing robes. There was also the persona of the solemn moralist exhibited by high officials of mainstream religious denominations.

Despite the overwhelmingly dominant cordial civility, I must report that this trait was not universally present. There was a very small minority of "hard radicals" who specialized a persona display of righteous anger. They were most prominently associated with the organization, No Business As Usual, one poster from whom was done in the style of a criminal wanted handbill and featured frontal and profile photographs of the U.S. president under the words "WANTED FOR INTERNATIONAL TERRORISM." These folks tended to show up at protest events dominated by the "gee-whiz enthusiasts" described previously, but their numbers were too small for their anger to be noticeable.[32]

With few exceptions, then, the personae of the peace movement were quite cordial and lacked the "edge of menace" more frequently observed as a prominent element of many other movements. Even the more radical leaders struck postures of religious contemplation and serenity. Many other leaders were trained as ministers or other church functionaries and had the platform and interpersonal styles of successful ministers, as seen in William Sloane Coffin. More secular leaders were not unlike corporate press spokespersons reading press releases or were otherwise text-dependent when speaking in public. Moreover, peace movement leaders with the flamboyant or dramatic public persona of people such as Adolf Hitler, Winston Churchill, John L. Lewis, Martin Luther King, Jimmy Swaggart, Molly Yard, Eleanor Smeal, or Desmond Tutu were decidedly rare. As mentioned, the few peace leaders who *did* strike somewhat more colorful or "hard edge" public postures generated criticism from within the movement on that account. For example, Helen Caldicott's talks were criticized for scaring and even "paralyzing" people. While her persona provided a certain unusual "toughness," it was, comparatively viewed, a rather mild toughness.

Relations

What I have just reported about *persona* implies a great deal about the relationships peace movement people carried on among themselves and with various categories of outsiders. To speak of personae, however, is not the same as speaking of relations. The unit of analysis for the former is the individual actor and the comport of her or his body in interaction. The unit of analysis for relations, in contrast, is the connection (or its lack) of a movement member to other movement members and/or to persons outside the movement. For persona, the vantagepoint is, metaphorically, the person in "full frontal" view. For relations, the vantage point is a bird's-eye view of two or more persons in association.

The personae I have described imply that these relations will be cordially civil as a class and varied in any of the several ways I have listed. But because it takes at least two actors to make a relation, we cannot assume that this will be the cultural reality.

As indicated, culture is, among other things, about positively valued or preferred modes of action that may or may not be enacted or rewarded with any regularity. Applied to relations, what are peace movement preferences and values with regard to relations, even if we do not observe these preferences regularly enacted? As is obvious, peace movement people were primarily in an advocate or *persuader relation* to the Goliath of the war system, the public at large, the electronic and print media, and so forth. Because of the centrality of this persuader relation — its virtually core status — I want to focus on the implicit culture that peace movement people brought to this relation (or absence of relation). I use the term *implicit culture* because the characterization I will now put forth consists of my inferences about largely unstated preferences and desires. This is my reading of culture preferences from broad tendencies of peace people behavior rather than from culture we can easily find written or otherwise clearly articulated. My "reading" of this implicit peace culture of relations consists of two simple declarations, the second of which is more complicated than the first.

1. Cordial face-to-face encounters with one's adversaries are the most desirable and, to the extent feasible, should be initiated and sustained.

2. When a face-to-face meeting is achieved, the encounter should involve an *equalitarian situation of civil influence* with these kinds of features:

    a. The participants should be personally acquainted with one another in the sense that each knows something of the other's personal biography and has a feeling for the other "as a person." They should address one another by personal names and not just by title.

    b. The physical situation should be equalitarian in the sense that both are on the same physical level and seated and seated in civil if not intimate proximity and configuration.

    c. They should discuss how they disagree on whatever war-peace topic then at issue and how such policies might be changed, as distinct from social chitchat or discussion of nonwar-peace topics.

    d. They should engage in dialogue, meaning that they should take turns talking, with one responding to what the other has said (as distinct from giving set speeches).

    e. The dialogue should be prolonged in the sense of going on for hours and over days and weeks at appropriate intervals.

    f. There should be symmetry in the facts available to both parties as opposed to one saying at critical points that the relevant justifying facts are secret and cannot be revealed. Put differently, authoritarian mystification is set aside.

g. Each should take the other seriously in the sense that each should recognize the objective need to deal seriously with the other because of the other's social standing and the support of a constituency that has to be taken into account.

These features of what I infer to be the implicit culture of persuader relations observed among peace people are, of course, also the features of interaction that powerful parties are forced to practice among themselves at private elite gatherings, political negotiations, and summit meetings between nations. It is also, interestingly, the situation of interaction that Mohandus Gandhi went to great pains to create between himself and his adversaries in his long years of campaigning on a variety of matters.

I "read" these preferences for such civil and equalitarian relations with adversaries, in part, from the fact that over the eighties some movement people tried quite assiduously to initiate encounters that they hoped would turn into such relations, even to the point of creating explicit programs to open dialogue. The sad larger fact, though, was that it takes two parties to make an encounter or relation and hardly anyone in the war system wanted such a relation with — or *any* relation with! — peace movement people. Near the height of the eighties surge of peace activism, a sense of frustration moved one peace intellectual to speak of the "extraordinary spectacle" of two "'universes of discourse' for what basically is the same topic," which "are not engaging with each other. Like the dog in the famous Sherlock Homes story that did not bark in the night, something of extraordinary interest is *not* occurring. . . . There is no 'Great Debate' occurring between the conflicting points of view" (Smoke 1984, 743). Knowing war system resistance to relations, most peace people did not even try to initiate them on the assumption that such effort would be futile.

Conclusion

I want to conclude with (1) a summary of what it means to say that a movement can display a relatively modest degree of culture, (2) some observations on the implications of sparse culture for other movement matters, and (3) a suggestion regarding how the present analysis relates to theories stressing a contrast between "old" and "new" social movements.

Civil, Uneven, Two-Tiered Culture

Our perception of the extent and character of the peace movement culture is sharpened by comparing its profile with an ideal typical depiction of a maximally developed movement culture. In an ideal typical *rich* or *developed* movement culture:

1. Participants *share* knowledge and veneration of a set of cultural items—values, iconic persons, key artifacts, historic events, places, features of occasions roles, persona, and the like.

2. These shared cultural matters are *distinctive* and not largely imported from the host culture.

3. The values and practices are wide in *scope.* The culture applies not merely to politics and public policy but also to the entire array of human activities and, most especially, to the conduct of economic institutions and to the organization of domestic or family life.

4. Cultural matters in all the areas just mentioned are quite complex and *elaborate,* including diverse and artful *dramatizations* of cultural themes, as in artistic performances and varied *roles* dedicated to cultural elaboration.

5. There is a great *quantity* of culture in the sense that we observe it prominently everywhere. It is expressed via diverse media of *dissemination* (publications, motion pictures, and the like).

6. Matters of cultural import are experienced by participants as the positive *emotional and symbolic expressions* of their highest aspirations, hopes, and longings.

I think it is clear from the analytic description I have given that, at the *movementwide level,* the American peace movement of the eighties had a quite limited degree of culture. However, this movementwide sparsity must also be contrasted to culture at the *cluster level* where it varied widely in substance and was developed to a much greater degree although unevenly. The movement was, in this sense, *culturally two-tiered.* Specifically,

1. Participants shared some basic and abstract values and the practices of a polite persona but little else. However, much more sharing of iconic persons, artifacts, etc. was found at the cluster level, although the clusters varied among themselves in this respect.

2. The small number of shared values and civil persona at the movementwide level were to a significant degree distinctive in the sense that in critical policy circumstances most members of the larger American society did not adhere to them. Fortunately for the movement, however, in less policy relevant contexts—and especially at Christmas time—most Americans also professed to desire "peace" and what it implied about how to act and interact. At the cluster level, some of the culture was distinctive, but much, if not most, was clearly imported; that is, it partook of the cultural patterns found in the larger society. Thus, one found the boosterism of transcenders, the communication earnestness of educators, the schol-

arly disciplines of intellectuals, the political practices of politicians, the civil disobedience of protesters, the radical religiosity of prophets.

3. The scope of institutional matters to which the core values were applied was quite narrow at the movementwide level. This was also true at the cluster-level except among the neocounterculture elements of the protesters and among the prophets, who led distinctive lives of dissent. That is, these two groupings seriously modified their economic and family lives in terms of peace movement values to a degree and in ways not seen in other clusters.

4. Movementwide culture was quite simple and lacking in dramatization and culturally enacting roles. This, again, was in very great contrast to the cluster level where intellectuals, especially, had produced enormously elaborate "erudite and scholarly" forms of culture. The intellectuals seemed to me, indeed, to be far and away the strongest, or "richest," cluster in the sense of sheer elaboration — which of course implies a relatively large quantity of cultural objects.

5. Perhaps befitting a movement in which a significant portion of the participants questioned materialism, except for the intellectuals, the movement was not overrun with "objects" at the movementwide or cluster level, nor were those that did exist especially wide in scope. I think of movements, in contrast, that develop distinctive attire either as accoutrements of daily life or for draping the body during ceremonial occasions.

6. Objects and occasions of symbolic expressiveness were quite evident although not abundant at the second-tier level of clusters. This was especially the case among the prophets and other clusters of explicitly religious peace movement people (who were using symbols, however, that were imported from other traditions rather than movement-generated).

Three aspects of this summary profile require underscoring. First, at the movementwide level, culture was relatively weak, sparse, or impoverished in the senses just elucidated. This is not to say, however, that what we found at this level was insignificant. A commitment to peace and the relative absence of abrasive persona may not have been much culture but was surely of importance for the *contrast* with other movements and social life that it presented us. Second, there was a quite clear contrast between the modesty of movementwide culture and its much greater development at the cluster level; that is, it was "two-tiered." Third, in the second tier, peace movement culture was *uneven* in the sense that sharing, distinctiveness, scope, elaboration, quantity, and symbolic expression were not equally developed across clusters. Overall, the neocounterculture protesters and prophets had proceeded furthest on these dimensions while clusters farther to the "right" had proceeded least. As a summary caption, then, we can think of the peace movement as exhibiting a *civil, uneven, two-tiered culture.*

A next question we might ask is Why was the culture so sparse at the movementwide level? Unlike the answers to a great many other causal questions, the answer to this one is rather easy. This social formation was growing very rapidly and springing from a variety of social groupings, occupations, and other enclaves. Focused on whatever the peace task at hand in one's cluster, there was no time or inclination to promote the culture of one's cluster to other clusters. Sparsity is, in this sense, simply another way of speaking of newness.[33] Such newness also meant that not enough time had yet passed for simple processes of diffusion to have occurred on any scale.

More Is Not Necessarily Better

Most of us tend to think that culture is a "good thing." As such, the more of it we have, presumably, the better off we are. Yet for movements, this does not appear to be the case. Cultures that are shared, distinctive, wide in scope, elaborated, large in quantity, and intensely expressive tend too often — and, perhaps, always — to be stifling and oppressive. To discuss culture in terms of its degrees of development, of richness or poverty, as I have done, is not to say that a culture is preferable simply because it is rich or that it is less than desirable only because it is, in the technical sense, poor.

More specifically, movement cultures that are especially rich tend also to be religious in the conventional sense and, along with this, intolerant of other perspectives. Outsiders apply such terms as *dogmatic, hard-eyed, sectarian,* and *true believer* to them, and these labels are often quite descriptively accurate as well as pejoratively appropriate. Consider a second kind of example, the highly developed culture of the military segment of the American military-industrial complex. It begins at the skins of its participants in the form of attire that is *uniform* in critical respects within organizational categories but quite dramatically *differentiated* from those who are not members. It continues through an enormously complicated panoply of *equipment* and *life-style.* Aside from the intriguing and challenging complexity of military gear, there are prolific forms of colorful insignia, flags, and regalia. To this is added a vast body of *celebratory traditions* (ceremonies, books, historical reenactments, etc.). Whatever else may be said of the military, its designers have proved experts in creating a "corporate culture" that is highly developed and *rich* in the technical sense I use that term here. Compared to it, the peace movement of the eighties was anemic.

I am not here advocating that peace movement people imitate the military by devising an elaborate counterculture with such things as peace uniforms. There seems to be, in fact, a "dilemma of culture:" Truly strong movement or organizational cultures tend to stimulate commitment and participation but to be authoritarian, while weak cultures, even though democratic and participatory, understimulate commitment and participation (Lofland 1985, chap. 9). Put differently, culture is a two-edged sword. On the one side, more culture probably means greater capacity for collective movement action, greater tenacity in the face of target resistance and campaign reversals, and a membership that derives greater satisfaction from movement participation. The obverse, however, is likely higher degrees of membership coercion, narrowing of the number and range of people who will participate, and reduction in the civility of the participants' persona and relations among themselves and with outsiders. The trick seems to be to elaborate culture that sustains participation without stifling democratic participation and sponsoring demeaning treatment of non-members. The likelihood that the peace movement would be stronger if it had "more culture" is, therefore, qualified by the realization that, like butter on toast, one can have too much of a good thing — that one can socially overdose with consequent social illness, so to speak. Further and finally, relations among degrees of movement culture and other ways movements vary are, of course, not necessarily linear. There might also be threshold effects in which culture can develop in certain ways and up to certain points without becoming stifling or oppressive.

A "New" Social Movement?

In recent years a number of, especially European, analysts of social movements have distinguished what they label "new social movements" from "old social movements." The labor movement and left political parties have been offered as leading instances of old social movements and the women's, environmental, and peace movements are cited as key examples of new social movements. The new social movements are said to be in several and radical ways different from the old social movements. The following features are often said to characterize new social movements:

- Antihierarchical and equalitarian in ideal and practice.
- Concern with private lifestyle issues as much or more than public policy and policies
- Proclivity to use nonviolent direct action tactics and not simply ordinary political strategies
- A concern to live a new lifestyle now — to be *prefigurative* — and not simply to work for one to be lived in the future.[34]

The profile of the cultural features I have constructed in the foregoing provides one basis on which to evaluate the characterization of the peace movement as a new social movement. Above all else, I have stressed the *diversity* of culture in the peace movement. That diversity *includes* the cultural (and organizational) features we find in the above profile, but the profile definitely does *not* fit the movement taken as a whole. I estimate, in fact, that the new social movement participants of the peace movement in the eighties were a decided minority of all participants and organizations. If such was the case, I think we must conclude that at least some theories of new social movements are overgeneralized. Some data on the peace movement fits this "model," but it is an inaccurate characterization of the entire movement.

Rather than describing a new type of social movement, these analysts are describing a particular approach or culture which can be found in a variety of movements but that is not distinctive to any specific movement. If this is the case, clarity would be better served by simply naming the approach rather than by trying to identify it with entire movements. Candidate names for this approach appear to include "nonviolent direct actionists," (Epstein 1991), "neocounterculturalists," and "Greens" (Galtung 1986).

There might be a way, however, in which to save at least one key part of new social movement theory. If we reduce our list of defining features of new social movements to the single criterion of an embracement and practice of nonviolence and enlarge that element to mean the practice of politeness and civility in the fashions I have described, then the peace movement is, in this delimited sense, "new." In so doing, however, we will have departed so far from the fuller set of features of new social movements that we might better think of the class of such polite movements under some new label, such as "civil movements" or "polite protester" movements. In view of the fact that the peace movement does not seem to be the only recent instance of this pattern, such a new and generic type merits further exploration.

Notes

1. These dimensions and the analyses to follow draw from and expand on Lofland (1985, chap. 9).
2. Gusfield (1981, 323).
3. Ibid., 329.
4. Ibid., 323.
5. Ibid.
6. The more prominent of these directories are discussed in chap. 7, this volume, regarding "Coalescing Events."

7. Selected from E. Boulding's (1990, 32) compilation of "key words."

8. Further, and in a "collective behavior" vein, citizens can sometimes believe that there is a movement "out there" that yet other people refuse to credit. Such appears to be the case with Satanism as a social movement in the American nineties, a putative movement organized against by the Anti-Satanism movement (Richardson, Best, and Bromley 1991).

9. One version of its origin and meaning held, however, that it was "designed in 1958 by Gerald Holtom in England for the 'Direct Action Committee Against Nuclear War.' The symbol is made from the semaphore signals for the letter 'N' and 'D' for Nuclear Disarmament" (Quoted from the back of a sheet of stick-on peace symbols sold by Donnelly/Colt).

10. The 1991 Christmas "wish book" of Sears and Roebuck fame offered a page of flags, one of which was called "peace" and contained a new and distinctive dove logo. Interestingly, this flag was one of nine in the catetory "special occasions" (distinguishing it from national flags). The other eight were "Its a Boy," "Its a Girl," "Party," "Halloween," "Smile" (the smiling, yellow, "happy face"), "Happy Birthday," "Merry Christmas Sleigh," and "Merry Christmas Reindeer."

11. The implications of these values are pursued further in chap. 4 on the organizational profile of the peace movement.

12. I treat artifacts further in connection with specialized cultural roles.

13. Peter van den Dugen (1986) provides an insightful survey of peace museums, monuments, and peace places more generally in international and historical perspective. In these perspectives, peace places is a surprisingly rich topic, making its neglect all the more mysterious. Perhaps, as van den Dugen (1986, 242) quotes Quincy Wright, "Peace is intrinsically less interesting to human beings than war. . . . The artist, sculptor, or poet can produce a work of art which the untutored can at once label 'war.' It is difficult, on the other hand, to imagine a painting, statue, or poem that the average man would unequivocally label 'peace.'"

14. Other such projects included Berkeley, California's, Peace Wall, a construction of some "100 curving feet of concrete layered with nearly 2,000 ceramic tiles hand-painted by nearly as many people" (Asimov 1988).

15. In this vein, it is of note that Stanley Kubrick's classic film *Dr. Strangelove* started out to be a serious treatment of nuclear war but the absurdity of the topic prompted Kubrick to recast it as a black comedy. Although otherwise a solemn lot, even the prophets developed a nice strain of humor, most notably in the "Dear Gandhi" column of the newspaper/letter *Ground Zero*. The column was a humorous take-off on advice columns in which Gandhi answered the questions of perplexed peace seekers (questions written, that is, by Jim and Shelley Douglass, who wrote the column). Several of these columns are assembled in Douglass and Douglass, 1988. A brief example follows:

> Dear Gandhi,
> I'm coming to you as a court of last resort on a question of civil disobedience. I'm confused as to why the media treats Martin Luther King as a hero and Colonel Oliver North as a criminal. Even granting what I don't grant in the case of Oliver, isn't it true that both men disobeyed the law for the sake of a higher cause?
> Sincerely,
> Patrick Buchanan

> Dear Patrick,
> Yes, but Martin Luther King's cause was higher than the next floor.
> Gandhi

16. Long-distance and long-term marching or walking are surprisingly important themes in many social movements and most especially in the peace movement where it has become

something of an art with a rich history that is only now being written. Accounts of peace marches include Leonard and McLean 1977; Folsom, Fledderjohann, and Lawrence 1988; Shay 1987.

17. Written by Julie Gold, the song was a professional success for singer Bette Midler and featured on her album "Some People's Lives." Except for "From a Distance," the songs mentioned can be found in Blood-Patterson, *Rise Up Singing: The Group-Singing Song Book* (1988), the all-purpose, all-left/progressive handbook of social movement songs.

18. Core associations included (and include) the International Peace Research Association, the Peace Science Society (International), the Consortium on Peace Research, Education, and Development, and the Peace Studies Association. However, many peace intellectuals were not members of these associations. If affiliated, they could be found in such organizations as the International Studies Association, the American Political Science Association, and the American Sociological Association. At the height of the surge, portions (or even close to all) of the energies of members of the Union of Concerned Scientists, the Federation of American Scientists, and kindred associations were devoted to peace intellectual concerns.

19. Blumer (1969a, 110) distinguishes between the "erudite and scholarly" and "popular" character of social movement ideologies. The former "is likely to consist of elaborate treatises of an abstract and highly logical character. It grows up usually in response to the criticisms of outside intellectuals, and seeks to gain for its tenets a respectable and defensible position in the world of higher learning and higher intellectual values."

20. This analysis of questions and roles is condensed from Lofland 1992a.

21. Compilations of these lines of thinking include Hollins, Powers, and Sommer 1989; Sommer 1985; Smoke and Harmon 1987; Barash 1991.

22. Reports on aspects of their activities include Strickland 1968; Primak and Von Hippel 1974.

23. Works exploring factors at these levels include Etheredge 1978.

24. Mr. Barash also provided his conception of the movement's iconic intellectuals by including pictures and biographical paragraphs on nine of them, who are, in the order of their appearance: Johan Galtung, William Sloane Coffin, Helen M. Caldicott, Roger Fisher, Randall Forsberg, Richard A. Falk, Kenneth E. Boulding, Aryeh Neier, Lester R. Brown.

25. For collections of these, see the references in n. 21, this chapter.

26. Green 1986. See also, Howlett 1991.

27. For an annotated listing of 173 of them, see Lofland, Johnson, and Kato 1989. See also, Atkins 1986.

28. Shah 1992 is a compilation of 1980s articles from the *Nuclear Times.* Farren 1991 performs the same task, covering two decades, for *Peacework,* one of the longest-running and largest regional peace newsletters, published by the New England Regional Office of the American Friends Service Committee. These anthologies are cultural events in themselves, memorializing and celebrating, as they do, peace activism of the eighties. I know of nothing comparable to them on earlier periods, and they might, therefore, signal a new trend in transmitting movement history. Such works might begin, that is, to confound a saying that arguably described the eighties: "A movement without a past is a movement without a future."

29. Implications of the fact that the overwhelming majority of movement people were unpaid, spare time volunteers are explored in chap. 4.

30. For example, in their respective soaring periods, the Black Panthers appeared to have sponsored a persona of anger and the "Moonies" promoted one of gung-ho bliss (Lofland 1985, chap. 9).

31. It is easy, however, to misread indications of a "carnival" atmosphere as frivolity.

Another and probably more valid way to view protest festiveness is as joy over the glimmer of liberation experienced in *acting* against what one regards as an oppressor. So regarded, the festiveness was deeply serious and profound rather than frivolous and in the vein of the mass jubilation expressed during national revolutions by people who are overthrowing an oppressive government.

32. On rare and unusual occasions, though, the percentage of hard radicals did become significant at peace rallies and produced on-the-scene conflict between them and mainstream peace people. Thus, the rally called on September 5, 1987, to protest a train running over and cutting off the legs of Brian Willson at Concord, California, drew hundreds of San Francisco Bay Area hard-left radicals who systematically dismantled the railroad track, ignoring pleas from rally organizers not to do so (Sturgeon 1987). Even a relatively unsympathetic study of eighties peace protest conducted by the RAND Corporation for the Sandia National Laboratories declared that there were "virtually no spontaneous anti-nuclear protest actions of any kind. All . . . have been meticulously planned and coordinated. . . . As a result, the massive confusion, uncontrollable outbursts, and lack of cohesion characteristic of many of the Vietnam era protests have been avoided, and even mild forms of confrontations with the police have been kept to a minimum" (Daubert and Moran 1985, 7).

33. I thank David Meyer for bringing this point to my attention.

34. Depictions of "new" social movements are reviewed by Klandermans (1991), who, using a somewhat different profile of features applied primarily to European peace movements and campaigns, reaches a conclusion similar to the one I offer here.

4

Organizational Profile
Scattered, Voluntary Organizations

Social movements are sprawling and complex ensembles of organizations. The forms of organizations in these ensembles are highly diverse, and the proportions with which different forms of them appear vary from movement to movement. Primary tasks in the analysis of these ensembles, therefore, include (1) elucidation of organizational forms per se, (2) assessment of the proportions of these forms in a given movement, and (3) comparison of such *organizational profiles* across movements.

There are few studies of the organizational profiles of social movements although a great many case studies treat them indirectly and in a glancing fashion. The strongest conceptual purchase we yet have on them is provided by McCarthy and Zald's idea of the "social movement industry," which is the "organizational analogue" of a social movement, meaning "opinions and beliefs . . . representing preferences for changing some elements of the social structure. . . ." (McCarthy and Zald 1987, 20, 21). Social movement industries are constituted of social movement organizations "representing" such a "preference." As developed by these authors, though, social movement industries are about cooperative versus competitive relations among organizations in a particular industry rather than about organizations per se (Zald and McCarthy 1987).

Also pertinent to thinking about the organizational profiles of movements is Gerlach and Hine's (1970, 1983) characterization of social movements as segmentary (divided into fragmented sets of organizations), reticulate (the organizations are, nonetheless, interlaced by personal relations) and polycephalous (having multiple heads or leaders). These concepts imply a particular kind of organizational profile, but Gerlach and

Hine do not develop them in that direction. Instead, they propose that the three are general features of social movements.

Among other discussions related to organizational profiles is Ronald Lawson's review of work on movement structure, which begins with the declaration that "the literature on social movements is noticeably deficient on the subject of . . . structure [which] . . . is ignored or treated only implicitly or in passing" (Lawson 1983, 119). The situation with regard to analyzing structure — which includes organizational profiles — has changed hardly at all since Lawson's 1983 declaration. This is true despite, oddly enough, the rise of "resource mobilization" thinking, which is frequently claimed to be about organization, but which is more about organization that is antecedent to movements rather than about organization that is constitutive of them.[1]

With the larger and longer-term aim of comparative analysis of organizational profiles, I want here to focus on two aspects of the American peace movement's organizational ensemble as it appeared in "full flower" during its eighties surge: its varied and distinctive organizational *forms* per se and its equally varied and distinctive modes of *funding* that were ancillary to organizational forms. Following presentation of these, I strive to set both in comparative movement organization perspective and in war system perspective.

My discussions of forms and funding will make more sense if grounded in what we know or can surmise about the sheer scale of the peace movement in surge. I want, therefore, to discuss numbers of organizations and participants as an introduction to my analysis of organizational forms and their profile. In introducing the topic of funding, I will also estimate — "guesstimate," actually — amounts of money spent in the eighties surge.

Numbers: Organizations and Participants

In order to construct an organizational profile with care, we must be able to say which organizations are "in" a movement and which are "out" of it. This task also implies that we are able to say how many people are in those organizations and in the movement as a whole. But, as I discussed in connection with peace movement culture in chapter 3, the "boundaries" of a movement are not at all clear and are, even, inherently unclear. It is important, moreover, that we clearly perceive this ambiguity. Therefore, let me preface my report of the movement's organizational profile with an analysis of the several ambiguities inherent in asserting particular numbers of organizations and participants.

Organizations

Two independently conducted censuses of eighties peace organizations tallied about 5,700 in mid-decade, rising to some 8,000, and then falling again by the end of the decade.[2] Because of the ad hoc and transitory nature of many peace groups and the limits of the canvasing methods used by both census takers, these figures need be treated with caution. In particular, the peaking of their numbers in the late-eighties likely measures wider and more aggressive canvasing rather than an increase in organizations. Taking account of these counting problems, I offer 7,000 as a working estimate of their number near the end of the eighties, down from perhaps 10,000 at middecade. All these numbers are, I must stress, only *order-of-magnitude* estimates, at best. And even such estimation is especially difficult because the target on which we are trying to fix was itself changing rapidly, shooting up in the early-eighties and plunging in the late-eighties.

The Institute for Defense and Disarmament Studies (IDDS) divided the organizations it counted in 1985 into *national* versus *local* groups, listing 384 groups as national in scope, defining *national* as "groups whose audience or activities are national in scope, or whose mailing list or membership is distributed throughout the nation" (Bernstein et al. 1986, 38). This is a very generous definition of national. It means a national headquarters that coordinates a vigorous set of locals and branches in only a handful of cases. Using a loose version of this latter criteria, IDDS reduced its list of national organizations to 48 groups (Bernstein et al. 1986, 39). Peace associations, therefore, were overwhelmingly local and freestanding in character.

In offering these numbers I am accepting the definitions of the IDDS and the Topsfield Foundation regarding what is a peace organization. For purposes of providing an order of magnitude number, this is not a problem. If we wanted to be quite exact, however, quibbling would be necessary. Thus, IDDS lists the League of Women Voters and the Council on Foreign Affairs as peace groups—discussable decisions, to say the least! Further, each of these and many other organizations founded before the eighties shifted their programs and addressed themselves to war-peace issues in distinctive ways that were responsive to the larger upsurge of peace concerns of the eighties. We might actually want to consider these organizational participants in the surge rather than peace movement organizations.

Participants

It is more difficult to count participants than organizations. Because of the enormous variability in individual activity, we are forced to begin with the question, What are the criteria of (1) participation in the surge as distinct from (2) membership in a peace surge organization?

An initial fact of key importance is that the vast majority of peace organizations in the eighties were voluntary in character; that is, most members/participants were not paid. This is in contrast to the American war system (the military-industrial complex), the largest portion of whose participants appeared on payrolls as monetarily compensated employees. We can develop a good estimate of the membership of that system simply by adding up the number of names on the payrolls of all the organizations preparing and organizing for war. (There were about eleven million of them in the eighties, by the way.)

Matters are far from that simple for the peace movement. We could, of course, simply add up the names on the paid membership rosters of all the organizations that made up the surge. This presents some complications, though.

1. As noted, the category "organizations making up the movement" is itself, in actuality, a variable rather than a category. There were some very clearly "peace" organizations in the sense that the word figured centrally in these organizations' expressed beliefs and virtually all their activities were focused on conventionally identified "peace issues." But, once beyond these, matters are more complicated because a second kind of organization only often or sometimes took up peace issues. Common Cause, the Union of Concerned Scientists, Greenpeace, and the National Resources Defense Council, among others, are examples of such groups. Each addressed one or more peace issues for a period of time, but the dominant programs of each, in the eighties and over the longer run, did not consist dominantly of war-peace topics. Are these organizations members of the peace movement? Or, are they simply participants in the peace surge of the eighties? To what degree do we count which of their members? The IDDS directory of American peace groups even included, as just mentioned, the League of Women Voters and, further, a category labeled "national organizations whose main constituency is teachers" (Bernstein et al. 1986, 38).

2. Many people on organizational rosters were "members" only in the sense that they had paid a membership fee of, perhaps, fifteen dollars or so. The notions of "member" and "participant" seem too strong for such "checkbook members."

3. Unknown and varying portions of such rosters continued to carry the names of people whose memberships, even in this minimal sense, had lapsed. Put differently, membership rosters were often inflated with lapsed "members."

4. An unknown but not insignificant portion of participants belonged

to more than one organization. Simply to add up rosters without correcting for duplication inflates one's estimate.

5. Many people who regularly engaged in peace activities were not paying members of any peace surge organization. A roster count would not include them.

6. Many thousands of people at one time or another participated in a *peace event* (such as a rally, a movie, a lecture, a vigil, or such) without necessarily and thereby being members of a peace organization, but they were in *some* sense participants in the surge. The ephemeral and scattered nature of their participation defies counting.

7. Among dues-paying organizational members, levels of activity varied over time. People came and went in their participation as a function of particular campaigns that might or might not fire their interest. When inactive, they considered themselves peace-concerned citizens who were only inactive at that time.

Therefore, and unlike the employee type of membership found in the war system, we require an image of a vague and indefinite membership and participation that ebbed and flowed. In the useful contrast expounded by Gusfield (1981) that I discussed in chapter 3, we require a conception that is "fluid" rather than "linear."

With these inherent ambiguities in mind, I venture a series of estimates that recognizes several levels of participation and membership.

The first most inclusive and loosest level counts anyone a participant who ever performed even a single, modest act that signaled support for peace, including attending a rally, writing a check in support of a peace activity, or even thinking or expressing a promovement opinion. Using this last indicator—thinking a promovement opinion (the least demanding possible measure)—one might claim that at the height of the Freeze campaign, when a great majority of Americans supported a freeze (chap. 7, section on "Public Opining Events"), the bulk of the adult population of some 175 million people were peace movement supporters, if not exactly members. Such a vastness and rapid increase—even if modest and transitory—goes to the heart, indeed, of a movement in a state of surge.

The second level, tightened somewhat to include only casting a vote in support of a peace electoral initiative, would probably still put surge participation in the range of twenty or so million. Several survey research studies have found on the order of 10 percent or more of their respondents in this range (Schatz and Fiske, 1992, 19). Projected to the adult population of the middle-eighties, this is slightly less than twenty million people.

At the third level, if we look for more than sentiment and an occasional vote, but not much more—such as writing a check supporting a peace activity or attending a peace rally—then the surging peace movement of the eighties could likely be said to have several million participants but, likely, not more than ten million. The number of participants at this level probably rose sharply in the early-eighties, peaking about 1983 or 1984 and declining erratically toward the end of the decade. It likely dropped sharply after the signing of the intermediate-range nuclear forces (INF) treaty in 1987 to, perhaps, no more than two million people.

If we tighten the definition in the fourth level to mean only those who held paid membership year after year in at least one unambiguously peace organization, in the mideighties there may have been between one and two million people, declining toward the end of the decade.

At the fifth level, an even more mobilized layer of members participated in surge activities with some regularity—perhaps three or four occasions or events a year. In the mideighties, this might have meant about a million people, declining to half a million in the late-eighties.

An estimated total membership of five hundred thousand in the late-eighties divided by the estimated seven thousand organizations yields an average organizational membership of some seventy people. Like many other averages, however, this is misleading because a few national organizations had relatively large memberships, and a large number of local organizations had very small memberships (on the order of twenty or so people, or much fewer).

I want to conclude this discussion of difficulties about how many people and organizations there may be in a movement (especially one in a stage of surge) by calling attention to a conception of "membership" that I believe fundamentally distorts the fluid, diffuse, and permeable character of movements in general and surges in particular. I refer to the conception that surging citizen actions have the same control over their members as do, say, business and government organizations, organizations that can select, train, discipline, transfer, fire, and the like. Only the tiniest portion of the participants in the eighties peace movement were subject to anything like procedures of these sorts. Instead, the vast bulk of participants were volunteers who came and went pretty much as they pleased and worked on whatever they elected at a level of competence of their own selection. The marvel, indeed, is that so many citizens did so much over the eighties on such terms of self-discipline and lack of compensation, paying their own expenses and those of the peace activity at hand.

It is, therefore, a misperception for analysts such as Daubert and Moran (1985, 11), for example, to characterize what they call the "anti-nuclear weapons movement" as having "an absence of selectivity in admissions," and a "policy of not excluding any group from membership and participation because of ideological beliefs or commitments" (Daubert and Moran 1985, 11, 34). The implication of their statements is that "the movement" had a *capacity* to establish "admissions" and to make "a policy" but elected not to. My point, in contrast, is that movements — especially movements in surge — have only the most limited kind of such capacities or *no* such capacities. Movement and surges are, more accurately, free-for-alls, albeit free-for-alls carried on by more-or-less organized groups. I do acknowledge that there were admissions criteria and policies at the level of *coalitions,* but such entities were most often quite short-lived and focused on staging a single event (normally a single march and associated rally), after which they disbanded. Or, if they were enduring, they had extremely limited capacity for collective action and engaged in only a minimum of the weakest undertakings. Therefore, decidedly protean, permeable, and diffuse conceptions of movements and their surges are more accurate.

Organizational Forms and Their Profile

David Knoke and David Prensky's (1984) incisive comparative analysis of what they label *firms, bureaus,* and *associations* provides a fruitful frame of reference for examining forms of organization found in the peace movement of the eighties. By *firms,* Knoke and Prensky mean organizations "distinguished primarily by the production of goods and services for sale in a marketplace in order to make profits." *Bureaus,* in contrast, "use tax revenues to deliver goods to citizens." The two are alike in that "most participants are financially compensated. . . . [Indeed,] ownership or employment are synonymous with membership." *Associations* are "formally organized named groups, most of whose participants do not derive their livelihoods from the organizations' activities" (Knoke and Prensky 1984, 3).

I venture the order-of-magnitude estimate that perhaps 1 percent of the organizations making up the peace movement of the eighties were firms, another 10 percent or so were bureaus, and something like 90 percent were associations. This is graphed in figure 4.1 as an "organizational profile."

Firms

While scarce, the peace movement did contain organizations offering a product or service to a market from which the revenues supported owners and/or workers. Oddly, almost all of them were instances of radical educators who were selling educational materials. The largest and most stable

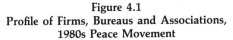

Figure 4.1
Profile of Firms, Bureaus and Associations,
1980s Peace Movement

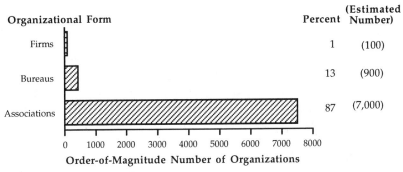

seems to have been New Society Publishers, a worker collective that specialized in peace movement and related books. It employed about two dozen people, which was large by movement standards but, of course, miniscule in the context of mainstream publishers.[3] The most publicly visible effort to operate as a firm was the magazine *Nuclear Times*, which aimed to be something of the *Newsweek* of peace affairs. For a time in the mideighties it was rather widely available on newsstands and circulated in the liberal clusters of the movement through dues tie-in arrangements. It was, however, also heavily subsidized by foundations, and it failed to reach solvency by the time its subsidizers decided to spend their money elsewhere. Without announcement or notice to subscribers, it abruptly ceased publication in 1989.[4]

Some other firms were simply one, two, or three people. These included Donnelly/Colt (Kate Donnelly and Clay Colt), who sold peace paraphernalia, and Felice Cohen-Joppa and Jack Cohen-Joppa, who eked a living publishing the *Nuclear Resister* (case 16 in figure 4.3). Such couple-centered businesses were truly "mom and pop" affairs (and especially so because both couples featured their children in their advertisements).

Bureaus

Knoke and Prensky use the term *bureau* to refer to entities of government in which employees are salaried staff. Taxes transformed into "appropriations" rather than market sales are the sources of funding. I adopt this meaning here, but I need to broaden it to include nongovernmental bureaucratic organizations, particularly religious denominations and educational institutions. From the point of view of organizational form and functioning, the distinction between taxes and other sources is less central. The key, instead, is that bureaus live on a yearly cycle of appropriations, be these taxes or not. They are also not "membership organizations" in the sense that anyone can join by writing a check or simply showing up at a meeting. Instead, "members" are "hired" and paid for their work.

There were on the order of a thousand such bureaus in the eighties movement. This was a significant political and consequential fraction of the movement but still a very small numerical proportion of it. These were the main categories:

1. Within the United States Government, the United States Institute of Peace (begun October 1984) would have to be counted — although control of it was contested by war system appointees. Parts of the staff organizations of close to a hundred members of Congress were, to varying degrees, peace movement bureaus, an infrastructure network formally expressed in the Military Reform Caucus and the Arms Control and Foreign Policy Caucus.

2. At the level of state and local government, several thousand elected or appointed officials devoted time to peace matters over the eighties. The most famous of these was Larry Agran, mayor of the city of Irvine, California, and moving spirit of the Center for Innovative Diplomacy and the magazine *Municipal Foreign Policy.*

3. Many of the large religious denominations had peace and justice commissions or departments that were staffed by full-time peace-oriented people. Likely *the* most important of these for the eighties movement — as well as for numerous social movements extending back several decades — was the Friends-associated American Friends Service Committee. In the late-eighties, the Northern California American Friends Service Committee even had a component called the Nonviolent Movement Building Program.

4. By the late-eighties, almost three hundred institutions of higher education had teaching programs in peace topics.[5]

5. Pertinent research institutions within and without the academy numbered close to a hundred. A large portion of these would have be conceived as "arena" organizations in that they had both war-leaning and peace-leaning intellectuals civilly sharing the largess of government and foundation appropriations.

6. There were a few free-standing and unaffiliated organizations that had paid staff engaged in peace promotional work. The Better World Society, the Carnegie Endowment for Peace, and the Institute for Policy Studies ("the think tank time forgot" [Blumenthal 1986]) were among these.

Viewed in the cluster terms described in chapter 1, a number of the liberal educators, intellectuals, and politicians were employees of bureaus. The fourth and fifth types on the list were, in particular, the homes of intellectuals. The most privileged were professors in research universities. Well-paid (relatively speaking) and staff-supported, we ought not, therefore, be surprised by the rates at which they produced their product—writings that addressed one or more of the ten subjects treated by intellectuals that I enumerated in chapter 3.[6] Indeed, peace intellectuals—along with peace educators—were perhaps the most securely and firmly situated participants in the peace movement. Supported by foundation grants, "membership" subscriptions, angels, and other sources (discussed later), "free-standing" research institutes were key suppliers of peace movement data and ideas. If it is sensible to speak of social strata in the peace movement, the topmost layer would consist of the assortment of politicians, educators, and intellectuals who populated these movement bureaus. Unlike the vast majority of peace workers, they were paid for carrying on movement activities.

As bureaus, these entities were structured much like any other bureaus: as hierarchies that were not seriously questioned, with appointed heads, job evaluation procedures, and the like. They were peace *movement* in the war-peace substance of what they believed rather than in the questions they raised about how to organize themselves.

Associations

As shown graphically in figure 4.1, the vast majority of peace movement organizations were *associations*. Most members were not paid, and programs were heavily or totally dependent on the uncompensated labor. Open membership was a key feature of these associations. In formal principle, anyone who subscribed to the purposes of the association could join. This principle also meant that anyone could also easily decide not to work or to leave the association—and many did.

We need to make a major distinction between associations that had paid staff and those that did not. Of the some seven thousand associations, about 90 percent had no paid staff (Colwell 1989). I depict this radical imbalance graphically in figure 4.2, which also shows estimated percentages of various types of staff- versus volunteer-managed associations.

I use the term *staff* rather than the more precise term *employee* to refer to paid employees because staff was the term used in movement circles. However, many associations had volunteers who functioned at the level of paid employees and who were, therefore, de facto staff. Such people were not called staff, though. Instead, they were referred to by their vol-

Figure 4.2
Profile of Staff- and Volunteer-Managed
Associations, 1980s Peace Movement

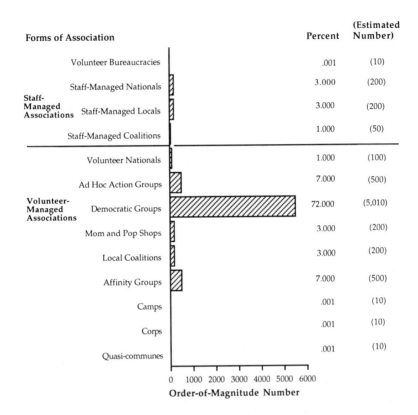

unteer titles, such as coordinator, (as in publicity or speaker coordinator), chair, spokesperson, president, secretary, or the like. For simplicity, I refer to such persons as *volunteer-managers*.

Staff-managed associations. Associations with staff varied quite considerably among themselves in terms of the degree to which their internal organization was mainstream in character and in the scale of their operations.

1. *Volunteer bureaucracies.* A handful of peace associations constructed a seeming contradiction in terms — staffed associations with the trappings of bureaucracy that were run by paid staff — but the largest number of the bureaucrats were volunteers who exhibited much the same commitment

of time and competence as paid employees. Beyond War was reported to be most successful at this feat of organizational wizardry (Faludi 1987; Brigham 1990; Gelber and Cook 1990). Their successful effort was centered in the Silicon Valley of California and was constructed from affluent upper-middle-class housewives and executive-level males who were willing to take leaves from their corporate employment in order to work as full-time volunteers. Such bureaucracies were structured much the same as ordinary American corporations, with several layers of authority, division of labor, and decision-making done largely at the top. Bordering on volunteer bureaucracies were organizations such as the Federation of American Scientists and the Union of Concerned Scientists, in which portions of a large membership could be organized by staff to carry on specialized intellectual analyses.

2. *Staff-managed nationals.* The kind of organization that most often comes to mind when thinking about citizen political groups is the national association that has an important component of volunteer labor and funding by member dues but is substantially managed by a national staff. Over the seventies and eighties, the National Organization for Women (NOW) was something of a prototype of such citizen action groups: numerous and vigorous purely volunteer local chapters, viable state organizations, and nationally coordinated programs managed by a paid, central staff.

The eighties peace movement had several organizations that approached this pattern and that were, indeed, the spearhead of the movement. The more prominent of them included the Nuclear Weapons Freeze Campaign, SANE, Physicians for Social Responsibility, Educators for Social Responsibility, and the Lawyers Alliance for Nuclear Arms Control. In my assessment, however, none (save perhaps Freeze for a brief period) achieved the national, state, and local vigor that an organization like NOW managed, even though they moved in that direction. More commonly, the members of these staff-managed nationals had a more marginal and episodically involved relation to local and state organization.

Staff-managed nationals were centered on lobbying and tended to be the largest, best-financed, and most stable peace associations, although, in comparative terms, they were not very stable. Based "inside the Beltway," to the slight degree there was a movement "elite," they were it. In addition to SANE and the Freeze, associations included the Council for a Livable World, Physicians for Social Responsibility, Women's Action for Nuclear Disarmament, and the Arms Control Association. This circle of associations had their own "all-volunteer coalition" (defined later) called the Monday Lobby Group, a weekly gathering to strategize lobby action for the week. In the mideighties, there were about a hundred full-time lobbyists employed by some two dozen organizations. They were the visible and continuing "peace" or "arms control" presence.[7]

Because they were centered on the legislative arena, the peace politician staff were less socially scattered and diffuse than most other peace activists. Having a geographic focal point in which virtually all of them were physically present, they were in a position to know one another better and had good reasons to seek one another's support in legislative campaigns.

The staff-managed national had many of the trappings of bureaucracy, but there was also dissent from the strict application of this model. Hierarchy existed but tended to be shallow — to have only two or so levels. People "higher" in these organizations were often expected to do their own "scut work," such as typing their own letters and placing and answering their own phone calls. High salaries and large differences in pay were likely to be resisted. At the SANE/Freeze merger convention of 1987, for example, one dissident faction circulated a leaflet titled "Are these peace movement salaries?" questioning a central office budget giving several staff average white collar salaries.

The Freeze campaign of the early-eighties managed to achieve a more or less viable national office from the alliance of its burgeoning local Freeze groups (and significant foundation underwriting). But, not all such efforts to create staff-managed nationals were successful. For example, paired Soviet-American cities efforts also burgeoned in the early-eighties, but they lacked national and staffed coordination. In Gainesville, Florida, Steven Kalishman and others sought to establish Citizen Diplomacy, Inc., as a national and staffed force that would provide such coordination and leadership. But the number of citizen groups who were willing to tax themselves was too small to support a staff-managed national.

3. *Staff-managed locals.* As the eighties began, there were at least several dozen "peace centers" scattered around the country. Many were affiliated with mainline church denominations, and some were allied with national peace organizations such as the American Friends Service Committee, the War Resisters League, and the Fellowship of Reconciliation. Through the eighties, these operated on a pattern of paid staff in association with local volunteers.

The swelling of the Freeze campaign in the early-eighties meant that *new* groups were founded in profusion. Some spun off from peace centers, but many also began as free-standing volunteer associations. By the late-eighties, a a portion of these had disbanded, but several hundred persisted. As time went on, these voluntary locals had increasing difficulty sustaining themselves on totally volunteer labor. The core of six to a dozen volunteer-managers who had forged the local found it difficult to replace themselves with equally dedicated volunteers. If the budget at all allowed, pressure mounted to hire at least one part-time staff person. The impetus to do this sometimes created conflict among core volunteers because the resolutely volunteer-oriented believed that this change marked the end of true and effective citizen organization. In particular, the need to raise staff salary became a high — if not the highest — priority in fund raising and supplanted program funding. In the extreme, dedicated voluntarists alleged, a staffed association became merely a means for raising staff salary, thus diverting the organization from its goals.

The fears of these dedicated volunteers were sometimes well founded. In some cases, these new peace employees did devote the largest part of their attention to raising their salaries. They became the peace movement version of what McCarthy and Zald (1987) have termed the *professional movement organization*. Such a development was not, nonetheless, entirely negative. Sometimes, the choice was between such a staffed organization and no organization at all or, at least, not much of an organization. Even if most of the activities of these staff-managed locals were merely salary raising, that task had to be clothed in program terms to have any credibility. The process of fund raising commonly involved public events and publicity. Therefore, *some* program work was necessarily accomplished, and a continued presence in the public realm was achieved. While not as ideal as the voluntarists would have liked, it achieved more than the realistic alternative of little or no action. (This is, once more, the half-full versus the half-empty glass.)

I have spoken of "national" staff-managed organizations and distinguished them from "local." However, there were, in addition, a number of regional and state-scale organizations that looked, for all practical purposes, like national staffed organizations. These were primarily focused on raising and spending money on political campaigns and deploying volunteers to campaigns. Freeze Voter was the preeminent instance.

4. *Staff-managed coalitions.* Several important movement associations had members who were organizations rather than individuals. A paid staff and office was created from assessments agreed to by participating associations. The Coalition for a New Foreign and Military Policy was the most impressive of these, for it was the joint product of many religious denominations and other associations. Others included the U.S. Comprehensive Test Ban Coalition, the Common Agenda Coalition, the Citizens Budget Campaign, and the Alliance for Our Common Future. Dependent on continued funding by participating organizations, these coalitions were vulnerable to subsidy withdrawals. Such a withdrawal struck the Coalition

for a New Foreign and Military Policy a rapid and fatal blow in September 1988. (A version of it was resurrected in 1989 as the Common Agenda Coalition.)

Geographically scattered affinity groups (described later) were assembled into "actions" by national or regional coalitions. The main national protest coalitions of this sort were staffed units of Mobilization for Survival (the Weapons Facilities Network) and the American Peace Test. Regional organizations included the Livermore Action Group (Epstein 1991) and the Snake River Alliance (Peace 1991, chap. 2). The staff coordinators of protests were engaged in the delicate task of fielding a complex and temporary coalition of affinity groups composed of neocounterculturalists and more conventionally organized groups composed of mainstreamed liberals (Epstein 1991; chap. 1, this volume, "Neocounterculturists and the Middle Class"). While sharing in sympathies for organizational equalitarianism and consensus process, liberals were not as enamored of these practices as radicals. This made for tension between liberals and radicals in large-scale actions. Nonetheless, as Epstein observes, "For several years, these disparate elements showed a remarkable ability to work together in spite of often deep differences" (Epstein 1991, 126).

Protest coalitions were the most fragile of national and regional coalitions. The Weapons Facilities Network of Mobilization for Survival (MfS), for example, was held together by national MfS staff work that published the *Mobilizer* and the *Weapons Facilities Network Bulletin* and organized conferences. Protester-oriented activists who worked against local weapons facilities around the country had a sense of "community" in part because of these publications and occasional conferences. Information on local campaigns was shared at the conferences and new plans of actions discussed and voted on, but as a group, the network had virtually no capacity for collective national action. Anyone could participate and vote in the conferences by simply appearing, and the network did not selectively dispense its meager resources to a set of ratified members (of which there were none), so collective decisions had the status of group sentiments rather than sanctioned and enforceable plans for action. For such reasons the term *network* in this formation's title was an unusually apt label.

Although unique in some respects, the well-publicized organization called 20/20 Vision was a variation on the staff-managed coalition. Invented by Lois Barber of Amherst, Massachusetts, and beneficiary of the promotional work and support of Jeremy Sherman, "a son of the founder of the Midas Muffler chain" (Bennett 1989), 20/20 Vision attempted to use a franchise structure. The effort was to form local congressional district "core groups," who researched peace issues to lobby and, for twenty dollars a year, each month sent subscribers a postcard with instructions on a specific action to take. The suggested action was itself supposed to take no more than twenty minutes, hence, the "20/20." The organization's slogans included "save the world in twenty minutes a month" and "defuse nuclear bombs on your coffee break." In 1990, this association reported somewhat more than a hundred of such franchised groups operating in the United States.

Volunteer-managed Associations

We come now to "hard core," "pure," or "true" citizen action, the realm of all volunteer citizens joining together to engage in public action for peace. Although I treat this realm second because of the logic of exposition on a continuum from "hard" to "soft" incentives and forms of authority, it was very far from second in the movement. Instead, it was the effervescent essence of the surging peace action of the eighties.

Contrary to some views of these matters, I think that all associations require management. One or a few people must take regular responsibility to initiate and organize joint activity. One of the great miracles of the eighties surge of peace action was that the largest proportion of peace organizations were volunteer-managed and (by definition) composed of volunteer workers. As we will see, though, volunteer management is fragile. It flowers best under the special conditions of a sense of urgency, or even emergency, and withers when that definition of the situation abates.[8]

In addition, in this realm, we encounter a greater degree of "form diversity" than seen among the major patterns discussed previously. In particular, we need to distinguish among volunteer-managed associations in terms of their attitudes toward how organizational decisions were to be made. The forms of organization considered previously were more likely to accept bureaucratic hierarchy, democratic majority rule, or both, as principles of organization and decision making. Among volunteer-managed associations, we find a third conception of organization and decision-making, that of equality and consensus.[9]

Volunteer nationals and regionals. The number of majority-run, all-volunteer associations that strove to operate with members on a national or regional scale was relatively small. The much greater costs of communicating and coordinating actions are among the likely reasons for this.

Unsurprisingly, the more stable of these nationals and regionals were composed of people employed in peace occupations, namely educators and intellectuals. The larger occupational milieux of these people provided hundreds, if not thousands, of examples of all-volunteer associations dedicated to myriad educational, academic, or scholarly topics. Little imagination was required to perceive how this form of association could be applied to such topics as "peace studies," "peace research," and "peace education."

It was also the case that a great many institutions of higher education employing educators and intellectuals felt an obligation to *subsidize* this kind of national association by means of released time, office space and equipment, student assistance, secretarial aid, and the like. Staff could be volunteers because the association was, thus, supported by these institutional angels. Prominent instances included the International Peace Research Association, the Consortium for Peace Research, Education, and Development, the Peace Studies Association, and the Peace Science Society (International).[10]

In addition, within the major professional associations of mainstream academic disciplines, suborganizations brought together peace educators and intellectuals and provided them platforms for developing and publicizing their work as in the Sociology of Peace and War section of the American Sociological Association, the International Conflict and Cooperation section of the Society for the Study of Social Problems, and similar specialized groups within political science, psychology, and anthropology.

Volunteer locals. The "core of the core" of peace organizations, so to speak, were citizens associated for peace activity in a local area. They were not only unpaid, they spent their own money in support of peace action. In surveying the gamut of these efforts, I have found it necessary to distinguish among at least eight forms minimally to capture quite significant variations in these local enterprises. I order them here in a general way from the least to the most enduring, stable, and involving.

The most primitive in the sense of brief and uncomplicated of peace organizations was the *ad hoc action-group.* One or a few peace activists who were not necessarily acting on behalf of a local peace organization would assume lead roles in organizing an ad hoc group to participate in an "action." He or she would begin to make the necessary arrangements for transportation to an action site and then set about recruiting.

The dozens of busloads of protesters that arrived at the Nevada Test Site (NTS) in the mid- and late-eighties were prime examples of such ephemeral and action-specific enterprises. American Peace Test (APT) organizers could "call an action" at the NTS and send notices to previous and prospective organizers of buses in communities across the country. From there on, APT was dependent on local people actually chartering buses and recruiting bodies to fill them. Local activists, of course, recruited among other already known groups and activists, but the ensemble thus constituted had little more internal organization than tourists assembled on a tour bus anywhere in the world. Unlike tourists, though, these bus-loads tended to be composed of small groups that were larger than those among tourists. They also tended at least to "know-of" many of the other participants, even if they had not met them before. But like tourists, there was no internal authority structure that united and hierarchically ordered them as a group.

The ideal type of the local peace group and the statistically most prevalent was the open-membership, public meeting, and *democratically organized citizen association*. At least on the surface, the officers were elected by ballot and decisions made by majority votes taken by the membership, an elected board, or some combination of the two.

As mentioned in connection with staff-managed locals, Freeze groups that burgeoned in the early-eighties were partial to this form of organization. Although many later moved to the staff-managed form, others held tenaciously to this early configuration. In so doing, they depended heavily on a few members being prepared to donate a large portion of their time and labor to function as elected, volunteer "staff."

Despite the fact that this was the overwhelmingly most common form of organization (figure 4.2), we have remarkably few descriptions or analyses of how these groups actually worked, including an assessment of just how democratic they may or may not have been. My guess is that be-cause their operations were mundane, the ethnographically inclined were not attracted to them or thought they had found little or nothing when they did try to study them.[11] Even so, we do have a picture of them of sorts — a picture of great differences in levels of involvement (e.g., Marullo 1990) and of frequent vacillation, indecision, and buffeting regarding courses of action (Wernette 1990; Benford and Zurcher 1990; Price 1990). Based on early- and mideighties organizational improvement workshops with many groups of this kind, Ayvazian formulated their "seven deadly sins," "sins" we can also view as simple descriptive characteristics. In her view, many tended to exhibit: "Founders' Disease [domination by the ini-tial members] . . . lack of long-range planning . . . burnout . . . growth with no plan . . . no clear lines of accountability . . . poor or nonexis-tent office systems . . . horrendous meetings" (Ayvazian 1986, captions pp. 3–15).

Democratic groups heavily dependent on a few core volunteers shaded off into and were difficult to distinguish from the pattern of the *"mom and pop shop"* or simply the *"pop shop"* or the *"mom shop."* By means of these labels I point to the pattern in which a local couple, a man, or a woman played a central role in conceiving, creating, and administering a peace group. The group might have had the trappings of a democratic association, but the enterprise had clearly come into existence and persisted primarily (or only) because of the focusing central couple or person.

Some of these groups did not bother with trappings of democratic structure. They might offer "membership," meaning one sent them a check each year and they called you a member, but little or no democratic process was otherwise practiced. In some forms, a husband and wife operated a nonprofit corporation participated in by supporters of these focusing figures. Among these was the Aquarian Research Foundation of Art and Judy Rosenblum, who promoted peace in 1987 by offering, for a one-dollar donation ("cash is fine") and an SASE, "an actual Samantha Smith stamp [from the Soviet Union] and a cassette tape of Armand Hammer."

Sometimes started as simply local mom and pop shops, the vigor, energy, and, sometimes, wealth of the focusing person or persons led to a national or quasi-national presence. Such a trajectory could be traced for Gen. Robert Bowman's Institute for Space and Security Studies, Barbara Weidner's Grandmothers for Peace, and Linda Smith's Women Embracing Nuclear Disarmament (Mehan and Willis 1988).

Other terms one might use to capture this kind of social formation include "focusing figure organization" or "the moving spirit and her or his circle." The key organizational feature of these associations was the inseparability of one or two persons and the organization, both at the point of founding and in later development. Prominent additional examples include Ted Turner and the Better World Society and Betty Bumpers and Peace Links.

Cooperation among local peace groups was commonly in the form of one group organizing an activity that it asked other groups formally to endorse and financially to support with at least a token amount of money. The most common activity involved in such a "signing-on" was as a speaker, rally, or other gathering. These multiple sponsorships were reasonably frequent and sometimes even termed *local coalitions*, giving the public impression of a high degree of cooperation. But, endorsing (cosponsoring) another group's effort was far from true joint planning and action. This level of cooperations appeared, in fact, to have been rather rare among local peace groups. Instead, groups often felt competitive with and resentful of one another, even among groups who were in the same cluster and shared liberal or radical orientations, as Benford and Zurcher (1990) have analyzed among the peace groups in Austin, Texas.[12]

Reported to have been invented (or at least crystallized) at the Seabrook demonstrations of the 1970s (Epstein 1991, chap. 2; Barkan 1979) an *affinity group* was, in ideal form, a named association of a dozen or so people who shared some nonprotest feature, such as belonging to the same church, working at the same place, or sharing a cultural style (such as being "punk"). In this way, movement involvement was built on an extramovement foundation — on an ordinary form of social organization.

As propounded in the numerous manuals and leaflets that told one how to form and "do" an affinity group, consensus — universal agreement — was the preferred form of decision making. This practice was supposed to strengthen the group itself and to have positive effects on the selves of group members because every member's feelings had be taken seriously. It was another source of the "empowerment" that was also said to flow from acts of protest.

Affinity groups were the "acting units" in protest action. The object was to assemble as many of them as possible in actions "called" by one of the staff-managed national or regional associations described previously. Many such "actions" involved thousands of people and hundreds of affinity groups, creating a problem of how to make decisions at the level of the overall action. For the purpose of making such decisions, a limited form of representation was allowed. Each affinity group elected (by consensus) a "spokesperson" — called a spoke — who represented the group at meetings of a "spokes council" that was itself, formally speaking, a volunteer coalition. Decisions at the spokes council level were also, ideally, by consensus.[13]

I have inserted the word *ideal* into this sketch because the reality was often different. In reality, consensus was very hard to achieve, and in order to avoid interminable meetings and organizational paralysis, compromises were made. Dissenters sometimes agreed to "stand aside" even though they disagreed with the majority. Some critics charged that the equalitarianism of consensus allowed stronger and more assertive persons to be de facto and unrecognized manipulators of the group. This was seen as bad because, unlike groups with formal leaders and hierarchies, there was no formal means of calling such hidden leaders to account. Because they did not occupy a formal role, one could not replace them by formal means.[14] In addition, the demand for consensus was alleged by critics to give the most ideologically extreme and/or mentally unstable members a license to dominate a group with their intransigence.

The volunteer locals I have just described made up the vast majority of all volunteer-managed associations — the democratic local likely being the statistically modal form. Three additional forms were infrequent but not unimportant or inconsequential on that account. By their rarity, however, they tell us something about what the eighties peace movement was *not* as well as what it was.

The first of these was the *camp* or, more precisely, what movement people called the "peace camp." These were places of quasi-permanent habitation established near military installations as forms of protest. The women who camped several years at Greenham Common in England provided the model for a number of American efforts, including the Seneca Women's Peace Camp, "a massive women's presence adjacent to the Seneca Army Depot in upstate New York, a facility used by the Department of Defense to store nuclear weapons" (Epstein 1991, 160). Others included the Peace Farm just outside and overlooking the Pantex final-stage nuclear assembly factory near Amarillo, Texas. Some were less permanent, fragile, and harassed by officials, as in the case of the camp by the Mercury gate to the Nevada Test Site.

No reasonably parsimonious effort to summarize a complex array of efforts can be totally precise. A protest at a particular place that is carried on long enough with enough people becomes a kind of de facto peace camp, or at least an ambiguous creature hovering between an activity and a form of organization. Such was the case for the vigil activities conducted at the railroad tracks leading from the Concord, California, Naval Weapons Station. While no one literally lived there in a full sense, people were on the scene around the clock for several years in the late-eighties and early-nineties, making it, perhaps, a quasi-peace camp. A similar social formation was also maintained for several years in Lafayette Park, just across from the White House.

In the social movement context, a *corps* is a geographically mobile tactical unit in which the full round of life activities is temporarily organized in pursuit of movement goals (Lofland 1985, 188). These are infrequent but by no means unheard of in social movements. In the eighties peace movement, corps took the form of long marches or walks in the name of peace. The most famous was the Great Peace March, which started from Los Angeles as PRO-Peace on March 1, 1986, collapsed in the Mohave desert near Barstow, California, was resurrected as the Great Peace March, and completed its journey in Washington, D.C., on November 15 of the same year (Folsom, Fledderjohann, and Lawrence 1988).

Corps *qua* marches were transcender and educator dominated in ethos. But, in 1987 and later, at least one group conceived the corps in more protest and prophet terms and called it the Peace Army. It was to be a mobile body that targeted weapons facilities with protest activities. Organizers were not able, however, finally to field this "army," and there was much criticism of the militaristic tone of its name and proposed operation.

Last, a very small portion of peace movement people organized themselves into *quasi-communes*. These were "quasi" rather than full communes because the pattern involved a set of families and individuals living in separate but relatively proximate households and regularly congregating in a "community" building in which joint activities were planned and conducted (Lofland 1985, chap. 8). (This contrasts with the full commune, which involves a single plan of household living.) The participants also tended to use the word *community* in the formal names of their associations, an infrequent practice in other peace movement clusters.[15] Examples of this usage included the Atlantic Life Community, the Kairos Peace Community, Aletheia Community, the Community for Creative Nonviolence, the Puget Sound Agape Community, and the Community of the Servant.[16] The movement cluster I have termed *prophets* in chap. 1 were most partial to quasi-communes and, as among the more radical and countercultural protesters, equalitarian organization and consensus decision-making were highly valued and practiced.

≪

These forms of organization are only one major part of the story of organizational profiles. The other major part concerns how all these forms were financed.

Funding Amounts and Philosophy

I want to discuss three aspects of funding peace organizations: yearly amounts spent, the language and philosophy of money, and the sources or forms of raising money — of funding.

Amounts

Estimating total movement expenditures for given years is even more difficult than estimating numbers of organizations and participants. Because of the dispersed, small, and even informal nature of many groups, budgets were not easily available, even if they existed. Only the large national organizations had accessible budgets, and their total spending was well less than half of overall movement spending. Moreover, and unlike the American war system, even organizational budgets were only a fraction of total spending. There was, for example, little or no accounting of the travel, lodging, and meal expenses of the hundreds of thousands of people who participated in peace events in a given year. Hardly any such participants were on expense accounts; they simply paid their own ways. Thousands of local peace activists also bought peace books, brochures, posters, flyers, and the like out of their own pockets. The accoutrements of peace events were commonly "out of pocket" (e.g., poster board for signs, photocopied announcements, refreshments for receptions, etc.). In addition, in some years, ad hoc contributions of substantial amounts of money were made to movement events by wealthy donors, and there was no public accounting of those amounts.

One simple means of estimating total spending is to gauge how much, on average, a movement participant likely spent in a year. Recognizing very wide variations in individual spending, I would estimate an average yearly expenditure of about two hundred dollars. If about one-half million people spent this much, this is aggregate spending of about one hundred million dollars.

Moreover, a significant portion of money was in the form of gifts from affluent members, grants from foundations, and appropriations for "bureaus" from religious, government, and educational organizations. The total from these sources was likely as much as two hundred million dollars, since we can document well over one hundred million from larger foundations alone (chap. 7, "Funding Events").

Taken together, total spending was at least in the range of 300 million dollars a year, a figure that accords with the independently arrived at assessment of Michael Shuman (1987, 46 n. 46), who has estimated that 305 million dollars was spent in 1984. (Shuman's estimate, however, concentrates on foundation and other more formal sources of funding and is, in this sense, conservative.) Taking yet other sources into account, a more generous estimate would set spending at about five hundred million (one-half billion) dollars a year, at least in the peak years.

I think it is important to appreciate that we are not, in relative terms, speaking about very much money. The American war system spent — at the very least — about half-a-trillion (five hundred billion) dollars in most years of the eighties. The formal Department of Defense budget alone was on the order of three hundred billion dollars and that left out a great deal of war spending. Such sums utterly dwarfed the peace movement even at its highest point of surge. Conceived in temporal terms and as calculated by Sam Marullo (personal communication, 1992), "The war system spent as much every six hours as the peace movement spent in a year."

Philosophy

The language of money and economic activity I heard in the peace movement was rather different than the language one hears in mainstream commercial society. In the latter, money and economic activity are commonly spoken of in such terms as "price comparison," "lowest bidders," "discounts," "sales," "price competition," "rate of return on investment," "sales incentives," "cost effectiveness," "efficiency," "cost cutting," "effective management," "market shares," "market niches," and "market saturation," among a host of allied terms. Commercial society, that is, expresses a philosophy of relations between monetary resources and economic action. It is a philosophy in which a person seeks to minimize cost per acquisition and to maximize income per action.

While the language and philosophy of commercial society were sometimes encountered in some peace movement clusters, neither was central in ordinary undertakings. Instead, at the level of language, people more commonly spoke of "funding," "fundraising," "contributions," "grants," "contributors," "canvasing," "fundraisers," "donations," "giving," "givers," "memberships," "supporters," "volunteers," "coordinators," "development officers," and the like. At the more inferential level of the philosophy expressed in these terms, many peace people had little concern with money-goods-labor exchanges in which equivalencies of remuneration among the three were to be calculated and negotiated. Such a concern was not entirely absent, but it was decidedly subordinated to moral commitments as the most significant component of the money-goods-labor trinity.[17] Thus, in making appeals to people to "give" money and/or labor, it was exceedingly rare for the requester to employ any of the sales devices of commercial society, such as providing price, service, and performance comparisons with other peace groups in order to show that one's money was better invested with the group in question rather than with a competing group. Notable for their rarity were evaluations such as those conducted by the progressive Christian magazine *The Other Side*, which, over several years in the eighties, assembled annual reports on dozens of peace and justice organizations and calculated proportions of their budgets spent on administration and fund raising as opposed to program work.[18] In fact, contributors (metaphorical "investors") were infrequently even given a report on how their money had been spent, much less any detailed specification of spending patterns and rationales of why the particular patterns were better than alternatives. Commercial society concepts of accountability, efficiency, and effectiveness simply did not come up very often although extravagant claims of success were frequently put forth. When, perchance, someone desired to press a closer and more searching assessment of comparative pricing and effectiveness, the topic was unlikely to be pursued with any depth or seriousness. To raise such issues was to introduce a kind of venal stink into the realm of high-minded self-sacrifice.[19]

From a commercial society point of view, the management of peace movement economic matters would be judged, in the aggregate, as something of a scandal because of lack of accountants' reviews, cost-effectiveness assessments, and return on investment calculations, if it was even possible to apply such ideas in this realm much less to calculate exact figures.[20]

Funding Sources

Peace activities were financed, or funded, in a great variety of ways, and I want now to map these, to relate them to forms of organization, and to develop the key theme that most enterprises had multiple sources of — often jerry-built — funding.

Even though I want to focus on money, an accurate account of the peace movement economy cannot be constructed on this basis alone. An enormous amount of peace activity and organization came from the working equivalent of money — donations of in-kind goods, services, and labor. Such donations could be just as (or more) useful as raw money, and our perception of economic scale and resources is distorted if these are not included. In my mapping, I will, therefore, first treat the several varieties of in-kind donations.

Within any source of funding, we need to distinguish between (1) those that were self-contained or self-terminating and (2) those that were understood as continuing or on-going, other conditions being constant. The first, or terminating, sources, came with the understanding that a specified amount of money, goods, or labor-hours constituted the entire obligation of the giver/provider. In addition, the amount was often clearly earmarked for a specific purpose, such as renting a bus, painting a set of signs, offering fellowships, or conducting a specific campaign. When the given short-term undertaking was completed, the donor had discharged the obligation. The second, or continuing, sources operated on the premise that, barring extraordinary circumstances, the funding would be forthcoming at the next budget juncture. This was the common circumstances of the various bureaus described previously.

This distinction between terminating and continuing funding is a critical one because it traced a central feature of peace movement economy. A very large portion of the sources of funding I am going to review were terminating rather than continuing, and within mixed sources, a high proportion was terminating. This, meant, of course, that the peace surge's economy was extremely fragile.

In-Kind Donations

Four varieties of in-kind donations were especially important.

Participation. Without being able to affix a very accurate dollar value, I would guess that the largest (and also unstable) source of in-kind donations were from the many millions of Americans who elected to pay their own travel, food, and lodging expenses to participate in a peace event. Referring back to my discussion of amounts, this might have come to something like a hundred million dollars in each of the peak years. Participation in local events was not expensive, but many other gatherings required hundreds or thousands of miles of travel. When thousands of people were involved in national events, these were, in the aggregate, substantial sums of donated money.

Affinity groups were among the most interesting "self-financing" entities. Each member provided his or her own costs of transportation, accommodations, and the like. An ordinary protest action was likely to cost about the same as an ordinary weekend away from home or on a vacation, an activity that could be accommodated to the budget of many Americans, especially if they camped out at or near the protest site, a practice that was rather common.

Work. Participation did not require the specialized or sustained performances we call work. Much peace activity did, though. As seen in the organizational profile I have presented, peace associations depended on large amounts of donated labor in such unskilled forms as answering telephones and acting as event helpers and in such skilled forms as designing and producing publications and organizing events. Very often this donated labor was not performed at the levels of competence and effectiveness likely to be demanded in commercial society, but work *did* more or less get done. Even if the quality was "worth" only something like the minimum wage, that value accrued to the movement and likely amounted to many millions of dollars a year.

Especially competent and skilled donated work were the hallmarks of the transcenders, whose volunteers were likely to be quite educated and to respect bureaucratic organization, hierarchy, and detailed planning. This meant that volunteer transcenders were fearsomely effective as organizers, and their organizational efforts were on larger scales and more impressive in important part because of this effectiveness. Here is a sketch of such a volunteer, one for the Center for U.S.-USSR Initiatives in organizing its Soviets Meet Middle America! (SMMA) scheme, a person referred to by that center as providing "the gift of carrying out the dream." "Without Barbara Machado, the idea of 400 Soviets trotting in and out of 300 cities and towns of middle America would have been relegated to the pile of unfulfilled visionary dreams. Her tenacious attention to details, infinite patience with frustrating mix-ups, ability to delegate to staff and volunteers, and her contagious enthusiasm for a nearly impossible task, combine to make her the perfect person to ride herd over Soviets Meet Middle America!" (Tennison 1988, 13).

Likely the most significant source of donated labor in terms of legitimizing the movement was provided by liberal office-holding politicians who, among many other agendas they of necessity pursued, also, in effect, donated their time to the movement by speaking in favor of one or another movement proposal at a variety of peace events. And, we would need to add to them elite ex-officials (e.g., Paul Warnke, Robert McNamara) who spoke free or for their expenses at peace gatherings.

Life-style. One small minority invested themselves in peace activities and organization to a degree that was discontinuously greater than simply "donated work." These were, generically, the activists. A great many of them were unpaid or paid only token amounts of money *and* constructed virtually their entire lives in peace movement terms. For them, peace work was not simply or merely a matter of "donating work" but of life itself.[21]

"Life-style donation" was clearest among the prophets. Their anti-materialist and anticonsumerist beliefs supported simple and subsistence living, and this considerably reduced the scale on which they needed to finance themselves. But, their materialist-minimalism seemed hardly at all to restrict the level of their movement activities. They still traveled and spoke widely and undertook a broad array of organizing activities. Supported by sympathizers, the simplicity of their living combined with their total availability made them, ironically, all the more potent as organizers and itinerant activists. In the same range of commitment were the upper-middle-class wives who, because of supportive and affluent husbands, could devote themselves almost totally.

A portion of those who donated their life-styles did, nonetheless, work, often at part-time and ordinary jobs. Ordinary work that was not demanding left time available for virtually full-time movement work. Such people were "self-financing" as activists and the logic of their life-styles seemed much like that of superdedicated hobbyists and recreationalists who elect to build their "real lives" outside a mundane job. Seen in this perspective, peace activism required resources on a par with (or less than) resources available to many families who are intensively involved in recreationalism (e.g., skiing, angling, boating).

Goods and services. Ordinary business people who were not otherwise noticeably "peace" in orientation were, in the eighties, unusually willing to donate equipment, supplies, and services to peace projects — especially to transcender peace projects. These donations were founded, in part, on the general willingness of businesses to contribute to public-spirited undertakings, both as a matter of conscience and as a not-too-expensive form of advertising. (*Who* contributed the equipment, supplies, or services was commonly acknowledged with frequency and care.) In this fashion, such contributions were not different from those commonly made to needy and worthy causes of other kinds, such as mental health associations and high school athletic teams and clubs.

For many transcender endeavors, such as visiting Soviet delegations in city twinnings, goods and service donations spelled the difference between carrying off the affair with dignity and flair or not. In one small West Coast city in 1987, for example, donations in support of hosting Soviet visitors included commercial lodging and the ingredients and skilled labor to stage a community dinner for some four-hundred people.

The Great Peace March born in the Mohave Desert in late-March 1986, had important angels and other sources of money. But also important, business in that corner of California and Nevada (and all along the route across the country) came forth with donations of specialized vehicles and other relevant equipment and food (Folsom, Fledderjohann, and Lawrence 1988).

Virtually all in-kind donations of goods and services were terminating, but some were continuing. Here and there around the country, ideologically sympathetic landlords, for example, provided either free or discounted rental space for movement offices.

Money

In theory, movements could be built entirely on in-kind donations. If the range of such donations exactly matched the range of activities, then little or no actual cash would be required. But, the practical fact is that such a match is rare, at best. An enormous range of things are not donated — from telephone service to "porta-potties" — and hard money is required to get them.

From where did this come in the eighties peace movement? In my accounting, there were fourteen main sources. They vary in monetary significance, but even the smallest required investment of energy despite being less than lucrative.

I want to review these fourteen with particular attention to the fact that many peace organizations relied on *several* sources — often in an ad hoc and jerry-built way — to get things done. The better to convey this diversity, I have assembled a spectrum of peace organization budgets in figure 4.3 that I will refer to as we proceed. The examples in figure 4.3 are

Figure 4.3
Funding Sources of Selected Peace Organizations
(in percentage)

1. Beyond War, 1985 income of approximately $2 million: Individual Contributions 66 Events 17 Sale of Materials 16 Other 1 100[a]	2. Physicians for Social Responsibility, 1986 income of $2,735,884: Contributions 58 Dues 35 Grants 6 Other 2 101[b]
3. Institute for Defense and Disarmament Studies, 1987, income of $486,770: Grants & Subscriptions 77 Subscriptions 15 Honoraria 4 Literature sales, royalties, other 4 100[c]	4. Clergy and Laity Concerned, 1986, income of $334,504: Grants and Bequests 33 Contributions 32 Member subscriptions 30 Other 5 100[d]
5. Union of Concerned Scientists, 1986, income of $3,359,032: Donations 70 Grants and Bequests 22 Other 8 100[e]	6. Center for Economic Conversion, 1989 income of $121,208: Contributions — individual 53 Contributions — foundations 12 Contributions — organizations 3 Benefits 18 Consulting and Honoraria 10 Publications 2 Interest 2 100[f]
7. SANE, Inc., 1986, total revenue of $3,538,192: Canvass 42 Grants and Bequests 25 Other dues and Contributions 33 Other 1 101[g]	8. SANE/Freeze 1988 Draft Budget totaling just over $4 million: Canvass and related 28 Mail Programs 21 Phonaton 28 Major donors 9 Sales/Subscriptions 1 Grants 8 Other 5 100[h]

[a] Beyond War 1985, 11 . The term "approximately" is used by Beyond War; exact figures not given.
[b] Percentages rounded to nearest whole number from Kraybill 1988a, 5.
[c] Calculated from Kraybill 1988b, 7.
[d] Kraybill 1988a, 5.
[e] Kraybill 1988a, 4.
[f] Center for Economic Conversion 1990, 5.
[g] Kraybill 1988a, 4.
[h] Categories grouped from Cottom and Cortright 1987.

Figure 4.3 — *Continued*

9. Sacramento, CA SANE/Freeze, 1988, budget of $50,409:		10. Santa Cruz County, CA, Nuclear Weapons Freeze,1987, dollar amounts not given:	
Membership	21	Membership dues and small contributions	43
Major donations and pledges	12	Business membership, advertising and subscriptions to the	
Big ticket raffle	25	Monthly Planet	28
Fundraising events	18	Fundraising events	20
Small ticket raffle	16	Sustainers	6
Sale of merchandise and literature	4	Literature and merchandise sales	3
Other	4		100[b]
	100[a]		

11. Freeze Voter Income of $863.468 for the two years, 1985-86:		12. Center for Innovative Diplomacy,1986-87, dollar amounts not given:
Direct mail	58	"Most of CID's support has come from foundations including [fourteen foundations listed]....A number of individuals have been extremely generous, particularly [ten people listed]....A final and increasingly important part our funding is membership dues....."
Phone banks	22	
House parties	6	
Major donors	9	
Special events	3	
Other	2	* * *
	100[c]	"CID currently has about 4,000 members."[d]

13. American Friends Service Committee, 1986-87 fiscal year income of $21,584,461:		14. Women's International League for Peace and Freedom, 1987-88 fiscal year income of $435,939:	
Contributions	54	Dues and contributions	61
Bequests	21	Foundation and JAPA grants	14
Fees and grants from government agencies	1	Bequests	11
Investment income	20	Literature sales amd subscriptions	11
Program service fees	2	Interest, dividends, reimbursements	5
Miscellaneous	1		100[f]
	100[e]		

15. War Resisters League, 1988 income of $368,458:		16. The Nuclear Resister, 1987 annual income of $26,250:	
Contributions	57	Subscriptions	43
Sales	27	Contributions	31
Foundation grants	5	Grants	5
Special events	8	Paraphernalia sales	20
Other	3	Back-issue sales	1
	100[g]		100[h]

[a] Sacramento SANE /Freeze 1988, 2.

[b] Teitelbaum 1987, 10.

[c] Simplified representation of Freeze Voter Statement of Receipts and Disbursements in Freeze Voter 1987, 12.

[d] Center for Innovative Diplomacy 1986-87, 2.

[e] Kraybill 1988b, 8.

[f] Women's International League for Peace and Freedom 1988.

[g] War Resisters League 1989.

[h] The Nuclear Resister 1989.

arranged, roughly, from "right" to "left" in the spectrum of six clusters explained in chapter 1: transcenders, educators, intellectuals, politicians, protesters, prophets. For the most part, the labels for income sources given in this figure are those used by the particular organization (which means that direct comparisons among organizations are difficult). Nonetheless, the degree of diversity both within single organizations and across them is striking.

Parent organizations. What I would regard as the most privileged stratum of the peace movement was dependent on donations of a sort, but donations that were appropriations within the hierarchy of a larger organization. Once a year, or on some similar cycle, movement bureaus (as defined and discussed above) came under review by their parent organizations and were funded. The negative side of this arrangement was that the parent organization could decide to reduce or eliminate that funding with disastrous or lethal consequences. The positive side was that, if funded, one only had to worry about the next budget cycle. Analytically, this arrangement was one of a small number of funders who made infrequent decisions that controlled (for the funded organization) a large amount of money. This was quite different from organizations I discuss later that were dependent on a large number of small funders (contributors) making — in the aggregate — frequent decisions on funding. For these, funding was a more continuing worry.

Having already discussed "bureaus," I need here only to recall that these were national peace and justice oriented commissions of mainstream religious bodies, peace education and research programs of colleges and universities, and the few government bodies dedicated to peace matters. These were the havens of the relatively small number of people who got paid to pursue peace matters more or less full time.

Grants. Foundations and other philanthropic entities have rather broad and flexible conceptions of what merits funding, and they are, therefore, able rapidly to shift their funding priorities in response to changing conceptions of pressing social problems. This is how they reacted to changes in U. S. defense (and domestic) policy in the early-eighties. A wide variety of peace organizations were beneficiaries of this shift, leading one observer to remark: "What makes this new round of peace activism unusual is their impressive financial backing, an anomaly among perpetually bankrupt peace groups."[22] One study of seventy-four foundations found that their grants tripled between 1982 and 1984, rising from 16.5 to more than 52 million dollars and even more in subsequent years (McCrea and Markle 1989, 117).

Even though the recipients were varied, the largest portions flowed to the three most conservative clusters: the transcenders, educators, and intellectuals (Wright, Rodriguez, and Waitzkin 1986). Larger mainstream foundations were particularly partial to funding university and allied research and educational programs on war-peace affairs.

This conservatism of mainstream foundations meant that the three clusters to the left—the politicians, protesters, and prophets—were hard-pressed as foundation applicants. However, there were a few "progressive" foundations that funded activities of a more political character, but they also gave relatively small amounts of money. (The three "left" clusters were, thus, more dependent on angels, solicitations to the public at large, and direct participant support.)

Foundation funding was overwhelmingly of the terminating sort. It lasted only for the duration of a specific project and period of time. Especially among the intellectuals but also among others, ambiguity about grant renewal—or certainty of nonrenewal—gave rise to the perpetual need to write and "hustle" project renewals or proposals for new projects. This left less time for currently funded projects, and the constant need to so hustle tended to sap morale.

Angels. In funding contexts, an angel is a person of some wealth who provides large lump sums that catapult a project from a mere good idea to reality.[23] An angel might not be underwriting all the costs but enough to make a dramatic difference in whether a project gets "off the ground" and how it is carried out. In addition, as private persons making donations, they are not constrained by laws—especially tax laws—that affect foundations nor need their donations be a matter of public record. Indeed, it was not easy in the 1980s to know the degree to which angels were operating in particular situations, an ambiguity that itself gave rise to many "rumors of angels" that may not have been factual.

The most publicly known and, perhaps, largest spending angels gifted the transcenders. Joan Kroc (widow of Ray Kroc, founder of McDonald's Hamburgers) appeared to be the most prominent eighties peace angel. Cordes (1985–1986) characterized her as putting "megabucks into peace efforts—the most visible a recent $400,000 one-day campaign consisting of full-page anti-nuclear war ads in 23 major newspapers." Among many other projects, she "financed the printing of 500,000 copies of Helen Caldicott's *Missile Envy*, which she's sending to influential people around the country" (Cordes 1985–1986, 9).

Transcender ranks were also populated with people of more modest wealth. Among them was San Francisco Bay Area entrepreneur Don Carlson, who did the following sort of small-scale angeling: "We had hardly transferred the Soviets Meet Middle America [SMMA] scheme from a paper table napkin to a legal pad before we cautiously approached Don to see if he would be the founding donor for SMMA. In a nervous hour-long breakfast one morning we laid out the 'maps across America' and waited for Don's response. After several penetrating strategic questions, he turned to his associate and said, 'It's a great possibility.' He absorbed the vision and pledged the first seed money of $36,000, without which SMMA never would have left the legal pad" (Tennison 1988, 13). Drawn heavily from the educated and technocratic upper–middle class, transcenders could raise millions of dollars when thousands of them were each prepared to donate several thousand dollars. Such an angel-like pattern seemed important in a number of transcender undertakings, especially those of Beyond War (see, e.g., cell 1 in figure 4.3).

Angels were less publicized in the three more-left clusters, but numerous rumors alleged that the largest "liberal protester" undertakings were significantly underwritten by Hollywood entertainment people and other pop media figures, such as astronomer-activist Carl Sagan. A number of the prophets also seemed to have less-than-evident angel support. For example, in 1981, Jim and Shelly Douglass discovered it was possible to purchase a house just outside the Trident submarine base near Poulsbo, Washington, and right beside the railroad tracks leading into that base. Desiring to acquire the building as a post from which to track and protest trains carrying nuclear missiles, by means of diligent phone calls to certain people, they were able to raise the funds in a short time. Or, in Jim Douglass's words: "Through the grace of God and the gifts of many wonderful friends, we were able to buy the house" (Douglass 1991, 61).

Operating foundations. A very small number of peace movement organizations were "operating foundations"; that is, they had an endowment they spent on their own internally staffed and conducted programs rather than making grants to applicants. The Nuclear Age Foundation and the Council for a Livable World were prominent among these. They are notable for this discussion because of their extreme rarity.

Dues. In one idealized image of citizen action, people ban together, impose dues and levies on themselves, and forge forth so supported. Such an image — and its reality — has been central to the workings of many movements, the cooperative and labor movements among them. Its elements even appear as defining features in the "classical model" of movements depicted by McCarthy and Zald (1987, 368–70).

This image of how movements are and should be funded was widespread in the peace movement but rather less than successful as a movement practice. Unlike associations that offer strong selective incentives (e.g., the closed shop for labor unions, strong solidarity bonds in other associations), few peace associations provided incentives that reliably ensured receipt of dues or levies. The more successful were groups whose members were also practicing an occupation in common, as with educators, intellectuals, and politicians (e.g., the International Peace Research Association and others discussed previously as volunteer nationals). And even among these, in-kind and angel donations figured importantly in organizational functioning.

Others, such as liberal politician groups, stressed dues but could not fund their activities with dues alone. For example, in the mid- and late-eighties a Freeze chapter reputed to be among the more stable and active in the nation budgeted dues as only about a quarter of its yearly spending, using, in addition, such sources as raffles, fundraiser admissions, and angels (case 9 in figure 4.3).[24]

Actually, the line between dues and angels was often blurred, a blurring that some groups encouraged by offering *many categories of dues*, especially "upscale" categories. In mail solicitations for his Search for Common Ground, John Marks, for example, offered five levels of membership, starting at the top with "lifetime" for $5,000, followed by "patron" for $1,000, declining to "Sponsoring" ("$1,000 or more"), "Sustaining" ($50), and merely "member" ($25).

Among organizations in clusters to the left, dues were deemphasized or even eschewed. Expressing the equalitarianism we have seen regarding other matters, dues were defined as inappropriately rigid or elitist. People should support "the work" with whatever amount was consistent with their economic situations and consciences. This was, most notably, the philosophy of the venerable War Resisters League (case 15 in figure 4.3).

Getting people to renew for the new year was among the main problems of dues. A single mailed renewal notice would result in checks from only a minority of the mailing (an experience of many nonpeace associations, however). Groups serious about collecting dues resorted to labor-intensive volunteer phone banks that solicited laggard renewers. An equal or more serious problem in collecting dues was the inability to keep accurate records of who had paid and who had not, to send renewal notices, and properly to record renewals. High turnover among staff and volunteers assigned such tasks, combined with the inherently boring character of membership record keeping, meant that membership records of many groups were almost always in disarray. Ironically, the largest peace group, SANE/Freeze, was among the most notorious and even scandalous for its inability to maintain member lists and otherwise to stay in touch with or service its mass clientele. Its massive slump in the late-eighties was due in part to managerial disarray and not simply the decline of public concern about war-peace matters.

Direct mail. As anyone in America who had a mailbox in the seventies and eighties well knows, mail solicitation became the technology of choice in raising money for an incredible variety of causes (as well as for marketing virtually everything else). Performed by people who knew what they were doing, it was very cost effective, that is, it produced a lot more money than it cost.

This social fact was not lost on the peace movement and virtually every organization of any size made repeated mail appeals. Relative to other and professional direct mailers, however, I have to judge peace group efforts to have been smaller and less "slick." Few if any organizations contracted with the high-technology professionals in the direct mail business. Preferring in-house (and, therefore, cheaper) operations, these tended to be less sophisticated in obtaining or constructing mailing lists and in the design of appeals. Sometimes, these efforts were unsophisticated or even crude. It took an exceptionally dedicated peace person to wade through multipage letters printed front and back that were single spaced in tiny print and crammed onto pages with the smallest of margins. As someone who tried seriously to read these appeals, in mystification I would declare to myself, "What *is* this about?" and "What *do* they want?" Nonetheless, some peace organizations did achieve—at least briefly—high degrees of sophistication and monetary success in direct mail, SANE and Freeze Voter among them (cases 7, 8, and 11 in figure 4.3).

Direct mail appeals were shaped by the fact that federal and state tax laws distinguished between tax-deductible contributions for charitable and educational purposes and nondeductible political donations. An appeal saying that a donation was tax deductible, therefore, sent two messages: the giver got a deduction and the donee organization was socially legitimate because it was not "political." These two incentives encouraged peace groups to incorporate themselves as educational rather than political entities. Some even maintained both kinds of corporate entities, one for "political education" and the other for "political action." Their direct mail solicitations could then provide the giver two options for writing checks, as in this language from a solicitation by Operation Real Security (ORS). "Checks should be made payable to 'ORS PAC' and mailed to. . . . Tax-deductible contributions to support the separate ongoing national educational work in the NATO Project should be made to the 'Center for Energy Research'" (ORS, mail solicitation, October 1989).

Phone banks. Occasionally, larger national as well as local volunteer associations organized phone banks in which paid or volunteer telephoners worked lists of current or lapsed members for renewals or simply for donations. Freeze Voter and SANE/Freeze were, for a time, effective in this (cases 8 and 11 in figure 4.3). Sometimes there were efforts to acquire the phone lists of similar organizations in order to expand the base of donors, but solicited organizations were understandably reluctant to allow others to prospect on their turf.

Fund-raiser events. The fund-raising event was the forte of, especially, local peace groups. This was a gathering for which admission was charged, but a fee often termed "suggested donation" (or such) in order to make it a tax deducible donation and in order to avoid the business law implications of charging admissions to events.

One common form was gathering to hear a speaker, a person who might be from out of town and who was well known. After the merger of SANE and the Freeze, a major activity of its president, William Sloane Coffin, was touring regions of the country making fund-raising appearances organized by SANE/Freeze chapters. Sometimes public talks were augmented with smaller wine-tasting or dinner parties before the talk. Admission fees to these were much higher than to the larger public talk. Other foci of fund-raising events included the showing of movies in receipt-splitting arrangements with theaters, dinners featuring speakers and entertainment, and receptions and poetry readings. A few fund-raising events were elevated to yearly affairs that were depended on as continuing sources of revenue, such as Santa Cruz, California's, twelve-hour dance marathon called "Give Peace a Dance" or "Dance Your Nukes Off" (case 10, figure 4.3). (As did a few other groups, this organization also sponsored a Freeze Walk-A-Thon.)

A successful variation on the fund-raising event, called house parties, was developed by Freeze Voter in 1984. It was modeled on the political fund-raising practice of recruiting a reasonably prominent local personage — not necessarily a peace activist, only a sympathizer — to provide her or his home for, typically, a cocktail party. Invitations were mailed and/or phoned to known peace-oriented or sympathetic people. Attendance entailed a donation on the order of twenty-five, a hundred, or more dollars — the attender deciding the exact amount. As middle- and upper-middle-class affairs held in spacious and well-appointed homes, several dozen or more participants providing at least twenty-five dollars each could generate more than modest sums of money.

Business revenue. As the dearth of "firms" in the peace movement signals, only a modest revenue stream flowed from the sale of goods or services. Even though almost every peace organization sold, for example, publications, buttons, and other paraphernalia, these retail activities were seldom subjected to an economic calculus of pricing, volume, and labor that produced a profit that could be invested in other activities. On the contrary, pricing was often haphazard and publications (especially leaflets) were simply given away, resulting in monetary loss rather than gain although this generosity may have resulted in peace gain rather than loss.

Among the peace organizations that were true "firms" (as described previously), if one accepted the accounts of these entities, volume and profits were often hardly sufficient to keep many of them afloat, and only a few could achieve even modest growth (e.g., case 16, figure 4.3).

Canvases. Within SANE and, then SANE/Freeze after their merger, there was a special unit called the canvas. Operating on a national scale with offices in several cities, it was a full-time door-to-door fund-raising force that, in the late-eighties, employed about two hundred people at its summer peak of activity. Using voting and other statistics to detect liberal neighborhoods and cities, canvasers solicited memberships in door-to-door sweeps. For example, going door to door in the early evening hours over a three-week-period, twenty or so canvasers could "work" fifteen thousand "doors" (residences) and produce some five hundred new "members." This operation yielded about a million dollars a year or more during the late-eighties. (Its role in budgets is shown in cases 7 and 8, figure 4.3). The canvas itself, however, *cost* about that much a year to run because canvasers were employees working for a small stipend and a percentage of their collections. Modeled on classic door-to-door sales strategy, this was salesmanship applied to citizen action.[25] Profits, therefore, only appeared if such front-door members renewed, a problematic matter, as indicated before regarding dues.

Tabling. The technique called *tabling* involved setting up a table (often a more handy ironing board, actually) in a high-traffic area for the purpose of collecting signatures on a petition or petitions. Solicitations for contributions were also made and this could sometimes result in reasonable amounts of revenue for a local group.

Games of chance. A few peace groups used games of chance to raise money. Mostly, these were raffles and other drawings offering various sorts of prizes (e.g., trips to vacation spots, dinners at restaurants, or articles of clothing). These seemed most prevalent among the liberal politicians, where one group even had a yearly "big ticket" raffle in which the tickets were $100 each and gave the winner a vacation trip to a specific locale or air travel for two to anywhere in the world. (The trips were either donated or sold at cost by a travel agency, see, e.g., case 9, figure 4.3.) Anomalous, to me at least, was the historic radical protester War Resisters League's yearly use of a raffle to raise money.

Passing the hat. The practice of "passing the hat" at meetings as a means of raising money is historically identified with religious groups but is also seen among ordinary political associations. Although not widespread, some peace associations passed the hat and one, national SANE/Freeze, developed it into something of a high art, using techniques reminiscent of more enthusiastic Christian churches. At its merger convention of 1987, for example, an anonymous "challenge donation" was announced. In order to receive it, a matching amount had to be raised from passing the hat. Time and again the hat was passed and the convention crowd exhorted to give more because the collection kept falling short of the magic matching number. A some ten-foot-tall drawing of a thermometer was affixed to the wall next to the podium and a rising red column painted in after each round.

Affinity credit cards. In the late-eighties, "affinity" Visa and Master cards became popular as fund-raising devices with many occupational and other associations. The affinity organization commonly received 0.5 percent of every credit card purchase and, with enough card holders, this could create a sizable yearly income. The Sierra Club, for example, was reported to have some twenty-six thousand holders of its affinity card. In the first years of operation, this generated about $250,000 for that organization (Tozian 1988, 16). Two of the most mainstream peace groups offered such cards, SANE/Freeze and the Physicians for Social Responsibility.

Source Profile and Funding Combinations

Following the logic of figures 4.1 and 4.2, which graph a conjectured organizational profile, I would venture profiles of funding for the eighteen sources I have reviewed. I need, however, to be more cautious about funding. Estimating amounts of money is much more difficult than numbers of organizations. With organizations, we at least begin with some serious counts and even published lists of them (e.g., Conetta 1988). These counts and lists were possible because organizations create easily located physical traces in the forms of names, addresses, phone numbers, newsletters, and the like. In contrast, in-kind and monetary funding do not leave physical traces that are anywhere near as easy to find. Therefore, estimations of funding are much more speculative than of organizations.

Nonetheless, at least two useful generalizations can be drawn from this review of funding. One, peace groups quite commonly funded themselves with several types of activities and sources of donations. Even many firms and bureaus did not sustain themselves purely on market revenue or appropriations, respectively. Instead, they used additional donated participation, work, life-style, goods and services, and even — for bureaus, especially — grants and angels. Diverse sources were even more evident among associations. Two, the largest portion of these sources were "one shot" or "terminating" in character as opposed to stably continuing. By inference, the monetary value of one-shot or terminating funding likely far exceeded that of continuous or stable funding.[26]

Comparisons

Using the foregoing profile of organizational forms and the discussion of funding, I want now to address two comparative questions. One, even though we do not yet have systematic organizational profiles on other social movements, What comparative similarities and differences are, nonetheless, evident based on what we know about movement organizations? Second, the main opponent of the eighties peace movement was the American war system. If we compare the two, how are they similar and different?

Social Movement Organizations

As key units of social movements, social movement organizations vary in terms of their *scope*, the increasing "number of activities in which . . . participants are jointly involved" (Etzioni 1961, 160). Along this variable, one can distinguish six basic levels of movement scope, of levels at which the lives of participants are organized:

1. Associations sustained by volunteers, which organize a small portion of most participants' lives.

2. Bureaus employing staffers, which organize only the work life of participants and do so along traditional, hierarchical lines.

3. Troops deploying soldiers, which temporarily suspend most aspects of the participants' lives in temporary and crisis-driven mobile units.

4. Communes composed of householders, which organize the domestic but not work lives of participants.

5. Collectives, consisting of workers, which organize work lives of participants along equalitarian or other innovative lines.

6. Utopias populated by utopians, which seek to organize the full round of participants' lives in a comprehensive scheme (Lofland 1985, 204).

Associations composed of volunteers are lowest in scope, and this was the form of organization that quite clearly dominated the eighties peace movement although there were some bureaus. The lack of bureaus contrasts, in particular, with labor movements, who tend to build a significant infrastructure of them — structures made possible by strict policies of collecting significant dues from members (Adamson and Borgos 1984). One sign of the weakness of peace of organizations was their fear of charging more than token dues that would make bureaus — or, simply, strongly staffed associations — possible.

Looking from the other end of these degrees of scope, the peace movement had a miniscule number and proportion of the more absorbing forms of movement organization. I know of no fully communal utopian settlements founded in the name of peace and virtually no collectives or communes. More broadly, there was a dearth of entities producing any kind of economic goods.

There were also no literal troops deploying soldiers, although the Great Peace March (Folsom, Fledderjohann, and Lawrence 1988) and the planned but never fielded Peace Army were metaphorical versions of this level of scope or mobilization. At these more absorbing levels, other movements sometimes develop a more challenging form of the *camp*, a form made more challenging by being large and proximate to a center of ruling elite power. As assembled on Beijing's Tiananmen Square in June 1989, for example, such a camp was the lead form of the Chinese student democracy movement. Chinese ruling elites quite accurately perceived it as a challenge — and acted accordingly. Save, perhaps, for the brief Poor People's encampment of 1968, the Bonus Army encamped in Washington, D.C., in June and July of 1932 was the last time a movement fielded such a serious camp in the American context. Not too unlike the Chinese ruling elite, the American elite ordered its removal, a military assault and forced dispersion led by no less than that great military hero, Douglas MacArthur (Lislo 1974; Waters 1969). In a perspective of this breadth, the organizational challenge presented by the peace movement was mild, indeed.

Focusing on mobilization *within* the lowest of the six levels of organizational mobilization noted — associations sustained by volunteers — there are five quite salient differences even at this bottom level:

1. Study group locals with student members, whose collective action is confined to assembling and talking as in consciousness-raising groups.

2. Fellowship locals with adherent members, who undertake external collective courses of action but lack a headquarters place and collectively owned equipment as with affinity groups and block clubs.

3. Congregational locals with parishioner members, who reach the level of sustaining a collectively operated headquarters building, a range of group-owned equipment, and a spectrum of program activities.

4. Sect locals with sectarian members, who boost the range of congregational forms to higher levels of scope or encompassment and who combine it with an ideology of a "unique and privileged access to truth or salvation" (Wallis 1977, 17).

5. Cell locals with conspirator members, who add secrecy, conspiracy, and illegal action to the sect level of mobilization (Lofland 1985, 205–16).

Holding aside questions of moral propriety regarding sects and cells, I think we can say that the peace movement had few if any of them. This is another way of saying that the highest levels of part-time involvement that can be generated in social movements were not achieved to any noticeable extent in the peace movement. Instead, volunteer groups were commonly at the lowest three levels, the levels of study groups, fellowships, and congregations. Even congregations were weaker versions of that form.

Finally, I want to mention as aspect of movements that is related to organizational profile but distinguishable from it: its strata of spokespeople and activists. Although the previous analysis does not address activists directly, its structure implies much about them that was, in fact, the case: they were numerous and varied, but hardly any had a wide movement following and none were well known to the public at large. This is in contrast to some other movements where one finds multiple and articulate activists with wide followings and authority — who may even be charismatic — and who become widely known to the public as speaking for the mass of surge participants. In my assessment, the peace movement fell far short of such a state. With the possible but short-lived exception of Helen Caldicott, no one came close to achieving media status as "the" or even "a" major spoksperson. (Consider, in contrast, the relation of Ralph Nader to consumer interests, of Cesar Chavez to farmer worker interests, or of Jesse Jackson to African-American interests.)

The American War System

Knoke and Prensky (1984) compare firms, bureaus, and associations with respect to their forms of power and authority, hierarchy and complexity, centralization and coordinated action, and technology and technical expertise. These points of comparison are also useful in thinking about the peace movement in relation to its chief opponent, the American war system.

Power and authority. There are three primary bases of power and authority: coercion, exchange, and persuasion. The first consists of force and threat of force; the second relies on exchange of goods, services, remuneration, or labor; and, the third appeals to moral commitment (cf.

Etzioni 1961; K. Boulding 1989). No system of power and authority relies exclusively—in the long run—on only one of these. All systems we observe in the real world are mixed. Nonetheless, systems vary in terms of the predominance of one or other of the three.

Persuasion was the *primary* principle of power and authority in the peace movement with a quite secondary role given to negotiation or remuneration (the exchange of material resources for member compliance). Of course, persuasion is the primary basis of power and authority, by definition, in voluntary associations, and the peace movement was simply no exception. Persuasion was, moreover, especially congruent with movement beliefs about preferred ways of organizing human society. Peace activity based on coercion or remuneration was, to many, a contradiction in terms (and many radicals hoped for a future society based entirely on persuasion).

These distinctions would be banal were it not the case that the war system and the peace movement were dominantly organized on *different* principles. Virtually all war system organizations and their members operated on the principle of *exchange*, that is, remunerative compensation. One large segment of it—the military—operated, indeed, on the principle of *coercion* mixed with remuneration.

War system *funding* was explicitly *coercive* in character, that is, by taxation. Persons who refused to pay for the military could expect government agents to extract payment, with force if necessary. Peace movement funding, in contrast, was premised on persuasion or moral commitment.[27]

Hierarchy, complexity, decision making. Viewed in the aggregate, peace movement organizations were, comparatively (1) uncomplicated in the formal or technical senses of having low degrees of internal differentiation in structure; (2) shallow spanned, in the sense of having only two or a few "levels" of internal hierarchy; and (3) democratic and ambivalent about hierarchy, if not overtly hostile to it. As just mentioned, these are all simply features of voluntary associations, and they also fit with ideological proclivities of many peace workers.

The contrast with the war system, though, was thoroughly striking. Its participants seemed even to relish organizational forms, practices, and philosophies that were opposite to those of the peace movement:

• Huge organizations—or what Knoke and Prensky (1984, 11) term *giantism*

• Many, many levels of organization

• Complexly differentiated internal structure

• Strict definitions of who was "under" and "over" whom

• Undemocratic decision making carried on by a few top "leaders"

The prototypic instance of this contrast with the peace movement was the military component of the war system in which hierarchy and complexity were so central that its members wore complicated and finely graded indicators of them on their bodies so that others could instantly perceive who was superior to whom and who performed what detailed function. These were called uniforms, of course, and they were only the most visible way in which principles of hierarchy and subordination were ingrained in the military.

The scale of the war system combined with its "deep" hierarchy, alerts us to it also being a system of layered social classes. Recognizing its internal segmentation by military, political, and economic realms, within each segment a similar scheme of layered social classes appeared. At the top, there was a ruling circle or class. Underneath it was a substantial technical and managerial strata that advised on policy, translated policy into operating plans, and oversaw policy execution. At the bottom, but numerically the very largest class, were the millions who were directed by the two upper classes. The military segment had the clearest specification of leaders, of course, a clarity that was regularly presented on wall chart "trees" studded with photographs (in such publications as the Department of Defense's *Defense*). Leadership hierarchy was not quite so codified in the political and industrial segments, but who the leaders were and how they ranked were not difficult to specify.

The American war system also had a well-developed culture of leadership and leaders. Leadership and leaders were celebrated a great deal — with the stress on military leaders (of course). Even something of a cult of leadership was institutionalized in a range of "leadership schools" and "colleges" and a scholarly literature dedicated to finding, expositing, and exhorting the features of "good leadership" (or, in more recent times, "management"). Leaders were accorded great deference, elaborate personal and bodyguard staffs, privileged living arrangements, and much higher than ordinary financial compensation.

The contrast with the peace movement in such respects was dramatic. First, and as I have discussed at several points, the peace movement did not have *a* leader at the top of a movementwide hierarchy. Second, associated with but not required by this fact, it was difficult even to say there was a small and identifiable inner circle of peace leaders, even if none in the circle was *the* leader. Third, extending the previous comparison with other social movements to institutional leadership, peace leaders did not develop a counterpart to the kind of presence achieved by people such as Ronald Reagan who was — in a strictly technical sense — a very successful leader. Fourth, the smaller size, voluntary, and decentralized nature of the movement also meant that it did not have a stratification system of the sort seen in the war system. There were certainly variations in power and wealth among participants, but these were imported into the movement as much or more as generated by the distribution and control of resources within it.

Centralization and coordinated action. The peace movement had vastly less centralization and capacity for collective action than featured in even the most pluralistic depiction of the American power elite or its war system.[28] At the end of World War II, American elites were able to initiate a "containment" foreign and defense policy that was executed with remarkable consensus and continuity to the end of the Cold War. To suggest a degree of centralization and capacity for coordinated action among U.S. elites is not to say they never disagreed among themselves. Such was obviously not the case, and one of the purposes of the debate processes observed within ruling circles (e.g., in the pages of a journal like *Foreign Affairs*) was to work out what the ruling elite position is to be on particular matters (Domhoff 1978). We must go further, though, and show that questions of policy were raised, debated and settled among a relatively small number of people after which successively lower levels of the war system executed them. Such a regular and centralized process has not been documented to the satisfaction of all observers, but a reasonable amount of plausible evidence has, in my view, been put forth.[29]

Peace movement people differed from the war system participants with respect to their attitudes toward centralization and capacity for collective action and the organizational reality of decentralization and extremely limited capacity for collective action. Some, especially liberally inclined members, perpetually lamented what they perceived as the pronounced fragmentation and decentralization and corresponding lack of capacity for collective action. This lament was not false consciousness. The movement's some eight thousand organizations were, in fact, an atomized scatter of independent creatures with little capacity for collective action. Even occasions of joint action requiring the least centralization – the mass rally – were not easy for peace groups to mount and occurred infrequently for that reason.

Technology and technical expertise. Knoke and Prensky (1984) suggest that firms and bureaus tend to use more, more innovative and sophisticated technology than associations. This also implies that firms and bureaus have relatively higher degrees of technical specialization and skill. Such contrasts were also evident between the peace movement and the war system.

Most narrowly, there was the technology and skill of military hardware per se. War system folk invented it, made it, trained on it, controlled it, and had a strata of technical specialists who justified it. Much of this technology was directly lethal, but some of the most important types involved more generally scientific matters (as in, e.g., seismic measurement regarding "verification," laser beams regarding Star Wars). Technologically, indeed, the war system was truly impressive at the levels of invention and development and a quite significant percentage of the Department of Defense budget was allocated specifically to these tasks.

Peace movement people had no, or a very marginal, relation to these several aspects of military hardware. Largely opposed to the existence of most of it, their marginality was consistent with their beliefs. Nonetheless, a few peace groups attempted critique with regularity and scientific credibility. Some made calls for individuals to "adopt a weapons system" and to learn all there is to know about it for the purpose of critiquing it with unassailable objections (e.g., Tobias et al. 1982). Few people responded to this urging, though, and some argued against it, suggesting that technical debate over weapons and hardware was a political dead end (e.g., Schwartz and Derber 1990). Irrespective of the merits of such debates, the social fact was that the movement had a very marginal relation to (and mastery of) war system hardware.

Military hardware was only an element of a larger intellectual enterprise commonly called strategic studies. Using technical vocabularies, defense intellectuals presented impressively arcane rationales of war policies. The military segment even operated an elaborate system of war colleges that invented and elaborated this kind of thought. A few peace intellectuals undertook to engage strategic studies directly, but, for many others, this was like trying to critique a religion from within. Once the assumptions were granted, one had already lost the debate — and defense intellectuals did not concede assumptions. Yet other peace intellectuals attempted to end run strategic studies by organizing efforts to rethink basic defense and security concepts.[30] But, relative to the war system, there were few of these.

Encompassing both hardware and strategic studies were broader war system perspectives traveling under such names as "international relations" and "foreign affairs." Numerous research centers were dedicated to elaborating these approaches, and such "realism" and "neorealism" dominated the teaching of "international relations" in college and university departments of political science. Comparatively, there were only a few peace research institutes and educational curricula.

In addition, there were very large differences in the technology and expertise of public promotion and persuasion. War system functionaries paid thousands upon thousands of technologically sophisticated people to work full-time at presenting war system views in myriad forms to numerous audiences. The more obvious forms of this included:

1. While ostensibly for recruitment, the military's constant advertising campaigns served to keep it before the public in an upbeat and positive light. Making regular high school appearances, thousands of military recruiters deployed around the country served the same function. (In the eighties, the military spent an estimated billion and a half dollars a year on recruitment alone [Davidson 1986]. Also, it had one recruitment officer for every 330 high school seniors and officers located *in* some high schools [Fitz 1986, 10].)

2. Every military installation of any consequence had a press and public information office and personnel assigned to disseminating favorable information on it. The Pentagon alone had hundreds of press relations people. Public relations programs of military installations included "open house" days, free availability of musical performance groups, and speakers who explained war system views. At the national level, cadre of the intellectually most able officers were sent on tours of college campuses to "explain" topics of current war system interest.

3. War system members controlled the U. S. government per se and used the apparatus of the presidency, the State Department and other government agencies to achieve privileged access to the media of mass communication.

4. The industrial segment of the war system had an extensive public relations structure and contracted with the most professional advertising firms to craft and disseminate its messages.

Compared to the above, peace movement public relations and communications were anemic. While the war system had many thousands of technically trained and proficient people working full time on public relations and media presence, peace groups had virtually none. Organizations of equivalent technology and skill sometimes donated these for a particular campaign, but such commitments were infrequent and short term. This extreme contrast in public relations and promotion was recognized and discussed in some movement circles. At least two organizations — the Ark Foundation and WAND (1986) — took up the problem as a major task, but both of their efforts came to little more than "calls to action."

<<<

There were, then, a number of quite profound, not simply belief, but organizational contrasts between the peace movement and the war system.

It was a contrast, in starkest terms, of sheer power, a "David-Goliath" disparity in which, unlike in the Bible, Goliath was not overcome by surprise and marksmanship.

Summary

I conclude with a summary of some of most important organizational, financial, and comparative features we have seen.

1. Viewed in the aggregate, the eighties peace surge was characterized by *associations*, as distinguished from *firms* and *bureaus* and, among associations, by a small number of national and local staff-managed associations. The modal peace organization was volunteer managed.

2. One prime meaning of the dominance of associations was that the movement's economy was donation driven rather than based in significant market-generated or appropriated income.

3. To a significant extent, movement funding was "terminating" rather than "continuing" in character, creating a pronounced vulnerability to "down swing."

4. Peace groups were likely to employ several rather than simply one source of funding.

5. Movement organizations tended to the simple and equalitarian — to have few levels of authority, low complexity, and modest amounts of technology.

6. Viewed as a social formation, the movement was loosely structured in having almost no hierarchy among organizations and relatively little coordination between them, albeit with weak coalitions. All of this was in radical contrast to the war system.

7. The level of absorption of most participants into organizations — the scope of most organizations — was relatively low.

8. Relative to the American war system, the movement had conspicuously small funding, technology, and organizational scale.

In the conclusion, I draw these features together in a more general depiction of the movement.

Notes

1. This imbalance is both documented in and illustrated by the comprehensive review by McAdam, McCarthy, and Zald 1988.

2. Detailed documentation is provided in chap. 7, "Coalescing Events."

3. Specializing in cultural materials more generally was the Syracuse Cultural Workers, "a non-profit publisher/distributor (founded in 1982) of materials which create a culture that supports and inspires the ideals of justice, liberation and peace" (Syracuse Cultural Workers 1991). Structurally, it was a worker's association of about a dozen people.

4. The Winston Foundation subsequently resurrected and issued it erratically.

5. Details are given in chap. 7, "Coalescing Events."

6. Chap. 2, section on the "Analytic" pattern of culture creators and elaborators.

7. Simply on the surface, this was a relatively impressive number of lobbyists, but, as pointed out by Sam Marullo (personal communication, 1992), these "full-time" lobbyists, even though given titles such as "legislative directors," usually also had several nonlobbying duties. Therefore, a typical day for them was quite different from the day of, for example, a McDonnell-Douglas lobbyist.

8. The sense of urgency or emergency is discussed in chap. 7, "Perceptions."

9. This difference can be, however, overstated. Marullo, Chute, and Colwell (1991) report, for example, a considerable frequency of consensus decision making in the "nonpacifist" groups of the 1988 Colwell survey of peace groups.

10. In deciding what pattern a peace organization may exhibit, one must, of course, proceed with caution. An association that seems superficially to be one pattern, may, on closer inspection, actually be another. For example, some seemingly volunteer national and regional associations of a democratic cast were arguably, in fact, very similar to the mom and pop shops I describe later. Or, they were complex blendings of these two patterns. In its early years the Peace Studies Association was arguably such a complex blending, or even a "pop shop."

11. In contrast, the more radical forms I enumerate generated a much richer literature in spite of their numerical infrequency. Such is the irony of the ethnographic imagination.

12. Although in one sense a "national coalition," the informal association of lobbyists in Washington, D.C., called the Monday Lobby (or the Monday Noon Lobby Group), was, as a local entity, also a local coalition (see Shuman 1991; Szegedy-Maszak 1989).

13. The functioning of affinity groups among middle-class residents of the San Francisco Bay Area is sympathetically depicted in Peter Adair's videos "Change of Heart," 1984, and "Stopping History," 1984.

14. Ryan 1983. Epstein (1991) provides a rich history of the development of affinity groups and their various practices, such as "the block."

15. Ironically, strong opponents of the peace movement seemed to use the term *community* more often than did peace activists, as in the *defense community* and the intelligence *community* — both of which are excellent examples of oxymoron.

16. All but the last of these associations are described in Epstein (1990); she also provides further references. The Community of the Servant is treated by Holworth (1989, esp. 142–43). For brief, formal descriptions of diverse other peace groups see Meyer 1988.

17. Because of this quite real difference between some social movements and commercial society, McCarthy and Zald's (1987) effort to conceive social movements as "industries" with "sectors" and the like strikes some readers as "novel" and "cute" but seriously misconceived. One *can*, of course, impose economic models on movements (or anything else), but that imposition suppresses the fact that people in movements may not so operate.

18. The July–August 1989 issue of *The Other Side* carried the third such evaluation, intended to guide giving in 1989–1990 (Olson 1989a). Editor Mark Olson's "Givers Guide," (1989b) provides an especially stringent (and appropriate) set of criteria for evaluating funding solicitations.

19. At the 1990 annual convention of SANE/Freeze, held in Oakland, California, the

executive director's report to the assembled convention did not include a monetarized account of the previous year's spending or a budget of spending proposed for the next year. I asked a senior SANE/Freeze staff member for a copy of the budget and was told that the staff had forgotten to bring even a single copy of it! He would send me one, though, if I desired it. (I requested it and received the copy some weeks later.)

20. Of particular notice to me as a person who joined a large number of peace associations and ordered books, kits, buttons, and other paraphernalia through the mail was the slowness with which groups banked their checks. While gas, electric, phone, credit card, discount, mail order, and other companies banked my checks the day they received them, many peace groups allowed them to lay about for weeks on end. I know this, of course, from the process of balancing my checkbook and perpetually having to carry forward uncashed peace group checks, some of which were *never* banked!

21. Several books published at or near the height of the eighties peace surge consisted of brief descriptions of many of these people. McGuinness 1988 contains almost fifty such profiles, complete with photographs, drawn from all six clusters of the movement. Totten and Totten 1984 is a similar compilation, with twenty profiles, also with photographs and representatives of all six clusters. See also Roberts 1991. (The fact that these authors researched and were then able to publish books of this kind is one measure of the existence of a "soaring" surge, as analyzed in chap. 7.)

22. Cordes (1985–1986, 8). See also Reed (1983) and chap. 7, "Funding Events."

23. Angels who provided continuing large sums of money were euphemistically termed *sustainers.* Other terms for angels included *major donors* or simply *contributor.* For other terms, see figure 4.3.

24. Marullo (personal communication, 1992) reports that fund-raiser events and angels accounted for more than half of the yearly budget of the large, midwestern Freeze organization he studied.

25. The canvas as a fund-raising practice was unusual in the peace movement, but it was not unique as a social movement activity. Said to have been invented in Chicago in the early-eighties by an encyclopedia salesman turned community organizer, it was used through the eighties by various kinds of citizen action groups in several U.S. metropolitan areas. Its generic features were the same as those described for the SANE/Freeze operation. As one of the few cities in America carried by Mondale in 1984 and Dukakis in 1988, Davis, California – the city of my residence – was for that reason frequently targeted by the canvas operations of movement organizations. The traffic to my front door was so heavy, indeed, that I became reluctant to answer it between six and eight o'clock in the evening – the peak period of canvas action. Aspects of the SANE/Freeze canvas operation are described in Gusterson 1989.

26. Published too recently for me to treat the findings properly in this chapter, I want, nonetheless, at least to note the pertinence of Jack Walker's *Mobilizing Interest Groups in America* (1991), a study finding, among other things, a general pattern of citizen group funding quite similar to the one depicted here. See, in particular, his chap. 5 and tables 5.1, 78 and 5.4, 82.

27. One ironic question is, To what degree would people contribute to the war system if it had the same voluntary character as the peace movement? Could the war system raise even the same amount of money as the peace movement if it had to compete on an even – moral commitment – footing? (One item of peace culture implicitly asked this in a declaration: "It will be a great day when our schools get all the money they need and the air force has to hold a bake sale to buy a bomber.")

28. Among numerous reviews of this debate, see Alford and Friedland 1985; Block 1987.

29. E. g., Domhoff 1978; Jenkins and Brents 1989; Jenkins and Eckert 1986.

30. Patterns of intellectual work, including this pattern, are described in chap. 3, in the section on "Roles."

Part Two

Processes in the
American Peace Movement

5

Citizen Surges

The Peace Surge in Movement Studies Perspective

The histories of human social organizations are punctuated by brief and intense periods in which significant numbers of citizens define some social situation as a dire threat, injustice, and/or opportunity requiring urgent action which will forestall the threat, right the wrong, and/or seize the opportunity.[1] The situations most commonly at issue in such periods are recent actions of political authorities or economic elites that are viewed as morally noxious.

We may think of the generic class of all such periods of upwelling urgency in a populace as *citizen surges*, using the term *surge* in its ordinary sense, only here applied to a distinctive moment in human collective life. A dictionary, thus, defines a surge as "a strong, wavelike, forward movement, rush, or sweep. . . . a strong swelling, wavelike volume or body of something. . . . [in electricity:] a sudden rush or burst of current or voltage."

The image — properly — is one of a more-or-less stable arrangement of forces (a structure) through which, or in which, there is a visible, upwelling change of state that rises and then subsides. As a phenomenon in human organization, the citizen surge forms an abstract and distinctive analytic class of human collective action.

Students of social movement, protest, revolt, insurrection, riot, collective violence, and the like immediately appreciate that citizen surges are intimately involved with these types of conflict. Students of social change efforts that are much less dramatic also recognize the surge as associated with the more prosaic efforts they analyze. In addition, scholars of *mobi-*

lization, collective action, and *collective behavior* can point to the citizen surge as integral to their investigations. Thus, the citizen surge analytically cuts across all these types of conflict and social processes, but it is not co-extensive with any of them. Indeed, *conflation* of the surge with a variety of other phenomena was a source of fruitless debate among researchers throughout the 1980s.

The Generic Citizen Surge and Its Contrasts

As a class, the citizen surge exhibits a small number of distinctive phases and features that provide an orienting profile to guide us. Citizen surges are marked by:

1. A rapid spread of the belief that a situation-at-hand is *urgent* and that people must, therefore, depart from action-as-usual because of new threats and harms that must be countered and/or new opportunities that must be seized before they recede;

2. A rapid increase in the number of people participating in forms of action that are *new* to them and that are directed to these dawning threats, injustices, or opportunities;

3. A rapid decline in the above beliefs and actions as a consequence of the success or failure of the new actions, the responses of authorities or countersurges, or the self-terminating nature of the actions themselves;

4. A residue of practices and institutions and other stamps on collective organization and memory.

These four "moments" describe a *surge curve*—a rapid rise to a peak and an even more rapid fall followed by a long tail with, perhaps, smaller "blip" curves in it.

The citizen surge and my treatment of it here contrasts with other patterns in a number of ways. First, the word *citizen* contrasts with *elite* and other labels denoting minorities with inordinate control of the economy, the polity, and other institutional orders. Citizens are the mass of the ordinary populace who take an interest in matters of public or collective significance but who are not in positions of economic and political power. Other terms that might be used include *public, popular, grassroots, mass,* and *populace.*

I do not treat them here, but elites, of course, exhibit their own surges. One example is the urgent effort of U.S. elites just after World War II to identify the Soviet Union as "the focus of evil in the world" and to coax the citizenry—successfully—into a surge with a similar outlook (Nathanson 1988).

Second, the term *surge* is intended to contrast with *wave* or *cycle* (e.g., Tarrow 1989). I do not use either of these terms because both imply a regularity of rising and falling — a cyclical hypothesis — that I want to avoid. The degree to which surges are cyclical should be a matter of investigation rather than built into one's initial conception. In fact, my impression is that most surges are "free-standing" and not part of any longer "wave" series of surges although some clearly are, as Tarrow (1989) and Tilly (e.g., 1986) have abundantly documented.

Third, the elements of urgency, crisis, and rapid adoption of new actions contrast with the more common circumstance of chronic, low-level, and protracted conflict. Thus, the various cases of citizens opposed to authorities that Deena Weinstein admirably analyzes in her book *Bureaucratic Opposition* (1979) show us a great deal about mobilization and collective action but very little about surges because each case is so quietly protracted or even carried on in a laboriously hidden and conspiratorial fashion.

Fourth, in surges, citizens respond to elites in order to create or deter social change. Such surges may be oppositional, affirmational, or mixed and are distinct from fads, fashions, and crazes, such as citizen responses to British royal weddings, Olympic Games, and periods of revivalistic fervor. These have some surgelike features, certainly (see, e.g., Aquirre, Quarantelli, and Mendoza 1988; Irwin 1977), but they are not aimed at achieving social change and are, therefore, not within our current domain.

Fifth, my focus in this chapter on the surge curve — the object itself and its varieties — contrasts with focus on its causes or consequences. I refer to causes and consequences, but the major effort in this chapter is to isolate the citizen surge itself as a topic of analysis.

Sixth, the basic imagery is that of citizens acting collectively against ensconced authorities who are larger and more powerful than citizens. This is in contrast to at least two other images of parties in conflict: two equally powerful and organized authorities or elites in opposition and two factions of the citizenry in conflict with one another while authorities or elites are only bystanders or tacit allies of one party.

Social Organizations Surging

As depicted thus far, nothing has been specified about the macro-micro levels of units of human association that embody the surge.[2] This ambiguity is intentional because the *acting units* comprising surges vary enormously and produce an array of forms that requires its own level of comparative surge analysis.

Surges are observed in terms of two basic acting units, the citizen *gathering* and the citizen *organization*. The former is defined simply as the face-to-face assembly of citizens (cf. McPhail 1990). The latter refers to any reasonably enduring (transassembly) association of citizens that is often named and is, at least, somewhat independent of control by authorities.

These two terms allow us to answer the question *What* is surging? We are "seeing" a surge when we observe among citizens a rapid increase in the sheer number of gatherings and/or organizations that they define in terms of urgency, threat, injustice, and/or opportunity.

Surges vary in the degree to which they are composed of gatherings or organizations. A lower form of surge consists of a rapid increase in selected types of gatherings rather than of organizations. One level up from this, other surges are an increase in numbers of given kinds of organizations (acknowledging that organizational surges likely presuppose and mask surges in gatherings). I call surges *uniform* if they tend to take either the single form of the gathering or the organization. A more complicated set of surges consists of upwellings of *both* gatherings and organizations as well as of additional dimensions of upswing to which we will come. These are, as a class, *multiform* surges.

Uniform Surges

Let us look first at uniform gathering surges and then at uniform organizational surges.

Gathering Surges

Gathering surges vary in two fundamental ways. First, there is the question of how many gatherings are involved and how sequential gatherings are related. The theoretical lower limit would appear to be a single gathering whose members act against an authority. Multigathering surges vary in organizational linkage through the sequence. Those lacking organizational linkage are a mere "set," whereas those following a sequential plan, or "campaign," are a "chain" (cf. Oliver 1989).

Second, gatherings vary in terms of contentiousness—the level and form of pressure brought to bear on authorities. The classification of such forms and levels is itself a topic of some contentiousness,[3] and I here use a traditional trinity. Forms of action in gatherings vary with respect to

• *Politeness of action.* Civil, restrained, and circumspect efforts to press a point or program of change or resistance to change.

- *Protest of action.* Ostentatious, dramatic, and ambiguously legal or illegal nonviolent efforts.
- *Violence of action.* Efforts that injure or destroy property or humans.

The cross-classification of the respective three possibilities on the two variables of *series* and *contentiousness* specifies nine types of uniform gathering surges, which range in seriousness and consequentiality from, at the low end, a single gathering in a surge of polite action to, at the high end, an extended chain of violent gatherings. For reference, these are shown in the left-hand portion of figure 5.1, "Uniform Surges."

The *primal surge*, if one can conceive such a creature, is likely the single instance of an agitated and ad hoc collection of citizens coming together to discuss some policy or action of an authority to which they object, including, perhaps, actually addressing that authority face-to-face in a polite manner—a kind of surge that occurs more frequently than one might at first blush surmise.[4]

Such single instances of assembly can, of course, move from the polite to protest to violent levels of contentiousness. Conceived in surge perspective and as the study of how surges are created in single assemblies that begin in states of compliance, William Gamson's work on *Encounters with Unjust Authority* is of signal significance as a base point for our thinking and all the more important because it is one of the very few investigations of primal surges (Gamson, Fireman, and Rytina 1982). In Gamson's "fabrications," the task was to create *compliant* assemblies that were manipulated into *polite* and, to some degree, *protest* levels of contentiousness, a set of fabrications that was, indeed, not completed because of investigator fears that *violent* action could well develop and/or that a net of surge-curve gatherings might emerge!

A variety of investigations have documented how some kinds of protest and violent assemblies occur in very clear surge-curve fashion. Among them, special note should be made of McAdam (1983) on the several tactics of the civil rights movements, Spilerman (1976) on ghetto rioting, Gambrell (1980) on issue dynamics in sixties student movements, and Jenkins (1987) on the global curve of sixties demonstrations.

In these studies we see a significant degree of modeling in which prior occurrences in the surge curve appear to serve as exemplars for later and increasingly numerous instances that rise to a peak before precipitous decline. The "collective actionists" are, of course, the champion students of oppositional gathering surges—or waves, to be more exact about the kind of materials they treat—at the "chain" level. Their theory implies that the series of contentious gatherings they have coded are more than simply

Figure 5.1
Uniform Surges:
Conjunction of Three Key Variables

		Social Organization					
		Gatherings			Organizations		
		Series			Series		
		Single	Set	Chain	Single	Set	Chain
Contentiousness	polite						
	protest						
	violent						

loosely associated sets but, instead, are politically interrelated and driven ensembles of assemblies (Tarrow 1989; Tilly 1986; Oliver 1989).

Organization Surges

Surges of oppositional organizations exhibit the same two variations in sequence and contentiousness. Regarding the variable of sequence, the *primal-organizational* surge is that of a single organization lurching into surge. More complicated, organizations of a given type burgeon fairly independently of one another or, at the third level, there is a strong degree of modeling or even franchising (McCarthy and Wolfson 1992).

Just as gatherings range from polite to protesting to violent, so do organizations. More familiar terms for each of these three include, of course, *interest or lobby group* for polite organizations, *movement organization* for protest groups, and *terrorist or guerrilla forces* for violent organizations.

Classification as one of these three requires, however, reference to more than sheer organizational action. Opposition organizations also have a general ideological orientation, one that varies as to how critical it is of the dominant ideology of the surrounding society. These ideological orientations are used by members of the organization and by their audiences to interpret the meaning of an organization's actions. Opposition groups with limited goals and mild definitions of threats can sometimes "get by with" protest actions without being defined as protest groups (see, e.g., Lofland 1985, chap. 14, on "crowd lobbying" by corporation executives and other mainstream lobbying groups).

Likewise, opposition organizations in surge with radical change goals and expansive definitions of threats may engage in no protest action yet be defined as movement or protest organizations. The case, however, is not so ambiguous when it comes to violence. Even the smallest amount of violence serves to define an organization as terrorist or the like, regardless of its ideology. (In this, I follow Useem and Kimball 1990, who sharply depart from the recent tendency to regard violence as merely another means of political action.)

The tendency of many social movement scholars to treat polite/interest group organizations as social movement organizations requires me to stress the distinction between them. The opposition to authorities pursued by *movement* organizations uses, by definition, strategies and tactics that are illegal or, at least, strain at the margins of legality, civility, or mainstream ideology. That is, mere collective opposition to authorities or their policies is not sufficient to warrant being called a movement organization (or a social movement). If it were, every interest, lobbying, and pressure group would have to be considered a movement organization or, by extension, a social movement. But organized opposition to one or more current policies is the warp and woof of civil, mainstream politics. If all such staid political activities were social movements, the concept would have no meaning. Opposition becomes *movement* opposition when it at least approaches the edges of the restrained and polite. Interest groups are careful to avoid such edges or manage their approach to them very carefully.

Just as with gatherings, organizations can be classified in terms of the same two variables of *series* and *contentiousness,* creating a hierarchy of series complexity and seriousness of contention. The nine basic types in this hierarchy are shown in the right-hand portion of figure 5.1.

The lowest level, or *primal organization surge* is, therefore, that of a single, polite organization snapping into surge. One of the more recent and closely documented instances is that of Mothers Against Drunk Driving (MADD), an entity that experienced phenomenal growth and penetration of its market in the mideighties (McCarthy and Wolfson 1992). Up one level, to the single *protest* organization, Lofland (1985, chap. 10) has, for example, analyzed the "white-hot mobilization" achieved by the Unification Church (the Moonies) for a period during the early- and midseventies. The single most famous surging protest organization in recent history was, likely, the Students for a Democratic Society, an upwelling chronicled (if not analyzed as a surge) in numerous studies (e.g., Sale 1974). Of course, violent organizations also surge (Gurr 1989).

A case such as MADD alerts us to how an organization can be a "surge isolate" or "sport" because it did not appear to have been accompanied by the surging of numerous other organizations of its kind. The Moonies, however, both were and were not surge isolates. During the period of their surge in the seventies, numerous other "new religions" (*aka* cults) were surging in the United States as well as in other countries. This burgeoning of new religions was simply a "set" because the individual religious organizations making up that surge did not appear to model themselves on one another or to draw inspiration and support from each other. While each was *aware* that there were other new religions, each did not conceive itself as part of a mutually supportive and broad "new religions movement." Members of each of these new religions could be encouraged to see other people defecting from mainstream society while, nonetheless, regarding these other groups as in fundamental error.

Similar set surges have occurred repeatedly in United States history, particularly with respect to interest groups, as noted by David Truman (1971, chap. 3), James Q. Wilson (1973, 198–211), and Arthur Stinchcombe (1965, 153–55).

At the third level of a "chain" relation, however, surges of interest groups and movement organizations may exhibit a *shared identity*. The participants see others as involved with them in pursuing related oppositional goals. In addition, among such organizations a degree of interactional "netness" is found that, in the cases of Black Power and Pentecostalism, Gerlach and Hine (1970) have called "reticulateness," that is, relations of cooperative association.

Surges have, of course, long been appreciated as key moments in the lives or natural histories of social movements, where they have been labeled, variously, the stage of "collective excitement" (Dawson and Gettys 1935, chap. 19), "popular," "mushroom" (Freeman 1975, chap. 5), "mobilization," "mass defiance" (Piven and Cloward 1979) or "insurgency" (e.g., Jenkins and Eckert 1986). The signal feature of these surges is a rapid growth in old and a burst of new protest organizations. Such a surge phase ought not, however, be confused with a movement itself as an ongoing entity which may precede or outlast the surge (Rupp and Taylor 1987). Among surging *interest groups*, such chain relations or netness appears to have obtained with regard to the large number of consumer groups founded by or associated with Ralph Nader (Griffin 1987).

An Aside on Surges of Mass Sentiments and Acts

I want to highlight uniform surges visible as gatherings and organizations, but we need also to recognize that in societies saturated with media of mass communication, dispersed persons can attend to the same objects without participating in gatherings or organizations. Media messages can generate the same sense of urgency about threats, wrongs, and opportunities. Or, at least, public opinion polls sometimes show rapid increases and declines in the proportion of citizens who are disturbed about some matter. When such surges represent only responses to a pollster on the telephone, we wonder how seriously to take these changes, except when public figures then act on the basis of the changes that are reported.

However, there is a second form of such mass behavior that ought to be taken more seriously in surge perspective. What is blandly labeled "consumer behavior" is of course a tracking of mass *compliant acts*. But, on occasion, an oppositional spirit is aroused, sometimes even taking the form of oppositional surges of mass action although these are infrequent. The boycott is, of course, a familiar mass action effort of movement entrepreneurs, even if rarely achieved on any significant scale. The rise of oppositional mass support for Ross Perot in 1992 was, as a type of political boycott, one that political entrepreneurs scurried to translate into surging chains of gatherings and organizations.

Multiform Surges: Profile Points and
Application to the U.S. Peace Surge

Multiform surges combine assemblies and organizations at various levels of "series" and contentiousness and they are "larger" and "longer" than uniform or simpler surges. Fruitfully to analyze them we must specify the particular character of their assemblies and organizations and the *beliefs* that citizens have about what they are doing. Moreover, for the sake of completeness, we need formally to incorporate additional major questions we should address in profiling surges.

With these specifications and additions, multiform surges require at least ten points of profile, which I elucidate at two levels, the abstract and the case study. I "ground" these abstractions with materials from the case of the surging of the American peace movement of the 1980s. In this profile, *peace surge* is abbreviated PS.

1. Change-Theories

Generic. The sense of urgency that is central to surges is associated with beliefs about *what kind* of urgent action one must take in order to stop a threat, realize an opportunity, and/or right a wrong. Surges, in this sense, embody *practical theories of social change*, a topic that was elaborated in chapter 1 of this volume. Participants in citizen action must, at least, assume a theory of how to act in order to achieve the social changes they desire. There are variations in *how many* such theories are used, what *particular* theories are employed, and what *proportions* of citizens hold the theories. Uniform surges are dominated by a single or very few such theories.

There are seven main theories of how to achieve social change:[5]

1. Transcenders. Promote rapid shifts of consciousness.
2. Educators. Communicate facts and reasoning.
3. Intellectuals. Produce new facts and reasoning.
4. Politicians. Undertake political electioneering and lobbying.
5. Protesters. Force issues by noncooperation and disruption.
6. Prophets. Affect deep moral regeneration.
7. Warriors. Engage in violent action.

Classified in terms of the trinity of polite, protest, and violent forms of action, the first four are all polite; numbers five and six are protest; and, the seventh is violent.

PS: Diverse and polite theories of change. Six of these seven theories — all except violence — were well represented in the U.S. peace surge. My estimates, or "guesstimates," of the relative number of people and organizations primarily committed to each of the six in the period close to or just past the peak of the surge are given in figure 1.1 of chapter 1. On the order of 90 percent of participants subscribed to one of the four versions of polite action. In comparative terms, the PS was, therefore, *diverse but decidedly polite-leaning* in its change-theories.

2. Beliefs

Generic. In analyzing multiform surges, we ask: What proportions of citizens surging think particular *kinds* of changes are needed, and *how much* societal change do they believe is required? Are such beliefs systemized into articulate and comprehensive packages, or "doctrines"? Do participants hold "liberal" aims? Are they more "radical"? or, Are they something else altogether?

Sometimes participants believe that the surge itself is a vehicle by means of which humans will catapult themselves into a new form of society. The electrifying whirl and intensity of the surge and its new forms of action and organization are thought to prefigure and model the leap that humans are then making (or are about to make) into a vastly improved, if not perfected, organization of human society. Such collective definitions — or "moments of madness" a la Zolberg (1972) — are reported to have obtained, for example, in the Paris Commune of 1848 and the surge of 1968 in that same city (Zolberg 1972). (See also, on Italy, Tarrow 1989 and Adler 1981 on the social psychology of the "momentum" that is ofttimes involved.)

PS: Liberal dominated policy beliefs. The PS was diverse but tended overall toward liberal beliefs. The kinds of threats it identified and changes it advocated were compatible with the existing order of things, and these beliefs were not "bundled" into rigid doctrinal packages. Primarily, the threat was seen as an increasing likelihood of nuclear war in the context of deteriorating East-West relations. This grave threat could be forestalled by social changes that did not require deep changes in U.S. society, especially by a "freeze" on nuclear weapons. However, the PS *did* also contain a substantial minority of radical participants who called for sweeping changes and held those beliefs as parts of comprehensive critiques of U.S. society or modern societies more generally.

3. Activities

Generic. The change-theories of a citizen surge reflect the various activities it actually fields. Four variations in these fielded activities are especially important. First, activities may primarily involve *talking*, speaking to one's own kind or to a generalized public, as opposed to *doing*, confronting one's opponents in ways they dare not or cannot avoid. Second, activities may be undertaken by everyone in the surge in a coordinated fashion, or they may be decentralized so that everyone "does her/his own thing" without much regard to what others are doing. Third, activities may be long-term campaigns, or they may be lone single-shot, short-term events (cf. Oliver 1989). Four, as I have discussed, activities may be contentious or not; they vary in degree from polite to protesting to violent.

PS: Sputtering and uncoordinated polite talking activities. The PS leaned toward talking rather than doing, dispersion rather than coordination, sputtering rather than persisting, and toward polite activity augmented by protest and with virtually no violence.[6] Statistical and other indicators of these main patterns are given in the sections that follow, and additional pertinent data appear in the other chapters of this volume.

4. Relations

Generic. Surges vary in *relations* between surge participants, authorities, and other opponents, bystanders, countersurges, the media, and the public at large. Quantitatively, how often is there interaction or contact of *any kind* between surgers and authorities? Qualitatively, what sorts of interactions transpire? Is the interaction typically equalitarian or hierarchical, amiable or abrasive, polite or protesting or violent?

PS: Scant and restrained targets and relations. As elaborated in chapters 1, 2, and 4, the PS had limited relations to its opponents, experienced little opposition from countersurges, and, except during its magic movement of peak, drew little response from the media. In the context of this relative isolation, relations were, however, qualitatively *civil or even cordial.* Advocates of the six change-theories formed themselves into clusters that tended to interact within their own clusters or with adjacent clusters, except that liberals and radicals tended to interact with like-minded participants in other clusters, a pattern described in more detail in chapter 1.

5. Organizations

Generic. Existing organizations that experience rapid spurts of growth in membership and the proliferating formation of new organizations are the backbones of multiform surges. Key comparative concerns about these organizations include detailing the particular *forms* and *substantive focus* of them and the nature and sources of their *funding.*

Among other ways, multiform surges vary in the sheer number of organizations that compose them; the "tightness" or "looseness" of relations among them; their economic bases; the degree to which they selectively interact with one another or "cluster"; and their "corporateness"—the degree to which members are "absorbed" by surge organizations.

PS: Modestly mobilized and funded equalitarian organization. Summarizing the documentation provided in chapter 4, on the "organizational profile," in these terms the PS was

• Relatively large in consisting of, perhaps, eight thousand organizations by the mid-eighties, up from about twelve hundred organizations in 1980 (Conetta 1988; Colwell 1989).

• Quite loosely organized in that there was virtually no hierarchy among any of the organizations and relatively little coordination, albeit there were many temporary and weak coalitions.

• Clustered in the sense that organizations dominated by particular change-theories and activities preferred interaction with one another.

• Volunteer and donation sustained as opposed to having significant market-generated or appropriated income, except for a brief period of significant foundation support primarily to educators and intellectuals.

• Relatively low in the level most participants were absorbed into surge organizations.

Gerlach and Hine (1970) have characterized citizen surge organizational arrangements of this sort as *segmented* and *reticulate*.[7] That is, a great many more-or-less free-standing organizations (segmentation), nevertheless, carry on some sorts of relations with each other (reticulate). I think this image is basically correct in the case of the PS but also too crude. Segmentation and reticulateness are variables rather than simply categories. So viewed, the PS was likely *more* segmented than reticulate and likely *more of both* than the two movements/surges on which Gerlach and Hine developed the concepts of segmentation and reticulateness — those of Pentecostalism and Black Power.

6. Activists

Generic. If threats are to be countered, wrongs righted, and/or opportunities seized, how and why these are to be done must be *articulated*, *organized*, and *presented* to authorities, surge participants, and other parties. Only a relatively few people in a surge engage in such work in a sustained fashion. These are, generically, *activists* — as distinguished from the mass of less-involved participants. They require analysis from two angles: the features of activists themselves as distinct from their relation as a class to the surge and the wider society.

PS: Many diverse activists of limited influence and visibility. Relative to the former angle of analysis, surges vary in the number of activists and in their diversity in class, ideology, and other characteristics. The PS seemed quite rich in the sheer number and variety of such people who took up leadership roles. Overall, as McCrea and Markle (1989) have described, activists were almost totally of the "new class"—well educated, white, middle-class persons of current or former professional employment.

Regarding the latter angle of analysis, activists in surges, nonetheless, vary in the degree to which any or many of them gain very wide followings, exercise much influence or power, and achieve recognition as spokespeople before broad publics in the society at large. In more developed surges we may expect to find multiple and articulate activists — who may even be charismatic — with wide surge followings and authority and who become widely known to the public as speaking for the mass of surge participants. In my assessment, the PS fell far short of such a state. It had a great many activists, but few if any had large surgewide followings. Further, one would require a very relaxed and sloppy conception of *charisma* to use that term in characterizing any of them. With the possible, but quite short-lived, exception of Helen Caldicott, no one came close to achieving media status as "the" or even "a" major spokesperson. Consider, in contrast, the relation of Ralph Nader to consumer interests (Griffin 1987) or the relation of Elizabeth Kubler-Ross to the death and dying surge (Lofland 1978).

Gerlach and Hine's treatment of surges, just referred to, actually contains three key structural concepts rather than only the two elements of segmentation and reticulateness. They call the third element "polycephalousness," meaning the presence of many heads rather than just one. On this score, too, I would say that polycephalousness should be treated as a variable and not simply a category. The PS was correspondingly quite polycephalous.

7. Participants

Generic. Surges have *participants* more than they have "members." Organizations and enduring small groups certainly have members, but the relation of most people to surges is too episodic and partial to be thought of as membership — even though most participants are also likely members of surge-involved organizations. Participants, along with activists, imbue the surge with differing features of *culture* and vary in the degree to which they are involved in creating *new culture*, especially as regards *motifs of emotional expression.*

PS: Liberal middle-class and counterculture participants. Every survey conducted on samples of PS participants and every observation of gatherings reported an overwhelmingly white, educated, middle- and upper-middle-class population that was almost equally divided by gender and somewhat older than the society as a whole. Public sector occupations were much more numerous than private sector ones, with the exception of an important component of the "liberal professions" of law, medicine, and teaching (which could be based in the public or private sectors). There also appeared to be disproportionate employment in various entities of the nonprofit sector (cf. McCrea and Markle 1989).

As implied by the detailed analysis of peace movement culture given in chapter 3 of this volume, the *culture* of the PS was in the main that of the larger liberal middle class from which most PS participants were drawn. These participants were critical of mainstream mass culture in the ways typical of the liberal middle class more generally and partial to such icons of that culture as the *New York Times,* the *Washington Post,* the Public Broadcasting System, National Public Radio, and C-SPAN as against their vastly more consumed mass media rivals and their cultural content. PS culture was in this sense a minority culture but still not so variant as to be beyond the pale of power.

This, however, was only the main tendency. Again exhibiting *diversity*, participant characteristics and culture varied as one moved to the right and to the left in the cluster spectrum of the PS. To the right, that is, among the transcenders, were significantly greater numbers of people in private sector occupations who embraced mainstream mass culture more fully, TV tycoon Ted Turner and the kind of television culture he promoted are the archetypical example. To the left were large numbers of people who were educated and middle class in origin but who had assumed a countercultural life-style in adult life. They espoused "green" or socialist values and advocated ecological responsibility and nonconsumerist modes of living. Located primarily among the radical protesters and the prophets, but also found as radical educators, intellectuals, and politicians, they were, perhaps, no more than one-quarter of PS participants — if that — but, because of their higher levels of involvement and activism, they had important impacts on the surge.

8. Causes

The seven classes of matters described furnish points of a more or less static profile of citizen surges, facilitating their scrutiny in comparative perspective. There are, however, at least three additional aspects that require attention in order to round out our understanding: causes, dynamics, and effects.

Generic. Often surges are causally attributed to societywide changes in which parts of the population are rising and others are falling in contests for the scarce goods of life. Such shifts are commonly viewed as effects of economic or military changes in the world system.[8] Although major historical trends and events obviously are relevant to many surges, at least some are also explicable in terms of smaller and more proximate changes.

Some surges do not seem to have any proximate factors to which they are responding. Their occurrence is, therefore, rather mysterious, and we must perforce invoke underlying and general background factors to account for them. For example, in the United States in 1969-1970 there was a vivid swell of alarm over environmental deterioration, but no compellingly clear proximate factor or factors to which this was a response has been identified. And, as a second example, there was a dramatic surge of new religions or cults in the early-seventies in the United States, again without any clear situational spur. In the absence of near-at-hand stimulants, analysts reasonably theorize on the evolving nature of American society itself.

PS: Proximate causes. Not all surges are so enigmatically responsive to the vague churnings and trends of modern life. Instead, their sources are crystal clear and vividly proximate. Such has been the case among many farmer-composed surges in responding to market forces (e.g., Schwartz 1976), and such was clearly the case for the onset of the peace surge of the eighties. Ronald Reagan's assumption of the U.S. presidency in 1981 began a new era of belligerency in American foreign and military policy. Such was the militancy and toughness that only the most obtuse of citizens could fail to notice that America had taken a startling warlike turn. In this context of provocation, the puzzle would be the *absence* of a powerful surge to counter such a change rather than the fact that one welled up.

I am not saying that background factors are irrelevant to understanding the PS. There were many such factors facilitating play, such as the decline of the political fortune of the "new class" sector (McCrea and Markle 1989) and of liberalism in general and a growing conflict between the eastern and western segments of the U.S. power elite. Still, I say that no PS of the sort we saw in the 1980s would have occurred if Ronald Reagan and his entourage had not conducted foreign and military policy in the way they did. Once the Reaganites were set on their path, background conditions affected the scale, content, and longevity of the surge, but they did not provide the occasion for it. Without Ronald Reagan and his gaggle (and had not the Soviet Union itself gone out of existence), Randall Forsberg might still be on the road speaking to tiny peace groups about something obscure called a freeze.

9. Dynamics.

Generic. The longer a surge lasts and the more numerous and diverse the forms of it (items 1–7 on the list given), the more complex are the *dynamics* of its rise and fall. By "complex" I mean, in particular, the curves of the rising and falling of the varying parts of the surge. The component parts of the surge do not necessarily rise and fall at the same rate or peak at exactly the same time (cf. Gambrell 1980).

Multiform surges vary in terms of their *relative* composition of gatherings and organizations and in the spacing of events through time. Thus, a few multiform surges consist of a rapid-paced sequence of assemblies, such as unbroken day-after-day protest marches over weeks or months. The marker events of other multiform surges consist more of organizational acts that occur at widely spaced intervals. The more rapid paced and assembly oriented the multiform surge, the more seriously and ominously elites and publics are likely to define it (cf. McAdam 1983 on the "pace of insurgency").

PS: Multicurved and spaced dynamics. The generic dynamic of the eighties peace surge was a rapid, urgent upsurge of concern and action on matters that reached a peak and then declined. At its peak in 1982–1983, on the order of ten million Americans were involved at more than a trivial level. Using a looser conception of involvement, the level was vastly higher. Polls in the period reported, for example, that over 70 percent of Americans supported a freeze — an *idea* that had been virtually unknown, much less accepted, only three or so years earlier (Milburn, Watanaba, and Kramer 1986). In 1982, "sixty percent of those who had a chance to vote on the Freeze (about 30% of the electorate), approved it" (McCrea and Markle 1989, 112). But, already by the 1984 elections, Freeze and related matters were no longer salient. This "mile wide and an inch deep" participation dwindled with some rapidity to, perhaps, a half-million people continuing some at least modest level of involvement by decade's end.

Very similar curves obtained for several other basic indicators that traced the surge. A wide variety of these are reported in chapter 7, including rapid increases in the number of peace organizations, amounts of foundation funding, number of nuclear-free zones, and numbers of educational and protest gatherings.

Although an overarching curve of peak and decline can be traced, when looked at more closely, we also see constituent curves that are not rising and falling at precisely the same pace. Thus, transcender, educator, and politician types of assemblies, organizations, and participants rose rapidly in the early phases of the overall surge. When these forms of action started to decline, protester and prophet activities were still rising, but then, too, began to decline as shown in figure 5.2, which shows decade trends in the numbers of arrests, actions, and sites.

Viewed against the theoretical possibility of an extremely rapid rise of an enormous number of gatherings and organizations of several types that are tightly spaced in time (such as seen in the several surges of tactics involved in the civil rights movement and depicted in McAdam 1983), the PS was rather slow and polite with only a modest amount of protest. Such a mild dynamic was likely related, further, to the rather mild reactions it drew from elites and bystanding publics who did not define the peace surge as ominous.

10. Effects

Generic. A master hypothesis about surges is that the larger, more rapid, prolonged, varied, and violent the surge, the greater the effects of all sorts, especially elite repression or capitulation and reform (cf. Piven and Cloward 1979; Jenkins and Brents 1989). As the magnitude increases,

Figure 5.2
Nuclear Resistance Arrests, Actions, Sites:
United States and Canada, 1983-1991

Year	Arrests	Actions	Sites
1983	5,300	140	60
1984	3,010	160	85
1985	3,300	170	120
1986	3,200	165	75
1987	5,300	180	70
1988	4,470	160	65
1989	5,530	150	75
1990	3,000	85	41
1991	2,250	65	32

Source: Cohen-Joppa 1992, 2.

so does the likelihood and scale of countersurges. Yet, at the same time, many other citizens withdraw from the fray (Brinton 1965, chap. 6, esp. 160–61). Conversely, the "smaller" the surge, the less the effects on elites, citizens, and social organizations.

PS: Clear institutional and unclear policy effects. People who have dedicated significant time, energy, and money to something commonly believe that their effort "made a difference," that their dedication was "worth the effort." Such is the estimate one ordinarily encounters among peace surge veterans. However, what can we say as social scientists? Tentative assessments can be ventured at two levels: the residue of institutions created by the surge and direct effects on U.S. foreign and military policy. Large numbers of organizations and practices that were quite consciously and conspicuously part of the PS *began* in the eighties and persisted into the nineties, albeit often in scaled-down form.

We are on less certain ground in attributing to the PS changes in U.S. foreign and military policy, which was influenced by many factors. Ronald Reagan at its helm, U.S. policy *did* become more conciliatory in the mid- and late-eighties. Not least among the causal factors was the changed behavior of the Soviet Union and nations aligned with it. Indeed, changes in the Soviet Union must surely have been vastly more significant than the impact of a PS that was well past its peak in the late-eighties. Further, the Eastern European revolutionary "civil" surges of late-1989 changed the international order and the U.S. role in it in such fundamental ways that assessment of PS effects have become ever more problematic. Many of the previously marginal peace surge proposals to reduce the military unexpectedly became mainstream topics of policy. In this sense, the peace surge won but for reasons that, perhaps, had less to do with its own actions than with what used to be called the "Soviet Bloc." The *framework* changed so radically that one could not estimate the effects of peace surge action within it. The old game abruptly ended, and a new and *different* game began. The world is likely better off because of that sea-change in international affairs, but it certainly rendered social scientific assessment of longer-term effects of the PS more difficult.

Forms and Scales of Multiform Surges

The foregoing depiction of the generic components of multiform surges and their grounding in the United States peace surge provides a base on which to explore multiform surges more generally.

Old Terms with New Meanings

There is a vast literature of case studies written largely by historians and mostly ignored by analytic social scientists which describes multiform surges involving armed force as *insurgencies, insurrections, risings,* or *uprisings, mutinies, revolts, rebellions,* or *seditions.* Mass oppositional surges of a milder cast use gentler labels, such as *dissent, protest, mass defiance,* or — reappearing in tempered guise — *insurgency.* [9]

Typically, the authors fail to see that the case at which they are looking and the category they apply to it might be conceived as part of a larger class within which that category is a subtype. The thousands of case study books and articles in which these labels are applied tells us that there is no shortage of studies of multi-, violent, oppositional surges. What is lacking is merely the conscious application of relevant theory to the cases.

Megasurges

The large differences in scale observed among uniform and multiform surges calls our attention not simply to the lowest end — the "primal surge" so adroitly installed in the literature by Gamson, Fireman, and Rytina (1982) and discussed previously — but also to the highest end. On rare occasions, societies appear to undergo successions of multiform surges that amount to something like *megasurges.* The succession of revolutions that swept across Europe in 1848 was perhaps the premier nineteenth-century instance of this kind of complex event (Stearns 1974). Over the sixties in the United States, there were, of course, several riot, interest group, and movement surges that composted into multiform surges, interesting surge-curves on which have been assembled by Jenkins (1987) and Gambrell (1980). Conceiving all humans on the planet as some manner of global society, worldwide student and other oppositional activities in 1968 might be seen as a type of *global surge* (Katsiafricas 1987). Similarly, the surges in China and Eastern Europe in late-1989 verged on global surges.

The most ambitious recent effort to chart forms in this upper range is that of Sidney Tarrow (1989), who has developed a complex cast of useful concepts organized around the ideas of "mobilization waves," or "cycles of protest." Four cases to which he has paid particular attention communicate the scale of surge he addresses: England, circa 1828–1832; France, circa 1934–1936; Italy circa 1965–1975; Poland, circa 1980.

Violent Multiform Surges and the Civil Surge

Multiform surges differ dramatically in contentiousness. In many of them, participants publicly advocate violence to achieve social change. There may be numerous violent assemblies; organizations dedicated to violence may form and act; and there are mass, individual acts of violence. Of course, even in the most violent of multiform surges most events are still at the levels of polite and protest forms of gathering and organization. Still, even a small amount of violence imparts a distinctive character to a multiform surge (see, e.g., Murray 1955 on the U.S. red scare of 1919–1920).

Multiform surges commonly, in fact, involve at least some violence or, at the very minimum, advocacy of violence. By definition, these surges lack central control and "anyone" can join in the "act," increasing the likelihood of violence-prone participants. Statistically, violence in espousal (and perhaps deed) is normal in multiform surges although scholars such as Gene Sharp (1973) have compiled many counterexamples.

I, therefore, view multiform surges that are low in contentiousness as anomalies — so anomalous that some scholars have even singled them out as a distinctive class of phenomena that requires its own special study.[10] This is the perspective I bring to the case of the U.S. peace surge. Taken as an overall pattern — as an enormous gestalt of features — it was quite remarkably "gentle" or "civil."[11] Although it involved, at its peak, on the order of ten million people at some reasonable degree of mobilization and involvement, it was strikingly restrained, amiable, and even affable. It was in some ways even a reticent or reluctant surge (cf. Walton 1984). It was a pattern marked by

- Diversity of change theories, policy beliefs, and activities that were acted on in a predominantly polite fashion with only a small amount of mild protest and practically no violence.
  - Insularity of relations and limited public visibility of activists.
  - Little coordination or persistence of activities.
  - Equalitarian organization.
  - Relatively narrow class base and culture.
  - Proximate and clear causes.
  - Indefinite effects on policy but clear institutional residues.

The American peace surge of the eighties might be the only instance of its type — the civil surge — although recent surges in other societies suggest otherwise. In any event, this is a pattern that now begins to be available to us as a case for comparison with other surges.

Confusing Surges with Intersecting Phenomena

I have formulated the idea of the citizen surge in response to a number of confusions in the literature on social movements and collective behavior/action. I propose the concept in the hope that it will help us escape several recent intellectual cul-de-sacs into which movement studies have driven in recent years. There are at least five of these conundrums that a surge perspective clarifies.

Confusing Surges with Interest Groups and Movement Organizations

Some analysts have confused surges with interest groups and movement organizations. Thus, what one might term the "McCarthy-Schwartz brouhaha" centers on John McCarthy (McCarthy and Wolfson 1992) wanting to conceive Mothers Against Drunk Driving (MADD) as a consensus movement, while others (Schwartz and Shuva 1992) want to deny MADD standing as any kind of movement at all or at least to downgrade consensus movements to an inferior phenomenon scarcely deserving attention. The simple solution is to acknowledge that while MADD is not a movement organization, it *does* present a genuine surge pattern. Even though it is not a *movement/protest* pattern, it *is*, nonetheless, a pattern of interest to students of surges — of collective behavior and action. Therefore, once we bring the surge into focus as a key object of attention, we need no longer try to read the work of scholars in or out of the movement studies arena on the question of whether or not they are studying interest groups versus movement organizations.

Confusing Surges with Movement Origins and Mobilization

In usual (and especially resource mobilization) treatments of the origins or mobilization of social movements, the quite specific and special period of surge is treated as synonymous with such origins or mobilization. This conflation is patently narrow and, therefore, quite misleading as an angle from which to attempt understanding of either origins or mobilization.

With respect to origins, we fortunately now have work such as that of Rupp and Taylor (1987) on the American women's rights movement, which documents how it existed in quite solid and specific forms prior to its 1960s–1970s surge. Mobilization is a phenomenon of *all stages* of a movement, not merely of a surge period. Indeed, mobilization during, especially, the upsweep stage of the surge is likely quite different than other periods. Pictures of mobilization based only or primarily on studies of upsweep phases of surges are therefore likely to be misleading etchings. Said differently, mobilization is commonly considered a synonym for surge mobilization and it ought not be. Surges involve, more accurately, a special form of rapid mobilization, one that features a sense of urgency in the upsweep phase.

Confusing Units That Are Surging

Surge activists and participants tend to overclaim and to exaggerate the extent and breadth of the surging that is afoot, for, among other reasons, the possibilities of self-fulfilling prophecies. Thus, members of the Unification Church — a single movement organization — strove during their seventies surge to present themselves to the world as a social movement surge and proliferated dozens of "front" organizations intended to give the impression of snowballing *multiple* movement organizations that constituted a "true" movement. The reality, however, was a single, rather small movement organization (in a surge state, however) that was simulating rather than exhibiting movement surge (Lofland 1985, chap. 10). Conversely and ironically, alarmed opponents of a single surging movement organization that is posing as a surging movement are likely to take such claims at face value and begin to act as though the threatening movement organization were, in fact, a movement. (Recall the oft-reported remark that J. Edgar Hoover was the most credulous consumer of the CP-USA's propaganda.)

At a broader level, members of surging interest groups and movement organizations who are part of *multiform surges* have an easily understood interest in construing the multiform surge as a manifestation of *their* particular interest group or movement organization. Thus, long-time peace movement intellectuals with historical knowledge and vision routinely construed the peace surge of the eighties as a new wave of *the* peace movement and some reckoned it as the fourth such wave (e.g., Boulding 1990). This is easily confused, however, for the historic peace movement itself was also surging to some modest degree as part of the larger multiform surge that was also much more vigorous. It is tempting and easy in the euphoria of multiform surge to code a wide variety of undertakings as "ours" even though more reflective accountings counsel caution and modesty.

To read a surge as more movement than is true is also to impute more capacity for unified collective action than is the reality and, therefore, to overestimate the possibilities for leaders to shape the course of a surge. We see this error of overestimation clearly in the work of Earl Molander and Roger Molander (1990) who construe the eighties peace surge as a movement that had leaders who failed correctly to strategize the movement through an "educational" phase before undertaking a "political phase" and, therefore, "failed." Such conceptions and fault-finding *might* have merit when applied to uniform surges of chained interest groups or movement organizations — since these are more homogeneous, smaller, and have more widely known and respected spokespeople — but are singularly misplaced when applied to multiform surges, which are fractionalized and even atomized far beyond the possibility of overall, guiding direction.

Confusing Surges with Irrationality

Studies of social movements and collective behavior and action over the last two decades have largely been framed as critiques of the alleged defects of something they term the *collective behavior* approach to social movements. This approach has been criticized for discrediting social movements by imputing irrational motives, perceptions, and actions to their participants thereby undercutting the substantive claims made by movement actors. I think this critique is wildly overgeneralized and that it has been applied too broadly to work labeled as collective behaviorist, but I must acknowledge its validity for at least a few works, most notably those of Smelser (1963).

The result of the critique, however, has been to throw the baby out with the bath. If we look at the specific social events that have attracted the attention of collective behaviorists — as distinct from how they interpret those events — we find that they have been scrutinizing instances of rapid changes of definitions of situations marked by a sense of urgency and the need for new forms of action combined with actual new action. These events, that is, commonly exhibit the surge pattern I have been discussing, be they—to use Smelser's terms—panics, crazes, hostile outbursts, or norm- and value-oriented movements.

Certainly, we can fault irrationalist characterizations of surges as in Smelser's statement that "collective behavior displays . . . crudeness, excess, and eccentricity . . . [and] is the action of the impatient. It contrasts with the processes of social readjustment that do not short-circuit the journey from generalized belief to specific situations."[12]

Possibly, the newer students of surge phenomena have so closely identified the subject matter with Smelser's kind of characterization that they have thought it impossible to examine surges except as irrational. A few newer students have even concluded that, because irrationalist depictions were wrong, there are no such things as surges! Most newer students are not this extreme, but their acceptance of the need to reject irrationalist depictions appears, nonetheless, to have blinded them to surges per se.

Confusing Surges with Civil Violence

Because collective or civil violence is so dramatic and threatening, scholars who study it easily perceive that a surge phenomenon is often involved. Indeed, James Rule concludes his review of literature on the subject with the suggestion that what I am calling surges—and that he calls "rapid 'change of state'"—is *the* "one topic [that] seems to offer particular promise for further inquiry" (1988, 271). His sketch of possible lines of study is studded with surge-relevant terms, including "chain reactions," "explosions of consciousness," "intense outbreaks," "abrupt upsurge," and "quick shifts in action and belief" (Rule 1988, 271-74).

However promising such insights and suggestions may be, they are, unfortunately, ghettoized. In Rule's case, they are ghettoized in the inner city of *civil violence*—"active . . . destruction of persons or property by people acting together" (1988, 10, 11). The implicit suggestion is that surges are mostly, if not entirely, about civil violence and that they should be studied mostly, if not entirely, in that context. The broader view I have put forth here recognizes surges involving civil violence as instances of a more inclusive category.

Concluding and Beginning

I hope that the concept of the citizen surge helps two important lines of analyzing social movements and collective action/behavior. One, I have tried to reassert, as a domain of study, rapid but brief episodes of collective action, varying from narrow microsocial events to wide macrosocial episodes. Such an analytic domain was well identified in earlier work (e.g., Turner and Killian 1957), but, under the sway of resource mobilization and collective action thinking, has faded from recognition in recent decades. Two, I hope that I have isolated the citizen surge as a phenomenon in its own right that, nonetheless, cross-cuts and integrally intersects with the other units I have discussed but is not the same as any of them. If I am correct, recent debates arising from the conflations I have enumerated can be ended.

I have concentrated on depicting the phenomenon of surges rather than explaining their occurrence or tracing their effects. These are, nonetheless, signal matters. High on the continuing agenda, in particular, is the question of why opposition assumes the form of a surge rather than of a much more slowly rising curve or a "flat" and continuous effort. Any answer to this question will likely require analysis of why all social organizations are prone to deadlocked stalemates of entrenched self-interest. The inability to act with effectiveness both creates crisis and the need for crisis — the citizen surge.

Notes

1. This chapter is revised, with a change of editorial voice, from publication as Lofland and Johnson 1991.

2. For simplicity's sake, here and after I often drop the term *citizen* modifying surge.

3. For a review, see Lofland (1985, 1-25). The term *contentiousness* is employed in a related way by Charles Tilly (e.g., 1986).

4. Case descriptions of *mini surges* may be found in Lofland (1985, chaps. 14, 15). Anyone who follows small-city politics and city council scenes is well aware that such mini-surges are the warp and woof of oppositional citizen action, or at least they are in Davis, California, where watching cable-cast proceedings of the city council as it copes with aggrieved citizen groups is a form of indigenous entertainment referred to locally as "the Wednesday night follies" (the evening of council meetings).

5. The first six of these seven are discussed in chap. 1, this volume.

6. The term *virtually* means: one, that there were *no* reports of violence in the sense of intentional bodily injury inflicted by any surge participant directly on another human; two, that a tiny minority infrequently and in a manner not regarded by most surgers as nonviolent engaged in property destruction (Sturgeon 1987); and, three, that in the name of religious nonviolence, a small minority of prophetic peace Christians ritualistically damaged nuclear weapons and ancillary equipment (Laffin 1987; Laffin and Montgomery 1987). The question of violence is discussed further in chap. 1 in the section on "Change Theories of the American Peace Movement."

7. Gerlach and Hine apply their analysis to social movements rather than to surges. They are, however, addressing the surge phase of the social movements they discuss, and their analysis is, therefore, as much of surges as of movements in a stable or establishment mode.

8. See, for example, Skocpol 1979; Tilly 1986; Walton 1984.

9. The number of existing but unheralded accounts of fairly large multiform surges can be gauged by means of title-word searches of books in library computer databases. Thus, an early-1990 search of the University of California's MELVYL, a systemwide listing of almost ten million books and other publications, generated these totals for the following surge-relevant terms/title-words of books: defiance — 88; dissenter — 475; dissent — 1,223; insurgency — 120; insurrection — 531; mutiny — 425; protest — 6,111; rebel — 4,370; rebellion — 2,060; revolution — 16,789; revolt — 1,661; rising — 919; sedition — 111; uprising — 244. For comparative purposes, consider the results of title-word searches for books with these words: collective action — 76; collective behavior — 37; social movements — 442; resource mobilization — 30 (only 2 of that 30 have anything to do with social movements, however).

10. The single most dedicated student of nonviolent surges — multi or otherwise — has been Gene Sharp, who has organized a complex research agenda and published prolifically on many aspects of them. See Albert Einstein Institution 1990.

11. I am indebted to Metta Spencer for pointing up the special merit of the term *civil* because of its relation to the idea of "civil society" as it is evolving in Eastern Europe. For a considered use of the idea of "gentle" as applied to social organization, see Boulding (1977, chap. 10, "The Coming of the Gentle Society").

12. Smelser (1962, 72–73). See also Rose 1982 on "outbursts.

6

Surge Stages
*Focusing, Soaring, Faltering,
Slumping, Percolating*

The most conspicuous feature of citizen action in general and social movements in particular is their soar and slump dynamic—the flashing rapidity of their onset and meteoric rise followed by an almost equally quick decline over a period of only a few years.[1] In the prototypic case, there is an initial period in which a particular topic is of little overt citizen concern. Then, suddenly, that topic is broadly believed to be of considerable or even momentous import, requiring urgent preventive or remedial change. Citizen actions to achieve such change are launched, rise quickly to a crescendo, and recede as swiftly from the center of public attention, sometimes having achieved the envisioned social changes and sometimes not. The rapidity with which such surges come and go have prompted some analysts to view them as spastic, mercuric, rippling twitches in the body politic.

To understand the soars and slumps of such citizen surges, we must, first, provide a precise elaboration of exactly what is meant by "soars and slumps," second, delineate their basic variations and forms, and, third, specify the phases and dynamics of their internal development and decline. I have addressed the first two of these in chapter 5, and I want here to take up the third, that of their phases and dynamics.

I propose to do this by first reviewing previous efforts to discern stages or phases of their operation and to draw pertinent concepts from those efforts. I want, then, to use that framework to dissect a specific case, that of the soar and slump of citizen actions opposing the East-West foreign and military policies of the United States government in the early- and mid-1980s.

Perspectives on the Process Dynamics of Surges

The generic phenomenon I am identifying as citizen surges featuring soars and slumps cross-cuts several substantive specializations in social science, most specifically, those of collective behavior, collective action, social movements, and the sociology of social problems. In all of these, scholars have noted the lack of attention to the internal processes of the major forms of citizen action found in those domains. For example, in a wide-ranging review of the literature on social movements, McAdam, McCarthy, and Zald distinguish between movement "emergence" and "development" and comment that scholars "have theorized more and amassed more empirical evidence concerning the early stage of a social movement. By comparison, we know . . . little about the dynamics of collective action over time. Specifically, we see a need for the creation of more systematic theoretical frameworks for studying movements over time" (McAdam, McCarthy, Zald 1988, 728–29). Indeed, a sociology of this neglect might be in order.[2]

As McAdam, McCarthy, and Zald show in their review, our understanding of preconditions or facilitants of emergence is especially impressive with respect to delineating *social organizational* arrangements that prefigure a surge of citizen activism and serve as vehicles of collective action. In several formulations, such vehicles have been referred to as *co-optable networks*,[3] *catness*,[4] and *movement halfway houses*,[5] among other specifications.[6]

As everyone recognizes, however, identifying such conditions of emergence still leaves us only with a "black box" labeled the citizen surge. The surge itself remains a mystery because it is treated as a fixed entity only the antecedents of which need to be specified. The neglect of process may, indeed, inadvertently incline us to view surges as ejaculations rather than as the tentative, fragile, and continuous constructions they more likely are. A processual, dynamic, or developmental view, in contrast, treats every increment of a surge as problematic, as a phase that might or might not form a "higher" step in an enlarging process. In switching to a process view, we look for facilitating and inhibiting social organizational, psychic, and other factors that operate *all along the way*. We shift from implying preconditions or precipitants of a process that unfolds by an interior dynamic that simply consumes resources and employs vehicles it had at the outset.

Although processual dynamics have not often been studied, there is, nonetheless, a useful literature that commands our attention. Two rather different conceptions of them have already emerged. Turner and Killian (1987, 253–55) have labeled these the typical *life history* and the fragile and problematic *interactive spiral*. As a class, life-history formulations posit a series of stages through which a citizen surge passes. These seem analogous to the life histories of living organisms, which are thought to exhibit a regularized set of stages of birth, growth, decline, and death. Such models have been formulated in at least three areas of the study of citizen surges. First and with regard to social movements, a formulation of quite amazing durability is that of Dawson and Gettys, first published in 1935, which was adopted by Blumer in the forties and fifties and repeated in the three editions of Turner and Killian's *Collective Behavior.*[7] It distinguishes the social unrest, popular excitement, formalization, and institutionalization stages of social movements. More recently, Armand Mauss (1975, 61–68) has offered the stages of incipience, coalescence, institutionalization, fragmentation, and decline.[8]

Second, students of citizen surges conceived as social problems have pondered the possibility of "natural histories." Fuller and Myers (1941) pioneered the idea and were criticized for doing so by Lemert (1951), who argued there was no typical life history. Blumer (1971) took up the task again in the seventies, suggesting the stages of emergence, legitimation, mobilization, formation of an official plan, and implementation of an official plan. And, Spector and Kitsuse (1977) propounded a competing four-stage view stressing the interaction of opposing claims makers. Most recently, case studies featuring phase depictions of social problems have been a flourishing cottage industry in the pages of the journal *Social Problems* and in such series as Holstein and Miller's (1989) *Perspectives on Social Problems.*[9]

Third, a few students have offered case studies of particular movements or movement organizations that have implications for life-history formulations, even if these were not fully realized by their analyses. Here we need to point in particular to Jo Freeman's treatment of the "mushroom effect" in the context of women's liberation.[10]

All these versions of surge life history need, as a set, to be contrasted with at least the logical possibility of the *interactive spiral* as termed by Turner and Killian.[11] Rather than viewed as a typical set of stages, the surge is seen as a "series of episodes" between and among which there are extremely problematic relations that can at any juncture result in escalation or deescalation. Each moment and its outcome is presumed to be radically problematic and contextually dependent. Turner and Killian offer

Max Heirich's (1971) analysis of citizen surging at the University of California, Berkeley, in 1964–1965 as among the few thorough applications of an interactive spiral view, and I would agree with their assessment. In this imagery, "instead of one grand analysis" of a surge, there is "a series of mini-analyses." "Rather than being predictable on the basis of a set of generalized stages, the course of a" citizen surge can "only be predicted from episode to episode." In situation after situation, surges are always changing and in the process of "establishing renewed ground for . . . development" (Turner and Killian 1987, 255).

While I am building primarily on research treating the trajectories of collective behavior events, social movements, and social problems, as just reviewed, my approach is additionally informed by several other traditions of research and theory. These include analyses of conflict as a generic in terms of escalation and deescalation,[12] depictions of the public arena and the dynamics of "agenda setting,"[13] and studies of micromobilization.[14]

My effort conjoins elements of all these traditions. Because each of them has tended to be carried on in relative isolation from the others, I hope here to draw a larger picture in which key parts of each appear prominently.

Dissecting the Surge Process

Let us press forward, then, with a processual dynamics analysis of citizen surges attuned to both interactive spiral imagery and a more flexible conception of life history. A surge is a process of interaction that is spiraling either "up" or "down" (or simply cycling in a stable pattern). There are likely to be several of these spirals linked in something like life-history fashion. In so moving, I think we must specify *who* is interacting, at *what levels* and forms of involvement, and over *what* sorts of issues.

Who Is Interacting: Major Actors and
Their Levels of Mobilization

Participants in and parties to surges are not an undifferentiated lot. Instead, surge spirals feature a rather complex but finite cast of characters. Let me discuss the nine main parties, with the understanding that all nine do *not* appear in every spiral of a surge (a central fact affecting spiraling) and that all need not be seen in all surges.[15]

In addition, as I introduce each of these "actors," I describe what it means for them to be "in surge." We can superficially characterize spiraling upsweeps and downsweeps in surges, but careful analysis requires a precise rendering of how it is we can know that a surge at a given time is higher or lower than at any time before or after it. That is, we require measurements that make assessments of "higher" and "lower" beyond simply impressionistic imputations. Devising a precise scale of surge size is a major task, and with the imperfect data available, I here only suggest items that might be used for such a scale. Determining the exact weights to give various items and how to combine them must be set aside as a separate task. Nonetheless, we can conceive, in ideal typical fashion, the kinds of measures for which we can look.

1. Primary in surges are *activists*, that class of persons who most frequently organize collective action and publicly speak and write on behalf of the surge. In measurement terms, we see surge-relevant activists beginning to involve themselves in the surge; entry of new activists into the surge arena — the coming of "new faces"; a rapid increase in the latter's numbers spread over wide geographical areas; and activists advocating the *urgency* of citizen action on behalf of the surge *and* the *urgency* of social changes that are proposed.

2. As is well articulated by the resource mobilizationists, there are recruitable pools of surge *predisposed organizations* with their leaders and members. This is, roughly, the surge's "constituency." Salient measures of this include rapid membership and contribution growth in already existing surge-relevant organizations and the almost simultaneous founding of many new surge organizations of various kinds (e.g., in the peace surge instance: transcender, educator, intellectual, political, protest, and prophetic).

3. Perhaps limited to instances of the kind I consider later, there is a class of *funders* who at propitious times have the financial means to provide predisposed organizations with significant underwriting. From a grassroots perspective, it will seem odd to single out a class of monied entities who play a critical role. However, though there may be widespread grassroots mobilization that is *a* source of funding, in some surges, specialized "big money" suppliers can also play a quite central role. To measure such funding, we look for conspicuous shifting in patterns of foundation funding toward the surge and wealthy individuals beginning to make large contributions to support surge events, publications, and other action.

4. Recent events *may* have created a stratum of *dissident elites*, people who previously participated at high levels of state policymaking but who have been "exiled" by political changes. Such persons are experts with portfolio sans ascendancy. As a class, some of them shade off into activists, but they are, nonetheless, distinguishable. In measuring that constituency, we attend to increases in the number of surge-supportive books and ar-

ticles published by dissident elites and rapid increases in their public appearances and their participation in films and videos.

5. Beyond activist leaders and members of predisposed organizations, philanthropic funders and dissident elites, there are — for many issues in American society — perhaps a million or more surge *disposed citizens.* These are people who can be coaxed into giving money for surge events and at least occasionally participating in them. Turner and Killian term these supporters *adherents.* Relevant measures of their activity include increases in contributions to surge organizations and names on membership rosters of surge organizations.

6. There is the great mass of *bystander citizens* who pay little attention to the surge except, perhaps, at its peak, where they are perforce involved by virtue of media coverage and telephone polling. One measure of their acting in the surge is public opinion polls showing large increases in the proportion of citizens who claim to be aware of the surge topic and who think it is one of the most important problems facing the country.

7. There are the *media* who are truly central figures in modern surge sagas and whose massive and rapid entrance itself creates a new interactive spiral. For measurement, we see an upsweep in coverage given the surge topic.

8. There are the targets of surge action, the policy-spawning and supporting *elites* themselves and their subordinates, the people pursuing policies to which the surgers object. Measures of their involvement include rapid increase in the number of negative statements elites issue on the surge; deployment of special personnel to speak against it, recruitment of countersurgers, and start-up of clandestine operations to spy on and disrupt surge activities.

9. Allied with but not necessarily a part of the elites are *countersurgers* who mobilize expressly to overcome the threatening action of the initial surgers. Measurements of countersurge activity include increases in published expressions of counterurgency to combat the surge, an upsweep in countersurge events, and activation of major countersurge actors.

What Is Interacting: Conditions and Events

From the point of view of surgers, the field of action is divided into the situation being confronted at any given time and the actions that might be undertaken with regard to that situation. More broadly, using common sense and Turner and Killian's model, this is a division between *conditions* of action and *events* created by surger action or by other parties.

By "conditions" I mean objective, standing states of social organization of all kinds and shared definitions of what is "real," timely, and feasible. Other labels for such conditions that seem not quite accurate include "context" and "situation."

By "events" I mean immediately recent, in-process, and serious-in-preparation courses of action mounted by surgers or other parties and defined by one or both as in-the-present objects of action. They are matters "around which," about which, or toward which, proximate action "must" be taken.

Conditions and events are not fixed categories. Time rushes on and today's events become tomorrow's conditions — or soon thereafter.

Surges are composed of several kinds of events and conditions that require some basic sorting, in terms of importance, effect, and sources.

Importance: Focusing or minor. Events (and, perhaps, conditions also) differ in terms of how widely they are defined as being of large or small importance and in terms of the length of time they serve as objects of concerted action. Those few events that are defined and acted on over relatively long periods of time (months or, perhaps, a year) serve as *focusing events.* They are relatively few compared to many *minor* events that serve to keep the surge afloat but do not provide signal markers around which to organize the action of large numbers of people.

Effect: Facilitating or inhibitive. Focusing events — and some conditions — differ in whether they facilitate or inhibit escalation or deescalation in a spiral period. There are, thus, four major kinds of focusing events or conditions: escalation facilitators, escalation inhibitors, deescalation facilitators, and deescalation inhibitors.

Focusing events that facilitate escalation are central to the first stages of surges. They are perceived as providing the possibility of great progress and *success* in the surge quest, and they are imbued with *hope.* An escalating interactive spiral is characterized by a propitiously spaced and paced sequence of such focusing events. Strengthening the perception of *feasibility* and *timeliness* characterizing such multiple, focusing and escalating events is a fundamental dynamic of surge expansion (Turner and Killian 1987, 241–42, 245–48). The auspicious occurrence and spacing of such hopeful events then become *iconic conditions* that strengthen perception of feasibility and timeliness. In the case I will discuss — the peace surge of the early-eighties — examples of major focusing-escalating events include winning a nuclear Freeze referendum in November 1980, the March 1982 introduction of Freeze legislation in the U.S. Congress, the June 1982 march and rally of three-quarters of a million people in New York City, and winning Freeze referenda across the U.S. in November 1982. Each was a key turn in the spiral that ratcheted the surge to a higher level that, also — ironically — made life more difficult for the movement. The higher the spiral, the harder to produce *new* focusing events for a further spiraling.

Conversely, an equally critical dynamic of surge *deescalation*, contraction, or "slump," is the lack of hope-inducing events — events imbued with feasibility and timeliness. More important, some events inhibit or interfere with an escalation process. Such events in the eighties peace surge included Reagan's Star Wars speech of March 1983 and the very poor showing of peace candidates and issues in the presidential election of November 1984, an event that sent the surge into pronounced decline.

Sources: Proponents, opponents, and others. Focusing events with facilitative or inhibitive effects on escalation or deescalation vary in terms of who is producing them — surge proponents, its opponents, or some other actor or circumstance. This is an obvious but not trivial observation because the central contest of a surge is about who can produce the most effective focusing events of which of the four major types. Obviously, proponents are in the escalating-focusing-event business, while opponents are otherwise disposed. What becomes more interesting, however, is that each group can and often does produce events that counter its own goals. That is, there is maneuvering over events in terms of seizing, retaining, or recapturing the initiative or control — if, indeed, any party can do so.

Consideration of the sources of events prompts us to look carefully at the ironic possibility that *opponents* can be *a* if not *the* major source of facilitating/escalating events — especially in the first and second spiral stages of surges. Let us call this class of happening *goading events*, these being episodes that produce fear and anxiety sufficient to stimulate focusing, surger events. All surges are likely built as much on a rich supply of opponent produced goading events as on events produced by early-surgers. Certainly, the eighties peace surge was amply helped or escalated in its focusing and soaring stages by a great many Reagan administration pronouncements and policy acts.

Surges, by definition, have a variety of opponents, but, because of the obscurity of the initial focusing phase and the lightning ascent of the soaring stage, these opponents are likely caught unaware, unprepared, and unresponsive. This, of course, is itself a facilitating factor in the vigor of both the focusing and soaring stages. But opponents soon begin to act and to produce events they hope will cause the surge to falter and slump. A classic ploy is, of course, the *discrediting event*, in which efforts are made to call into doubt the wisdom of the surge proposals or the moral character of its proponents. The former tactic sends one's countersurge agents on tours of talk shows and the like. The latter offers up versions of redbaiting and accusations of personal, often sexual, misconduct. More subtle and, perhaps, more effective are *reframing events*, in which the opposition stresses agreement with the goals and philosophy of the surgers but adroitly substitutes contrary means and programs of its liking for achieving the goals or realizing the philosophy. Reagan's Star Wars speech of March 1983 was one such event. Further, if goading events emanating from surge opponents are eventually recognized as such by them, they can stop the supply. Or, at least, produce them in much less galvanizing form. This is exactly what the Reagan administration did — together with *defusing events* it produced, such as Reagan's trip to Moscow in June 1988 and his announcing that the Soviet Union was no longer an "evil empire."

Note on measurement. Bringing forth my subsidiary concern with measurement, expressed just above, key measures of surge enlargement or contraction through *events* should include

1. The sheer *number* of substantive surge events taking place.
2. The *rapidity* with which they occur over units of time.
3. The *number of people* directly participating in them.
4. The level of *contentiousness* of actions composing the events — polite versus protest versus violent action.[16]
5. The proportion and spacing of those events widely defined as major or focusing.

The "higher" the number on one or more of these dimensions, the "larger" the surge overall, and vice versa, and the "larger" the particular spiral of the surge we may be examining.

The specific measurements of events and major actors I have suggested are diverse and complex. There are at least a dozen quantitative series of changes we need to examine in assessing a surge's size, level of mobilization, or strength. The question, then, becomes one of how most appropriately to weigh and combine these items into a single quantitative expression of activity level in each spiral that could be summed over time to produce a surge "curve." I recognize this as an important task, but in the context of the data and foci I have set here, I can only acknowledge its appropriateness.

⋘

Although indispensable as analytic tools, the critical feature of a surge is neither the interaction of conditions and events nor the participation of the nine major actors in some object of social change contention. These two matters are also the stuff of ordinary political and other life and, therefore, not distinctive to surges. What *is* distinctive is the *rapid change* from a state of not (or barely) attending some noxious elite policy or action to a state of wide and urgent attention to that object. And in the case we

will now analyze, as well as in many other cases, there is also a rapid decline in that attention — a precipitous "downsweep spiral" or slump.

Thought of in the terms noted, then, in addition to having a conspicuous and overall upsweep and downsweep dynamic, surges are a sequence of interactively spiraling cycles of conditions and events in which
some or all of the nine major actors participate in either surge-facilitative
or -inhibitive ways at different times.

The Focusing Spiral in a Surge of Polite Protest

Let us now use this framework to understand a specific body of data.
Development of a single overarching process model for all forms of citizen
surges is desirable as a larger goal, but I think this is premature and fruitless to attempt at this time, as witness the lack of follow-up on the several
existing such models I have reviewed. Instead, more progress can be made
by carefully studying well-documented cases, or, at most, delimited classes
of cases. This is the course I elect here.

A Surge of Polite Protest

The case is, of course, that of U.S. citizens surging in opposition to
newly militant U.S. government foreign policy in the early- and mid-
eighties. As simply one case, a number of its features need to be understood as likely limiting and qualifying my analysis of it. Quantitatively
and set in the context of surges as a general class, this was a medium-size
citizen surge, at most. At its peak, it involved citizens ranging in the several millions. Core activists likely amounted to no more than a third of
a million dispersed in approximately eight thousand organizations. Well
less than a billion dollars a year — perhaps half a billion — were being spent
in furthering it. Such numbers qualify it as more than trivial, but, by way
of contrast, we need to consider surges in the United States over the sixties
and in diverse revolutionary situations around the world. In length it was
also a medium surge in that it lasted longer than several months or a year
but less than a decade (depending on what one counts as part of it).

Qualitatively, and as I have stressed in several other chapters, the dominant forms of oppositional action in this surge were polite, conciliatory,
and affable. It was a remarkably *civil* surge. The forms of protest action
that emerged with some prominence were decidedly restrained and frequently choreographed. Even the conspicuously nonviolent American civil
rights movement of the sixties was dramatically more "protestful" than the

eighties peace surge, involving, as major features, the tactical forms of bus boycott, sit-in, freedom ride, and community campaign (McAdam 1983, 740–50). Levels of contentious protest action such as these were simply not seen in the peace surge. Instead, its major activities were extremely restrained and constrained, a character I have tried to capture with the term *polite protest.*

Quantitatively and qualitatively, then, we are inspecting a special creature. The distinctiveness of this constellation of features could well mean that the analysis I abstract from this case fits only this case or only a few cases of its general type. However, such uniqueness can also be overstressed. This surge *also* exhibits the salient features of the general construct of the citizen surge as these were set forth in the opening paragraphs of chapter 5.

Five Spiral Periods

The November elections held every second year in the United States were central focusing events in either escalating or deescalating peace surge activism. The second Tuesday of November in each even-numbered year closed one spiral round and opened another moving toward either a higher or lower level of surge mobilization. What we saw at the end of each period, which makes each a period, was a sharp change in level of mobilization — up or down. More precisely, new major events and the expansion or contraction of the participation of one of the major actors punctuated time in ways that suggest periods. We observe these differentiations in two kinds of facts. First, looking at the historical record, we see how, objectively, the state of the surge changed dramatically at or after a certain point — hope was soaring or dashed, money came cascading in or "dried up," and so forth, through many items in the list of ways to measure the actions of major actors described previously. Second, leading participants also often had such a perception of change at the time. They perceived that "the situation is now different" and expressed alarm over new threats to the movement that were upon them and/or exhilaration over new opportunities that had just opened. Thus, in the eighties peace surge data, there are five periods:

1. Focusing, in which a set of social change actions opposing nuclear weapons and the arms race came to be seen as feasible and timely (1979–1980);

2. Soaring, in which there was a very rapid expansion and "rise" of these social change actions (1981–1982);

3. Faltering, in which the surge reached a peak and began to decline (1983–1984);

4. Slump, in which concern and actions went into steep decline (1985–1986).

5. Percolating, in which decline leveled off and a residue peace-focused milieu resumed something like its previous state, only at a more complex level (1987–1990).

My guiding assumption is that there is no a priori reason for there to be a set number of spiral-periods in a soar-slump process. If we attend to critical changes and turning points, different cases are likely to vary in numbers of periods. Further, criteria of periodization, while reasonably clear in the abstract, are subject to quite different interpretation in specific cases. Therefore, the five periods I suggest for the peace surge case are not offered as a general model and different sets could surely be constructed for this case (and have been by several authors, including Molander and Molander [1990]).

The five I propose, however, do have a simple and attractive logic and, I think, fit the data. The focusing and percolating periods are the opening and closing phases that flank the three dynamic "moments" of soar, falter, and slump. In the faltering phase, escalation stalls and something like a "peak," or zenith, is identifiable. In this case, several observers have, indeed, cited the specific date of May 4, 1983 – the day the House passed a Freeze resolution – as *the* precise apogee of the surge.

The three center periods of soar, falter, and slump are, however, founded on and only possible because of the prior "focusing" period where, as its label seeks to signal, major coalescing elements came together and formed a platform, so to speak, from which the soaring phase could spring. Let us seek now to understand this first and critical phase.

The analysis I develop uses data on the single largest campaign of the eighties peace surge, the Freeze. This was a major activity of the politician cluster and participated in by people from other clusters. In addition to being important for the size it would attain in the second, or "soaring," phase, the Freeze is also the best documented case we have on a focusing phase and therefore the most available for scrutiny. I want to stress, however, that it was far from the only activity afoot in the focusing phase of 1979–1980. Peace activism of other political forms was stirring as were activities distinctive to other clusters. Educators, in particular, were "on the move," especially in the Physicians for Social Responsibility and in the person of Helen Caldicott (Neal 1988). Therefore, while the Freeze was important in this period, it was but one of a variety of efforts that were beginning to focus.

The Focusing Phase and Six Principles of Facilitation

The focusing phase of 1979–1980 exhibited several key conditions and events, the confluence of which crystallized into a sharp sense of threat and urgency, on the one hand, and hope for success of citizen action, on the other. This facilitating mix of conditions and events reveals to us, I think, at least six generic principles of first-phase focusing dynamics that I draw from a review of the relevant history.

Processual accounts of citizen action are often begun with a statement of distress, unrest, milling, grievance, or kindred conception of social strain or frustration as it is found among large sectors of a population. It is entirely logical to do this because — common sensually — we as readers "naturally" wish to know the motivations behind a new and burgeoning line of action. While I certainly do not discount the general relevance of grievances and unrest in the population at large, I think that in the case at hand it is more useful in tracing the causal chains from which surges are woven to begin with those conditions and events in the historical record that provide the *mesostructural vehicles* for the expression of unformed and, therefore, "unactionable" mass grievances. Grievances must be crystallized in actionable form and such *focusing* is achieved by certain mesoscopic conditions and events. Mass grievance has a causal role that is once removed from those focusing conditions and events. It shapes them and, of course, enters with full causal force in later surge stages — both as an expander and constrictor.

In the eighties peace surge, the mesoconditions that provided the context in which grievances could be focused in actionable ways were the constellation of organizations commonly termed "the historic peace movement," the several dozen stable organizations that focused on achieving disarmament or, at least, a significantly scaled-down military. Most prominent among them were (and continue to be) the American Friends Service Committee, the War Resisters League, the Fellowship of Reconciliation, Mobilization for Survival, Women's International League for Peace and Freedom, Sojourners, local peace centers, and church peace and justice commissions. These organizations formed a milieu of publications, conferences, and personal relationships.[17] Such a social world has otherwise been called a "co-optable preexisting network,"[18] inappropriately so in my view, since the peace milieu was not slyly diverted from central purposes into a novel undertaking, as is implied by the term co-optation. Instead, people in the peace milieu were, at the time we are examining, *searching* for surge vehicles, and when they found one that appeared timely and feasible, they plunged into it willingly and enthusiastically. Elevated to a first principle — the *preexisting supportive milieu principle* — we can say that the focusing of surges is facilitated by a preexisting social milieu already preoccupied with the topics of the surge that will emerge and is routinely in search of vehicles for a surge.

Such a supportive social milieu is a hothouse for possible lines of campaign action in its general realm of activity. In a different imagery, it is a percolator of possibilities. Allied only in loose ways, the diverse organizations that made up the peace milieu were continually devising and launching diverse ideas, conceptual approaches, and campaigns. Virtually all of these proposals, tryouts, and campaigns came to rather quick and sputtering ends if launched at all. A Darwinian image of nature producing random genetic combinations in reproduction provides, I think, an appropriate metaphor. Variations are thrown into the world. Those that somehow have a competitive advantage are the ones that survive to reproduce their own new kind and yet additional random variations. Such a process was going in the peace milieu of the late-seventies in the United States.

Among the *macroconditions* that were background to this percolation of possibilities in 1979–1980 were the failure of SALT II, the militaristic turn of then President Carter and the new militarist platform of presidential candidate Ronald Reagan.[19] In this context, the peace milieu was especially beleaguered and unable to inspire widespread enthusiasm. At the mesoconditional level of resources and organization, the peace milieu was, nonetheless, facilitatively postured. Its beleaguered and directionless state meant that it had slack resources. Its participants were concerned about militarism but lacking in compelling notions of how to act against it. This state of the milieu suggests a second principle of surge dynamics — *the slack resources principle*. Surge focusing is facilitated by preexisting supportive milieux whose resources are not at the time already deployed in a taut fashion in existing campaigns.

What I have just sketched are two mesoscopic conditions of *readiness*. They, however, only set the facilitative stage and do not in and of themselves ensure that Darwinian percolation will result in a larger, uniting focus. Percolation could, in theory, simply continue indefinitely. There is, nonetheless, pressure to find a program that can become an object of focus and joint action among the many possibilities.

At the level of lived experience in the peace milieu of the late-seventies, the percolating parade of Darwinian possibilities was in the form of individual or group proposers promoting one or another peace-action scheme. Each proposal was more or less seriously evaluated by those attending to these proposers. Most of them were rejected in the sense that only a few people responded. Conceived more abstractly, even though most initiatives in a supportive milieux are not adopted, a third principle — the Darwinian parade of proposers principle — is that surge focusing is facilitated by a supportive milieux in which there is a continual parade of action proposals.

But, then, lightning of some social alchemic sort strikes. In 1979–1980, this mysterious and focusing lightning struck twice in the peace milieu, both times in Massachusetts and both times with persons whose first names were Randall (Forsberg and Kehler). What kind of events did they create that catapulted them from the chorus line of scheme-proposers to star performers?

Forsberg and Kehler had in common the fact that, in their different ways, they proposed a bilateral Freeze on nuclear weapons testing, production, and deployment. Critical features making the Freeze idea pragmatically attractive as a vehicle of action included the following: it was, first, bilateral (allaying fears of Soviet advantage); second, it focused on nuclear weapons (which were thought more fearsome and less legitimate than other weapons); and, third, it called for cessation rather than disarmament. It is important to note that this was *not* a new idea, which may have, paradoxically, been one of its strengths in the peace milieu of the time. It had been "kicked around" in the Darwinian parade of proposers for many years, even attracting a considerable congressional following (Leavitt 1983, 14–15). What *was* new was *how* the two Randalls proposed the idea, *who* they were, and the *events* their proposing created.

Randall Forsberg was in but not of the peace milieu. She was not a "peace diaper baby," and came instead from a mainstream arms control (i.e., "legitimate") background, having worked at the Stockholm International Peace Research Institute, done graduate work on arms matters at the Massachusetts Institute for Technology, and coauthored a progressive book on national defense (Boston Study Group 1979). However, she quite purposely set out to promote Freeze ideas in the peace milieu, attending and speaking before gatherings of its major groups. She possessed legitimating educational and work credentials, knew her subjects, and by all accounts was an articulate and skillful speaker. She was then "thirty-something" and, in the view of many, physically attractive. She dressed more conservatively and "smartly" than the "informal/shabby left" commonly observed in the peace milieu. By mainstream standards, she was "impressive." Moreover, she dedicated herself to speaking to a great many peace milieu gatherings so that she became quite well known in a relatively brief period. The fact that she lived in the Boston area, a hotbed of major peace milieu organizations, eased her traveling and association task.[20]

Her Freeze promotional work in the Darwinian parade had a rather dramatic turning point at the annual convention, in December 1979, of a coalition of peace groups called Mobilization for Survival. The delegates at that convention are reported to have had, in the words of one person present, a "moment of redefinition" (Leavitt 1983, 15). Lightning may not literally have struck, but something metaphorically like it seemed clearly to have occurred and less dramatically at a large number of other peace milieu gatherings Forsberg addressed in 1979 and 1980.

In the same period, the other Randall, Mr. Kehler, was at the other end of Massachusetts, in Deerfield, on the staff of the Traprock Peace Center. Interestingly, he took his conception of the Freeze, not from Forsberg, but from the Sojourners circle in Washington, D.C., and Senator Mark Hatfield, who was associated with it. While Forsberg promoted her version to the peace milieu, Kehler thought a local citizen referendum asking state senators to call for a Freeze was an appropriate route. The necessary signatures to put such a resolution on the ballot in three western Massachusetts state senate districts were successfully collected in late-1979 and early-1980 and a campaign for adoption was conducted for the November 1980 election. The three districts approved the resolution and also gave majority votes to Ronald Reagan for president.

Other accounts of this 1979–1980 period have tended to offer Forsberg rather than Kehler as the central activist in initiating the Freeze element of the eighties peace surge. Without denigrating Forsberg's obvious importance in all of this, I suggest the need for a more balanced and synergistic analysis. In my view, the emergence of the two Randalls in the roles they played was an extraordinarily surge-facilitating coincidence. The level and shape of the surge would have been very different had either been absent. Indeed, contrary to other accounts, I am inclined to think Kehler and his activities were as or more important than Forsberg's in ratcheting the surge to the next level. Kehler brought a kind of evidence (and at the right time) that arms control thinking and argumentation could never produce. The referendum adoption proved that, despite the election of a conservative president, ordinary people were ready to support arms control and perhaps reduction. Even if public opinion polls ran in that direction (and they did not at the time), any theoretical popularity of a Freeze proposal could not be convincing because it had not been tested in the polling booth. In the absence of this critical, *positive* test, Forsberg's elegantly penned and arrestingly titled "Call to Halt the Arms Race" was simply one more episode in the Darwinian parade of presenters described. She might even, by personal intellectual force, have assembled a body of "Forsbergites" around her. But such personal surges do not easily and necessarily build into a full surge. They tend, instead, to remain marginal and encysted social formations.

What is required, in addition, to break out of that encystment are signals in the experience of existing activists that the *feasibility* of social change action has now radically changed and that such action is *timely* to a degree it was not previously—the key variables pinpointed by Turner and Killian (1987, 245–48). As simply an idea, an argument, and a convincing presence, Forsberg alone, or with her new following, could not provide such a signal, only the exciting glimmer of it. What at this time differentiated her and her program from many other proposals was the signal of likely *wide public support* that could be read from the western Massachusetts referendum.

Fully to appreciate the special significance of a new perception of feasibility and timeliness in the peace milieu, we need also to understand a major theme that pervaded its "culture." Its participants were acutely aware that most if not virtually all their proposals tended to be "out of step" with mainstream thought. They were very conscious of a large political and intellectual gap between them and most Americans. The Darwinian parade of proposers, therefore, was not simply a search for good ideas but for ones that could bridge that gap. Good ideas were abundant and not intellectually difficult to evaluate. What *was* hard was arriving at a grounded assessment of how an idea might attract wide support. Without actually trying to develop such support, one could not know, and even actual trials were not successful on any significant scale. Randall Kehler's achievement was that he put an idea to the test and succeeded. Political propriety of the Freeze aside (and many peace milieu people were troubled by its narrow and single issue framing), he had apparently found a solution to the problem of the peace milieu's marginality. With the Freeze, they could bridge the gap.

The activities of each of the Randalls suggest further principles of surge dynamics. The fourth on my list is *the principle of the attractive public intellectual.* In the focusing period, a surge is facilitated (and, perhaps, absolutely dependent on) the coming forth and active promotional work of an intellectually and personally credible and skilful intellectual articulator and advocate of a change-idea that pointedly responds to elite behavior widely perceived as threatening.

I add to this the related fifth principle of *the dramatic demonstration of feasibility and timeliness.* Initially, a surge focuses and achieves a mobilization platform with a critical success event signaling an idea is feasible and timely. Otherwise stated, surges need and use early and major success events.

I view these fourth and fifth principles as refinements of Freeman's (1983, 22–27) third condition for starting a social movement, the need for skilled organizers. What she says about the role of such organizers is correct but imprecise. Pushing on, we need to specify the *kinds* of skilled organizing required, as in principles four and five. Note, however, that principle five points to feasibility-demonstrations rather than organizers. Feasibility-demonstrations may or may not be produced by specific organizers, but if they are, many social-emotional and political skills are necessary to pull them off, skills different from those of the intellectual articulator and promoter.

A sixth principle pertinent to the focusing period concerns features of the idea that survives a feasibility-timeliness test and will, therefore, be subsequently promoted. A feasible proposal must respond to threat but not itself also raise obvious new threats. The Freeze proposal moved in this direction by avoiding, specifically, threatening endorsement of unilateral disarmament, reduction of conventional forces, and notions of the United States as an imperial world power. Further, the Freeze idea was not overly complicated and could be claimed to be a matter on which every reasonable person can agree (cf. Wright, Rodriguez, and Waitzkin 1986). Initially and later it was, indeed, promoted as "not a matter of politics but of humanity." We might think of this, then, as illustrating the *principle of the feasible proposal*.

This sixth principle leads me to take issue with models of surge action that feature radical shifts of cognitive orientation as requisites for surges. I am struck in particular by "political process" models which posit a moment if not a stage of "cognitive liberation," by which is meant "a transformation of consciousness" in which people "collectively define their situations as unjust and subject to change through group action" (McAdam 1982, 51). I think that this too dramatic and wide-ranging a characterization of the cognitive change observed in at least the focusing stage of the eighties peace surge, which primarily involved participants in the peace milieu. Those members had for the most part far earlier gone through such a "cognitive liberation." The liberation peace milieu people *did* achieve in the focusing period was from problematic action rather than from self-blaming world views. All labels are elastic, of course, and if one insists on thinking of new vehicles of action as "cognitive liberation," we might distinguish between more general and more specific liberation.

≪

What, in composite, do we *see* and *not see* in this initial spiral of the peace surge?

Central facilitating *conditions* of the first escalating spiral were a pre-existing supportive milieu with unengaged resources in which participants were scrutinizing a parade of Darwinian proposers. Major focusing and, hence, escalating *events* were the appearance of a striking intellectual articulator and proposer of a central concept and a dramatic demonstration of the feasibility of a proposal that fit in an unthreatening way with public fears and proclivities for safe change proposals. The electoral triumph in western Massachusetts in November 1980 served to ratchet the nascent surge to a new and higher level.

This period is notable for the number of important types of actors who were *absent* as important players. At that point, the most prominent actors were peace activists, disposed organizations, and some disposed and bystanding citizens. Major funders had yet to appear, dissident elites to "sign on," media to go into their typical surge frenzy, elites to take much notice and react, and countersurges to be activated.

The ratcheting achieved in this period, however, would shortly change all this in the most dramatic fashion that is analyzed in chapter 7.

Conclusion

I have proposed a framework for analyzing surges of citizen activism as interactive spirals of conditions and events in which several types of actors differentially participate. I have applied this framework to the initial, or focusing, stage of American citizens surging for peace in the 1980s.

There are two major directions to take an effort of this kind. If this approach seems fruitful, next tasks obviously include its application to other stages of the same surge and to other cases. This is the scholarly approach, and I take one more step on this path in chapter 7. But, there is also an activist direction. From the point of view of planning and doing citizen action, I am impressed with the framework's possible value as a guide. In one sense, the previous discussion is simply a crystallization or systemization of (1) factors that activists take into account and (2) goals they strive for in devising their actions. My statement, however, is obviously only a beginning.

Notes

1. Revised from initial publication as Lofland 1992b.
2. Other discussions of this neglect include McAdam (1983, 735), who provides a list of yet others who have puzzled about it.

3. Freeman (1983, 8–27).

4. Tilly (1978, 52–63).

5. Morris (1984, chap. 7).

6. See also Oberschall (1973, 120) on "communal ties"; McAdam (1982, 43–48), on "indigenous organizational strength"; McAdam, McCarthy, and Zald (1988, 709–11) on "micro-mobilization contexts."

7. Dawson and Gettys (1935, chap. 19); Blumer (1969, 102–3); Turner and Killian (1987, 253).

8. See also, Moyer 1988.

9. Holstein and Miller 1989. See also Best (1987, 1989).

10. Freeman (1975, chap. 5). See also Lofland (1977, 279–344), on the "boom and bust" pattern of a movement and white hot mobilization; Downs 1972; Jackson et al. 1960, on stalling in the initial spiral; Molander and Molander 1990 on "thresholds."

11. Turner and Killian (1987, 253–55). See also, McAdam's (1983) use of the ideas of "tactical interaction" and "interactive dynamics."

12. Kriesberg 1982.

13. Hilgartner and Bosk 1988; Kingdon 1984.

14. McAdam, McCarthy, and Zald (1988, 709–16).

15. In addition to my own observations of peace movement action, this enumeration of major actors is informed by Michael Lipsky (1968, 1144–58); Turner and Killian (1987, 225); Lofland (1985, 10–22); Snow et al. (1986, 465 n. 2). Curiously, there have been rather few efforts systematically to treat the question of who are major classes of actors in surge situations.

16. Lofland (1985, 1–10, 260–69) and chap. 5, this volume.

17. The characterizing assertions in this section are derived from diverse primary documents, interviews with the participants, and from published accounts such as Leavitt 1983; Kennedy and Hatfield (1982, chap. 7); Waller (1987, chap. 2); Solo (1988, chaps. 2, 3); Meyer (1990, chap. 9).

18. Freeman (1983, 22–27).

19. These and additional macroconditions are summarized in Chatfield (1992, 151–52).

20. The Boston metropolitan area seems to have had the highest peace group density, diversity, and membership in the United States, far exceeding even New York City and Washington, D.C., the leading centers of social activism.

7

Surge Soaring
Peace Activism, 1981–1983

with Sam Marullo

The histories of social movements and other forms of citizen action often exhibit a phase of extremely rapid growth and rise in public attention that participants and observers alike find quite miraculous, mysterious and even enthralling. Unexpected and unpredicted, such a meteoric change in social movement fortune has elicited diverse labels that isolate it as a phase, including popular excitement (Dawson and Gettys 1935), emergence (Blumer 1971), popular (Turner and Killian 1987), mobilization (Smelser 1963), coalescence (Mauss 1975), mushrooming (Freeman 1975), mass defiance (Piven and Cloward 1979), outbreak (Rose 1982), takeoff (Morris 1984), explosion (Rupp and Taylor 1987), moment of madness (Zolberg 1972), and (our preference) soaring.

All of these are captions for what is most often conceived as the *second* phase in a multistage "natural history" of a social movement or other collective action. In these models, the prior *first* phase points to macrosocial background, organizational, and resource mobilization factors that make possible or "cause" this second "outbreak" phase. The third, fourth, or more phases depict faltering, slump, decline, fragmentation, institutionalization, or other kinds of outcomes.

Perhaps not surprisingly, most analysts have focused on the first or underlying causes stage rather than on the second soaring or mushrooming stage (McAdam, McCarthy, and Zald 1988, 728–29). This is an unfortunate neglect, and we want here to help remedy this oversight by providing a case study analysis of a second stage in a way that draws out how it may operate more generally in social movements.

The case of a second stage we will examine is, of course, that of the peace surge of the 1980s. As reported in chapter 6, a *first* stage of citizen dissent achieved focus in 1979–1980, soared in its *second* phase (1981–1982) and peaked in 1983 during its *third* phase (1983–1984). It began to falter in this *third* phase when its flagship activity—a Freeze on nuclear weapons—was unsuccessful in the U.S. Congress and the Reagan administration launched deescalating counterinitiatives, the Strategic Defense Initiative (Star Wars) being among the more important. Peace activists pressed forward in the hope of significant gains in the November 1984 elections, but Reagan's landslide reelection precipitated steep decline in 1985–1986 (the *fourth* phase). A new period of fairly stable percolation was achieved by 1987 and continued through 1990 (the *fifth* phase).

Concepts

In order to examine soaring stages, we require a conception of their constituents; a delineation of the elements that compose them at or near their fullest development. If we took metaphorical photographs of a series of them at "full flower"—at or near peak points—what would we see? What elements would be evident? And, by extension, if we photographed them at various earlier times, what elements appear at what points and grow at what rates over different phases and within phases? Drawing from movement and collective action literature, there appear to be four major categories of elements: *actors, perceptions, events,* and *conditions.* Elaborated, these provide us with depictions of who is interacting, at what levels and forms of involvement, over what sorts of perceptions, events, and conditions.

Utilizing our data on the United States peace soar of 1981–1983, we begin with an enumeration of the actors in that surge as they were drawn from elites, active citizenry, and the public at large. We then report perceptions that animated the soar of activism and gave it the direction it took. Our analyses of actors and perceptions set the stage for our central focus, the synergistic interaction of *events.* Following this analysis, we report conditions from the prior, or focusing, phase of the surge that served as the facilitating circumstances, or platform, from which the soar phase sprang.

We conceive our focus on events as a type of *event analysis,* using this term more broadly than do some other researchers. It is, specifically, an *event synergy* analysis. We recognize that the term event analysis has at least two other referents, and we, therefore, want carefully to distinguish what we are doing here from these two other approaches. In the approach called event-history analysis, the occurrence of a discrete phenomenon is explained as a probabilistic function of a series of other factors (Allison 1984; Tuma and Hannan 1984). The model implies that the dependent variable is conceptually distinct from the explicands. A second approach, that can be termed *event series analysis*, primarily consists of frequency counts of categories of events over time coded from the public press or similar public or archive record, most notably from the index of the *New York Times.*[1] Both these forms of event analysis are quite useful for several purposes but differ in focus and logic from the event synergy approach we use here. In particular, the present approach points to the reciprocal or synergistic interaction of several different classes and sequences of events at a level of complexity and "spiraling" that is not modeled in event-history or event series analysis. Unlike event-history analysis, we make no prior designation of exogenous variables that explain a discrete outcome. Instead, the surge outcome is itself a confluence of events that continuously and simultaneously cause each other. Further, we attend to how events are related to major categories of actors who may or may not appear at particular points in various phases of social movements. Finally, we stress that events can only be understood through proper elucidation of perceptions that are facilitating or inhibiting their synergy.

Actors: Elites, Citizenry, the Public

As discussed in chapter 6, we must attend to nine major categories of actors as participants in or parties to citizen surges in general and social movements in particular. All of them appear — at least minimally — in the analysis that follows, but it must be understood that all nine do not appear in every phase of every surge.[2] Described in chapter 6, we here simply repeat their names: activists, predisposed organizations, funders, dissident elites, disposed citizens, bystander citizens, media, ruling elites, and countersurgers.

As we show in the conclusion to this chapter, it is sometimes helpful to think of these nine actors as instances of only three basic social locations in this fashion:

Elites	*Citizenry*	*Public*
funders	activists	bystander citizens
dissident elites	disposed organizations	
media	disposed citizens	
ruling elites	countersurgers	

To point to nine major categories of actors is not to say that this is an exhaustive list. We require an "other" category in order to recognize that yet other collective forces can and do come into play. Two such "other" actors were particularly important in the case of the United States peace surge. One, the actions of the Soviet Union were relevant in all stages and especially after 1985 when its new leader embarked on radically modified policies regarding the United States and other countries. Two, peace action in Europe appears to have had at least some modest effects on several actors in the American arena.

Perceptions: Danger, Urgency, Simplicity, Effectiveness, Legitimacy

The explosion of opposition to official policies and other actors' reactions to that explosion, which are the essence of social movement soars, are accompanied by *perceptions* of the meaning of that opposition and its meteoric rise. Aside from the substance of the perceptions, the most important shared perceptions that take hold are of opportunity, danger, and, most especially, *urgency*. It is thought necessary to act with haste because of new threats and harms that must be countered and/or new opportunities that must be seized before they recede. In the terms offered by Turner and Killian (1987, 245–48), there is a radical revision of the sense of "feasibility and timeliness." Movements in soar vary, of course, in terms of particular *substantive* beliefs, but all center — analytically — on a sense of actual or imminent crisis, fear, danger, and/or opportunity.[3]

A Galvanizing Constellation of Beliefs

Let us try to understand these beliefs through posing and answering this question: What varieties of perception are most likely to give rise to quick and urgent action? Considered in a simply logical fashion and attuned to previous analyses,[4] such a galvanizing constellation likely includes these elements:

1. A previously contained or controlled danger has suddenly gotten out of hand and while it has not yet caused the threatened damage, the likelihood it will is *rapidly increasing*.

2. The danger in question is much more than minor; in this case it is the *ultimate threat*; it portends the obliteration of humanity itself or at least a gigantic catastrophe.

3. There is only a *short time* in which to take action, so one must act *now*. This is an *urgent* matter.

4. The actions required to reduce this danger are uncomplicated and can be performed without enormous effort, inexpensively, and close at hand.

5. The simple and safe actions are an *effective* means to address the danger.

6. Large numbers of other people, many of whom are experts or otherwise knowledgeable regarding the danger, are also acting to reduce this threat. One is not acting alone and this increases the effectiveness and *legitimacy* of one's actions. Furthermore, one need not feel foolish undertaking these actions.

Such a logically constructed set of beliefs has the propitious feature of combining a very high degree of danger with a very easily performed but effective set of remedial actions that are sanctioned by authorities. One might even say there is a considerable disproportion between the magnitude and urgency of the danger and what one must do in order to reduce or eliminate it. Such a disproportion can be very attractive, indeed. It provides, in the slogan of one peace lobby, a way to "save the world in twenty minutes a month."

These six beliefs are not simply a logical exercise in how to galvanize action. As a package and with varying approximations, they were observed in the soar phase of the United States peace surge. Let us briefly examine their specific forms in that case.[5]

Doomsday Talk: Crisis, Fear, Urgency

The wide array of changes we witness in the soaring (and faltering) period were not animated by merely dispassionate cognitive assessments of the parade of goading events presented by the Reagan administration (described later). Quite the contrary, activists, dissident elites, the professional pundits, and others began to define the national — nay, species — situation as one of truly profound danger that required urgent human activity to ward it off. In collective behavior language, the "keynoters" of this emergent definition of the situation included Jonathan Schell (author of *The Fate of the Earth*, 1982) and Helen Caldicott (author of *Nuclear Madness*, 1978, and called caustically by her detractors "Helen Holocaust"). But these were only two leading voices in a chorus of apocalyptic warnings about the vivid and proximate threat of nuclear war. The message conveyed by these keynoters is summarized by Caldicott and Schell:

The individual would misconceive the nuclear peril if he tried to understand it primarily in terms of personal danger, or even in terms of danger to the people immediately known to him, for the nuclear peril threatens life, above all, not at the level of individuals, who already live under the sway of death, but at the level of everything that individuals hold in common. Death cuts off life; extinction cuts off birth. . . . Death is only death; extinction is the death of death (Schell 1982, 117, 119).

To be unemotional about the end of the earth approaching is mentally sick. To feel no feelings about it, to be uninvolved is inappropriate, to be psychologically comfortable today is absolutely inappropriate (Caldicott in Thierman 1984).

Every person is the right person to act. Every moment is the right moment to begin (Schell 1982, 226).

In an older and now surprisingly lapsed tradition of collective behavior studies in sociology, attention was given to "collective fears" or "scares" or even "panics" of various kinds (Smelser 1963, chap. 6; Lofland 1985, chap. 1). We think it is not inappropriate to resurrect at least some aspects of that tradition in order to highlight the degree to which the soaring surgers of 1981–1983 were cognitively and emotionally constructing the situation in a collective behavior fashion, that is, as a circumstance in which the attitude of everyday life is suspended, there is widespread and intense emotional arousal, and out-of-the-ordinary activities are pursued (Lofland 1985, 37–38). Of the three emotions seen most frequently as either dominant or mixed in instances of collective behavior — those of fear, hostility, or joy — fear was clearly the emotion that dominated the peace surge.

Such an emergent atmosphere — one centerpiecing crisis, urgency, and fear — has a great deal to be said for it in terms of "getting on" the social agenda. As Hilgartner and Bosk (1988), among others, have brought to our attention, the public arenas of modern societies are not especially permeable. Hundreds if not thousands of promoters of issues try constantly and unsuccessfully to achieve public arena space. Entry is extremely tricky, and how it is achieved is not well understood. In a general way, we know, though, that dramatic devices of some sort are a great help in breaking through the barriers into the public arena (Hilgartner and Bosk 1988, 61–62). But, the question is What at any given time will suffice as a dramatic device that will serve as a vehicle to entry? In the case at hand, the atmosphere of crisis, urgency, and fear exhibited by surgers was such a device.

If (at some psychic level) a great many people have such doomsday concerns, perhaps we should not be surprised that media and others begin to pay attention when doomsday talk started to be expounded by increasing numbers of educated, credible, and expert people. This, of course,

combined with the reality that the political elites who can create doomsday were *themselves* talking about its possibility!

We should note that even during the soaring phase, some observers
began to criticize nuclear doomsday talk, arguing that rather than scaring
people into action, such talk scared people into numbness, apathy, or mere
inaction (Coles 1984; Sandman and Valenti 1986). Its sheer negativism,
said others, was not a solid motivational base on which to mount and sustain citizen action (Meyer 1990b). Without denying the possible validity
of these assertions and concerns, we believe there would have been no peace
surge soar in 1981–1983 without doomsday talk. We accept the Hilgartner
and Bosk proposition that access to the public arena requires a dramatic
device. The danger of nuclear extinction and doomsday talk fulfilled that
role.

Consensus Problems and Solutions

What dissident elites said in a technical fashion about the likelihood
of nuclear war, the adequacy of a Freeze, other arms control proposals,
and consequences of nuclear war was, likely, less important than the mere
fact that they were disputing the Reagan administration. For, at the popular, mass level, the major themes at play were not particularly technical
or treated as complex disputes. Instead, concern focused on an unrestrained
arms race (in which nuclear weapons were the most prominent element),
the growing likelihood of nuclear war, the undesirability of such a war,
and the need to find a way to stop or, at least, slow these drifts. As such,
these were highly consensual problems and solutions that were viewed
widely as "above politics" and simply "for humanity." Among old-line left
and peace activists, the prominence of consensus themes was a matter of
considerable discomfort in that such a formulation left out questions of
American imperialism, exploitive relations with the Third World, militarism, and the like, that is, divisive issues of politics. But surgers were
often quite explicit about distancing themselves from the left (Lofland 1989,
and chap. 2, this vol.; Wright, Rodriguez, and Waitzkin, 1986). And as
many observers have suggested, it was exactly the consensual quality of
the leading ideas of the soar that must be reckoned as figuring centrally
in the rapid enlargement of the eight classes of events we analyze later.[6]

Perception of Soaring

A process can "feed on itself" in at least two ways. First, an initial
burgeoning class of events witnessed by people in a second class of events

inspires people in the second class to greater effort and action, which, in turn, inspires people in the initial class to greater action. In the case at hand, this ratcheting effect was multiplied over *several* classes of events. Once this ratcheting mutual reinforcement is underway, a second level of "feeding on itself" can take hold as participants begin to perceive that the first effect is afoot. They achieve the perception, to use the vernacular, that they are "on a roll" and that perception becomes *itself* a new kind of energizer, a derived kind of stimulating or facilitating factor in soaring.[7]

Leading activists began to form this perception in late-1981, and by early-1982, perception of surging was significantly facilitating the soar. Here is how it was expressed by national coordinators of the Nuclear Weapons Freeze Campaign in a memo to nationwide Freeze contacts dated March 19, 1982:

> Since the conference in Denver [in February, 1982] . . . the campaign has received unprecedented media attention. The Conference itself was covered by NBC and CBS. . . . Then came the Vermont and New Hampshire town meetings; launching a new series of national media attention. . . . Then the news of the joint Senate-House resolution set off a new wave of network and newspaper coverage. . . .
>
> All this is to say that our decision for coordinated press conferences on April 26th is riding the wave of more national attention than we ever expected this early in the campaign. We are *news!* We can proceed with confidence that our press conference can build on all this and will be taken seriously (Ramsey and Kehler 1982, 1, emphasis in the original).

Activists such as these were, of course, not the only source of the perception of soaring. Media, in particular, were a critical source of it. Indeed, as Ramsey and Kehler quite accurately perceive in the passage, it is the behavior of the media that largely stimulated the perception of soaring even though the media did not create it. Notice that the excitement of Ramsey and Kehler centers on "We are *news!*" In so asserting, the media importantly functioned to create *both the perception and reality* of soaring. While it is rarely true that phenomena are purely "media creations,"[8] there is a significant sense in which media are at least key helpers in creating social forms. (And, as we see later, what the media gives, they can also take away.)

Events: Eight Types in Spiraling Synergy

Perceptions are, most saliently, of *events*. An event is any space-time locatable occurrence to which people refer as a forthcoming matter about which there is an anticipation *or* as a past matter that is used as orientation to the present and future. As anticipation, events are in-process objects of proponent action. They are matters around which, about which, or toward which proximate action "must" be taken. As the past, events are the elements of the common history and folklore that help define what a movement is about.[9]

Perceptions carve out a realm of relevance and sensitize people to respond in certain general ways, but it is the continuing flow of events that determines whether any set of perceptions will be supported or contradicted, inflated or deflated, inflamed or extinguished. People tend to reespond, that is, to what is actually happening, and the beliefs we have just described persisted, spread, and grew stronger over the soar phase as a function of the occurrence of events that supported these perceptions.

The relations (1) among perceptions and events and (2) among events themselves are exceedingly complicated and synergistic in character. This fact poses a special problem of exposition that we need to address prior to discussing the soaring of eight classes of events.

Synergistic Interaction and Linear Exposition: A Conundrum

The eight sets of events described next that mainly made up the peace soar present a problem of linear exposition. Inspected as they operate in the historical record, one or another sometimes, in some ways, tends to "run ahead" of or to cause changes in other event sequences. But, more commonly, each is in a synergistic or feedback fashion responding to the others. Many are very often feeding off each other and mutually causing enlargement of the other. Because this is so thoroughly the case, reality is distorted by presenting the eight kinds of events in a linear fashion as a simple "one to eight" list. Such a list implies (if not asserts) either, one, a causal order among the eight and/or, two, a co-equal list of causes that play upon the dependent variable of soaring. Neither implication of a linear exposition is accurate. It is more accurate to depict all operating on the others simultaneously, or at least in numerous and complicated feedback loops that we can glimpse in the available data but for which we do not have detailed documentation. Further, it is not clear how one should model or otherwise visually depict these "interactive spirals," especially in view of the abstractness of recent efforts (e.g., Hilgartner and Bosk 1988; Turner and Killian 1987, 253–55).[10]

It is virtually impossible to document all these possible feedback loops since the eight sets of events can act on each of the other sets in at least fifty-six ways. The total number of synergistic paths is geometrically greater when we consider that they are time dependent and that they are likely to change at different stages of the development of the soar. We have tried to illustrate this synergy graphically in figure 7.1. Each of the eight types of events is connected to the other seven types of events at a given time (Cross Section), which can be thought of as an arbitrarily selected point of the soar phase. As each connection fuels the soar, the events change and become larger in their subsequent effects. This is depicted in Dynamic Surge, which uses time as the vertical dimension and the increasing circumference of the spiral to depict the increased intensity of the effects. Theoretically, cross-sections of the spiral would represent the nature of the connections among the eight types of events at a given moment. The connecting lines here represent both the intensity of the effects and their substantive nature — an analytical distinction we cannot capture graphically. Short of an enormously more detailed specification of effects (most likely beyond human comprehension as well as graphic explication), we undertake here but the first step of specifying what the events are and offering illustrative synergistic effects.

Focusing Events That Facilitate Soaring

Structurally, events are commonly and narrowly *encounters* (two or a few people maintaining a single face-to-face object of engrossment), otherwise termed *gatherings* (or *crowds* if numerous people are involved). Some few gatherings are marked by special actions that single them out as *an event* in the sense that larger and signal consequence is imputed to them. Hotly contested balloting that is won or lost, acts of violence, and unusually large or small numbers of participants in a gathering relative to anticipation are three typical forms of creating major or *focusing* events that can importantly either *facilitate* or *inhibit* surging soars. That is, events differ in terms of how widely they are defined as of large or small importance and in terms of the period of time over which they serve as objects of concerted action. There are relatively few focusing events compared to a multitude of minor events that serve to keep the surge afloat but do not provide signal markers. Events are the stuff of moving social life from which optimistic or pessimistic perceptions are formed, participants are emboldened or demoralized, and soaring facilitated or inhibited.

Combining the major versus minor importance dimension and facilitating-inhibiting effect dimension of events with the nine major categories of actors specifies for us thirty-six different types of events as associated with who is creating them. In our data on the soaring phase of the U.S. peace surge, though, we need not be concerned with most of the classes of events specified in such a cross-classification, for only eight major

Figure 7.1
Graphic Portrayal of
Peace Movement Surge Synergism

Cross Section

At a given time, the eight types of events positively affect each other.

Dynamic Surge

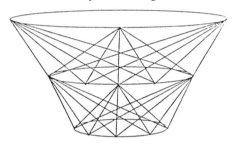

The effects change over time as well, leading to expansion or soaring.

categories of them stand out as embracing almost all the critical activity that made up the soaring phase: (1) ruling elite goading events, (2) local dissenting events, (3) dissident elite legitimizing events, (4) national dissenting events, (5) coalescing events, (6) media events, (7) funding events, (8) public opining events.

Thought of in a different perspective, these eight varieties of sequences of events answer the question "What happened in the soar of peace activism?" Or, in generalized form, "What *can* happen in the soar of a surge"? The eight specify for us the main ingredients of a movement soar, or explosion. The presence and expansion of each answers the question What *is* a surge in the concrete sense of what kinds and magnitudes of series of events take place that lead us to isolate a surge itself as a distinctive type of very complex event (or "episode," a la Smelser 1963). In addition, because we have differentiated these eight classes of events, we can track the behavior of each over time and therefore identify differences in how each is rising or falling in response to the rises and falls in each of the other classes.

Soaring Events

Even though there is a strong synergy among events, this does not necessarily mean that all eight classes of them are of equal importance in the dynamics of the soaring of events or that they all came into play (or play through time) simultaneously. Some are probably more consequential than others, and some are activated earlier than others in temporal synergies. Despite the reality of ratcheting mutual enlargement, all events (and associated classes of actors) are not equal in escalating import. If that is the case, virtue can be made of the necessity of doing a serial exposition of the eight classes of events.

Without saying that all eight can be firmly ranked in consequential and temporal terms, at least three of the eight *do* seem to have been of greater consequence and earlier in critical activation. These three are ruling elite goading events, local dissenting events, and dissident elite legitimizing events. Without these three happening early and in strong form, the other five were less likely, or would have been weaker.

Because all eight are burgeoning in very close temporal sequencing, we are making, of course, very tricky and hazardous judgments. But, the substance of goading, local, and dissident elite events gives some assurance. First, without ruling elite goading events, all the rest make little sense. Second, it is the early spread of local events — already underway in the prior focusing period and given inspiration in the soaring period by them — that gives rise to the possibility of national events as well as to other kinds of events farther down the list: coalescing, funding, media, and public opining. Third, the early legitimation provided by dissent elites is likewise important in the burgeoning of these "further on" classes of events.

We think, nonetheless, that beyond — or "below" — the first three, the ranking becomes murkier as the synergy among them becomes stronger. Therefore, although we discuss coalescing, media, funding, and public opining events in that order, we are not certain that they ought to be so ranked.

1. Ruling elite goading events. The class of events of most central significance in both precipitating and feeding the soaring of peace dissent was the new Reagan administration's provision of an ongoing and diverse parade of *goading* events in 1981–1982. Thus,

February 1981. Administration proposes largest peacetime military budget in United States history.

August 1981. Administration announces neutron bomb assembly and stockpiling.

Fall 1981. Frequent talk of the possibility of nuclear war. President Reagan says that he is an *optimist* that a limited nuclear war will remain limited.

October 1981. Secretary of State Haig talks about firing nuclear warning shots across the bow of advancing enemy troops.

October 1981. Vice-president Bush publicly discusses the possibility of winning a nuclear war.

October 1981. Plan to modernize nuclear forces announced.

January 1982. Defense Department proposes a budget for nuclear force modernization to achieve superiority over the Soviet Union.

January 1982. Deputy Under Secretary of Defense Jones says if there are enough shovels to go around, everyone will survive a nuclear war.

Spring 1982. Continuing talk of the possibility of nuclear war.

Spring 1982. Air Force General James Stansberry confirms that there is a shift in strategic warfare policy; that the U.S. must be prepared to fight a protracted nuclear war.

June 1982. Just prior to the Second United Nations Special Session on Disarmament, Secretary Haig reiterates the U.S. refusal to renounce the policy of first use.

August 1982. Secretary of Defense Weinberger talks about nuclear war as the biblical Armageddon.

This list contains only military and foreign policy matters. Domestically, there were attacks on significant elements of the "welfare" state and regulation of business and the economy. These attacks on domestic institutions were themselves a secondary set of goading events, with some of that concern channeled into the peace surge. Contextualizing all these events was nervousness generated by an economic recession in 1980 and 1981.

The Reagan administration was not simply more militaristic across the board although it was certainly that. More specifically, it began to *speak* about an aggressive conception of the role of *nuclear* weapons in the "world struggle." Although, for example, nuclear war fighting capability, scenarios such as nuclear "warning shots" over Europe, and civilian shelters to be used in nuclear war had previously been part of U.S. military battle plans, Reagan people began *publicly to talk*—even *casually* to talk—about these and related matters. Although clearly not invented to be, the Freeze was tailor-made as a counter to this new kind of public talk. That is, the Freeze as a mobilizing vehicle was underway prior to much Reaganite loose talk about nuclear war, and the Freeze plan was conceived as a general, proactive program of "arms control." For the purpose of a movement soar, however, it functioned superbly as a mobilizing vehicle that replied to the Reaganites precisely because it was focused on nuclear weapons. It was an auspicious congruence of (1) new and dangerous ruling elite talk and (2) an already underway credible form of opposition. Let us, indeed, lift this connection to the level of a *principle* of movement soaring. We label it the *already launched pointed response:* a soaring curve of mobilization against ruling elites is facilitated if a newly minted, pointed response to elite actions has already begun to gain significant citizen attention and following. That existing response becomes a platform on which already recruited activists can stand in recruiting additional activists and others. In addition to contributing synergistically to local dissenting events of the soar, this loose talk was an easy target for dissident elites' criticisms and focused some media attention on these issues.

2. *Local dissenting events.* Local dissenting events are all those occasions of citizens gathering for educational, political, protest or for other surge-involved purposes that are promoted over only a small geographical area and that draw participants from only that area. They generate only local press notice if they generate media notice at all.

The feasibility and timeliness of such events regarding United States foreign policy was clearly established by the November 1980 Freeze resolution triumph in western Massachusetts. It sent the critical message that local populations would respond positively to antinuclear weapons appeals. This, combined with the radical increase of ruling elite goading events, began to galvanize local peace-concerned activists in settlements across the United States. In something of the same manner in which the Chinese character for danger is also the character for hope, the advent of the Reaganites was accompanied by an early hopeful sign that citizen activism could effectively rouse disposed and even bystanding citizens.

This activism took two main forms, political and educational. The political form adopted the Freeze referendum tactic directly and followed or slightly adapted the western Massachusetts model. Existing and newly recruited activists began to promote freeze and nuclear free zone resolutions and referendum in hundreds of local governmental units. This began in New England town meetings in early 1981, where resolutions were successful and such successes began to feed upon themselves: the more governmental bodies that had already adopted a freeze resolution, the more legitimate it was — the more pressure there was — for one's jurisdiction also to do so. This "snowballed" so that by the spring of 1982, freeze resolutions had been adopted by 309 New England town meetings, 33 city coun-

Figure 7.2
New Nuclear Free Zones, 1978-1989

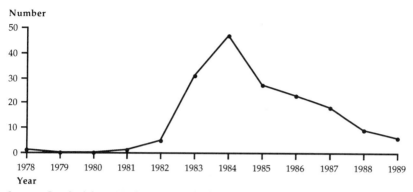

Source: Graphed from Nuclear Free America 1990, 12.

cils, 10 county councils and one or both houses of 11 state legislatures. There began, in addition, local campaigns for nuclear free zones which got off the ground in the soaring period before achieving its peak in the 1983–1984 faltering stage as shown in figure 7.2.

The educational form of local events focused heavily on the nature and dangers of nuclear weapons and wars and were often staged on college campuses and in churches. The single most used educational item is reputed to have been a videotaped program titled "The Last Epidemic," which is a compilation of nuclear war "expert"—dissent elite—figures who appeared at the 1980 national convention of the Physicians for Social Responsibility. Edited by Ian Thierman, it was made available free or cheaply to whomever requested it and by the fall of 1981 it was being viewed widely in churches and on campuses around the country. It and the hundreds of other videos of its ilk that circulated were the centerpiece of many local events. (The videotape may be the "postmodern" version of the broadside. Instead of Tom Paine's manifestos, we now have the Center for Defense Information's outpouring of half-hour video shows.)

A quantitative glimpse of this educational activity is shown in event-by-year counts of the extensive listings of upcoming events appearing in the pages of the surge's major and only slick paper publication, *The Nuclear Times* (an entity that was foundation subsidized and put out its first issue in July 1982—two facts that themselves express soaring). As figure 7.3 shows, events listed were heavily educational and peaked in 1983.

Three analytic features of educational and political events need to be

Figure 7.3
Events Announced in *The Nuclear Times,*
1982-1988

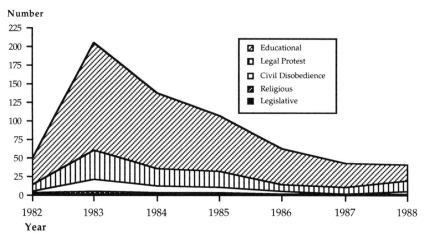

Note: Figures for 1982 cover July to December; those for 1988 cover January through October.

underscored. One, these acts were, in overwhelming proportion, extremely institutional, polite, civil, and staid acts that carried little or no social or physical risk or stigma and that were at the same time not very difficult to perform. They were *simple* as well as *legitimate.* These acts were the very "stuff" of American good citizenship — albeit, perhaps, a dying art: collecting signatures on petitions, signing petitions, offering resolutions, speaking at town meetings, arranging to show a video, attending a video viewing, and the like. Part of the explanation of soaring is that its main vehicles were very mundane, proper, and easy to do but seemingly effective in the context of 1981–1982. It is on this score that we take strong issue with Pam Solo's (1988) characterization of the Freeze in this period, in particular, as moving "from protest to politics," the title of her book on the Freeze element of the peace surge. More accurately, what we saw was simply "from local staid politics to national staid politics" without involving much "protest" in any meaningful sense.[11]

Two, such simple and proper activist actions *legitimized* foreign policy dissent. By being so simple and proper, activism avoided or forestalled counterattacks or shunning on the grounds that improper means were being employed to further opposition to foreign and military policies.

Three, the foreign policies of nations are abstract and remote in ways that other kinds of government policies are not. They are, therefore, more difficult to "bring home," to "make real," to *concretize*. Local events of the sorts just described served to at least reduce if not eliminate the problems of abstractness and remoteness. Consciousness was, thus, raised and facilitated further and wider citizen action.

Overall, then, in tandem with consensus problems and solutions perceptions (discussed previously), the "formula" for local events centered on relatively simple acts that could be performed by millions of people to register their concern about nuclear war. Propitiously, foremost among these was petition signing for one or more of several campaigns in the soaring period, which were primarily drives to have units of government endorse a Freeze and drives to place referenda on election ballots. Such drives to collect signatures also, of course, provided a central, nonthreatening form of activity for citizen activists.

Events required stagers — actors who were going to "arrange" matters so that they would "happen." In the prior focusing phase of 1979–1980, such actors were importantly drawn from the staffs of the classic peace organizations, most especially from the American Friends Service Committee. This involvement continued and widened in the soar phase but remained, nonetheless, a relatively small number, albeit an extremely important small number.

But, most auspiciously to facilitate soaring, cadre of local event organizers must be quite considerably if not vastly enlarged. New people must hear and respond to the challenge. They must be prepared to give a significant portion of each week if not their entire work lives to "making events" and doing other of the work we are describing. It is not necessarily the case that a population will contain enough people willing to so change their lives. If a population does not, then we ought to expect a surge to be small and to lack energy if not to falter entirely.

Propitiously, the American population did contain, in the early 1980s, a distinctive strata that was already sensitive to questions of war and peace and who were "prepared" in several ways to take up the task of intense local (and national) activism. Although this strata did not exhaust the ranks of the new activists, it was likely the most prominent part of it: thirty-something, college educated, white, middle-class men and women who were of college age during the Vietnam War.[12] One of the ironic legacies of the Vietnam War was a class of articulate persons who were, from their experience, suspicious of U.S. military policies. Edward Price's survey of national and local Freeze participants is among several documenting this background.

Most of the respondents in my survey [of a local Freeze group's members] were clearly from the generation of the Sixties. Fifty-six percent were between the ages of thirty-five and forty-four in 1985. The same percentage had a postgraduate degree, and ninety percent had at least a bachelor's degree. . . . [T]he most striking things about [national] Freeze board members were their age and educational distributions. Seventy two percent of the respondents were born during the ten years following World War II. . . . Eighty-one percent had at least a bachelor's degree, and forty percent also had a master's or Ph.D. degree. . . . [T]hey would have been college . . . students during the late 1960s and early 1970s, at the time of the anti-Vietnam war movement (Price 1990, 212, 214).

The findings of Price and others both agree and disagree with "new class" theory interpretations of eighties peace activism such as that offered by McCrea and Markle (1989), who propound that the social base was simply the white, professional, upper–middle class. This is largely true, we think, as far as it goes, but imprecise at the level of indicating which parts of the new class itself were more and less active in the surge. After all, the vast portion of the so-called new class likely had little or nothing to do with eighties peace action, and that variable cannot, therefore, do a great deal in accounting for it. Such additional, selective factors have not, however, been identified and likely involve mundane and situational variables, such as who happened to be in what social networks at particular and critical times (cf. McAdam, McCarthy, Zald 1988, 707–11). For example, in his survey of local freeze group members in a midwestern city, Marullo (1990) found that 64 percent of the respondents learned of the Freeze from social contacts (friends or members of church groups or other voluntary associations to which they belonged).

In stressing these features of main local event-makers regarding the Freeze, we do not want inadvertently to imply that they exhausted the ranks of peace soaring, for they clearly did not. As explained in other chapters, there were several additional "clusters" or modes of action and participants of differing social characteristics involved in them. Among the protesters, for example, there were what Barbara Epstein has labeled "the nonviolent direct action movement" and that we might otherwise call the "neocounterculture." In alliance with more mainstream people, they mounted protest campaigns against nuclear and military installations. The Women's Peace Camp begun July 1983 at Seneca, New York, was among these as were the campaigns of the Livermore Action Group (Epstein 1991) and the Honeywell Project (Rogne and Harper 1990), both of which peaked in 1983 and declined thereafter. A cluster of prophets also undertook directly to obstruct the military as acts of religious ritual. What is important about them in this context is that they were encouraged by goading elite events and the upwelling of other classes of events to initiate their own new campaigns and to step up existing ones. In 1988, a member of one of these networks issued a chronology of its "actions" which, when graphed in figure 7.4 shows an increase in their activity that parallels those of other networks of prophets. (We note that the curve peaks somewhat later — in 1984–1985 — than the curves of some other types of events, as we would predict from the enormous commitment to antiwar issues among the prophets.)

All of these local dissenting events synergistically fed back on the other soaring events. Local media coverage of them fed into national media coverage and brought issues home to the local level for people to consider. Local dissenting events provided ready audiences for dissident elites and prepared people for national dissenting events. Leaders of local events knew that they had become the news, further fueling perceptions that the soar had penetrated into local communities across the country. This is illustrated by a local Cleveland Freeze Campaign coordinator's statement made shortly after the U.S. House of Representatives and the Ohio state legislature passed Freeze Resolutions in the summer of 1983. "We've got the [local] media people coming to us now for stories. This win [in the Ohio state senate] means that we have the clout to get rid of any of the local politicians who voted against our resolution. Even on the national scene, the country is looking to us [the Ohio state and Cleveland Freeze Campaigns] for our judgment on [Senator and presidential candidate John] Glenn's position on arms control. We really turned him around on the Freeze."[13]

3. Dissident elite legitimizing events. Even though the political success in western Massachusetts in November 1980 was critical for galvanizing further political action of its sort, people most central to organizing the Freeze did not all throw themselves into organizing ballot and related actions. Instead, they embarked on actions the importance of which are obvious only in retrospect. They began a campaign of getting peace organizations, peace sympathetic organizations, recognized arms control "experts," and prominent individuals of many sorts to endorse the concept of freezing the arms race. Thus, when the first "Call to Halt the Nuclear Arms Race" was circulated in 1980–1981, it contained the endorsements of 66 individuals and organizations, most of them affiliated with churches, peace groups, or liberal political organizations (American Friends Service Committee 1980). However, when a new "call" was issued in February 1983, the "prominent endorser's list" contained the names of 148 national and international organizations, 30 arms control experts and ex-governmental officials, 32 artists and performers, 26 business executives, 320 city coun-

Figure 7.4
Plowshares Arrests and Actions, 1980-1987

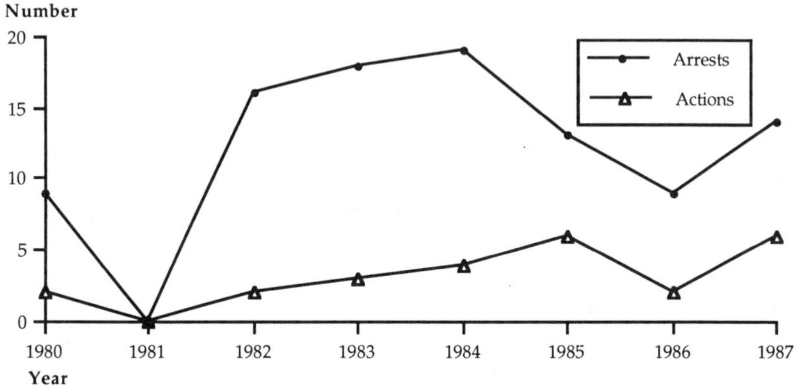

Number

cils, 444 New England town meetings, 11 state legislatures, 6 additional state houses, 10 mayors, 10 Republican officials, 32 educators and educational institutions, 2 Nobel laureates, 40 labor unions and leaders, 13 medical professionals, 17 ex-military officers, 19 minority group leaders, 50 religious bodies and leaders, 15 other professionals, and 21 other local and regional organizations (Nuclear Weapons Freeze Campaign 1983).

Working in ratcheting tandem with all the other classes of events we are reporting, this turns out to be an enormously important component of soaring. In fact, it may have been especially important in this surge because of the special character of foreign policy matters in relation to the population at large. We believe the conventional wisdom about opinion formation and change to be true — that the less direct experience people have with a topic, the greater is their tendency to defer to expert and other elite opinion. Further, the more complicated and inaccessible the topic, the more likely are people to defer to experts and elites. Foreign policy and arms control are remote and complicated topics for most people. These are matters, therefore, in which people who claim expertise and elite competence have particular influence — as opposed to many matters of domestic policy in which lay people have direct experience against which to judge the claims of experts and other authorities.

Therefore, the strategy of recruiting profreeze endorsements and statements critical of U.S. foreign policy from dissident elites was particularly important. The long lists of such endorsements and statements developed and publicized in 1981–1983 served to send the message that the views of the current administration were not necessarily the only valid and legitimate *expert and elite* way to think about American foreign and military policy.

This Freeze-supportive effort was, however, but one form of elite dissension. Concern with nuclear foreign policy burgeoned as a more general topic among many elite occupations, in particular, scientists, physicians, and religious leaders. Among scientists, for example, the prestigious *Bulletin of the Atomic Scientists*, which had published a Doomsday Clock since the start of the nuclear age, moved the clock's minute hand from 51 to 53 minutes in 1980 (the first change since 1974) and then to 56 minutes in 1981, and even to 57 minutes in 1984, the closest to midnight the minute hand had been since 1953 (*Bulletin of the Atomic Scientists* editors 1990, 58; and depicted in figure 7.5). Among physicians, a rejuvenated association of doctors called Physicians for Social Responsibility undertook well-publicized, large, and very elaborately staged local symposia on nuclear war as shown in figure 7.6.

Such dissident elite legitimizing events were critical in fueling the soar phase. The split between the Reaganite far Right and moderate arms controllers provided much grist for popular media coverage as well as specialty foreign policy journal debates. *Foreign Affairs*, one of the most widely read and influential foreign policy journals among policymakers, illustrated the increased attention paid to nuclear weapons issues during this period. We counted the number of articles that focused on U.S.-USSR relations, nuclear arms control, and the U.S. debate over strategic policy in the journal and found that the number of articles on these topics dramatically increased during the soar phase (and then remained at relatively elevated levels.)[14]

This increased interest among dissident elites helped to place the issue on the public agenda and forced the public to consider the threat of nuclear weapons. Dissident elites also opened the door for foundation and other funders' support for peace movement related activities since they were credible, politically safe, and even prestigious recipients of such support. These elites were also seen as legitimate and desirable representatives of opposition to U.S. foreign policy, which further facilitated media coverage of the movement.

4. *National dissenting events.* A surge "comes alive" in myriad local events, some of which are seen as major in the local context, even if they have little national impact. But soaring cannot be constituted of only such major but simply local events. More national and larger-scale foci are

Figure 7.5
Minutes on the Doomsday Clock, 1978-1990

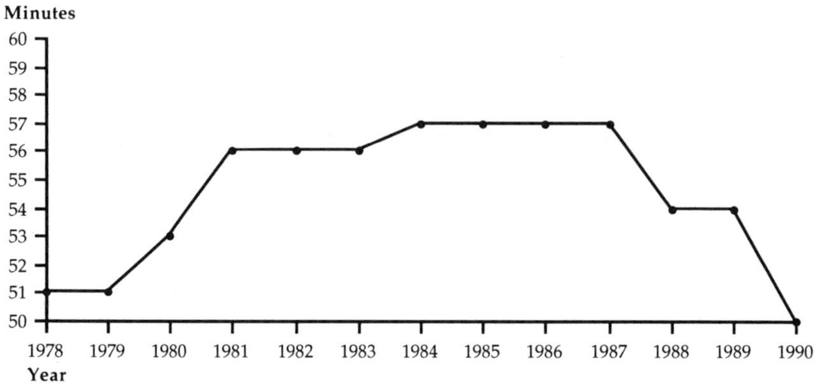

Source: Charted from *Bulletin of the Atomic Scientists* Editors 1990, 57.

needed to imbue the surge with grand significance and consequence. By definition, such events are publicized and promoted nationally (or at least over regions) and draw participants on that scale, resulting in coverage by national media. Further, such national, focusing events should be matters toward which (or "around" which, in organizer jargon) people can prepare and organize. In order most strongly to energize and mobilize people, focusing events should be conceived as within the control—or possible control—of actions undertaken by ordinary citizens.

In the major inflection year of the soaring period, 1982, there were at least five such major focusing events—events providing something to "look forward to" with positive expectancy and to "look back on" with pride and energized hope.

1. *March.* Unveiled at a major press conference event (Waller 1987, 67), the Kennedy-Hatfield Freeze resolution was introduced with 165 House and 24 Senate cosponsors.

2. *April.* Ground Zero Week, in which there were meetings on the nuclear threat in some seven hundred communities; its organizers claimed that about one million people participated in at least one event of the week.

3. *April.* In California, some 700,000 signatures were ceremoniously presented to state officials in order to place a Freeze resolution on the ballot of the November election.

4. *June.* Timed to coincide with and to support new United Nations

Figure 7.6
National and Local PSR Symposia,
1980-1983

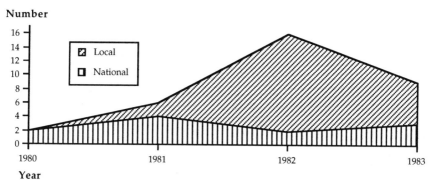

Number

Source: Neal 1988, 330-31, table 4. National means organized by the national office; local means organized by a local chapter.

talks on arms control and disarmament, close to a million people rally for a nuclear Freeze in New York City.

5. *November.* Freeze resolutions adopted by the electorates of eight states and the District of Columbia and about thirty cities. Overall, 18 million vote on Freeze resolutions (about 30 percent of the electorate), 10.8 million in favor, 7.2 million opposed.

It is critical to stress that each of these events (and myriad lesser-scale undertakings) were the end products of an enormous amount of local citizen effort and/or dissident elite planning and enterprise. None simply "happened." For weeks and months beforehand, people were focusing ahead to these events, constructing plans to ensure their success, and carrying out those plans.

It is the assertion that there *will be* such events and their actualization that is at the core of soaring when combined with and fed by other of the classes of events discussed. (Conversely, the *absence* of the assertion of such events and/or the failure of their actualization is at the core of failure to soar, faltering, and slump.)[15] Such events also become topics around which local events were organized and for which fundraising was undertaken. Dissident elites were provided national forums from which to espouse their opposition, and the media had newsworthy events on which to report. More and more of the public was touched by these activities as they spread beyond movement spheres of influence and into everyday life.

In addition to these preeminent events of the major inflection year (just listed), a range of lesser, but still national or quasi-national, events were occurring in that year and in 1981 and 1983, events signaling diversified actions that moved in both more consensual and more conflictful directions. Here is a sampling:

September 1981. National conference on war tax resistance held, the first since 1974.

November 1981. First Union of Concerned Scientists national teach-in on nuclear war by means of satellite down links to 150 locations, with an estimated one hundred thousand participants. This form was repeated in subsequent years with larger numbers of participants.

October 1982. The White Train Campaign begins, tracking and protesting trains leaving Amarillo, Texas, the site of nuclear warhead final assembly, and traveling through U.S. communities.

December 1982. A man seizes and threatens to blow up the Washington Monument unless the arms race is stopped. He is shot and killed by police in the process of capturing him.

August 1983. Ground Zero's city-pairing project is launched.

November 1983. Network prime time broadcast of the movie, "The Day After."

The December 1982 event bears special discussion. At first glance, the actions of the presumably deranged individual at the Washington Monument may not appear pertinent, especially not in the context of national events. The incident was, however, national news and was, perforce, a relevant national event. And, we think, it tells us something about the higher escalated phases of the soaring stage. Individuals who focus their mental difficulties on public events and debates are not, unsurprisingly, likely to select topics of the most intense civil concern at the time they are constructing their personal troubles as public issues. Further, nuclear weapons and the arms race are themselves topics that likely touch the "deep mythic themes" of human societies themselves (the universal deep themes of death and renewal) (Hilgartner and Bosk 1988). The surprising aspect, actually, is that so few disturbed people seemed to have responded in as innovative a fashion as the gentleman at the Washington Monument.

5. *Coalescing events.* Coalescing events are all the occasions in which people undertake to name and otherwise formalize their surge interactions with one another into enduring associations. The term *organizing* would be an appropriate caption for this kind of event were it not so commonly used in a much broader sense to mean all activities attendant to promoting a social movement. The particular significance of coalescing events is that they publicly assign responsibility for further collective action—further

events — and, thereby, increase the *capacity* for creating local, dissident elite, and national events and the *likelihood* that they will occur.[16]

Both responding to and encouraging the other classes of events, in 1981–1983 new organizations came onto the scene and existing organizations experienced membership spurts. Looking first at sheer numbers of nuclear war–related — or more broadly, peace — organizations, a first fact of note is that no one appears to have had an interest in counting American "peace groups" until the late-seventies, when Randall Forsberg began her own "small survey" of, initially, only some ten organizations that she rapidly expanded in 1978 and 1979 as she discovered many additional local groups in the course of her Freeze-promoting travels in those years (Forsberg 1984, vii).

The initial surge of the focusing period (1979–1980) and the founding of her Institute for Defense and Disarmament Studies in 1979 provided the stimulus and vehicle for the first concerted national count by means of questionnaires circulated to groups (Forsberg 1984). Published as the *American Peace Directory 1984* (Fine and Steven 1984), it listed 1,350 groups enumerated in 1983. The 1986 update lists 5,700 groups counted in 1985 (Bernstein et al. 1986) and the 1988/1989 version enumerates some 7,000 counted in 1987 (Conetta 1988). Such numbers are an amalgam, of course, of an actual increase in the number of groups and increasing sophistication in identifying groups missed in earlier counts. (The last pages of all three editions of this directory were a questionnaire that asked unlisted groups to report themselves, thus increasing the rate of reporting.)[17]

A different measure of the rate of coalescing into new organizations is provided by a survey of 414 peace groups conducted by Mary Anna Colwell in 1988. In her survey of all large, national peace groups combined with a randomly selected sample of smaller groups, Colwell asked groups the year in which they were founded (Colwell 1989). Figure 7.7 shows the number and percentage founded in each decade of this century, indicating that over half of all groups existing in 1988 were founded in or after 1980. Another quarter of them were founded since 1970, suggesting that while peace activism may be a persistent social force, only a very small proportion of its specific vehicles have any historical depth. If we look at the most recent years of peace group foundings (1977–1987), as in figure 7.8, we see that the peak year was 1982. We have here, indeed, a clue about the fragility and instability of peace organizations that foreshadows phases to come.

A determinedly nonpartisan research and information organization called ACCESS (itself funded by major mainline foundation grants), un-

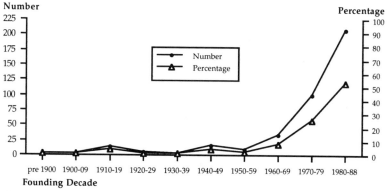

Figure 7.7
Founding Decade of 414 Peace Surge
Organizations Surveyed in 1988

Source: Colwell 1988.

dertook, in 1987, to enumerate what it defined as "information source" organizations on "war, peace, and security" matters. By "information source" ACCESS meant largely research organizations and associations of scholars. This survey resulted in two kinds of founding-date-rate information — by decade and by year in the 1980s. It is noteworthy that the decade percentages parallel Colwell's findings for peace groups more generally: almost half were founded in the eighties and another quarter or so since 1970. The year in the 1980s data shows an ascent in 1979 and 1980 and a soar in 1981, the year with the largest number of foundings (Kincade and Hayner 1988, xi, xiii, table 1, and figure 3).

The coalescing of national organizations directly fueled several of the other events. As national groups formed and undertook operations, they promoted the creation and expansion of local groups by providing information and advice for conducting local dissenting campaigns, by hiring field organizers to promote additional activity at the local level, and by coordinating activities to increase their visibility to the public. The national coordination of events facilitated increased media coverage of movement activities by making the stories and spokespersons more accessible to the media. The growth of national organizations was supported, to some degree, by foundation funding, but, more importantly, they provided a safe (tax deductible) corporate structure to which foundations and wealthy donors could make grants and major donations. Finally, dissident elites were provided with an operating base in some instances and, more gener-

Figure 7.8
Founding Years of Peace Surge
Organizations, 1977-1987

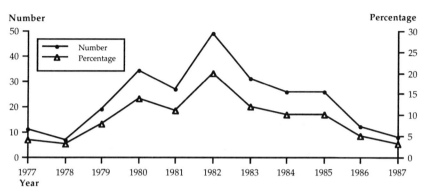

Source: Colwell 1988.

ally, were assured audiences for their speeches, articles, and other statements opposing the Reagan buildup.

6. *Media events.* Coverage by any of the media of impersonal or "mass" communications is very much an event in the sense of a space-time isolated occurrence even if it does not literally involve people gathering in a face-to-face manner. It is in one sense unfortunate that the term *media event* has come to mean an occurrence contrived for coverage by the media. In our usage, in contrast, a media event may or may not have been so contrived. What is important, instead, is that media provide coverage. In common usage, media increasingly means only newspapers and television, and as important as they are, they are hardly the only mass media. Also salient are books and magazines and, increasingly, video tapes.

Analysts of media perennially debate the question of whether media construct what are widely perceived to be issues in public life through their selective reporting or if they merely reflect and report what is already happening in public life. Media critics of the Left and Right alike incline to the former view while people in the media, naturally enough, prefer the latter view. Our view is that one or the other of these views may be most accurate depending on the period and case we are inspecting at any time. The media certainly are selective in their coverage, which, in turn, raises the visibility of certain issues, but their coverage is often also a reflection of what is already going on.

However, in the case of the eighties peace surge, it is clear that a stir-

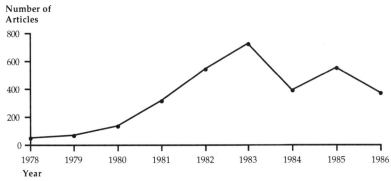

Figure 7.9
Magazine Articles on Nuclear Weapons
and Related Issues, 1978-1986

Source: McGrea and Markle 1989, 143, table 6.1.

ring of peace action in the United States began (in 1979–1980) well before significant media interest and the surge's advance was retarded by media inattention. This continued to be the case to a significant extent even through 1981 but then changed radically in 1982 when the media lurched into their "blitz" mode with respect to citizen peace action. Among other statistical series that document this, those compiled by David Meyer show very clear "jumps" in coverage on CBS national news, in the *New York Times,* and in periodical articles compiled in the *Reader's Guide* (Meyer 1990b, 123–125; figures 2, 3, 4).

Reports of citizen dissent are, of course, only one component of the larger topic of the problematic character of the American war policy per se. One measure of media response to this more general topic is shown in figure 7.9, which shows steep increases in yearly number of articles on nuclear war matters that peaked in 1983 and then declined.

There are two further indications that the issue had "arrived" in the media. The first was that the threat of nuclear war became the cover story of both *Time* and *Newsweek* in the spring of 1982, titled, respectively and tellingly enough, "Thinking about the Unthinkable" (March 29) and "A Matter of Life and Death" (April 26). The second was that the media become aware of its own role in covering the nuclear threat and began writing about its own coverage of the issue. Rather than reporting only on the substantive issues, they also produced self-reflective pieces discussing and analyzing how the media went about covering the nuclear question. The Center

Figure 7.10
Articles on How the Media Cover
the Nuclear Question

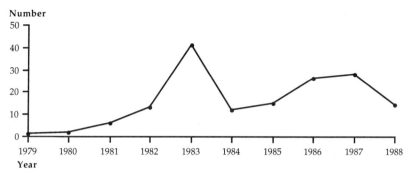

Source: Graphed from Dorman, Manoff, and Weeks 1988, 38-50.

for War, Peace, and the News Media compiled a comprehensive bibliography of articles and books that examined media coverage of the nuclear issue. Our count of the number of items published in each year is presented in figure 7.10 (Dorman, Manoff, and Weeks 1988). We see the peak of these articles in 1983, at the height of the soar, suggesting the media's awareness and concern that its own coverage of the issue had contributed to public concern over the nuclear threat.

The logic and impact of media coverage is an ironic two-edge sword because of what we might call the "spigot treatment."[18] In spigotlike fashion, for a great many topics, the media tend to be either "full on" or "full off." With regard to an enormous range of matters in life, the media spigot is, of course, virtually or fully off all the time. With some few topics it suddenly gets turned almost fully on. The critique of the media is that many realities "out there in the real world" do not themselves turn fully on or fully off in their operation. The spigot operation of the media, therefore, distorts what is a slower changing reality by depicting it as "not there" one day and "enormously there" the next day.

In the case of peace activism, the media first acted—in 1979, 1980, and 1981—as if hardly anything at all was "out there." But then it turned the spigot almost fully on, projecting a picture of peace action as a mighty force sweeping the country. Both were enormous exaggerations—of underestimation at first and of overestimation second.

But, of course, the second distortion, of overestimation, produced, in part, its own confirmation by falsely exaggerating peace activism, which served to mobilize people into peace action! The very fact of projecting a mighty force operated to energize, to ratchet, various of the other classes of events and actors we are describing. It had, that is, an enormous facilitative effect on soaring. The media are the creators of reality and legitimacy par excellence, and when the media blitz began in 1982, the soaring phase kicked into all out ahead — meaning up.

Moreover, this media blitz was in an auspiciously synergistic relation to the nationwide network of activists that was already emerging. That is, the several classes of quieter events and plans for events underway when the media blitz hit were likely ratcheted by the focus and publicity that the media were now providing. In particular, meticulous documentation that there were elite organizations and persons already on record as opposing Reaganite war-peace policies was available so that peace dissent could now "go public" with a bevy of intellectual and political "heavies" that provided *credibility*. They could not be dismissed as a mere gaggle of marginal fuzzy-minded peaceniks with nothing better to worry about. Important experts on military matters and significant political figures were reasonably concerned with the direction of foreign and war policy. Thus, for the simultaneous press conferences of all Freeze groups held on April 26, 1982, the national freeze coordinating organization constructed its press conference to "include the release of a paper on the Freeze and National Security Issues." The planners arranged that "the paper will be backed by prominent experts and the press conference will also be a place for national figures to announce their endorsement" (Ramsey and Kehler 1982). The activists were quite carefully ready when the media seriously came calling, and this preparation served to make the media even more serious. It also had the effect of stimulating further foundation support for peace and arms control issues because not only did the opposition to the Reagan buildup have credible opposition, but it was also a "hot topic" as evidenced by media coverage.

Materials on the operation of the media in this period suggest that its role was not, however, *only* that of a mechanical on-off spigot. At least one important form of the media — book publishers — were themselves active promoters of and participants in the peace surge, not simple responders to events. When war-peace matters had only begun to stir, a large number of publishers were already beginning to prepare a bevy of books on nuclear war and related topics. Reports of this development suggested that publishers were embarked on this activity not merely because of money to be made on book sales but because of a personal commitment to the importance of the topic (Davis and Smith 1982; Blooston 1982). Indeed, the Book of the Month Club took the exceedingly unusual if not unique step of offering Jonathan Schell's apocalyptic *Fate of the Earth* (1982) at cost to facilitate its purchase by large numbers of people (McGrath 1982). Wealthy donors and funders made large bulk purchases of Schell's book, Ground Zero's *Nuclear War: What's In It for You?* (1982), Helen Caldicott's *Nuclear Madness* (1978), and Ken Keyes' *The Hundredth Monkey* (1982) and either sold them at cost or gave them away at movement events.

7. Funding events. There are four major sources of funding for citizen action (or most other) activities: government (either national or local); for-profit private organizations: nonprofit organizations, including foundations; or individuals. Each of these can be divided into providing "large" versus "small" amounts of funding per funding event and total funding.

The soar phase of the eighties peace surge appeared to have received little or no funding from the first two of these sources. This is a banal finding except when placed in comparative movement and citizen action perspective and alongside such soars as the Earth Days of 1970 and 1990 or the anti–drunk driving campaigns of the 1980s, which were quite conspicuously financed by government and for-profit corporations. Eighties peace activism was financially based, instead, in nonprofit organizations, most particularly in churches, colleges/universities, and foundations, and dependent on the amity of wealthy individuals.

Foundations were an especially important source of funding because, even though their controllers were members of elite classes, many of them were also frightened by the new U.S. government and responded by increasing the number of peace and security programs they funded and amounts of funding.[19] Thus, a survey of prominent foundations done in the late-eighties found that over half of all programs they were currently funding were started in the eighties and another almost 30 percent had started since 1970 (figure 7.11).

The amount of foundation funding increased dramatically as well from $16.5 million in 1982 (McCrea and Markle 1989, 117), to $52 million in 1984, to $123.8 million in 1988 (Allen 1990, 11). The largest increase in funding occurred in 1983–1985 and continued to increase through the late-1980s, peaking later than most of the other events discussed here. Despite the important role of foundation seed money in the formation and operation of peace groups, a great portion of the funds went to larger, already established arms control organizations and individuals (dissenting elites). This pattern is seen clearly in the data of Wright, Rodriguez, and Waitzkin (1986), which shows foundation support going largely to educational and research programs in universities and research centers rather than to political or protest undertakings. The Wright, Rodriguez, and Waitzkin (1986) data also show that foundation support tended to go to educator

Figure 7.11
Decade Major Foundations Started
Programs Funding War-Peace Projects

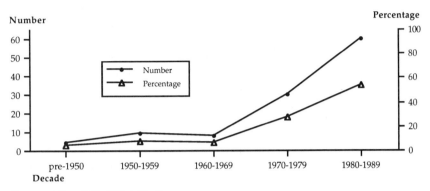

Source: Allen 1990, 185, table 8.

and research organizations that conceived the "problem" in largely United States–Soviet Union terms and as a matter of the "nuclear arms race" rather than in frameworks that would stress the United States' imperialistic relations with Third World nations and the power of a "military-industrial complex" (Wright, Rodriguez, and Waitzkin 1986). Within educational institutions, the growth in numbers of peace studies programs was notable, increasing from 90 in 1978 (Feller, Schwenninger, and Singerman 1981) to 140 in 1982 (Wien 1984) to 216 in 1989 (Thomas and Klare 1990).

Because of its dispersed, ad hoc, and personal contact character, it is difficult to form a clear picture of the role of large-scale private individual donors. We do know, however, that people such as Howard Willens both gave and raised very substantial sums in the California referendum drive, that Allan Kay contributed sizable sums to launch the Freeze campaign and hold its early national conferences, and that Joan Kroc, the McDonald's magnate heir, donated literally millions to the movement's soar.[20] Beyond lending their endorsement to peace activities, liberal personalities of the entertainment industry are also said to have contributed generously.[21]

8. *Public opining events.* For whatever reasons, the cognitive maps of citizens and elites alike have come to feature the public as a major actor to whom one makes reference in deciding one's own actions. The level of its knowledge and information on a given topic and the direction and strength of its attitudes and opinions on those topics are subjects of more or less constant monitoring and concern in the calculus of political actors'

next, best course of action. Functioning mystically much the same as the oracles and soothsayers of bygone societies, in U.S. society public opinion is held, superficially at least, as the final arbiter of public policy and, therefore, of the feasibility and timeliness of all projected courses of political action. The most recent opining of the public is, therefore, an event in a sequence of events that interacts with the other seven in synergistically facilitating or inhibiting the number and kinds of the other classes of events. If it speaks in your favor, you are energized to further effort and vice versa.

Public opining comes, of course, in two main varieties, one much more consequential than the other: poll reports and election results. The former is scrutinized for what it might portend about the latter, and the latter plays decisively on the facilitation or inhibition of surges. As reported, the surge "kick off" public opining event was provided in November 1980 by the electorate of western Massachusetts and was supported by local votes in various other jurisdictions, events treated previously as legitimizing local events.

On a national scale, beginning in 1981, credible pollers of public opinion began to report that the "American public" favored nuclear disarmament, arms reductions, or a nuclear freeze in overwhelmingly large percentages. A 1981 Gallup poll showed two-to-one support of disarmament and 80 percent support for the United States to negotiate with the Soviet Union (Gallup 1981); a 1982 Harris poll showed 73 percent support for all countries banning production of nuclear weapons, and 86 percent wanting U.S. and Soviet arms cuts (Harris 1982); and, a 1982 *New York Times* poll showed 72 percent support for a nuclear freeze (Miller 1982; see also Smith 1988). These results were reported in the public press and circulated widely in peace surge circles.

In retrospect, however, we, as analysts of surges of citizen action, are required also to point out that public opinion polls were consumed rather selectively by peace proponents. For, while the "peace positive" results of the polls just recounted are surely true, there were other results at the time that are not easily read as intense public concern over foreign and military policy or as unambiguous support for a Freeze or other such initiatives. In the *New York Times* poll, for example, support for a Freeze drops from 72 percent to 30 percent or less if the respondents believe the Soviets would gain an advantage or could cheat through a Freeze (Miller 1982; A22). In addition to many polls showing a strong and unwavering distrust of the Soviet Union, the "most important problem" series of questions that has been put to the American public for almost fifty years show a relatively small percentage of the public ranking foreign affairs as "the most important problem facing the country" in 1981 and 1982. The percentage climbs to the mid-30 range in late-1983, the time of showing the ABC broadcast film, "The Day After" (Smith 1985). However, percentages in the thirties are still quite low when compared to the war years of World War II, Korea, and Vietnam, when the percentages regularly ran along in the fifties and sixties (Smith 1980, 1985). Ironically, the percentage ranking foreign policy as the most important problem climbs and peaks after other, and more salient, classes of events have faltered, peaked, and gone into decline (Smith 1985; Schuman, Ludwig, and Krosnick 1986).

Nonetheless, credible polls showing public support were available in the soar period. Moreover, the November 1982 elections resulting in 60 percent support of Freeze referenda on state and local ballots did indicate a significant degree of peace policy support, however "soft" this might have been.

Conditions: Glossed Past Events

We have focused on the interplay of several classes of actors, a constellation of perceptions, and the synergy of events. This formulation as yet lacks, however, a necessary fourth element: a specification of conditions that play on and affect how these elements interact. We think it is helpful to think of conditions as accumulated past events that are "glossed" in the memory and actions of participants. So amalgamated, multiple events of a given sort become standing states of social organization that constrain or facilitate action. Nonetheless, not all amalgamated events/ conditions of importance need clearly or at all to appear in the explicit perceptions of participants. Thus, such accumulated events as "co-optable preexisting networks" and "slack resources" often appear as facilitating conditions in the focusing phase of movements (e.g., Freeman 1983, chap. 1; chap. 6, this volume), and they have an analytic meaning and importance independent of any participants' perceptions of them.[22]

Conditions and events, therefore, are not fixed categories. Time rushes on and today's events become tomorrow's conditions. Taken together, events and conditions in movement soars are about the production, control, or prevention of events as these are seen to relate to emerging conditions, into which events are always receding.

In the case at hand, it is important to appreciate that the soar phase we have dissected here was in part reacting to and building on conditions established in the first and focusing phase of 1979-1980. That is, the focusing phase contained several critical events that passed into facilitating conditions. First, in the soaring phase, the resources of the peace milieu were no longer "slack," as they were in most of the first phase, but dedicated to promoting a nuclear Freeze resolution and, more generally, alarm about the dangers of nuclear war. Second, the highly effective public intellectuals who appeared in the focusing phase continued their work and were joined by many additional spokespeople. Third, the triumph of the western Massachusetts Freeze referendum in November 1980 continued to be drawn on as a major facilitating event — now condition — that had radically altered participants' assessments of the feasibility and timeliness of movement action.[23]

Conclusion

Social movement soars consist, then, of an expanding number and array of *actors* who are sharing or reacting to *perceptions* of danger and urgency and contesting what will be the character of a burgeoning panoply of diverse *events* built in response to and on changing *conditions*. Soars are contests over the sheer existence of events and whether they will be major or minor (providing foci of attention and action or not), facilitative or inhibitive of the surge, and produced by the surgers, their opponents, or a third party. Movement surges soar (or slump) as a function of who can produce or prevent which of several kinds of events.

Although indispensable as analytic tools, taken alone, an elaboration of actors, perceptions, events, and conditions such as this does not make a surge. For, and as stated in previous chapters, these are also commonly the stuff of ordinary political and other life. What *is* distinctive is the *intensity* of threat/opportunity perceptions combined with the extremely *rapid and synergistic proliferation* of events pursuant to those perceptions.

This case conjoined with the analysis we offer of it points to several kinds of conclusions about the origin, growth, and faltering of citizen actions generally and social movements specifically.

On-Going and Not Simply Initiating Causes

The first and focusing phase of eighties peace activism (1979–1980) and the second and soar phase (1981–1982, extending into 1983) involved different kinds of events and categories of actors. We might best think of the two phases as qualitatively distinct in their specific dynamics and, certainly, in their scale and complexity. We would, in particular, be hard put to predict the second phase from the first. If we undertook to predict the second phase from knowledge of the first phase, collapse or dissipation is likely our best forecast. This is, of course, the fate of most potential social movements which contend for public attention but never advance beyond the first stage. The peace surge moved on, in contrast, because a wide variety of new classes of events began to happen and new actors entered. Such new entries are extremely difficult to foresee. To us this means that the course of a social movement and other collective action must be understood as a function of the operation of continuously changing and ongoing variables and not simply of those at play in early stages (cf. Turner and Killian 1987, 253–55).

Synergy

The eight classes of actors and events were operating in a nonlinear and synergistic fashion. Each was having an enlarging impact on the others. Each was in this sense "ratcheting" the other. Each grew stronger *because* each of the others was growing stronger and *as* each of the others grew stronger. The advancement of each was facilitated by advancement of at least some of the others, and vice versa. We have tried to specify a number of these synergistic relations, such as how "local events" grew in number and spread because of "media blitz," the "media blitz" grew in response to the spread of "local events," and both benefited from (and contributed to) large financial donations to the movement. What we had, then, was an exceedingly complex set of feed and feedback loops that were spiraling upward and outward as depicted in figure 7.1. The phrase "on a roll" is an effort to capture this dynamic as is the idea of "momentum" (Adler 1981), and both should be kept in mind in this context and not merely in the sports contexts where we usually encounter them. Both notions are helpful in that each refers to those unusual situations where all or many of the relevant factors begin to work together in an especially well-meshed and mutually strengthening fashion, thus producing or allowing performances and coordinations beyond those ordinarily achieved.

Why Eight and Why These Eight?

One can and should properly ask, Why these particular classes of events? and Why eight and not some other number?

With respect to the first question, let us in turn ask, if there is to be, considered generically, a challenge to authority, what tasks have to be accomplished? William Gamson has offered a useful answer to this question in his *Encounters with Unjust Authority*, specifying the three key tasks of rebellion as (1) forming a perception, a frame, that an injustice is, in fact, taking place; (2) psychologically breaking the bonds to authority, the premise that one will obey or concur with authority; and (3) organizing an actual challenger of the perceived injustice (Gamson, Fireman, and Rytina 1982). The eight classes of events we have been analyzing are operationalizations of one or more of these three generic tasks.

1. Goading events supplied the materials for a perception of problematic authority in the first place, and their continuing flow sustained and enlarged that perception. The "injustice frame" itself came from enclaves of entrepreneurs who were already and broadly disposed to doubt the propriety of given authorities and who "focused" such a frame in the initial phase of the surge as described in chapter 6.

2. The legitimacy of the obligation of obedience — or, at least, of acquiescence — was thrown into doubt by dissident elites, the increase of media events, and dissenting shifts in public opinion.

3. Actual challenges required the very concrete resourse of money or funding. At large system levels of action such as described here, the socially sanctioned means of expression were national and local events. Funding, local, and national events were, as a pragmatic matter, deployed through coalesced organization. The point of events was, of course, to achieve consideration in the public arena, and media events were primary routes to that achievement.

These eight, then, are ways in which the generic tasks of dissent and challenge are operationalized at the level of a large society that operates in the manner of the United States.

But why eight? The answer is that there likely are more than eight. Our claim is simply that these are the main eight, the eight that serve analytically to capture the primary substance of the surge we have described and that serve to accomplish the three tasks of rebellion.

The Particular Importance of Elites

Reviewing these eight classes of events as an overall pattern and taking account of analyses stressing relations between elites and social movements (e.g., Jenkins and Eckert 1986; Jenkins and Brents 1989), we are impressed with the central roles played by elite actors. In this case, elites, indeed, were virtually the dominant actors. They exhibited such dominance in at least four kinds of events.

1. The ruling elites were auspiciously providing a continuing supply of *goading events*. Without such a supply, the claims of danger, injustice, and crisis made by citizen surgers lacked evidential credibility. In this sense, ruling elites cooperated by antagonizing citizens and other categories of

elites. Conversely, ruling elites might cease to supply goading events and actively undertake to mount *curbing events* that served to undercut the possibility and vigor of surger events (as they, in fact, did).

2. We may posit that citizens did not easily and lightly undertake active opposition to ruling elites.[24] In order to become actively oppositional, it helped to be encouraged and legitimated by people endowed with the power to do this. In surge-analytic terms, legitimate and knowledgeable elites expressing dissent helped to furnish the evidence one needed. More helpful still was to have this happen publicly at an event. Gatherings that featured dissident elites, in fact, occurred in profusion. (In a different context, consider the following preachment of Martin Luther King, Jr., before a meeting the evening of December 5, 1955, the event at which the Montgomery bus boycott was publicly begun: "We are not wrong in what we are doing. If we are wrong, the Supreme Court of this nation is wrong. If we are wrong, the Constitution of the United States is wrong. If we are wrong, God Almighty is wrong.")[25]

3. Financial subsidy by wealthy individuals and foundations made an enormous difference in the frequency with which (1) local, (2) national, and (3) coalescing citizen events happened, the scale on which they were mounted, and the diversity seen in them. Although we do not usually think of funding as an event, it, in fact, was in both the narrow sense of people gathering and "funding"[26] and in the broader sense of the good news creating emboldening elations among its beneficiaries. This "angeling" critically fueled the soar phase (and its subsequent withdrawal likewise "fueled" the plummeting or slumping seen later).[27]

4. The national media were very much elites in the sense of having a great deal of power to decide what actors, events, and issues were given public attention and the kind of attention each was accorded. To a significant degree, there was a surge of citizen peace activism of the magnitude seen because the media decided there was one, thereby contributing to the scale of the soaring phase.

Using the term *elite* to encompass the collective actors just indicated, half of our eight key categories of events were *elite events*. This surge of citizen action was, therefore, very much *about* elites and not simply about citizens and consisted *of* elites. We might suggest, indeed, that citizens were dancing to the tunes played by contesting elite factions. In such a view, funding elites, dissident elites, and media elites were promoting citizen peace activism as a strategy in their contest for power with the ruling elite.

≪

The first and second phases of the peace surge of the eighties have been analyzed in this and chapter 6. These, obviously, provide only about half of this story of the soar and slump of polite protest. Combined with a characterization of the surge overall, the rest of the story is told in the Conclusion.

Notes

1. This genre is reviewed by Olzak 1989, who discusses many examples, including McAdam 1982.

2. As elaborated in chap. 6, only a few appeared in the first focusing phase of the eighties peace surge.

3. Neglected in the recent period, this aspect is stressed in the classic literature by, in particular, Neil Smelser (1963, 8, chap. 4). Recast and muted, such perceptions are, however, assumed in more recent "frame analysis" as in Snow et al. 1986.

4. This formulation is informed by Max Heinrich's (1971, esp. 19–25) discussion of perceptions involved in deciding to undertake collective action.

5. In the following, we provide only the briefest documentation of these beliefs. Happily, Benford (1993) provides rich documentation, thus relieving us of that responsibility. Moreover, Benford makes us more confident that there is a real world out there because, independently, he formulates a classification of beliefs that is very similar to the one we present here. His categories are severity, urgency, efficacy, and propriety.

6. We, therefore, disagree with those analysts who claim the Freeze failed because it was too watered down a program and did not centrally confront the "real issues" (e.g., Solo 1988). In contrast, we suggest that the very watered-down character of the peace surge is one major reason it got as far as it did—a distance that was not, actually, insignificant. "Stronger" programs, that is, would have had very little broad appeal, and, therefore, there would have been no peace surge of the eighties. Compare, in these terms, the size of the Freeze with the movement against intervention in Central America.

7. Cf. Aldon Morris's account of the soar of lunch counter sit-in demonstrations, involving the perception, in the words of a key activist: "This is it, let's go" (Morris 1984, 202). Neil Smelser's distinction between the "real" and "derived" phases of collective behavior episodes is a broader and more abstract formulation of the perception of soaring (Smelser 1963, 154).

8. Although infrequent, some phenomena are pure media creations. Fishman (1978) provides a case study of one—a crime wave against the elderly.

9. An "event" thus parallels in human constructions the phenomenon of "an experience" in John Dewey's sense as interpreted and applied to culture by Jaeger and Selznick 1964.

10. Max Heirich's (1971) effort to depict events processes akin to the kind discussed here comes the closest to a usable model, but, alas, his construction is overwhelming complex.

11. Differences between *politics* and *protest*, analytically understood, are detailed in Lofland (1985, 1–10, 260–69). Solo (1988) inaccurately uses the term *protest* to refer to grassroots or local politics, and by *politics* she means political action at the national center, Washington, D.C.

12. Although we lack systematic data, we are also impressed with the strong presence of retired middle-class people in local and national peace organizations. The Center for De-

fense Information even featured the fact that it was led by retired naval officers. See, further, Blumberg and French 1992 and Watanabe and Milburn 1988.

13. Extract from the field notes of Sam Marullo.

14. Various additional forms of elite legitimizing events are assembled and reviewed by Meyer (1990b, chap. 6), whose book is the most comprehensive historical account of the eighties peace surge thus far available and one to which we are greatly indebted.

15. Note, once more, that all these (and lesser) major focusing events were staid, polite politics.

16. Conversely, in slump phases "dispersing" events sever or discontinue such interactions.

17. The Topsfield Foundation (1987) *Grassroots Peace Directory* counts parallel those of IDDS and are slightly larger because that organization deliberately included organizations "such as churches and civic groups which do not have a primary focus on peace, but have a committee or task force doing peace work" (Colwell 1989, 11).

18. Jo Freeman (1975, chap. 5) has otherwise referred to this aspect of media behavior as "the mushroom effect" as it operated in the case of the media blitz regarding women's liberation in 1970.

19. In addition, Ferguson and Rogers (1986, chap. 5) argue that "multinational Democrats" and interests with which they were allied had economic (and not simply species survival) interests in opposing the administration's military buildup. The unusual generosity of these elites in funding peace activism was but one strategy in their struggle against the Reagan administration over patterns of government spending (especially in cities) and relations to international markets.

20. The significant financial support of a wide variety of prominent Democratic persons and groups and interests allied with them is detailed in Ferguson and Rogers (1986, chap. 5), "The Democrats' Response (1981–1982)."

21. Such supporters are reported to have included Paul Newman, Joanne Woodward, Hume Cronin, Jessica Tandy, Susan Sarandon, and Martin Sheen.

22. Other terms for *conditions* that are useful but are seen as not quite as accurate include "context," "situation," "constraint," and "opportunity."

23. Details on these events and their analytic meaning are provided in chap. 6.

24. Acute analyses of this fact are provided by Gamson, Fireman, and Rytina 1982.

25. Transcribed from the sound track of "Awakening," the first segment of the television series "Eyes on the Prize: America's Civil Rights Years 1954–1965."

26. Reed (1983) and Ferguson and Rogers (1986) roster some important such elite funding meetings of the peace surge, including those of "The Yacht Club," so named for the place of gathering.

27. Of course, many funding events also take place at the grassroots and consist of large numbers of people each giving relatively small amounts.

Conclusion

I conclude with remarks on two aspects of the foregoing studies. First and continuing from the introduction, I provide further explanation of the approach represented by these studies and I compare that approach to other vantage points. Second, I sum up major features of the eighties surge of peace activism, I suggest some meanings of those features, and I treat aspects of its falter and slump phases.

Mapping the Mesoscopic

The seven main chapters of this book are the reports of a mesoscopic mapping expedition, "mesoscopic" here referring to social matters between the micro- and macroscopic. Each of the seven seeks to depict the same social terrain, but each highlights different sections or features of that terrain. In the same way that there are different cartographical representations of a physical area (e.g., elevation, soil types, or whatever), these seven efforts bring different features to the foreground. Conceived most basically, I have mapped peace terrain for four kinds of features: change-theories, culture, organization, and surges.

Change-Theories

In chapter 1, I mapped the American peace movement in terms of its participants' beliefs about how to go about achieving social change and in terms of how this variation was embedded in the structure of the movement. This mapping draws our attention to the nature of movement activity and its rationales, specifically, the activities and rationales of transcending, educating, intellectualizing, politicking, protesting, and prophesying. Chapter 3, on city twinning and its consensus themes, is a closer or more fine-grained mapping of the specifically transcender segment of the peace movement. By casting that closer inspection in terms of the more general idea of the consensus movement, I also pointed out that transcender themes are not unique to the American peace movement but are found in at least several other movements and forms of collective action.

Culture

Broader than change-theory beliefs but involving them, every movement is a social terrain of culture, a terrain that itself varies in the several generic ways described in chapter 3. In the instance of the American peace movement of the eighties, that culture was sparse at the movementwide level but much richer in some of the six change-theory clusters of the movement.

Organization

Social movements *are* movements (that is, more than simply disparate collective actions), importantly by virtue of their new, named, and enduring human associations — associations commonly termed *organizations*. The typography of these organizations is itself an important topic for mapping. One form of such mapping has been provided in chapter 4, where we see the overwhelming prevalence of very small, voluntary, and democratic citizen groups. Questions of funding or financing are closely allied with but different from organization and might, in fact, be thought of as a distinct form of mapping although I elected to treat the matter of funding as closely related to organization.

Surges

In ordinary meanings, a cartographical map is static in character, a frozen-in-time depiction of an arrangement of objects in space. The three forms of social mapping just summarized are that kind of frozen-in-time representation, a representation I spoke of in the introduction as the study of *structure*.

Allow me now to take a bit more liberty with the analogy to cartographical mapping and extend it to the depiction of social objects as they succeed one another over time. This is the kind of mapping that I spoke of in the introduction as the study of "process" and that I undertook in chapters 5, 6, and 7. As yet lacking appropriate mapping tools for such processes, chapter 5 was primarily addressed to clarifying the nature of the mapping task itself. Chapter 6 followed chapter 5 in offering yet more detailed mapping devices and in beginning to apply them to the terrain of the American peace movement—in particular, to its first, or *focusing*, phase. And, chapter 7 was a detailed effort to display the internal dynamics of the eighties American peace movement in its period of soaring.

The Approach

These four mappings represent one sociological approach to studying the American peace movement as well as to studying social movements more generally. Let me here indicate ways in which a mapping approach is both similar to and different from other approaches.

First, a mapping approach is very much addressed to a movement per se as distinct from its causes or its consequences. Indeed, most studies of social movements, including the American peace movement of the 1980s, are addressed to why there was a movement, the macrostructural factors that caused its surge, and the effects it did or did not have on social policy.

I have no quarrel with causes and consequences foci in and of themselves. These are both proper aspects of the full study of social movements. I demur, however, when analysts become so concerned with either of these questions that they neglect to develop an understanding of what they want to explain or what it is that they think has consequences. Such neglect, I think, cripples most causal and consequential accounts because their authors fail to understand their main variable, that of the characteristics of a movement itself.

Second, analyses of social movements are commonly classified as being either *macroscopic* or *microscopic* in focus. The former looks at the broad conditions of society that prompt or facilitate movements and that movements, in turn, try to affect. The latter scrutinizes individual involvement at the level of biographical characteristics. Almost all work on social movements is one or the other of these. But, as investigators have increasingly realized, these foci neglect a broad range of matters that take place in between them, a middle level termed the *mesoscopic* (McAdam, McCarthy, Zald 1988). The macro and the micro are, in fact, linked at the meso level, and we have only begun to understand how these links occur or even what kinds of structures and process we find there. The mappings I offer here are efforts empirically to investigate and to conceptualize this mesoscopic level of movement reality. More broadly, I hope each of these map-pings contributes to the enlargement of a much-needed mesoscopic sociology. We are locked into a mindset of "right here" (microscopic) ver-sus "out there" (macroscopic) and sorely need cognitive constructs that at least bridge this division even if they do not transcend it.

Third, among accomplished mesoscopic analyses, there has been a significant amount of one special form of mapping to which I want to call attention so as to distinguish it from the forms I have attempted in this volume. This is the mapping of ideological systems, beliefs, or traditions. Relative to the American peace movement, for example, we have several chartings of the various approaches to peace, and one of these has even been called "an intellectual map" (Thompson and Jensen 1991). While these maps vary among themselves, they are alike in differentiating substan-tive goals and foci of peace thinking. In addition to those mentioned in discussing the work of peace intellectuals (in chapter 3, "Creators"), such mapping efforts include Nigel Young's (1987, 142) depiction of ten "peace traditions" (which include "liberal internationalism," "anticonscriptionism," "feminist antimilitarism," and "nuclear disarmament"). For other social movements, this kind of map commonly depicts ideological positions on a right to left continuum. In the history of the study of social movements, the mapping of ideological camps was, indeed, once *the* dominant form of mapping.

Of late, such efforts have fallen out of favor among most social scien-tists possibly for the same reason I have not attempted an ideological map of the 1980s peace movement. If one attends to movements at the level of lived, practical experience, ideological camps *can* be observed, but they are not all that articulate and central to the way people talk and act. To feature them as a map is, therefore, to articulate them well beyond the level of consciousness and the degree of ideological crystallization and systematization among ordinary participants. (Nonetheless, careful map-pers of the activities of the *intellectuals* of a movement can and do cor-rectly discover coherent ideological positions.)

In one sense, then, the mapping I have done here is in a line of histori-cal continuity with mapping of ideological positions or traditions. The change is that I have turned to additional matters — to the matters, specifically, of beliefs about how to achieve social change, to cultural form, to varieties of organization, and to processes of movement change.

≪

I turn now to the question of what, considered in a summary way, has been mapped?

Features Mapped

The seven chapters that I have characterized as four kinds of "mapping" of the American peace movement of the eighties provide rather complex depictions of many features of that movement. It would be redundant and wasteful to conclude by simply recapitulating these chapters, but a composite formulation of the more important of these features is in order.

Let me begin by recalling that the social terrain being mapped is the surging and then slumping of the entire spectrum of peace activism in the eighties. We need clearly to bear the words *entire spectrum* in mind because other analysts tend to reduce eighties peace activism to only that of the campaign for a nuclear freeze. This is an understandable tendency because the Freeze was, in fact, the most publicly visible part of the surge, and it was the focus of the iconic New York City Rally of June 1982. But, as I have tried to make clear in the preceding chapters, there was vastly more to the peace surge of the eighties than Freeze activism. The entire spectrum — that "vastly more" — is the focus here, not merely the Freeze.

Abstracting from the seven main chapters of this volume, I think nine reiterated or composited features stand above others as "mapping" this quite unusual and fleeting social formation.

Crisis

Although I have not documented it in this volume as thoroughly as might be desirable, participants in the surge exhibited a strong sense of fear, gravity, and urgency that is difficult, from a distance, to comprehend. Imagine, thus, two academic editors beginning an issue of a staid scholarly journal with these sentences: "Humanity is on the edge of its existence. Never before this half of our century have we been so close to our destruction and the destruction of all life." But, these are the sentences with which Marvin Wolfgang and Robert Kupperman began the September 1983 issue of *The Annuals,* an issue on "Nuclear Armament and Disarmament."[1] Sentiments like theirs were published and broadcast broadly and were registered in a wide variety of public opinion polls.[2]

Doomsday perceptions and fears were the proximate engines or drivers of the eighties surge of peace activism. Perceptions of crisis had, of course, their own causes, the bellicose behavior of the Reagan administration foremost among them, as was discussed in chapter 7.

It is important also to understand that several other emotions and perceptions tended to go along with those of fear and urgency. These included a sense of seriousness, importance, and (possible) personal consequence. Movement work was *important* work. One's movement actions were not simply the routines of ordinary life; instead, they were contributing to saving human life itself. In fear and urgency, the participant was lifted out of the humdrum of everyday life and into a realm of serious actors dedicated to achieving the most important of human missions — the prevention of ultimate destruction.

Explosion

As documented in previous chapters and in other studies, a great many people who were not involved in peace work became so involved. Precise numbers are debated, but participation in the range of ten million by the mid-eighties is well documented.[3] Against a baseline of a quarter of a million peace workers in the late-seventies (at best), this is an impressive change.[4] This explosion of participation was accompanied by (and partly caused by) a similar explosion in foundation and wealthy donor money used to pay for staff and other costs of activist projects.

In chapter 7, I treated this "explosion" more technically as a process of the synergistic expansion of eight classes of events. This conception of synergistic interaction is a critique of cruder explosion imagery, and I use the word *explosion* here in a cautious and qualified way. While there were clearly very rapid rises in all manner of movement activities, these rises were taking place in very close interaction with nonmovement changes that were themselves working to "increase the increases" of the movement during the process of soaring. This is quite different from any analysis of explosion which focuses only on movement activity and makes reference only to the internal dynamics of a movement and how it deploys the resources it has at the outset. At least in the peace surge case, the process was more like that of a marching army organized to live and thrive on the land than like a marching army requiring resupply from a previously amassed resource base.

One of the most important meanings of soaring was the *radical discontinuity* in "who" peace workers were in terms of their social characteristics and philosophies. The preexisting stalwarts were still there, of course, but their movement world was now quite new.

Diversity

This explosion of participation was expressed in a wide variety of forms, the six basic categories of which I treated in chapter 1 as transcending, educating, intellectualizing, politicking, protesting, and prophesying.

Though these six participation forms were quite different, they even over-simplify the extremely wide variety of concrete activities that took place. In addition, these six forms of change-making activities were themselves associated with wide philosophical, life-style, and social categorical differences among participants (even acknowledging that most participants were white, of more than average education, and of middle-class stand-ing, origin, or aspiration).

Clustering

These points of strategic, philosophical, and social diversity were not randomly associated with one another. Instead, people of kindred disposi-tions on strategic actions, philosophies, and social features clustered to-gether while maintaining significant distance from participants not like themselves. Moreover, and as I discussed in chapters 2, 3, and 4, many people often seemed unaware of the existence of distant clusters. Or, if they had heard of some given other people, they knew little and were not especially concerned to learn about them. Taken together, the two features of diversity and clustering are sometimes spoken of as a condition of *fragmentation.*

Rigidity

Conceived ideal-typically, there are at least four prominent patterns that strategies can exhibit as they are enacted over time by participants in a social movement.

1. Successive Unified Strategies. Everyone in a movement takes up the same strategy and pursues it until it is successful or fails, and then every-one changes to another strategy. This is the pattern to which the civil rights movement of the sixties tended, McAdam (1983) has suggested. In its "tac-tical innovation," it exhibited a chesslike succession of new strategies that were responsive to the changing strategies of its opposition.

2. Unified to Diverse Strategies. Everyone starts with the same strat-egy in a unified front, but as that strategy fails or declines in effectiveness, people fragment into varied and disparate strategies. A metaphor for this pattern is a hurled mass that spatters on hitting a wall.

3. Persistently Diverse Strategies. From the start, diverse strategies are pursued, and their enactors respond in only modest ways to opponent re-actions. Over time, people stop participation in the movement rather than switch to one or more other strategies.

4. Diverse to Dominant to Diverse Strategies. People begin with di-

verse strategies but also participate in one strategy that is dominant for a time. As that fails, people continue with diverse strategies, and these decline.

Although it is to difficult to assess, I think the peace surge of the eighties was closer to the third or or fourth patterns than to the first two. The six classes of change activity described in chapter 1 and in other chapters began to increase at about the same time and soared, peaked, and slumped at somewhat different paces over the early and middle years of the decade. Early in the decade, though, one of them — the political strategy of the Freeze — drew in some people from some of the other clusters, even as these other clusters continued alongside politics, including the Freeze. After the peak of the Freeze, all six continued.

It must be acknowledged, though, that in public or popular perception the surge *appeared* to approximate the second pattern of unified followed by disparate strategies. It had this public appearance because the Freeze received intense media coverage, while other forms of peace activism did not. But, as the statistics on founding and growth appearing throughout this book amply document, *all* forms of peace activism were soaring right along with the political forms or, at least, not lagging very far behind. And, as political forms — including the Freeze — began to slump, so did all the others. In addition, the second pattern implies a pronounced flow of individuals out of the former unified strategy and into many different strategies. It is a hydraulic image of the movement of bodies in a closed system. They start out in one strategy, but then flow into several strategies. Some people certainly did move in this way or engaged in several strategies. But the more dominant trend was for people to begin in one of the six major forms of action, to stay there, and, over time, simply to stop peace activism.

The pattern of successive unified strategies (number one) was clearly not seen. As depicted by McAdam (1983) and others, in this pattern we observe chains of moves in chesslike tactical innovation. In contrast, the peace surge is better likened, I think, to the image of a flower in the process of blooming, the image being that of a complex process of enactment, albeit a process of synergistic-interactive enactment.[5] Actually, given the diversity, the more accurate image would be a thousand flowers blooming. (I do not think Mao had peace surges in mind, though.)

Viewed in this perspective, the strategic structure of the peace surge was relatively rigid. Politics in the form of the Freeze had a temporary dominance, but there were also persistently diverse strategies that simply rose and declined over the decade.

Restraint

By joining the contradictory words *polite* and *protest* into a label for a key feature of the peace surge, I sought to identify the paradox that a movement energized by a crisis mindset (feature one) was, nonetheless, quite restrained and civil in its actions. Not only was there virtually no physical violence, there was even very little verbal violence, by which I mean the kind of angry, fist-shaking rhetoric that is fairly common in at least some segments of many other movements. One might say, indeed, that there was something disproportionate in the relation between the gravity of the crisis mind set and the restraint of politely protesting action. If matters were really as dangerous and threatening as many people asserted, perhaps much stronger and "radical" actions were in order. Interestingly enough, I rarely encountered much evidence of anyone perceiving this inconsistency or being concerned about it. Such an absence is perhaps evidence of the thoroughly pacific dispositions of peace surge participants.

Amorphousness

Many of the features of culture, organization, and other matters I have described are appropriately brought together as depicting a general condition of movement amorphousness. Despite the fact that one could discern clustering, which constituted a degree of order and coherence, the size and degree of explicit articulation of order at this level was, nonetheless, very limited. Both within clusters and between them, the order was close to a condition of anarchy, a term I select with care and use in its technical meaning and without any pejorative intent. I definitely do *not* use this term to mean the disorder of the "war of all against all" in a "nasty, brutish, and short" state of nature. Instead, the idea of anarchy points to the relative absence of ordering relations among entities making up the surge. The terms *decentralization, sprawling, diffuse,* and *scattered* are sometimes also used to indicate this state. Each is helpful but limited, especially the concept of decentralization, which often refers to dispersed units that are, nonetheless, held together in an overarching and hierarchical order.

But even the term anarchy is too strong because in other uses — especially in international relations discourse — it implies well-defined entities among whom there is no governing order. In the peace surge, even such well-defined entities were not abundant. As the statistics of organizational foundings (and disbandments) we have reviewed well attest, just who the players were, what they were doing, and how long they might be around were all problematic. Therefore, we had a condition, perhaps, that did not even reach anarchy, one tending to the amorphousness of the shapeless, the vague, the inchoate, albeit with some stable "kernels" delicately linked together with easily broken gossamer.

I need again to say that amorphousness was a characteristic of *the surge* itself. At the level of single associations and of specific campaigns and coalitions among a limited number of organizations and persons more definite order could be seen. It is when we expand our view in space and time that the object of our attention comes to lack shape and coherence.

Amorphousness is likely a matter on which movements vary considerably. At least, this is the impression one gets from such analysts as Luther Gerlach and Virginia Hine (1970), who have been impressed that movements are segmented but are also what they term *reticulate*, by which they mean that the segments are woven together by interaction among members — particularly leaders — of different segments. In comparative movement perspective, though, I think the peace surge would rank as quite low on reticulateness.

Fragility

At least three additional features mapped in earlier chapters suggest, in composite, a structure/process feature of pronounced fragility. One, a work force overwhelmingly composed of volunteers (who are acting in a crisis mind-set) is a highly unreliable way to ensure that tasks are performed over extended periods of time. Such workers are held by their sense of crisis rather than by their ideological commitments or money, and when the crisis seems to pass, they can easily "walk," as they largely did. Two, a sense of crisis was all the more important for the surge as a whole because of the relative sparseness of culture at that level. Three, limited-term and one-shot-at-a-time funding decidedly circumscribed and limited the stability and longevity of projects. The situation was, thus, set up for radical rip-saw effects — for soars when there is crisis and funding and for slumps when these are withdrawn.

In comparative movement perspective, the peace surge may be among the more fragile for the reasons just mentioned, but we do not want to underestimate the extent to which *all* surges may be fragile even though varying in degrees. By definition (chap. 5), all surges are predicated on a shared definition of a situation as extraordinary or as, at least, highly unusual. This means that action in all of them has an ad hoc and jerry-built quality that is appropriate to the need to act *now* and not simply with the slow and routine foot dragging of ordinary life. Hence, volunteer labor and special donations become the order of the day in order to *act*. So constructed, their fragility — and, hence, *brevity* — ought not surprise us.

In proposing this view, I am disagreeing with those strategically minded peace activists who think of the surge as aborted, and who argue that this abortion was avoidable. It was aborted, they say, because of a failure to build organization, a failure properly to frame the issues, a too-fast movement to national prominence, a failure to educate its participants or otherwise outflank its opponents.[6] The implicit assertion is that if only leading activists had done one or more things "right," the surge of activism would have continued longer, reached ever higher levels of mobilization, and have consolidated those gains at the level reached. A comparative movement perspective, however, throws doubt on this hypothesis. While the surge might have been a bit longer, higher, and consolidated at a higher level had other factors been different, I doubt its shape would have been significantly altered. For, surges, in general, display, albeit with some variation, this kind of rapid upsweep followed by rapid downsweep. The peace surge simply played a basic pattern one more time.[7]

Eclipse

While it is accurate to characterize the surge as fragile in the senses that it consisted of crisis-driven volunteer labor and one-shot funding, this characterization is also incomplete. We must go on to ask, Why did the sense of crisis and the funding subside with all the concomitant declines that these changes brought?

The answers can be thought of in terms of changes in the eight classes of events described in chapter 7. The first of these eight — elite *goading* events — changed from goading to assuaging or curbing events. The ruling elites of the United States and the Soviet Union, were, of course, the elites whose behavior started all this in the first place. Among the U.S. ruling elite, one person requires our special attention: Ronald Wilson Reagan. According to *Washington Post* journalist Don Oberdorfer, Reagan held "dichotomous . . . views" on the Soviet Union and his relation to it.

On the one hand, he could condemn Soviet leaders with sincerity and zeal, using the harshest rhetoric ever heard from a U.S. President, and on the other he could express a persistent willingness, even an eagerness, to reach out to them in constructive discussion. To some extent Reagan's duality of mind arose from his . . . experiences as president of the Screen Actors Guild . . . , which left him with two vital convictions. One was a passionate opposition to [C]ommunists . . . ; the other was an unbounded confidence in his own ability to convince others of the rightness of his positions. . . . According to [Secretary of State] Shultz, the President never wavered or hesitated . . . to engage in dialogues with the Soviets. . . . [One of his advisors] . . . ascribed some of his willingness to engage to a "self-confidence that he was an historic figure and that he was terribly effective in persuasion. . . . He had enormous self-confidence in the ability of a single heroic figure to change history" (Oberdorfer 1991, 22).

To this we need to add the fact that Reagan had a long-standing and apparently real and deep antipathy to nuclear weapons and the possibility of nuclear war (Oberdorfer 1991, chap. 1).

But, over the first years of Reagan's presidency, there was a "vacuum at the top of the Soviet power structure" (Lapidus and Dallin 1989, 16). Therefore, his antipathy toward communism could not be matched by effective direct engagement of its leaders on war-peace matters. In brief and disruptive succession, three aging and ailing Soviet leaders died over the first years of his presidency. He could, though, act on his dislike of nuclear weapons and did so. In his "Star Wars" speech of March 23, 1983, he effectively seized the moral high ground with his SDI answer to the question: "Wouldn't it be better to save lives than to avenge them?" (Oberdorfer 1991, 27). Also in 1983, Reagan "and his administration backed away from the cavalier rhetoric about nuclear warning shots, recallable missiles, improvised fallout shelters, and limited nuclear wars that had characterized the early years of his administration and animated the movement" (Meyer 1991, 12–13). Concomitantly, many foreign policy actions of the administration become more moderate, signalling a "trend toward greater pragmatism" (Lapidus and Dallin 1989, 15; Meyer, 1990a).

With these and other moderations, the administration "prevented the 1984 election from serving as a referendum on Reagan's nuclear policy" (Meyer 1991, 13). He was reelected in a landslide, an event that deeply demoralized peace workers and precipitated a broad and steep decline in movement activity and funding (much of which is displayed in the later years of the figures in the last chapter).

All of this was only the beginning of the remarkable changes we now saw in the behavior of ruling elites. In Mikhail Gorbachev, who became general secretary of the Soviet Union in March 1985, Reagan finally found someone on whom he could practice his belief in his "ability to convince others of the rightness of his positions in face-to-face encounters" (Oberdorfer 1991, 22). Auspiciously, Gorbachev seemed more than ready to be convinced of all manner of things regarding weapons and defense (as well as much else) and the two men met face-to-face five times over the four years from 1985 through 1988. These meetings and others were elements of a change that Don Oberdofer (1991) labels *The Turning*, the process of moving "from the cold war to a new era." One high-point event of these years was the December 1987 signing of the Intermediate Nuclear Force Treaty, the "first-ever treaty cutting nuclear arsenals" (Schwartz 1991, 8). This was, of course, only the start and was followed by many other weapons cuts, the collapse of Communist Eastern Europe (1989), and the dissolution of the Soviet Union itself (1991). While visiting Moscow in May 1988, Reagan declared that the Soviet Union was no longer an evil empire.

Stated in the terms used in previous chapters, there was a precipitous decline in surge-facilitating events of a goading variety with regard to nuclear weapons and Soviet-American relations. Ruling elites produced a dramatically *focusing* and fast-paced series of surge-*inhibiting* events – a succession of summits, trips, moratoria, and agreements quite explicitly intended to reduce people's fears about nuclear matters and foreign affairs.

Paralleling the central role of elite goading events in 1981–1983 in fueling an *expanding* synergy in the other seven classes of events, moderated administration behavior and the advent of this sea-change in elite assuaging events fueled a *contracting* synergy in these same seven kinds of events. In addition, the categories of participating actors changed as did perceptions.

Regarding perceptions, elite assuaging events were greeted with approval and apparent enthusiasm in peace circles, tempered with the caution that we were still a very long way from abolishing nuclear weapons and from a world free from war and related worries and evils. Nonetheless, the atmosphere of fear, urgency, and crisis subsided.

Lacking crisis, local dissenting events were fewer and harder to organize. Freeze Voter director Chip Reynolds encapsulated this change well in a 1988 interview in which he recalls that "between spring 1982 and spring 1983 . . . you could literally walk into town, hang up a leaflet and hundreds of people would show up. By the latter part of 1983 . . . the sheen was no longer there for the media and to get a meeting going they had to hammer the telephones" (quoted in Ferguson 1988, 28) (see also Hertsgaard 1985). Committed peace workers were still in evidence and a variety of campaigns were carried on, but funding was scant or nonexistent. Organizations were folding or retrenching – prominent among them, the Coalition for a New Foreign and Military Policy (disbanded, September 1988), *Nuclear Times* (ceased publication, April 1989),[8] and Freeze Voter (absorbed by the Professionals' Coalition, February 1989). As late as October 1987, a thousand peace activists could gather enthusiastically to merge SANE and the Freeze into the single largest American peace group. But in 1989 the convention was down to hundreds and, in 1991, down to a few dozen.

The movement in its diverse manifestations was still there, but the scale of enterprises and the heady atmosphere of 1982 and 1983 were now only some people's distant memories. Public opinion polls reported very large percentage declines in people concerns about nuclear matters and fears about the Soviet Union (Schatz and Fiske 1992). In November 1991, *The Nation* editorialized under the caption "Movement Gap:" "Just when it should have had its moment of triumph, the peace movement is feeble and wan. 'There *is* no peace movement,' one of the most effective movers and shakers of the antinuclear campaigns of the 1980s said dispiritedly last month. 'There's just a bunch of people who are still interested in the issues.'" (*Nation* Editors 1991, 539).

In early December 1989, I noticed that magazines, newspapers, and other forms of the mass media were starting to issue retrospectives on the 1980s. I began to look at these chronologies of the decade in terms of what media thought were and were not the most important events, people, and the like. Immersed in thinking about the eighties peace surge, I was very curious to see how media would represent it. What and who did they think was important? I assembled some two dozen of these that were published or aired in the last weeks of December 1989. What I found is surprising, to me at least. For, I read or saw *almost nothing* about eighties peace activism! In media memory, the peace surge simply did not happen, save for only the briefest of occasional mentions, mostly of the June 1982 rally in New York City. There was an enormous amount about Reagan and his administration, of course, but not of citizen opposition to his foreign and military policies. There was an enormous amount about Gorbachev and the end of the Soviet Empire and Union, but not of U.S. citizen action relating to these. In Orwellian *1984* fashion, the peace surge had been put down the "memory hole."

My experience with these decade retrospectives is similar to my experiences with many people to whom I speak about the peace movement in general or the eighties surge in particular. "What's that?" people ask me, even young people who were activists against the Gulf War.

I suspect, indeed, that the peace surge of the eighties has been eclipsed in the historical consciousness of all but longer-term peace activists, scholarly specialists, and a few others with eccentric interests. The irony is that it was eclipsed by the very momentousness of the success with which its aspirations became reality. Had the movement's goals not been so dramatically realized, we might still nurture its memory as a strong and worthy crusade that failed, but one whose time will come again. Instead, it is shrouded in the shadow of a great turn of history.[9]

My inspection of these eighties retrospectives prompted an additional appreciation: one must take care not to become myopic. The years of the eighties were filled with all manner of events and problems aside from nuclear weapons developments and hostile Soviet-American relations. These other matters quite properly energized surging citizen action. To mention only a few and in no special order: U.S. actions in Nicaragua, other Central American countries, and developing countries in general; AIDS; South Africa; antilabor trends; drugs; myriad environmental depletions, pollutions, destructions; corporate greed and crime; Iran-Contra; Ethiopian famine; Tiananmen Square. If even people who are socially conscious and active do not remember the peace surge of the eighties, perhaps it is because there is no shortage of other important matters to recall that preoccupy them into the nineties. The problems dwelled on by peace activists have been (and are) extremely important, but they are not the only such problems. Activists in other movements argue, in fact, that many of these other problems are *more* important. In this perspective, then, we can understand peace surge eclipse as a consequence of the large number of yet other socially consequential matters that are confronted by thoughtful people. In a world of a great many problems, cognitive limits on attending and recalling mean that many things are not attended to or, if perceived, are soon forgotten in the on-rush of attending to new problems.

⋘

The first purpose of the mapping approach I have described and just summarized for the peace surge of the 1980s is to expand the scope and sharpness of our perceptions of social movements. This has been my central task in this volume, but this is only the first of several additional tasks that I leave for other occasions and researchers. The first of these additional tasks is to make *comparisons* of movements in terms of their mesoscopically mapped features in order then to be able more fruitfully, second, to link such differences to differential *causes* and, third, to differential *consequences*.

Movements of the characteristics I have documented may have quite different main causes and consequences than movements of other features. For example:

1. Diverse, clustered and strategically rigid surges that are amorphous, restrained, and fragile may have more transient and elite-policy causes than movements of a harder and grittier texture who adopt more protestful and flexible strategies.

2. Situational goads to action (as opposed to more structural and deep grievances, such as the system of militarism itself) may gave rise to mild forms of movement action that are, therefore, more easily placated and

becalmed. The editors of the *Nation* put this proposition in these terms: organized in terms of "easy targets" rather than on a broader program of targeting the military-industrial complex per se, "when the easy targets moved out of the cross-hairs, there was nothing but blankness at which to aim" (*Nation* Editors 1991, 539).

3. Movements of polite protest may have more modest, superficial, and diffuse consequences than movements of harsher textures, and they are likely to slump as quickly as they soared when the conditions that caused them have changed. This leaves them with scant capacity for immediate new mobilization. "[F]or the most part [peace movement people of the 1980s] . . . were out of touch with the crises of class, race and social decay that affected the most potentially powerful sectors of change in the country. When war really came – in Panama and then in the Persian Gulf – the peace movement had neither the program nor a solid base to make a dent in the Pentagon's plans for battle. It was a profoundly depressing failure. . . . A movement that was born of a fear of destruction will be reborn only by a commitment to change" (*Nation* Editors 1991, 539). (In the politically incorrect language of King James English, "Whatever a man soweth, that shall he reap.")

Whatever may turn out to be the case regarding such characteristics-causes-consequences linkages, the main agenda is to compare movements on which we have nuanced mappings of their structures and processes and, thereby, to move beyond the cruder formulations with which we have been working.

Notes

1. Academics, indeed, may have been among population segments most caught up in a sense of threat and urgency. The faculty committee recommending establishment of a University of California Institute on Global Conflict and Cooperation declared in its March 15, 1982, formulation of the organization's research agenda that "while all the causes and conditions [of international conflict] demand study, none is as important as the conditions that may trigger the most destructive of wars. . . . Unless energy is devoted to study of the immediate causes of war and methods of conflict management appropriate to them, there may not be time to study the more remote causes" (Special Committee 1982, 2).

2. References to and discussion of these polls appear in the "Public Opining Events" section of chap. 7.

3. See discussion, chap. 4, "Number of Organizations and Participants."

4. Some analysts, nonetheless, regard ten million or even much more as a "little segment of the population," amounting, as it does, "merely" to some 10 percent of the adult U.S. population if one uses the most liberal estimates (Schatz and Fiske 1992, 19).

5. Independently, John McCarthy and Ronald McCarthy suggested this analogy to me.

6. See, for example, Solo 1988; Molander and Molander 1990; Meyer 1990b.

7. In broader perspective, Jack Walker has documented the dependency of all citizen action on diverse sources of patronage, concluding that "if all sources of patronage suddenly disappeared, the interest-group system would immediately shrink until it included only a small set of highly unstable insurgent groups that would remain in existence only as long as they were able to command the loyalty of some aroused segment of the public and another set of more stable associations that represented only small, tightly knit, commercial, occupational, ethnic, or religious communities, those groups also able to draw successfully upon the resources of their members to meet their operating needs" (Walker 1991, 101–2).

8. The Winston Foundation resurrected it as a quarterly in 1990 but stopped publication again in 1992.

9. As is evident, I am not here asserting a causal relation between the peace surge and the Reagan administration moderation of its policies or between the surge and the subsequent end of the cold war. I am, however, very much aware that peace activists and scholars alike commonly argue that the surge contributed to moderating the Reaganites and to ending the cold war (e.g., Meyer 1991). My view is that the evidence so far available does not demonstrate either of these causal relations or, at least, no relation that is more than quite modest and indirect. I believe, though, that such evidence *might* be developed by future researchers. My position, therefore, is that of "not yet shown" rather than "there are no causal links." In my view, people adamantly asserting a causal relation are committing the error of asserting that because B follows A, A must be the (or a) cause of B. But, obviously, B can be caused by all sorts of yet other factors that might be at play. Even though A precedes B in time, A can have nothing to do with the appearance of B. It is sad that the desire of some serious scholars to promote and justify peace activism leads them to reckless and even irresponsible disregard of this elementary rule of causal inference. (Cortright [1991] provides a detailed and responsible scholarly view of this matter.)

References

Index

References

ACCESS, The Forum Institute. 1985. *Search for Security: A Guide to Grantmaking in International Security and the Prevention of Nuclear War.* Washington, D.C.: ACCESS.

Adamson, Madeleine, and Seth Borgos. 1984. *This Mighty Dream: Social Protest Movements in the United States,* Boston, Mass.: Routledge and Kegan Paul.

Adler, Peter. 1981. *Momentum: A Theory of Social Action.* Beverly Hills, Calif.: Sage Publications.

Agger, Ben. 1991. "Critical Theory, Poststructuralism, Postmodernism: Their Sociological Relevance." *Annual Review of Sociology* 17:105–31.

Aguirre, B. E., E. L. Quarantelli, and Jorge L. Mendoza. 1988. "The Collective Behavior of Fads: The Characteristics, Effects, and Career of Streaking." *American Sociological Review* 53, no. 4:569–84.

Albert Einstein Institution. 1990. *Thinking About Nonviolent Struggle: Trends, Research, and Analysis.* Cambridge, Mass.: Albert Einstein Institution.

Alford, Robert A., and Roger Friedland. 1985. *Powers of Theory: Capitalism, the State, and Democracy.* New York: Cambridge Univ. Press.

Alger, Chadwick. 1985. "Creating Local Institutions for Sustained Participation in Peacebuilding." Paper presented at the annual meeting of the International Society of Political Psychology, Washington, D.C.

Alinsky, Saul D. 1969 (op 1946). *Reveille for Radicals.* New York: Vintage Books.

———. 1972. *Rules for Radicals: A Practical Primer for Realistic Radicals.* New York: Vintage Books.

Allen, Anne. 1990. *Search for Security: The ACCESS Guide to Foundations in Peace, Security, and International Relations.* Washington, D.C.: ACCESS, A Security Information Center.

Allison, Paul. 1984. *Event History Analysis: Regression for Longitudinal Event Data.* Sage University Paper Series on Quantitative Applications in the Social Sciences, no. 46. Beverly Hills, Calif.: Sage Publications.

Alpern, D. 1982. "This is Only a Game, But . . ." *Newsweek,* May 23, 22.

American Friends Service Committee. 1980. *Call to Halt the Nuclear Arms Race.* Philadelphia, Pa.: American Friends Service Committee. Mimeograph.

American Peace Test. 1987. *History of Civil Disobedience at Nevada Test Site and Chronology of APT Actions.* Salem, Oreg.: American Peace Test National Clearinghouse.

————. 1988a. "Message from Our Friends." *Test Banner* (Apr.): 1.

————. 1988b. *Reclaim the Test Site Action Handbook.* March ed. Salem, Oreg.: American Peace Test National Clearing House.

————. N.d. *The American Peace Test International Call Newsletter.* Las Vegas, Nev.: American Peace Test.

Asimov, Nanette. 1988. "Building a Wall for Peace." *San Francisco Chronicle,* Aug. 25.

Associated Press. 1985. "Thousands Rally Against Reagan." *Sacramento Bee,* Apr. 21.

————. 1988. "Protest, Vigils Mark Hiroshima Anniversary." *Davis Enterprise,* Aug. 7.

Atkins, Stephen. 1986. "Arms Control, Disarmament, and Peace Newsletters." *Behavioral & Social Sciences Librarian* 6, nos. 1, 2:58–75.

Ayvazian, Andrea. 1986. *Organizational Development: The Seven Deadly Sins.* Amherst, Mass.: Peace Development Fund.

Barash, David P. 1991. *Introduction to Peace Studies.* Belmont, Calif.: Wadsworth Publishing.

Barash, David P., and Judith Eve Lipton. 1982. *Stop Nuclear War! A Handbook.* New York: Grove Press.

Barkan, Steven E. 1979. "Strategic, Tactical and Organizational Dilemmas of the Protest Movement Against Nuclear Power." *Social Problems* 27, no. 1:19–37.

Benford, Robert D. 1993. "You Could Be the Hundredth Monkey: Collective Identity and Vocabularies of Motive in the Nuclear Disarmament Movement." *Sociological Quarterly* 34, no. 2:195–216.

Benford, Robert D., and Louis A. Zurcher. 1990. "Instrumental and Symbolic Competition among Peace Movement Organizations." In *Peace Action in the Eighties: Social Science Perspectives,* edited by S. Marullo and J. Lofland. 125–39. New Brunswick, N.J.: Rutgers Univ. Press.

Bennett, Amanda. 1989. "The Next Step Is to Get Someone to Read the Post Cards for Them." *Wall Street Journal,* Apr. 25.

Bernstein, Elizabeth, Robert Elias, Randall Forsberg, and Matthew Goodman. 1986. *Peace Resource Book: A Comprehensive Guide to Issues, Groups and Literature.* Cambridge, Mass.: Ballinger Publishing.

Best, Joel. 1987. "Rhetoric in Claims-Making." *Social Problems* 34 (Apr.): 101–21.

————, ed. 1989. *Images of Issues: Typifying Contemporary Social Problems.* New York: Adline de Gruyter.

Beyond War. 1985. *Beyond War.* Palo Alto, Calif.: Beyond War Foundation.

Block, Fred L. 1987. *Revising State Theory: Essays in Politics and Postindustrialism.* Philadelphia, Pa.: Temple Univ. Press.

Blood-Patterson, Pedter, ed. 1988. *Rise Up Singing: The Group-Singing Song Book.* Bethlehem, Pa.: Sing Out Corporation.

Blooston, George. 1982. "Are Nuclear Books Doing Well in Bookstores?" *Publishers Weekly* 221 (Mar. 26): 53–56.

Blow, Richard. 1988. "Moronic Convergence: The Moral and Spiritual Emptiness of New Age Thought." *New Republic* 198, no. 4: 24, 26–27.

Blumberg, Herbert H., and Christopher C. French, eds. 1992. *Peace: Abstracts of the Psychological and Behavioral Literature, 1967–1990.* Bibliographies in Psychology no. 10. Washington, D.C.: American Psychological Association.

Blumenthal, Sidney. 1986. "The Think Tank Time Forgot." *Washington Post National Weekly Edition* (Sept. 1): 8–10.

Blumer, Herbert. 1969a. "Collective Behavior." In *Principles of Sociology*, edited by E. A. M. Lee. 65–121. New York: Barnes and Noble.

———. 1969b. *Symbolic Interactionism.* Englewood Cliffs, N.J.: Prentice-Hall.

———. 1971. "Social Problems as Collective Behavior." *Social Problems* 18 (Winter): 298–306.

Bobo, Kimberley. 1986. *Lives Matter: A Handbook for Christian Organizing.* n.p.: Sheed and Ward.

Bost, Eric. 1987. "National Grandparents Day at Nevada Test Site." *Grandmothers for Peace* (Nov.–Dec.): 1, 6.

Boston Study Group. 1979. *The Price of Defense: A New Strategy for Military Spending.* New York: Times Books.

Boulding, Elise. 1977. *Women in the Twentieth Century World.* New York: Wiley.

———. 1990. "The Early Eighties Peak of the Peace Movement." In *Peace Action in the Eighties: Social Science Perspectives*, edited by S. Marullo and J. Lofland. 18–28. New Brunswick, N.J.: Rutgers Univ. Press.

Boulding, Kenneth E. 1989. *Three Faces of Power.* Newbury Park, Calif.: Sage Publications.

Boyle, Anthony Francis. 1987. *Defending Civil Resistance under International Law.* Center for Energy Research. Dobbs Ferry, N.Y.: Transnational Publishers.

Brians, Paul. 1987. *Nuclear Holocausts: Atomic War in Fiction, 1895–1984.* Kent, Ohio: Kent State Univ. Press.

Brigham, William. 1990. "Noncontentious Social Movements: 'Just Say No to War'." In *Peace Action in the Eighties: Social Science Perspectives*, edited by S. Marullo and J. Lofland. 155–66. Rutgers Univ. Press.

Brinton, Crane. 1933, 1965. *The Anatomy of Revolution.* Rev. and exp. ed. New York: Vintage Books.

Bromely, David, and Anson Shup. 1979. *"Moonies" in America: Cult, Church, and Crusade.* Newbury Park, Calif.: Sage Publications.

Bulletin of the Atomic Scientists editors. 1990. "43 Years of the *Bulletin* Clock: A History of the Cold War." *Bulletin of the Atomic Scientists* 46, no. 3:57.

Burnham, Walter Dean. 1982. *The Current Crisis in American Politics.* New York: Oxford Univ. Press.

Caldicott, Helen. 1978. *Nuclear Madness: What You Can Do!* New York: Bantam Books.

Cantril, Hadley. 1941. *The Social Psychology of Social Movements.* New York: Wiley.

Center for Economic Conversion. 1990. *1989 Annual Report.* Mountain View, Calif.: Center for Economic Conversion.

Center for Innovative Diplomacy. 1986–1987. "CID's Fifth Year." *The CID Report* 3, no. 1:1–2.

Chatfield, Charles. 1992. *The American Peace Movement: Ideals and Activism.* New York: Twayne Publishers.

Citizen Diplomacy, Inc. 1985. *American Soviet Sister Cities: A Bridge Toward Peace.* Gainesville, Fla.: Citizen Diplomacy.

Coffin, William Sloane. 1984. "William Sloane Coffin, Jr." In *Facing the Danger,* edited by S. Totten and M. Totten. 89–94. Trumansburg, N.Y.: Crossing Press.

Cohen-Joppa, Jack, and Felice Cohen-Joppa. 1992. "Nuclear Resistance, 1991." *Nuclear Resister* 65 (Feb. 28): 1–2.

Cole, Nancy. N.d. *INFACT mail fund and pledge solicitation letter.*

Coles, Robert. 1964. "Social Struggle and Weariness." *Psychiatry* 27 (Nov.): 305–15.

———. 1984. "Freezeniks Are Elitists." *Washington Post,* Nov. 11, D1, D4.

Colwell, Mary Anna. 1988. "The 1988 Survey of Groups and Organizations Working for Peace." Unpublished. (Available from the author, 1628 Jaynes Street, Berkeley, Calif. 94703.)

———. 1989. *Organizational and Management Characteristics of Peace Groups.* Working Paper no. 8, Institute for Nonprofit Organization Management, Univ. of San Francisco.

Conetta, Carl. 1988. *Peace Resource Book: A Comprehensive Guide to the Issues, Organizations, and Literature 1988–1989.* Cambridge, Mass.: Ballinger Publishing.

Cordes, Helen. 1985–1986. "Yuppie Peaceniks." *Utne Reader* (Dec.–Jan.): 8–9.

———. 1988. "A Field Guide to the New Activism." *Utne Reader* (Mar.–Apr.): 74–77.

Cortright, David. 1991. "Assessing Peace Movement Effectiveness in the 1980s." *Peace and Change* 16, no. 1:46–63.

Cottom, Carolyn, and David Cortright. 1987. "Draft 1988 Budget, To National Congress Participants, for Your Information." Memorandum, Nov. 5.

Crews, Robin. 1986. "Comments on COPRED Meeting." *COPRED Peace Chronicle* 11, no. 1:3–4.

Daubert, Victoria L., and Sue Ellen Moran. 1985. *Origins, Goals, and Tactics of the U.S. Anti-Nuclear Protest Movement.* Santa Monica, Calif.: RAND Corporation.

Davidson, Osha. 1986. "On Guard: Peace Workers Lay Siege to a Military Stronghold—The Public Schools." *In These Times* (Oct. 1–7): 23–24.

Davis, Joann, and Wendy Smith. 1982. "A Checklist of Nuclear Books." *Publishers Weekly* 221 (Mar. 26): 45–51.

Dawson, Carl A., and Warner E. Gettys. 1935. *An Introduction to Sociology.* Rev. ed. New York: Ronald Press.

DeBenedetti, Charles. 1980. *The Peace Reform in American History.* Blooming-ton: Indiana Univ. Press.

Divoky, Diane. 1980. "Hunger Project: A Crusade for est Leader's Devotees." *Sacramento Bee,* Jan. 5, A26.

Domhoff, G. William. 1978. *The Powers That Be: Processes of Ruling Class Domination in America.* New York: Vintage Books.

Dorman, William, Robert Karl Manoff, and Jennifer Weeks. 1988. *American Press Coverage of U.S.-Soviet Relations, the Soviet Union, Nuclear Weapons, Arms Control, and National Security: A Bibliography.* New York: Center for War, Peace, and the News Media.

Douglass, James W. 1983. *Lightning East to West: Jesus, Gandhi, and the Nuclear Age.* New York: Crossroad.

———. 1987. "Civil Disobedience as Prayer." In *Swords Into Plowshares: Nonviolent Action for Disarmament,* edited by A. Laffin and A. Montgomery. 93–97. New York: Harper and Row.

———. 1991. *The Nonviolent Coming of God.* Maryknoll, N.Y.: Orbis Books.

Douglass, Jim, and Shelley Douglass. 1988. *Dear Gandhi: Now What? Letters from Ground Zero.* Santa Cruz, Calif.: New Society Publishers.

Downs, Anthony. 1972. "Up and Down with Ecology—The 'Issue-Attention Cycle'." *The Public Interest* 28 (Summer): 38–50.

Epstein, Barbara. 1985. "The Culture of Direct Action: Livermore Action Group and the Peace Movement." *Socialist Review* 82/83 (1985): 31–61.

———. 1990. "The Politics of Moral Witness: Religion and Nonviolent Direct Action." In *Peace Action in the Eighties: Social Science Perspectives,* edited by S. Marullo and J. Lofland. 106–24. New Brunswick, N.J.: Rutgers Univ. Press.

———. 1991. *Political Protest and Cultural Revolution: Nonviolent Direct Action in the 1970s and 1980s.* Berkeley: Univ. of California Press.

Etheredge, Lloyd. 1978. *A World of Men: The Private Sources of American Foreign Policy.* Cambridge, Mass.: MIT Press.

Etzioni, Amitai. 1961. *A Comparative Analysis of Complex Organizations.* New York: Free Press of Glencoe.

Faludi, Susan. 1987. "Inner Peaceniks: Can We Move Beyond War with the Power of Positive Thinking?" *Mother Jones* (Apr.): 20–25, 51–53.

Farren, Pat, ed. 1991. *Peacework: 20 Years of Nonviolent Social Change.* Baltimore, Md.: Fortkamp Publishing.

Fay, Brian. 1987. *Critical Social Science: Liberation and Its Limits.* Ithaca, N.Y.: Cornell Univ. Press.

Feller, Gordon, Sherel Schwenninger, and Diane Singerman, eds. 1981. *Peace and World Order Studies: A Curriculum Guide.* 3d ed. New York: Institute for World Order.

Ferguson, Bruce. 1988. "Different Agenda, Styles Shape SANE/Freeze." *Bulletin of the Atomic Scientists* (Apr.): 26–30.

Ferguson, Thomas, and Joel Rogers. 1986. *Right Turn: The Decline of the Democrats and the Future of American Politics.* New York: Hill and Wang.

Fine, Gary. 1979. "Small Groups and Culture Creation." *American Sociological Review* 44 (Oct.): 733–45.

Fine, Melinda, and Peter M. Steven. 1984. *American Peace Directory 1984.* Cambridge, Mass.: Ballinger Publishing.

Fishman, Mark. 1978. "Crime Waves as Ideology." *Social Problems* 25, no. 5:531–43.

Fitz, Dawn. 1986. "Educating For Peace." *The Mobilizer* (Fall): 10.

Folsom, Franklin, Connie Fledderjohann, with Gerda Lawrence. 1988. *The Great Peace March: An American Odyssey.* Santa Fe, N.M.: Ocean Tree Books.

Forsberg, Randall. 1982. "A Bilateral Nuclear-Weapon Freeze." *Scientific American* 247, no. 5:52–61.

———. 1984. "The Shared Origins of the Directory and the Nuclear Freeze Movement." In *American Press Directory 1984,* edited by M. Fine and P. M. Steven. vii–viii. Cambridge, Mass.: Ballinger Publishing.

Freeman, Jo. 1975. *The Politics of Women's Liberation: A Case Study of an Emerging Social Movement and Its Relation to the Policy Process.* New York: David McKay.

———. 1983. *Social Movements of the Sixties and Seventies.* New York: Longman.

Freeze Voter. 1987. *Freeze Voter Report and Prospectus, 1986–1988.* Washington, D.C.: Freeze Voter.

Freeze Voter Education Fund. 1986. *A Peace Activist's Political Organizing Manual.* Washington, D.C.: Freeze Voter Education Fund.

Fuller, Richard, and Richard Myers, 1941. "The Natural History of Social Problems." *American Sociological Review* 6 (Feb.): 320–28.

Gallup, George. 1981. "Wide Support Found for World Referendum on Nuclear Ban." *Gallup Poll,* June 21.

Galtung, Johan. 1986. "The Green Movement." *International Sociology* 1, no. 1: 75–90.

Gambrell, Richard. 1980. "Issue Dynamics in the Student Movement." *Sociological Focus* 13, no. 3:187–202.

Gamson, William, Bruce Fireman, and Steven Rytina. 1982. *Encounters with Unjust Authority.* Homewood, Ill.: Dorsey Press.

Gelber, Steven M., and Martin L. Cook. 1990. *Saving the Earth: The History of a Middle-Class Millenarian Movement.* Berkeley: Univ. of California Press.

Gerlach, Luther, and Virginia Hine. 1970. *People, Power, Change: Movements of Social Transformation.* Indianapolis, Ind.: Bobbs-Merrill Educational Publishing.

———. 1983. "Movements of Revolutionary Change: Some Structural Characteristics." In *Social Movements of the Sixties and Seventies,* edited by J. Freeman. 133–47. New York: Longman.

Gitlin, Tod. 1987. *The Sixties: Years of Hope, Days of Rage.* New York: Bantam Books.

Goffman, Erving. 1961. *Asylums: Essays on the Social Situation of Mental Patients and Other Inmates.* Garden City: Anchor Books.

Grandmothers for Peace. 1987. *Grandmothers for Peace*. Sacramento, Calif.: Grand-
mothers for Peace. Brochure.
Green, Marguerite. 1986. *Peace Archives: A Guide to Library Collections of the
Papers of American Peace Organizations and of Leaders in the Public Effort
for Peace*. Berkeley, Calif.: World Without War Council.
Griffin, Kelley. 1987. *Ralph Nader Presents More Action for a Change*. New York:
Dembner Books.
Gromyko, Anatolii, and Martin E. Hellman. 1988. *Breakthrough: Emerging New
Thinking*. New York: Walker.
Ground Zero. 1982. *Nuclear War: What's in It for You?* New York: Pocket Books.
————. 1984. "First Strike Status Report." *Linkages* 2 (Jan.): 1.
Gurr, Ted Robert. 1989. "The History of Protest, Rebellion, and Reform in Amer-
ica: An Overview." In *Violence in America*. Vol. 2, *Protest, Rebellion, Re-
form*, edited by Ted Robert Gurr. 11–22. Newbury Park, Calif.: Sage
Publications.
Gusfield, Joseph. 1981. "Social Movements and Social Change: Perspectives of
Linearity and Fluidity." *Research on Social Movements, Conflicts and Change*,
4:317–39.
Gusterson, Hugh. 1989. "Knock Knock: Door-to-Door Canvassers Are the Foot
Soldiers in the Fight for Disarmament." *Nuclear Times* (Jan.–Feb.): 18–19.
Halmos, Peter. 1966. *The Faith of the Counsellors*. Boston, Mass.: Schocken Books.
Harris, Ian M. 1990. "Principles of Peace Pedagogy." *Peace and Change* 15, no.
3:254–71.
Harris, Louis. 1982. "Presentation by Louis Harris." *Harris Surveys*, July 27.
Heard, Alex. 1989. "Rolfing with Yeltsin: The Soviet Opposition and the Califor-
nia Cult." *New Republic* (Oct. 9): 11–13.
Hedemann, Ed. 1981. *War Resisters League Organizer's Manual*. New York: War
Resisters League.
Heirich, Max. 1971. *The Spiral of Conflict: Berkeley, 1964*. New York: Columbia
Univ. Press.
Hertsgaard, Mark. 1985. "What Became of the Freeze?" *Mother Jones* (June): 44–47.
Hilgartner, Stephen, and Charles Bosk. 1988. "The Rise and Fall of Social Prob-
lems: A Public Arenas Model." *American Journal of Sociology* 94 (July): 53–78.
Hochschild, Adam. 1986. "Slow-Scan to Moscow." *Mother Jones* (June): 28–38.
Hoge, Patrick. 1988. "Sacramento Man Plants the Hope of Peace." *Sacramento Bee*,
Oct. 17.
Hollins, Harry B., Averill L. Powers, and Mark Sommer. 1989. *The Conquest of
War: Alternative Strategies for Global Security*. Boulder, Colo.: Westview Press.
Holstein, James A., and Gale Miller. 1989. *Perspectives on Social Problems*. Green-
wich, Conn.: JAI Press.
Holworth, Robert D. 1989. *Let Your Life Speak: A Study of Politics, Religion, and
Antinuclear Weapons Activism*. Madison: Univ. of Wisconsin Press.
Howlett, Charles F. 1991. *The American Peace Movement: References and Resources*.
Boston, Mass.: G. K. Hall.

Howlett, Charles F., and Glen Zeitzer. 1985. *The American Peace Movement: History and Historiography.* Washington, D.C.: American Historical Association.

Institute for Soviet-American Relations. 1987. "Trips." *Surviving Together: A Journal of Soviet-American Relations* 11 (March): 55.

Irwin, John. 1977. *Scenes.* Beverly Hills, Calif.: Sage Publications.

Irwin, Robert A. 1989. *Building a Peace System.* Washington, D.C.: Expro Press.

Jackson, Maurice, E. Peterson, J. Bull, S. Monsen, P. Richmond. 1960. "The Failure of an Incipient Social Movement." *Pacific Sociological Review* 3 (Spring): 35–40.

Jacobson, Jim. 1988. "Activists Make Waves." *Nuclear Times* (Sept.–Oct.): 9.

Jacoby, Russell, 1987. *The Last Intellectuals: American Culture in the Age of Academe.* New York: Basic Books.

Jaeger, Gertrude, and Philip Selznick. 1964. "A Normative Theory of Culture." *American Sociological Review* 29, no. 5:653–69.

Jenkins, J. Craig. 1987. "Interpreting the Stormy 1960s: Three Theories in Search of a Political Age." *Research in Political Sociology* 3:269–303.

Jenkins, J. Craig, and Barbara G. Brents. 1989. "Social Protest, Hegemonic Competition, and Social Reform: A Political Struggle Interpretation of the Origins of the American Welfare State." *American Sociological Review* 54, no. 6: 891–905.

Jenkins, J. Craig, and Craig M. Eckert. 1986. "Channeling Black Insurgency: Elite Patronage and Professional Social Movement Organization in the Development of the Black Movement." *American Sociological Review* 51, no. 6:812–29.

Jergen, Mary Evelyn. 1985. *How You Can Be a Peacemaker: Catholic Teachings and Practical Suggestions.* Liguori, Mo.: Liguori Publications.

Katsiafricas, George. 1987. *The Imagination of the New Left: A Global Analysis of 1968.* Boston, Mass.: South End Press.

Katz, Elihu, and Paul Lazarsfeld. 1955. *Personal Influence.* Glencoe, Ill.: Free Press.

Keller, Audrey. N.d. *The Ribbon.* Leaflet published at 525 Homer Ave., Palo Alto, Calif.

Kennedy, Edward M., and Mark O. Hatfield. 1982. *Freeze! How You Can Help Prevent Nuclear War.* New York: Bantam Books.

Kenney, Ruth. 1988. "UCD Grad Samuels Works on U.S.-Soviet Relations." *Sacramento Bee,* Aug. 18.

Keyes, Ken. 1982. *The Hundredth Monkey.* Coos Bay, Oreg.: Vision Books.

Kincade, William H., and Priscilla B. Hayner. 1988. *The ACCESS Resource Guide: An International Directory of Information on War, Peace, and Security.* Cambridge, Mass.: Ballinger Publishing.

Kingdon, John W. 1984. *Agendas, Alternatives, and Public Policy.* Boston, Mass.: Little, Brown.

Klandermans, Bert. 1991. "The Peace Movement and Social Movement Theory." *International Social Movement Research* 3:1–39.

Knoke, David, and David Prensky. 1984. "What Relevance Do Organization Theories Have for Voluntary Organizations." *Social Science Quarterly* 65 (Spring): 3–20.

Kraybill, Charlie. 1988a. "Financial Statements." *Peace Activist Review* (Sept.–Oct.): 6–9.

———. 1988b. "Seven Large National Peace Groups Compared By Total Revenue/Expenses." *Peace Activist Review* (Jan.–Feb.): 3–7.

Kriesberg, Louis. 1982. *Social Conflicts*. Englewood Cliffs, N.J.: Prentice-Hall.

Laffin, Art. 1988. *Plowshares-Disarmament Actions, September, 1980–December, 1987*. New Haven, Conn.: Art Laffin/Isaiah Peace Ministry.

Laffin, Arthur J., and Anne Montgomery. 1987. *Swords into Plowshares: Non-violent Direct Action for Disarmament*. San Francisco, Calif.: Harper and Row.

Landau, David. 1984 "Citizen Diplomacy." *New Age Journal* (Jan.): 35–45, 93–95.

Lapidus, Gail, and Alexander Dallin. 1989. "The Pacification of Ronald Reagan." *Bulletin of the Atomic Scientists* 45 (Jan.–Feb.): 14–17.

Larson, Jeanne, and Madge Micheels-Cyrus. 1987. *Seeds of Peace: A Catalogue of Quotations*. Philadelphia: New Society.

Lawson, Ronald. 1983. "A Decentralized but Moving Pyramid: The Evolution and Consequences of the Structure of the Tenant Movement." In *Social Movements of the Sixties and Seventies*, edited by J. Freeman. 119–31. New York: Longman.

Leavitt, Robert. 1983. *Freezing the Arms Race: The Genesis of a Mass Movement*. Cambridge, Mass.: John F. Kennedy School of Government—Case Program, Harvard Univ.

Lemert, Edwin. 1951. "Is There a Natural History of Social Problems?" *American Sociological Review* 16 (Apr.): 217–33.

Leonard, Vickie, and Tom MacLean, eds. 1977. *The Continental Walk for Disarmament and Social Justice*. New York: Continental Walk for Disarmament and Social Justice.

Lipsky, Michael. 1968. "Protest as a Political Resource." *American Political Science Review* 62 (Dec.): 1144–58.

Lislo, Donald J. 1974. *The President and Protest: Hoover, Conspiracy, and the Bonus Riot*. Columbia: Univ. of Missouri Press.

Lofland, John. 1977. *Doomsday Cult: A Study of Conversion, Proselytization, and Maintenance of Faith*. Enl. ed. New York: Irvington Publishers.

———. 1985. *Protest: Studies of Collective Behavior and Social Movements*. New Brunswick, N.J.: Transaction Books.

———. 1989. "Consensus Movements: City Twinning and Derailed Dissent in the American Eighties." *Research in Social Movements, Conflicts and Change* 11: 163–96.

———. 1992a. "The Intellectual Structure of Peace Studies: Questions and Social Roles in the Recent Period." *Sociology of Peace and War*. Newsletter of the Section on Peace and War, American Sociological Association, Spring/Summer 1992, 1, 4–7.

———. 1992b. "The Soar and Slump of Polite Protest: Interactive Spirals and the Eighties Peace Surge." *Peace and Change* 17, no. 1:34–59.

Lofland, John, Mary Anna Colwell, and Victoria Johnson. 1990. "Change-Theories and Movement Structure." In *Peace Action in the Eighties: Social Science Perspectives,* edited by S. Marullo and J. Lofland. 87–105. New Brunswick, N.J.: Rutgers Univ. Press.

Lofland, John, and Victoria Johnson. 1991. "Citizen Surges: A Domain in Movement Studies and a Perspective on Peace Activism in the 1980s." *Research in Social Movements, Conflicts and Change* 13:1–29.

Lofland, John, Victoria Johnson, and Pamela Kato. 1989. *Peace Movement Periodicals: An Annotated Bibliography.* Davis: University of California, Davis Main Library JX1961.U6 L642 1989.

———. 1991. *Peace Movement Organizations and Activists: An Analytic Bibliography.* New York: Haworth Publishers.

Lofland, John, and Lyn H. Lofland. 1984. *Analyzing Social Settings.* Belmont, Calif.: Wadsworth Publishing.

Lofland, Lyn H. 1978. *The Craft of Dying: The Modern Face of Death.* Beverly Hills, Calif.: Sage Publications.

———. 1990. "Is Peace Possible? An Analysis of Sociology." *Sociological Perspectives* 33, no. 3:313–25.

MacQueen, Graeme. 1991. "Marking and Binding: An Interpretation of the Pouring of Blood in Nonviolent Direct Action." *Peace and Change* 17, no. 1:60–81.

Marullo, Sam. 1990. "Patterns of Peacemaking in the Local Freeze Campaign." In *Peace Action in the Eighties: Social Science Perspectives,* edited by S. Marullo and J. Lofland. 246–64. New Brunswick, N.J.: Rutgers Univ. Press.

Marullo, Sam, Alexandra Chute, and Mary Anna Colwell. 1991. "Pacifist and Nonpacifist Groups in the U.S. Peace Movement of the 1980s." *Peace and Change* 16, no. 3:235–59.

Mauss, Armand L. 1975. *Social Problems as Social Movements.* Philadelphia, Pa.: J. B. Lippincott.

McAdam, Doug. 1982. *Political Process and the Development of Black Insurgency 1930–1970.* Chicago: Univ. of Chicago Press.

———. 1983. "Tactical Innovation and the Pace of Insurgency." *American Sociological Review* 48 (Dec.): 735–54.

McAdam, Doug, John D. McCarthy, and Mayer N. Zald. 1988. "Social Movements." In *Handbook of Sociology,* edited by N. J. Smelser. 695–738. Newbury Park, Calif.: Sage Publications.

McCarthy, John D., David W. Britt, and Mark Wolfson. 1991. "The Institutional Channeling of Social Movements by the State in the United States." *Research in Social Movements, Conflict and Change* 12:45–76.

McCarthy, John, and Mark Wolfson. 1992. "Consensus Movements, Conflict Movements, and the Cooptation of Civic and State Infrastructures." In *Frontiers of Social Movement Theory,* edited by A. Morris and C. M. Mueller. 273–97. New Haven, Conn.: Yale Univ. Press.

McCarthy, John D., and Mayer N. Zald. 1987. "The Trend of Social Movements in America: Professionalization and Resource Mobilization." In *Social Movements in an Organizational Society,* edited by M. Zald and J. McCarthy. 337–91. New Brunswick, N.J.: Transaction Books.

McCrea, Frances B., and Gerald E. Markle. 1989. *Minutes to Midnight: Nuclear Weapons Protest in America.* Newbury Park, Calif.: Sage Publications.

McGrath, Peter. 1982. "The Nuclear Book Boom." *Newsweek* 99, Apr. 12, 21.

McGuinness, Elizabeth Anne. 1988. *People Waging Peace: Stories of Americans Striving for Peace and Justice in the World Today.* San Pedro, Calif.: Alberti Press.

McNeal, Patricia. 1992. *Harder Than War: Catholic Peacemaking in Twentieth-Century America.* New Brunswick, N.J.: Rutgers Univ. Press.

McPhail, Clark. 1990. *The Myth of the Madding Crowd.* New York: Aldine de Gruyter.

Mechling, Elizabeth Walker, and Gale Auletta. 1986. "Beyond War: A Socio-Rhetorical Analysis of a New Class Revitalization Movement." *Western Journal of Speech Communication* 50 (Fall): 388–404.

Mehan, Hugh, Charles E. Nathanson, and James M. Skelly. 1990. "Nuclear Discourse in the 1980s: The Unraveling Conventions of the Cold War." *Discourse and Society* 1, no. 2:133–65.

Mehan, Hugh, and John Willis. 1988. "MEND: A Nurturing Voice in the Nuclear Arms Debate." *Social Problems* 35, no. 4:363–83.

Meyer, David S. 1990a. "Peace Movement Demobilization." In *Peace Action in the Eighties: Social Science Perspectives,* edited by S. Marullo and J. Lofland, 53–71. New Brunswick, N.J.: Rutgers Univ. Press.

———. 1990b. *A Winter of Discontent: The Nuclear Freeze and American Politics.* New York: Praeger.

———. 1991. "How We Helped End the Cold War." *Nuclear Times* (Winter): 9–14.

Meyer, Robert S. 1988. *Peace Organizations, Past and Present: A Survey and Directory.* Jefferson, N.C.: McFarland.

Milburn, Michael A., Paul Y. Watanabe, and Bernard M. Kramer. 1986. "The Nature and Sources of Attitudes Toward a Nuclear Freeze." *Political Psychology* 7, no. 4:661–74.

Milich, Nick. 1986. "David Thompson: Man of Many Talents." *Davis Daily Democrat,* June 23, 1, 8.

Miller, Judith. 1982. "72% in Poll Back Nuclear Halt if Soviet Union Doesn't Cheat." *New York Times,* May 30, A1, A2.

Molander, Earl A., and Roger Molander. 1990. "A Threshold Analysis of the Anti-Nuclear Weapons Movement." In *Peace Action in the Eighties: Social Science Perspectives,* edited by S. Marullo and J. Lofland. 29–42. New Brunswick, N.J.: Rutgers Univ. Press.

Molander, Roger. 1982. "How I learned to Start Worrying and Hate the Bomb." *Washington Post,* March 21, D1.

Morris, Aldon D. 1984. *The Origins of the Civil Rights Movement: Black Communities Organizing for Change.* New York: Free Press.

Motley, Sandy, Ann Evans, and Joan Poulos. 1984. "Peace." Letter to the editor, *Davis Enterprise,* May 8.

Moyer, Bill. 1977. *A Nonviolent Action Manual: How to Organize Nonviolent Demonstrations and Campaigns.* Philadelphia, Pa.: New Society Press.

———. 1988. *Movement Action Plan (MAP)*. San Francisco, Calif.: Movement Impowerment Project.

Murray, Robert K. 1955. *Red Scare: A Study in National Hysteria, 1919–1920*. Minneapolis: Univ. of Minnesota Press.

Myer, Donald. 1965. *The Positive Thinkers*. Garden City, N.Y.: Doubleday.

Nathanson, Charles E. 1988. "The Social Construction of the Soviet Threat: A Study in the Politics of Representation." *Alternatives* 13:443–83.

Nation, Editors. 1991. "Movement Gap." *Nation* 253, no. 15:539.

Neal, Mary K. 1988. *Balancing Passion and Reason: A Symbolic Analysis of the Communication Strategies of the Physician's Movement Against Nuclear Weapons*. Ph.D. diss. in Medical Anthropology, Univ. of California, San Francisco. Ann Arbor, Mich.: UMI Dissertation Information Service.

———. 1990. "Rhetorical Styles of the Physicians for Social Responsibility." In *Peace Action in the Eighties: Social Science Perspectives*, edited by S. Marullo and J. Lofland. 167–79. New Brunswick, N.J.: Rutgers Univ. Press.

Nuclear Free America. 1990. "Nuclear Free Zones in the United States." *New Abolitionist* 7, no. 1:12.

Nuclear Resister. 1989. *General Budget*. Tucson, Ariz.: Nuclear Resister.

Nuclear Weapons Freeze Campaign. 1983. *Prominent Endorsers List*. St. Louis, Mo.: National Clearinghouse of the Nuclear Weapons Freeze Campaign.

Oberdorfer, Don. 1991. *The Turn: From the Cold War to a New Era: The United States and the Soviet Union 1983–1990*. New York: Poseidon Press.

Obershall, Anthony. 1973. *Social Conflict and Social Movements*. Englewood Cliffs, N.J.: Prentice-Hall.

Oliver, Pamela E. 1989. "Bringing the Crowd Back In: The Nonorganizational Elements of Social Movements." *Research in Social Movements, Conflicts and Change* 11:1–30.

Olson, Mark. 1989a. "A Giver's Guide: An Introduction." *The Other Side* 25, no. 4:16–21.

———. 1989b. "A Giver's Guide: The Listings." *The Other Side* 25, no. 4:22–64.

Olzak, Susan. 1989. "Analysis of Events in the Study of Collective Action." *Annual Review of Sociology* 15:119–41.

Panapoulos, Frank. 1986. "Plowshares: Disarmament by Example: *Weapons Facilities Network Bulletin* 1, no. 3:1, 6.

Paulson, Dennis, ed. 1986. *Voices of Survival in the Nuclear Age*. Santa Barbara, Calif.: Capra Press.

Peace Links Connection. 1988. "Annual Day of Peace." *Peace Links Connection* 4, no. 2:4.

Peace, Roger C. 1991. *A Just and Lasting Peace: The U.S. Peace Movement from the Cold War to Desert Storm*. Chicago: Nobel Press.

People Weekly. 1986. "Main Street: By a Show of Hands, America Takes a Stand for the Hungry and Homeless." *People Weekly*, June 9, 139–41.

Piven, Frances Fox, and Richard Cloward. 1979. *Poor People's Movements: Why They Succeed, How They Fail*. New York: Vintage Books.

Plesch, Daniel. 1982. *A Disarmament Action Manual: What Do We Do after We've Shown 'The War Game'?* London: Campaign for Nuclear Disarmament.

Plowman, Brenda. 1986. "Beyond War Foundation." *PEACE in Action* (Jan.–Feb.): 1.

Price, Edward. 1990. "Historical Generations in Freeze Member Mobilization." In *Peace Action in the Eighties: Social Science Perspectives*, edited by S. Marullo and J. Lofland. 207–216. New Brunswick, N.J.: Rutgers Univ. Press.

Primak, Joel, and Frank von Hippel. 1974. *Advice and Dissent: Scientists in the Political Arena.* New York: Basic Books.

Ramsey, Bill, and Randall Kehler. 1982. Important Notice: April 26 Plans. *Nuclear Weapons Freeze Campaign*, March 19.

Reed, Susan K. 1983. "Nuclear Anonymity—The Role of Foundations Has Been as Influential as It Has Been Unpublicized—Which Is to Say Considerable." *Foundation News* (Jan.–Feb.): 42–49.

Reeves, Richard. 1986. "Volunteerism Is a Crock." *San Francisco Chronicle*, June 30.

Rice, Jim. 1987. "Catholic Bishops Arrested at Nevada Test Site." *Sojourners* 16, no. 7:11–12.

Richardson, James T., Joel Best, and David G. Bromley. 1991. *The Satanism Scare.* New York: Aldine de Gruyter.

Roberts, Nancy L. 1991. *American Peace Writers, Editors, and Periodicals: A Dictionary.* New York: Greenwood Press.

Roberts, Ron E., and Robert Kloss. 1979. *Social Movements: Between Balcony and the Barricade.* 2d ed. St. Louis, Mo.: C. V. Mosby.

Robinson, Betsy. 1984. "Sister-City Program is Non-Political." *Tallahassee Democrat*, May 26.

Robinson, Chris. 1982. *Plotting Directions: An Activist's Guide.* Philadelphia, Pa.: RECON Publishers.

Rogers, Everett M. 1983. *Diffusion of Innovations.* 3d ed. New York: Free Press.

Rogne, Leah, and Bradley Harper. 1990. "The Meaning of Civil Disobedience: The Case of the Honeywell Project." In *Peace Action in the Eighties: Social Science Perspectives*, edited by S. Marullo and J. Lofland. 191–203. New Brunswick, N.J.: Rutgers Univ. Press.

Rose, Jerry D. 1982. *Outbreaks: The Sociology of Collective Behavior.* New York: Free Press.

Rosen, Jay. 1986. "Ted Turner: 'Captain Outrageous' or an Ambassador of Goodwill?" *Deadline* (Sept.–Oct.): 6–8.

Rule, James B. 1988. *Theories of Civil Violence.* Berkeley: Univ. of California Press.

Rupp, Leila J., and Verta Taylor. 1987. *Survival in the Doldrums: The American Women's Rights Movement, 1945 to the 1960s.* New York: Oxford Univ. Press.

Ryan, Howard. 1983. *Blocking Progress: Consensus Decision-Making and the Anti-Nuclear Movement.* Berkeley, Calif.: Overthrow Cluster.

Rytina, Steven. 1992. "Social Structure." In *Encyclopedia of Sociology*, edited by E. Borgatta and M. Borgatta. 1970–1976. New York: Macmillan.

Sacramento SANE/Freeze. 1988. *General Fund Balance Statement as of October 31, 1988.* Sacramento, Calif.: Sacramento SANE/Freeze.

Sale, Kirkpatrick. 1974. *SDS*. New York: Vintage Books.

Sandman, Peter M., and JoAnn M. Valenti. 1986. "Scared Stiff—Or Scared into Action." *Bulletin of the Atomic Scientists* 42, no. 1:12-16.

Sasson, Ted, Pam Solo, and Paul Walker. 1988. *Letter to "Dear IPIS Friend."* Boston: Institute for Peace and International Security.

Schatz, Robert, and Susan Fiske. 1992. "International Reactions to the Threat of Nuclear War: The Rise and Fall of Concern in the Eighties." *Political Psychology* 13, no. 1:1-29.

Schell, Jonathan. 1982. *The Fate of the Earth*. New York: Knopf.

Schuman, Howard, Jacob Ludwig, and Jon A. Krosnick. 1986. "The Perceived Threat of Nuclear War, Salience, and Open Questions." *Public Opinion Quarterly* 50, no. 4:519-36.

Schwartz, Michael. 1976. *Radical Protest and Social Structure: The Southern Farmers' Alliance and Cotton Tenancy, 1880-1890*. New York: Academic Press.

Schwartz, Michael and Paul Shuva. 1992. "Resource Mobilization versus the Mobilization of People: Why Consensus Movements Cannot Be Instruments of Social Change." In *Frontiers in Social Movement Theory*, edited by A. Morris and C. M. Mueller. 205-23. New Haven, Conn.: Yale Univ. Press.

Schwartz, James. 1991. "Key Events in the Gorbachev Era." *Washington Post National Weekly Edition*, August 26-September 1, 8-9.

Schwartz, William A., and Charles Derber. 1990. *The Nuclear Seduction: Why the Arms Race Doesn't Matter—And What Does*. Berkeley: Univ. of California Press.

Shah, Sonia, ed., 1992. *Between Fear and Hope: A Decade of Peace Activism*. Baltimore, Md.: Fortkamp Publishing.

Sharp, Gene. 1973. *The Politics of Nonviolent Action*. Boston, Mass.: P. Sargent.

Shay, Kevin. 1987. *Have Feet, Speak Truth*. Dallas, Tex.: Melchizedek Free Press.

Shuman, Michael H. 1987. *Building Municipal Foreign Policies: An Action Handbook for Citizens and Local Elected Officials*. Irvine, Calif.: Local Elected Officials Project, Center for Innovative Diplomacy.

———. 1991. "Main Street U.S.A.—Lobby or Lose It." *Global Communities: A Quarterly Newsletter of the Institute for Policy Studies* (Autumn): 1-5, 8.

Shuman, Michael, and Jayne Williams. 1986. *Having International Affairs Your Way: A Five Step Briefing Manual for Citizen Diplomats*. Palo Alto, Calif.: Center For Innovative Diplomacy.

Skocpol, Theda. 1979. *States and Social Revolutions: A Comparative Analysis of France, Russia, and China*. New York: Cambridge Univ. Press.

Smelser, Neil J. 1963. *Theory of Collective Behavior*. New York: Free Press.

Smith, Tom W. 1980. "America's Most Important Problem—A Trend Analysis, 1946-1976." *Public Opinion Quarterly* 44, no. 2:165-79.

———. 1985. "American's Most Important Problem, Part 1: National and International." *Public Opinion Quarterly* 49, no. 2:264-74.

———. 1988. "Nuclear Anxiety." *Public Opinion Quarterly* 52, no. 4:557-75.

Smoke, Richard. 1984. "The 'Peace' of Deterrence and the 'Peace' of the Antinuclear War Movement." *Political Psychology* 5, no. 4:741-48.

Smoke, Richard, and Willis Harmon. 1987. *Paths to Peace: Exploring the Feasibility of Sustainable Peace*. Boulder, Colo.: Westview Press.

Snow, David, Burke Rochford, Steven Worden, and Robert Benford. 1986. "Frame Alignment Processes, Micromobilization and Movement Participation." *American Sociological Review* 51:464–81.

Snyder, Edward F. 1988. *Mail Solicitation for the Friends Committee on National Legislation, October*. Washington, D.C.: Friends Committee on National Legislation.

Solo, Pam. 1988. *From Protest to Policy: Beyond the Freeze to Common Security*. Cambridge, Mass.: Ballinger Publishing.

Sommer, Mark. 1985. *Beyond the Bomb: Living Without Nuclear Weapons, A Field Guide to Alternative Strategies for Building a Stable Peace*. Boston: Ex-Pro Press.

Special Committee of the Academic Council on Global Security and Cooperation. 1982. "Report of the Special Committee of the Academic Council on Global Security and Cooperation." Oakland, Calif.: Univ. of California Academic Council. Typescript.

Spector, Malcolm, and John I. Kitsuse. 1977. *Constructing Social Problems*. Menlo Park, Calif.: Cummings Publishing.

Spilerman, Seymour. 1976. Structural Characteristics of Cities and the Severity of Racial Disorders." *American Sociological Review* 41 (June): 771–93.

Staples, Lee. 1984. *Roots to Power: A Manual for Grassroots Organizing*. Westport, Conn.: Praeger.

Stearns, Peter N. 1974. *1848: The Revolutionary Tide in Europe*. New York: W. W. Norton.

Stinchcombe, Arthur. 1965. "Social Structure and Organizations." In *Handbook of Organizations*, edited by J. March. 142–93. Chicago: Rand McNally.

Strickland, Donald A. 1968. *Scientists in Politics: The Atomic Scientists Movement, 1945–46*. Lafayette, Ind.: Purdue Univ. Press.

Sturgeon, Noel. 1987. "Concord Demo Raises Hard Questions." *Monthly Planet* (October): 18–19.

Syracuse Cultural Workers. 1991. *Catalogue*. Syracuse, N.Y.: Syracuse Cultural Workers.

Szegedy-Maszak, Marianne. 1989. "The Movement: Rise and Fall of the Washington Peace Industry." *Bulletin of the Atomic Scientists* 45 (Jan.–Feb.): 18–23.

Tarrow, Sidney. 1989. *Struggle, Politics and Reform: Collective Action, Social Movements, and Cycles of Protest*. Western Societies Program Occasional Paper no. 21. Ithaca, N.Y.: Cornell University Center for International Studies.

Teitebaum, Terry. 1987. "Where It Comes From, Where It Goes." *Monthly Planet* (Sept.): 10.

Tennison, Sharon. 1988. "The Gift of Carrying Out the Dream . . . The Gift of Making It Possible to Carry Out the Dream . . ." *When the People Lead* 1, no. 2:13.

Thierman, Ian. 1980. *The Last Epidemic*. Videograph. Impact Productions. 35 minutes, color.

————. 1984. *If You Love This Planet: Dr. Helen Caldicott on Nuclear War.* Film produced by the Educational Film and Video Project. 26 minutes, color.

Thomas, Daniel, and Michael Klare, eds. 1990. *Peace and World Order Studies: A Curriculum Guide.* 5th ed. Boulder, Colo.: Westview Press.

Thompson, S. Scott, and Kenneth M. Jensen, eds. 1991. *Approaches to Peace: An Intellectual Map.* Washington, D.C.: United States Institute of Peace.

Tilly, Charles. 1978. *From Mobilization to Revolution.* Reading, Mass.: Addison-Wesley.

————. 1986. *The Contentious French.* Cambridge, Mass.: Harvard Univ. Press.

Tobias, Sheila, Peter Goudinoff, Stefan Leader, and Shelah Leader. 1982. *What Kinds of Guns Are They Buying for Your Butter? A Beginners Guide to Defense, Weaponry, and Military Spending.* New York: William Morrow.

Tokar, Brian. 1987. *The Green Alternative: Creating an Ecological Future.* San Pedro, Calif.: R and E Miles.

Topsfield Foundation. 1987. *Grassroots Peace Directory: An Information Guide to Resources and Groups Working in the Areas of Peace, Disarmament, and International Security.* Pomfret, Conn.: Topsfield Foundation.

Totten, Sam, and Martha Wescoat Totten. 1984. *Facing the Danger: Interviews with 20 Anti-nuclear Activists.* Trumansburg, N.Y.: Crossing Press.

Tozian, Gregory. 1988. "Affinity Credit Cards Offer Plastic with a Purpose." *Local Endeavor* (Nov.): 16.

Traugott, Mark. 1978. "Reconceiving Social Movements." *Social Problems* 26 (Oct.): 38–49.

Truman, David B. 1971. *The Governmental Process: Political Interests and Public Opinion.* 2d ed. New York: Alfred A. Knopf.

Tuma, Nancy, and Michael Hannan. 1984. *Social Dynamics: Models and Methods.* New York: Academic Press.

Turner, Ralph, and Lewis Killian. 1987. *Collective Behavior.* 3d ed. Englewood Cliffs, N.J.: Prentice-Hall.

U.S. Out of Central America. 1983. *Recipes for Organizing: The USOCA Cookbook.* San Francisco, Calif.: U.S. Out of Central America.

van den Dugen, Peter. 1986. "Peace Museums." In *World Encyclopedia of Peace.* Vol. 2, edited by E. Laslo and J. Y. Yoo. 234–43. New York: Pergamon Press.

Useem, Bert, and Peter Kimball. 1990. *States of Siege: U.S. Prison Riots 1971–1986.* New York: Oxford Univ. Press.

Walker, Jack L. 1991. *Mobilizing Interest Groups in America: Patrons, Professions, and Social Movements.* Ann Arbor: Univ. of Michigan Press.

Wallensteen, Peter. 1988. *Peace Research: Achievements and Challenges.* Boulder, Colo.: Westview Press.

Waller, Douglas C. 1987. *Congress and the Nuclear Freeze: An Inside Look at the Politics of a Mass Movement.* Amherst: Univ. of Massachusetts Press.

Wallis, Roy. 1977. *The Road to Total Freedom: A Sociological Analysis of Scientology.* New York: Columbia Univ. Press.

Walton, John. 1984. *Reluctant Rebels: Comparative Studies of Revolution and Underdevelopment.* New York: Columbia Univ. Press.

WAND, Women's Action for Nuclear Disarmament. 1986. *Turnabout: Emerging New Realism in the Nuclear Age.* Boston, Mass.: WAND Education Fund.

War Resisters League. 1989. *War Resisters League 1989 Annual Report.* New York: War Resisters League.

Warner, Gale, and Michael Shuman. 1987. *Citizen Diplomats: Pathfinders in Soviet-American Relations and How You Can Join Them.* New York: Continuum Publishing.

Wasserman, Harvey. 1979. "The Nonviolent Movement versus Nuclear Power." In *Nonviolent Action and Social Change,* edited by S. T. Bruyn and P. M. Rayman. 147–62. New York: Irvington.

Watanabe, Paul, and Michael Milburn. 1988. "Activism Against Armageddon: Some Predictors of Nuclear-Related Behavior." *Political Psychology* 9, no. 3:459–70.

Waters, W. W. 1969. *B. E. F.: The Whole Story of the Bonus Army.* New York: Arno Press and the New York Times.

Weinstein, Deena. 1979. *Bureaucratic Opposition: Challenging Abuses in the Workplace.* New York: Pergamon Press.

Wernette, D. R. 1990. "The Freeze Movement at the Local Level." In *Peace Action in the Eighties: Social Science Perspectives,* edited by S. Marullo and J. Lofland. 140–54. New Brunswick, N.J.: Rutgers Univ. Press.

Wien, Barbara, ed. 1984. *Peace and World Order Studies: A Curriculum Guide.* 4th ed. New York: World Policy Institute.

Wilson, James Q. 1973. *Political Organizations.* New York: Basic Books.

Wolfgang, Marvin, and Robert Kupperman. 1983. "Preface." *Annals of the American Academy of Political and Social Science* 469 (Sept.): 9–10.

Wollman, Neil. 1985. *Working for Peace: A Handbook of Practical Psychology and Other Tools.* San Luis Obispo, Calif.: Impact Publishers.

Women's International League for Peace and Freedom. 1988. *Financial Report, October 1, 1987 – September 30, 1988.* Philadelphia, Pa.: Women's International League for Peace and Freedom.

Wright, Talmadge, Felix Rodriguez, and Howard Waitzkin. 1986. "Corporate Interests, Philanthropies, and the Peace Movement." *International Journal of Health Services* 16, no. 1:33–41.

Young, Nigel. 1987. "Peace Movements in History." In *Toward a Just World Peace: Perspectives from Social Movements,* edited by S. H. Mendlovitz and R. B. J. Walker. 137–69. London: Butterworths.

Zald, Mayer N., and John D. McCarthy. 1987. "Social Movement Industries: Competition and Conflict among SMOs." In *Social Movements in an Organizational Society,* edited by M. N. Zald and J. D. McCarthy. 161–84. New Brunswick, N.J.: Transaction Books.

Zolberg, Aristide R. 1972. "Moments of Madness." *Politics and Society* 2, no. 2: 183–207.

Index

311

*This Mighty Dream: Social Protest
    Movements in the United States*
    (Adamson and Borgos), 17–18
Time (magazine), 260
Topsfield Foundation, 136
Track Two diplomacy, 53–55
Transcenders, 3, 39, 41, 49n. 4, 53, 105,
    154, 161, 196; cultural values of, 93,
    95–96; and educators, 43–44, 47–48;
    funding from, 165–66; persona of,
    119–20, 126
Transcender theory, 25–26
Trident II Plowshares, 35
Trips (to Soviet Union), 57, 58, 82n. 3
Troops, 172, 173
Tucson, Ariz., 57
Turner, Robert E. ("Ted"), 121, 152, 201
Turner Broadcasting, 121
Turning, The (Oberdofer), 285
20/20 Vision, 148–49

Uman-Davis Pairing Project, 15, 53
Unification Church, 193, 194, 208
Union of Concerned Scientists, 112,
    118n. 18, 137, 145, 256
Unitarians, 65
United Nations, 14, 101, 255
U.S. Comprehensive Test Ban Coalition,
    147
U.S. Congress, 219, 234
United States Institute of Peace, 142
University of California, 12
University of California, Davis, 14, 15
USA for Africa, 51
Utopias, 172, 173

Values, 101; shared, 92–96, 126–27
Verdon-Roe, Vivienne, 47, 121
Vernon, Rama, 121
Vietnam War, 10
Violence, 33, 191, 192, 193, 206–7, 210,
    211n. 6
Voice, 11–12
Voluntary associations, 42
Volunteers, 172–73, 198, 282–83; associa-
    tion management by, 149–55; in bu-

reaucracies, 144–46; donated labor
    of, 159–60; in Freeze campaign,
    146–47; and phone banks, 168–69;
    as staff, 143–44

Walks, 106–7, 131–32n. 16
WAND, 179
War, 26, 93, 103–4. *See also* Nuclear war
"War Is Like Slavery" story, 103
Warnke, Paul, 160
War Resisters League, 15, 44, 97, 116,
    146, 167, 225
Warriors, 196
War system, 182n. 27; American, 174–80
War tax, 256
Washington, D.C., 101, 119–21, 145–46,
    154
Washington Monument, 256
Washington Post (newspaper), 200
Waterville, Maine, 57
Weapons Facilities Network Bulletin, 148
Weapons Facilities Network of Mobiliza-
    tion for Survival (MfS), 148
"Weight of Nothing, The," 103
Weinberger, Casper, 245
Weinstein, Deena. *See Bureaucratic Op-
    position* (Weinstein)
Welfare, 93
"We Shall Overcome," 108
White Train Campaign, 256
Wiedner, Barbara, 37, 120, 152
Willens, Howard, 264
Windstar Foundation, 106
Wolfgang, Marvin, 277
Women Embracing Nuclear Disarma-
    ment, 152
"Women for America, For the World," 47
Women's Action for Nuclear Disarma-
    ment, 145
Women's International League for Peace
    and Freedom, 66, 116
Women's Peace Camp, 47, 154, 250
Women's Pentagon Action, 47, 107
Workshops, 14, 151
"World Future Society," 73–74
World Peace Rose Gardens, 102
World War I, 9–10
World War II, 10

Syracuse Studies on Peace and Conflict Resolution

HARRIET HYMAN ALONSO, CHARLES CHATFIELD, and LOUIS KRIESBERG, Series Editors

A series devoted to readable books on the history of peace movements, the lives of peace advocates, and the search for ways to mitigate conflict, both domestic and international. At a time when profound and exciting political and social developments are happening around the world, this series seeks to stimulate a wider awareness and appreciation of the search for peaceful resolution to strife in all its forms and to promote linkages among theorists, practitioners, social scientists, and humanists engaged in this work throughout the world.

Other titles in the series include:

Polite Protesters
was composed in 10 on 12 Palatino on Digital Compugraphic equipment
by Metricomp;
printed on 50-pound, acid-free Natural Smooth,
Smyth-sewn and bound over binder's boards in Holliston Roxite B,
and with paper covers printed in 1 color
by Braun-Brumfield, Inc.;
and published by
Syracuse University Press
Syracuse, New York 13244-5160